# New Security Challenges

Series Editor
George Christou, University of Warwick, Coventry, UK

The security agenda has become increasingly complex in recent years, with the war in Ukraine that began in February 2022 reminding us that we cannot take sustainable peace for granted, and that traditional concerns focusing on the state, war and military defence that came with the Cold War, remain important. It has also highlighted, however, the interconnectedness of the traditional and issues that are now of equal and indeed more significance to the security of the collective and the individual in the 21st Century, including, for example, human, food, cyber, health, environmental, economic, and energy security. Such issues have also seen a proliferation of a multiplicity of actors – state and non-state – as well as institutions at different levels – local, national, regional, global – in the performance of security. Moreover, the construction, contestation and practice of security is increasingly playing out across many new 'spaces' and 'sites' to address new types of risks and threats that are far from straightforward, including bioterrorism, cyber-attacks, climate change, interference in democratic processes and global pandemics. The increasing complexity and dynamism of the unfolding security agenda is what the *New Security Challenges* series seeks to capture and reflect, whilst not neglecting the importance of the relationship between the traditional and the new, for the contemporary global security environment.

For an informal discussion for a book in the series, please contact the series editor George Christou (G.Christou@warwick.ac.uk), or Palgrave editor Lucy Everitt (lucy.everitt.1@palgrave.com).

This book series is indexed by Scopus.

Abdul L. Abraham Jatto

# Oil and Gas Pipeline Infrastructure Insecurity

Vandalism, Threats, and Conflicts in the Niger Delta and the Global South

Abdul L. Abraham Jatto
School of Social and Political Sciences
University of Lincoln
Lincoln, UK

ISSN 2731-0329        ISSN 2731-0337   (electronic)
New Security Challenges
ISBN 978-3-031-56931-9       ISBN 978-3-031-56932-6   (eBook)
https://doi.org/10.1007/978-3-031-56932-6

This Palgrave Macmillan imprint is published by the registered company Springer Nature Switzerland AG
The registered company address is: Gewerbestrasse 11, 6330 Cham, Switzerland

Paper in this product is recyclable.

*This book is dedicated to God Almighty for giving me good health, the will, resilience, and finances that made it possible for me to complete this rigorous academic research.*

### *Also,*
*To the unforgettable memory of my mother: Madam Kelimatu Agnes Oseni Jatto for her wise counsel, meticulous guidance, unrelenting prayers, and unflinching faith and conviction about providence in my life. Being the spark of light that has led me through the unpredictable path of life. Honing my invaluable quest for knowledge, and what I came to achieve.*

### *Equally to a Part of Me:*
### *Mrs. Edidiong Abdul Lamidi Abraham Osiorenuah Jatto*

### *More importantly, to my Posterity:*
*Mr Anabulu Osiokwah, Miss Oghieghie Efwah, and Mr Imouedemeh Enakhe*
*Abdul L. Abraham Osiorenuah Jatto*

*For their Ever-attractive, Exciting, and Energetically Charming Sparkles.*

# FOREWORD

Always a pleasure when asked to write a forward for a book by authors, but for such a request to come from a mentee, is a double honour and a joy fulfilled. The book dwells on one of the most intractable and intricate security challenges in Nigeria, focussing on the entanglement underpinning oil pipeline infrastructure insecurity and conflict in Nigeria's historic Niger Delta region. The author shows this entanglement constituting a 'Gordian knot' of deeply interconnected social, economic, environmental, political, and security challenges. Through extensive first-hand empirical research engaging an array of stakeholders on the ground, this eye-opening book provides illuminating and essential insights into the dynamics of these issues from the perspectives of those directly impacted. The in-depth interviews spanning key players ranging from impoverished community members to civil society activists, security forces, and oil company executives represent a profoundly valuable contribution distinguishing this text. Unlike abundant prior academic analysis of Nigeria's petro-insecurity dilemmas which has relied on secondary data and macro analysis, this book uniquely prioritises amplifying the voices of those experiencing these challenges first-hand in the affected communities.

Giving primacy to these local Niger Delta viewpoints enriches understanding of the context-specific frustrations and disparities which simmer below the surface before potentially manifesting in pipeline vandalism, oil bunkering, illegal refining, and the spectrum of threats to human and critical infrastructure security. Whether due to perceived social injustice and economic marginalisation, the unbearable burden of the environmental impacts of incessant oil spills and gas flaring, or the rural perspectives revealed in this book, add essential nuance regarding what fuels regional instability and infrastructural risks.

In addition to its empirical foregrounding of diverse qualitative insights from the bottom up, another signature hallmark of this text lies in its application of relevant theoretical propositions to logically explain the conflicts documented. The foundational Frustration-Aggression Displacement Theory first posited by Yale sociologist John Dollard and extended more recently by criminologists and human security scholars provides a cogent explanatory framework. Within Nigeria's oil-producing Delta communities long afflicted by abject poverty and lack of basic infrastructure despite providing the lion's share of government foreign exchange revenues, this analytical model illuminates logical linkages in how chronic unresolved development grievances psychologically give rise to anger, then aggression, often directed through displacement at the structures of powerful external oil interests.

As a compelling supplement to such established conceptual models, an additional seminal theoretical contribution of this text comes through the author's proposed Community Neglect Aggression Displacement Theory. This integrates environmental considerations by highlighting how sustained degradation of the local livelihoods and ecology essential for subsistence fishing and farming also fans community frustrations which at boiling point bubble over into destructive backlash. Hence the book provides actionable policy insights by tracing a circular cascade spanning socio-economic and environmental drivers of perceived neglect, eliciting hostility channelled toward the infrastructure enabling exclusion amid plenty.

For its grounded empirical enrichment of the discourse and novel theoretical explications, this book represents essential reading not only for academic researchers but for policymakers, development institutions, and industry leaders keen to get to grips with the 'hydropolitics' of energy insecurity. All have integral roles to play in dissolving rather than tightening the 'Gordian knots' of risk. Indeed, objective diagnosis here of the underlying societal malaise points the compass for how remedial interventions ought to be reoriented toward actualising comprehensive seaport, rail, and road infrastructure modernisation for Niger Delta region and its infrastructure-deprived population. This blueprint articulated at the community level serves as a microcosm for the urgency of reforms from the highest levels of political leadership down to multinational oil conglomerates and even small-scale illegal bunkering entrepreneurs. What is clear in this book is how technical pipeline security solutions or rhetorical amnesty gestures alone cannot hope to sustainably redress accelerating pressures without a holistic understanding of their root sociological and environmental drivers.

The clarity of the book leads me to conclude that it contributes long overdue enlightened perspectives toward solving the notoriously complex security problems that have bedevilled the Niger Delta region of Nigeria for decades. Additionally, the transferable insights the book provides are of critical relevance from Latin America's resource-rich Amazon to the Caspian's hydrocarbon hotspots anywhere vulnerable populations perceive pipeline corridor protection initiatives as instruments of exclusion and socio-ecological subjugation. This is a book for state and non-state actors contending with local, national, regional, and global environmental degradation and attendant socio-economic and political effects.

Prof. Obas John Ebohon
Dean of the Academy for
Sustainable Futures
Canterbury Christ Church
University
Canterbury, Kent, UK

# PREFACE

This book explored the causes of onshore oil and gas pipeline infrastructure insecurity in Bayelsa state as a lens to understand the oil and gas infrastructure insecurity problems in the Niger Delta and the Global South. Its aim focused on the critical analysis of the vandalism of the Nembe Creek Trunk Line which has also experienced several operational blowouts. Although oil and gas infrastructure insecurity and pipeline vandalism in the Niger Delta has fascinated many scholars who have focused on the political and economic perspectives, and socio-economic dimensions of the problem. Most scholars have shielded away from exploring a range of underlying socio-economic issues, poor governance, environmental conditions, and politics that are responsible for the vandalism of the NCTL. This book explored the borderline areas. It drew on inferences from both political socio-economic, and environmental factors and linked them to structural issues to reveal the causes of onshore pipeline vandalism, and oil and gas infrastructure insecurity in Nembe Bayelsa and most petrostates in the Global South. Many works of literature, documentary, and regulatory framework policies were reviewed, scrutinised, and analysed to have a broader understanding of oil and gas operations, and the dynamics of the insecurity problems in the sector. The book applied the frustration-aggression displacement theory to explain how various regulatory policy frameworks implemented by the oil and gas operators, the regulators, and the government represent the instrumental triggers that lead to anger and frustration resulting in aggression and vandalism. FADT is supported by a theoretical model called Community Neglect Aggression Displacement Theory. The proposed CNADT explains that the collective neglect to resolve the underlying socio-economic and environmental issues in communities led to poverty, unemployment, and a decrease in household incomes provoking anger and aggression that led to vandalism. FADT and CNADT established that a person, group, or community that has experienced extreme depravity, marginalisation, and obstruction to their source of wellbeing, happiness, and livelihood will be frustrated, angry, and turn to aggression. This book found that the heightened cases of pipeline vandalism and oil and gas insecurity problems in Nembe-Bayelsa, and most local communities across petrostates in the Global South are due to decades of collective neglect of many issues that concern local communities, poor governance, corruption, and environmental devastation.

January 2024

Dr. Abdul L. Abraham Jatto,
Ph.D., FHEA
AdvanceHE Teaching Fellow
in Politics & International
Relations, Political Security/
Resilient Oil and Gas Security,
Nigeria, Sub-Sahara Africa &
Global South, UK

# ACKNOWLEDGMENTS

I acknowledge the School of Social and Political Sciences ethics committee at the University of Lincoln, UK, for their rigorous ethical approval processes. It formed the basis for the doctoral fieldwork from where a substantial part of the data that formed this book was obtained. I appreciate the contributions of the book editor, Dr. Anietie Isong, an international oil and gas professional, a scholar, and an award-winning British author. He leveraged over 10 years of professional experience with world-leading multinational oil and gas corporations, to edit this book. Particularly, for integrating his wealth of practical knowledge in writing reports on the oil and gas industry and participating in many cross-sectoral and international oil and gas conferences. Editing this book demonstrates his unrelenting desire to contribute to the body of knowledge. As an author, Dr. Anietie Isong has been a guest speaker at the London Book Fair, the Ake Arts and Book Festival, the Henley Literary Festival, Marlborough Literature Festival, among other literary festivals across the world. He has also been a judge of the Society of Authors' Awards in the UK.

Also, I am extremely humbled by the unflinching support of my family, my wife, and my children, for being consistent, and persistent in their prayers, faith, loving care, kindness, and belief in me throughout my never-ending search for advanced knowledge. I express my gratitude to Professor Pat Utomi, Political Economist, at Lagos Business School and Management, Fellow of the Institute of Management Consultants of Nigeria. Scholar-in-residence at the Harvard Business School and the American University in Washington D.C., and currently the Chairman, of United Niger Delta Energy Development Security Strategy for his gate-keeping role. He used his vast contact network to introduce and link me with vital professional independent civil society organisations repre-sentatives and environmental activists in Bayelsa and the wider historic Niger Delta region. I thank all the professional participants, Senior oil and gas executives, Directors of oil and gas regulatory agencies, and Senior security officials from the Operation Delta Safe OPDS headquarters. I also want to appreciate all the community participants such as Kings, Paramount rulers, High chiefs, Youth leaders, and High-profile commu-nity leaders for volunteering their participation in the fieldwork. Their support, stories, and narrations gave the detailed insights needed to shine a new light into this dark area of onshore oil and gas pipeline vandalism, focusing on the NCTL and insecurity in Bayelsa-Nembe. It would have been difficult, if not impossible, to understand the complexities of the underlying issues of vandalism, threats, tensions, conflicts, and insecurity in the Niger Delta and perhaps the Global South through the lens of poor governance and socio-economic, political, and environmental challenges.

# Contents

# Abbreviations

| | |
|---|---|
| AFC | Armed Forces Council |
| AOGR | Africa Oil and Gas Report |
| BANGOF | Bayelsa Non-Governmental Organisation Forum |
| BTCC | Baku-Tbilisi-Ceyhan Corporation |
| BWF | Bayelsa Women Forum |
| CCECC | China Civil Engineering Construction Company |
| CDS | Chief of Defence Staff |
| CJD | Criminal Justice Decree |
| CNADT | Community Neglect Aggression Displacement Theory |
| CPGC | Contemporary Poor Governance Cycle |
| CSPDM | Community Stakeholders' Policy Development Model |
| DDRD | Disarmament, Demobilisation, Reintegration, and Development |
| DMI | Directorate of Military Intelligence |
| DPR | Department of Petroleum Resources |
| DRMS | Downstream Remote Monitoring Systems |
| DSA | Development of Special Areas |
| DSS | Department of State Security |
| EFCC | Economic and Financial Crimes Commission |
| EM | Exxon Mobil |
| ERA | Environmental Rights Action |
| FADT | Frustration-Aggression-Displacement Theory |
| FAT | Frustration-Aggression-Displacement |
| FEDAL | Federation of Female Lawyers |
| FET | Forcados Export Terminal |
| FIIB | Federal Intelligence and Investigation Bureau |

| FME | Federal Ministry of Environment |
| FMPR | Federal Ministry of Petroleum Resources |
| FPS | Floating Production Storage |
| GAM | General Aggression Model |
| GDP | Gross Domestic Product |
| GDPR | General Data Protection Regulation |
| GEIL | Green Energy International Limited |
| GMO | Genetically Modified Organisms |
| GMOU | General Memorandum of Understanding |
| GN | Global North |
| GPPAC | Global Partnership for the Prevention of Armed Conflict |
| GS | Global South |
| HCDT | Host Community Development Trust |
| HDI | Human Development Index |
| HNDR | Historic Niger Delta Region |
| HPS | Heads of the Paramilitary Services |
| ICC | Intelligence Coordinating Committees |
| ICPC | Independent Corrupt Practices Commission |
| ICR | International Centre for Reconciliation |
| IMF | International Monetary Fund |
| INEC | Independent National Electoral Commission |
| IPCC | Intergovernmental Panel on Climate Change |
| MEND | Movement for the Emancipation of the Niger Delta |
| MORETO | Movement for the Reparation to Ogbia |
| MOSIEN | Movement for the Survival of the Izon (Ijaw) Ethnic Nationality |
| MOSOP | Movement for the Survival of the Ogoni People |
| MOU | Memorandum of Understanding |
| MSSL | Maritime Support Services Limited |
| NA | Nigeria Army |
| NB | National Budget |
| NBC | National Bureau of Statistics |
| NC | Nigeria Customs |
| NCHRE | National Committee on Human Research Ethics |
| NCTL | Nembe Creek Trunk Line |
| ND | Niger Delta |
| NDA | Niger Delta Avengers |
| NDDC | Niger Delta Development Commission |
| NDLEA | Nigeria Drug Law Enforcement Agency |
| NDM | Niger Delta Militants |
| NDPVF | Niger Delta People Volunteer Force |
| NEITI | Nigeria Extractive Industries Transparency Initiative |
| NFEPA | Nigeria Federal Environmental Protection Agency |

| NG | Nigeria Government |
|---|---|
| NIA | Nigeria Intelligence Agency |
| NIS | Nigerian Immigration Service |
| NMDPA | Nigerian Midstream and Downstream Petroleum Authority |
| NN | Nigeria Navy |
| NNPC | Nigeria National Petroleum Company |
| NOA | National Orientation Agency |
| NOSDRA | Nigeria Oil Spill Detection and Response Agency |
| NPF | Nigeria Police Force |
| NPSCL | Nigerian Pipeline Storage Company Limited |
| NSA | National Security Adviser |
| NSC | National Security Council |
| NSCDC | Nigeria Security and Civil Defense Corps |
| NUPRC | Nigerian Upstream Petroleum Regulatory Commission |
| NURC | Nigeria Upstream Regulatory Commission |
| OGHC | Oil and Gas Host Communities |
| OGMNC | Oil and Gas Multinational Corporations |
| OML | Oil Mining Lease |
| OMPADEC | Oil Mineral Producing Area Development Commission |
| OOGIIN | Onshore Oil and Gas Infrastructure Insecurity Nexus |
| OPDS | Operation Delta Safe |
| OPEC | Organisation of Petroleum Exporting Countries |
| OV | Offloading Vessels |
| PHCD | Petroleum Host Community Development |
| PIA | Petroleum Industry Act |
| PICD | Pipeline Implementation and Community Development |
| POCD | Pipeline Operation and Community Development |
| POCDLC | Pipeline Operations and Community Development Life Cycle |
| PPCD | Pipeline Planning and Community Development |
| PPDA | Petroleum Production and Distribution Act |
| PSSC | Pipeline Surveillance Security Contractors |
| QIT | Qua Iboe Terminal |
| SCP | State Commissioner of Police |
| SDG | Sustainable Development Goals |
| SDNSA | State Directors of National Security Agencies |
| SPDC | Shell Petroleum Development Company |
| SPI | Social Performance Interface |
| SSR | Special Status Recognition |
| TNOG | Total Nigeria Oil and Gas Limited |
| TROMPCON | Traditional Rulers of Oil Mineral Producing Communities of Nigeria |
| UK | United Kingdom |
| UNDEDSS | United Niger Delta Energy Development and Security Strategy |

| | |
|---|---|
| UNDP | United Nations Development Programme |
| UNEP | United Nations Environmental Programme |
| UNHDR | United Nations Human Development Report |
| UNOCHA | United Nations Office of Coordination of Humanitarian Affairs |
| UNODC | United Nations Office on Drugs and Crime |
| UNSDG | United Nations Sustainable Development Goals |
| USA | United States of America |
| USAID | United States Aid for International Development |

# LIST OF FIGURES

# CHAPTER 1

# Introduction

## Introductory Statement

The novelty of this book is the 41 face-to-face professional and community stakeholder interviews that validate the use of the Frustration-Aggression Displacement Theory (FADT). Other scholars before now have neither interviewed this nature of population samples nor interrogated a combination of this type of stakeholders, CSO, villagers, policymakers, or operators. Oil and gas exploration and production have led to many disparities in trickle-down socio-economic benefits between the privileged few and many host communities in Nigeria (Collier, 2007; Hammond, 2011: 348; Okonofua, 2016). An additional novelty of this book is its structured and systematic outlining of underlying root causes that trigger socio-economic, corruption, and organised crime, and cursed leadership factors that cause vandalism and insecurity of the NCTL onshore pipelines and oil and gas infrastructure. There is no isolated factor(s) that cause oil and gas pipeline vandalism. The problem is a combination of factor(s) that are reinforced by a combination of underlying issues as alluded to by Umar and Othman (2017). Evidence shows that other petrostates in the Global South such as Venezuela, Myanmar, and Angola to name a few experiences the same problems leading to tensions). Oil and gas and other extractive activities are responsible for the devastating environmental and negative human development incidents

A. L. A. Jatto, *Oil and Gas Pipeline Infrastructure Insecurity*, New Security Challenges, https://doi.org/10.1007/978-3-031-56932-6_1

ravaging many host communities in Nigeria and across many other countries in the Global South (Dodd & Merwe, 2019; Loft & Brien, 2023; Olawuyi, 2012; Onuoha, 2007, 2008; UNEP, 2012; UNSDG, 2016).

This chapter provides a synopsised summary of onshore oil and gas pipeline vandalism and infrastructure insecurity problems in Bayelsa, Niger Delta region of Nigeria; threats, tensions; and conflicts which are problems also found in the Global South (Alagoa, 2005; Dollard et al., 1939; Hammond, 2011; Igbinovia, 2014; Okumagba, 2013; Onuoha, 2007, 2008). It discussed historical changes and challenges that occurred in the decades leading up to 2021 in the Nigeria petroleum industry. This is followed by an introductory search of some literature and a range of conceptual perspectives that herald many oil and gas exploration, and infrastructure security policies. The purpose, scope, and originality of this book are outlined across all sections of the book as demonstrated by the chosen research design strategy and data collection methods. This is followed by the concluding section which details a breakdown of the chapters and a summary of their content.

The book uses Bayelsa Nembe Creek Trunk Line (NCTL), in Nigeria, as a lens to understand the various issues of vandalism, threats, tensions, and varying degrees of insecurity problems in most petrostates in the Global South. It deconstructs the "resource curse" hypothesis advanced by Collier (2007) and Ross (2012, 2015). It argues that the issues of socio-economic stagnation and conflicts in many Global South countries are not due to the natural resources under the soil that these countries are endowed with, far from it. The evidence presented throughout the book supports the conclusion that the cyclical nature with which incompetent political leaders emerge in the Global South, which has assumed a "leadership curse", is the problem. The "curse" is the inability to break away from the negative trend of cases of incompetent political leaders in the Global South, like Myanmar. Who constantly create the impression of degrading the socio-economic opportunities for their citizens. This "curse" phenomenon also suggests that there is a supernatural power preventing the majority of citizens in Nigeria from comprehending the harm that the recycling of incompetent political leaders inflicts tensions, conflicts, and insecurity problems on them (Chapters 3, 4, 5, and 8). This book interrogates the views of different stakeholders to gauge their views, and those of professional civil society representatives working with the host communities, on the impact of collective neglect by the government and oil firms. This is to find out the underlying reasons for vandalism of the onshore NCTL oil and gas pipeline infrastructure in the Nembe case study area as well as explain reasons for other tensions leading to insecurity in Bayelsa state.

The book is structured around two distinctive areas: (1) it starts with an analysis of oil and gas infrastructure insecurity in Nigeria and the Global South, its midstream and downstream petroleum regulatory policies and operational activities of oil and gas multinational organisations coupled with the security architecture deployed drawing on professional civil society organisations, partly discussed in Chapters 2, 3, 4 and throughout Chapter 6; and (2) a study of the impact of oil and gas regulatory policies and activities of multinational oil and gas operators on host communities, by interrogating representatives of local NGOs, discussed in Chapters 6, 7, and 8. It draws on this structure to advance three main arguments which are (1) the instrumental policies of the government and their implementation; (2) along with the non-adoption of best international practices and some unethical behaviours, by oil and gas multinationals and; (3) on top the devastating impact of oil activities on the environment, suffered by the communities, caused tensions between individuals, communities, oil companies, and the government which cascades to varying degree of insecurity problems. These tensions and their wider socio-economic impact on host communities are not isolated to Nigeria and Africa, but are also prevalent in many countries in the Global South (Collier, 2007; Hammond, 2011).

The aims, objectives, and questions the book addresses are a reflection of the above two broad areas and the three arguments. Throughout the whole book chapters, the nexus between petroleum regulatory policies, security architecture, and the onshore pipeline structural resilience as well as the impact of oil and gas operations is considered. This book established that the failure to address underlying causes of socio-economic, environmental, political, and poor governance issues makes resolving the insecurity problems difficult. Scholars have always focused on the symptoms, random and sometimes reactive government regulatory policy frameworks, and the operationalisation of the regulations by oil and gas multinational corporations. They neglect the views of different community stakeholders and therefore fail to identify the underlying root causes of onshore pipeline vandalism in the Niger Delta. Reports, gazettes, and published statistical data in this area have neglected to undertake empirical interviews with the stakeholders to gauge their perspectives on the impact of oil and gas activities and government policies on their lives and collective communities. Therefore, creating a substantial gap in the literature around the empirical data that highlights the underlying reasons that motivate communities to aggress against onshore oil and gas pipeline infrastructure in Nigeria's Niger Delta, and other oil-producing countries in the Global South (Ross, 2012).

The context for this book is thus set based on observed and identified gaps in the literature which is the neglect of the views of different stakeholders, particularly the Bayelsa community stakeholders. The book filled the gap in the literature by undertaking empirical fieldwork and engaging in face-to-face semi-structured interviews to gather data from 41 different oil and gas and community stakeholders including professional civil society, security, and oil and gas executives. It draws on a variety of 41 respondents with representatives of oil and gas companies, security agencies, climate change and civil society/NGO professional representatives, community leaders, high-profile community members, and local environmental activists. It used the thematic analysis technique to analyse the patterns and themes that emerged from the qualitative data reduction, coding, and categorisation processes. Critical Discourse Analysis (CDA) was also used throughout the study as an analytical tool to explain the relationship between power, language, and social conflicts, as explained in detail in Chapter 5. The triangulation of thematic and critical discourse analysis enriched the outcome of the book, giving the student and reader a comprehensive understanding. Using both techniques did not reduce the relevance of any but corroborated the significance of the result.

The data gathered supported the richness of this book and the argument made. The Frustration-Aggression-Displacement Theory (FADT) provides the theoretical and explanatory framework for the book (Dollard et al., 1939). Applying FADT theory to the data gathered illuminates a deeper understanding of the reasons and mechanisms by which the underlying causes of discontent and resentment are understood. Whether they be socio-economic, environmental, or political, and highlighting how this led some individuals and local communities to support violent aggression and vandalism of the NCTL pipelines. The book builds on and complements FADT by proposing the Community Neglect Aggression Displacement Theory-CNADT model (Bergstresser, 2017; Coleman, 2015; Etemire, 2016; Etete, 2017; Okonta, 2016). Applying CNADT reveals deeper insight into why the aggressive reactions of some individuals and local communities are predicated upon frustration and anger due to collective neglect and poor human development index that has been suffered in the case study area and the Global South for many decades. In short, the arguments put forward are that the negative impact of oil and gas extraction combined with the other underlying causes mentioned above leads to frustration and displacement of aggression against onshore oil and gas pipeline infrastructure. In other words, creates tensions and exposes the infrastructure to poor resilience. This violence has serious socio-economic, security, and environmental implications thus, triggering a vicious cycle of violence and insecurity problems that is difficult to break.

## THE AIM AND ACADEMIC CONTRIBUTION OF THE BOOK

The book aims to explore the oil and gas pipeline infrastructure insecurity in Bayelsa state focusing on the vandalism of the NCTL pipeline in Nembe, threats, and conflicts in the historic Niger Delta area within the broader context of the Global South. Many underlying issues are the root causes of the vandalism of the onshore oil and gas pipeline infrastructure in the case study area. This book highlights that there are many innovative instrumental policies in the oil and gas sector as found in the recent Petroleum Industry Act 2022. But this Act, like many other policy instruments, contains inherent policy and organisational tensions and conflicts that are problematic to disentangle and resolve. These tensions and conflicts directly impact the host community's perceptions leading to resistance and thus the potential success of oil activities in Bayelsa host communities. Scholars argue that these tensions and insecurity issues in the Niger Delta have wider contextual implications across resource-rich host communities in the Global South (Rutten & Mwangi, 2014: 52–55). Some of these issues are socio-economic disparity and resource exploitation, land and fishing water displacement and loss of legitimate sources of livelihood, cultural and socio-cultural displacement, and inequitable distribution of benefits amongst others (Collier, 2007; Okumagba, 2012, 2013).

Although there have been research and papers written on pipeline vandalism in Bayelsa and the Niger Delta (Igbinovia, 2014; Mathias, 2015; Onuoha, 2007, 2008, 2016). None has used FADT to explain how oil and gas pipeline infrastructure vandalism and insecurity problems occur or interviewed different stakeholders on why they aggress against onshore and offshore oil and gas pipelines (Anderson & Dill, 1995: 365; Dollard et al., 1939; Krueger, 1996; Lazarus, 1994). Their tension and anger lead to a transfer of frustration against the oil and gas pipeline infrastructure (Berkowitz, 2011; Okumagba, 2013; Sanderson, 2010). Bayelsa was chosen for this research because it has one of the largest onshore oil fields, producing oil wells, and pipeline networks while the NCTL in Nembe is the most expensive and ironically the most vandalised onshore pipeline in Nigeria, which is the largest producer of crude oil and gas in Africa. Natural resources, especially, hydrocarbon minerals placed the historic Niger Delta at the forefront of political, economic, and environmental tensions in Nigeria for many decades (Alagoa, 2005; Alamieyeseigha, 2008a, 2008b; Douglas & Okonta, 2003; Ibaba, 2012; Igbinovia, 2014; Mathias, 2015; Onuoha, 2016). This book fills the gap in the academic literature through the professional and community stakeholders' interviews and analysed data. Previous studies have not done this before but mainly focused on the symptomatic outcome of oil and gas activities in Nigeria's Niger Delta. However, some reports have reviewed the inhuman environmental disaster and destruction in the Niger Delta area for over 63 years.

A study by Buzan (1984a, 1984b) and Waever (1998) provides a critical and vital insight into human/political security that focuses on the citizen as the central referent, which is a nonconventional approach to studying security. Thus, contributing to international security and international relations. This book examined some of the policymaking documentary evidence, its impacts, and processes, and the undercurrent dynamics that interact to instigate the factors that lead to tensions, threats, conflicts, and vandalism. Security seamlessly serves social, economic, climatic, environmental, moral, political, human, and religious justice to all citizens (Emmers, 2016; Hudson, 2010; Irvine, 2018; Neocleous, 2007; Schwegler, 2017; see Chapter 2). Suggesting that security should be practiced as a "process" rather than as an "assumption".

This study defines security as the effectiveness of established structures and instruments that are created to transparently address internal threats and conflicts between citizens and resolve environmental tensions. At the same time, protecting the state from external aggressions, and attacks. Unlike other oil and gas literature, this book explores the inherent tensions, and underlying background issues that interact with policies and procedures to impact host communities leading to tensions, oil theft, and vandalism. This book is more comprehensive because it analyses the entire spectrum of oil and gas issues from policy agenda setting, formulation, and implementation to its impact on host communities, the national budget, and defense security. This book, rather than focus on the underlying causes of onshore oil and gas pipelines alone, drills deeper and broadens its analytical scrutiny into the policymaking processes and how the tensions, resistance, and aggressive reactions from host communities have affected the implementation of various oil and gas policy regimes. Interrogating different community stakeholders is an additional contribution that this book makes to this field. Other areas of contributions made by this book are:

Political Security: A new perspective was introduced to the causes of pipeline vandalism and the onshore oil and gas infrastructure insecurity debate. By focusing on the vandalism of the NCTL this research contributes to the body of knowledge on political security.

Security and Insecurity Debate: The Community Neglect Aggression Displacement theoretical model contributes to the nonconventional approach to security debates that focuses on the rights of the citizens. The nonconventional—Copenhagen security approach ties security to the socio-economic, human, environmental, and climate rights of citizens (Haq, 1995; Owen, 2004). This agrees with Cordesman's assertion that the individual is the irreducible unit for discussing security (2016). This has relevance to human security which Haq described as the freedom of the citizens from fear and wants (1994). To the United Nations Human Development Report (UNHDR), human security is a people's safety from chronic threats and protection from sudden hurtful disruptions in the patterns of their daily lives (1994). This study contributes to the insecurity debate by proposing a Community Neglect Aggression Displacement theoretical model. The factors that define CNADT lean towards factors identified by Haq, Owen, UNHDR, and Codesman's postulations on (in)security. CNADT theoretical model explains that the failure of the private sector and the government's negligence in providing basic human needs leads to frustration. The failure to address food scarcity, shelter, employment, and health, halt environmental degradation impoverishing local communities. As well as addressing the consequences of climate change is responsible for the aggression, vandalism, and insecurity problems across the six geopolitical zones of Nigeria.

Theoretical Framework: This study uses the frustration-aggression-displacement theory to explain the vandalism of the NCTL pipelines. By explaining that when people are prevented from achieving their goals and set objectives they are bound to be frustrated and angry and in turn aggressively react overtly or non-overtly against the source of their frustration (Dollard et al., 1939; Okumagba, 2012; Sanderson, 2010). This study contributes to the body of knowledge by proposing CNADT to support the FADT hypothesis. While FADT points out that people reactively when prevented from achieving their set objectives. CNADT notes that people will react aggressively when displaced from sources of their socio-economic independence and issues are neglected and unresolved by the government and private oil firms. When local communities suffer more hunger, decreased income, unemployment, and impoverishment they will become reactive. This provokes them to displace aggression against oil firms and the government by vandalising pipelines.

Pipeline Vandalism and Oil and Gas Infrastructure Insecurity: There is an inherent correlation between the factors and actions of the actors in the Niger Delta's insecurity problems (Umar & Othman, 2017). This study asserts that the factors that cause onshore oil and gas pipeline vandalism and infrastructure insecurity problems, such as poor governance and politics; environmental degradation; leadership curse; socio-economic issues; and corruption and organised crimes highlighted and discussed throughout this book, and the micro-foundational variables that trigger those factors are found in the micro-foundational variables that underpin CNADT.

Structural Integrity of the Pipeline: Timashev and Bushinskaya (2016a, 2016b) say materiality, design code, as well as technology, are major determinants that ensure the structural integrity of oil and gas pipelines (see Chapter 5). This study contributes to knowledge by highlighting the dark spot underlying the structural weaknesses of pipelines.

## THE PURPOSE OF THE BOOK

The purpose ties in with the rationale for this book which draws on the "Bottom Billion" hypothesis proposed by Paul Collier (2007). He outlined reasons why natural resource wealth has neither percolated to the grassroots nor translated into socio-economic growth and critical infrastructure development in poorer countries in the Global South as observed in Bayelsa state. The assertions of Collier are reflective of the present-day realities in the historic Niger Delta region of Nigeria and some other natural resource-rich poor countries in the Global South (Moyo, 2011; Rodney, 2012). This book further highlights ways of approaching pipeline security in Nigeria that could be mirrored by countries in the Global South facing similar challenges which Mathias (2015) and Onuoha (2008) pointed out constitutes critical national infrastructure. Many random and unethical policies implemented by the government and oil firms are not reflective of the socio-economic and environmental realities of the people across host communities. Oftentimes, their views, economic and environmental, are neglected and the anger and frustration resulting from this create an atmosphere of resistance and resentment to policy implementation that triggers vandalism, political tensions, and risks to lives and properties. As Egbe and Thompson as well as Omoweh stated, the situation is worse because there is no reliable model for gathering or sampling different views or calculating the level of damage of oil activities on impacted host communities (2010; 2008).

This book is designed and structured around two central elements (1) an analysis of oil and gas activities, infrastructure resilience security, and its implications in the Global South, and; (2) an evaluation and discussion of tensions around policy implementation and the impacts these have on host communities. These two central elements are distilled and arranged around the following four critical objectives:

1. Identifying the causes of onshore oil and gas pipeline infrastructure insecurity in Bayelsa state (Chapters 2, 3, 6, and 8);
2. Evaluating how the government and oil and gas companies respond to oil spillage, in particular, vandalism of the NCTL pipeline infrastructure (Chapters 2, 3, 4, 6, and 8);
3. Identifying the strategies deployed in protecting oil and gas pipeline infrastructure from vandalism and the impact on local communities in Bayelsa (Chapters 2, 6, and 8);
4. Exploring the impact of the construction of the NCTL onshore pipeline on local communities (Chapters 2, 3, 4, and 7).

These four objectives are addressed individually across the subsequent Chapters and represent the centre of discussion and analysis across the entire book as it relates to the case study area. The challenges and success of oil and gas infrastructure security policies in Nigeria's Niger Delta as well as the Global South are gauged side-by-side with these highlighted aims and set objectives, although analysis and evaluation are a matter of perspective and therefore continually contested and debated. The structure and frame of the book raise some very critical and vital overarching questions across the entire Chapters focusing on the vandalism of the NCTL in the historic Niger Delta region such as:

- Have socio-economic, environmental, and political issues contributed to oil and gas pipeline infrastructure vandalism and insecurity problems in Bayelsa State, Nigeria's Niger Delta? (Chapters 2, 3, 4, and 8);
- What impact have regulatory policy guidelines on oil and gas extraction and production, and pipeline operations in terms of responses to vandalism and oil spills in Bayelsa State, Nigeria? (Chapters 2, 3, 4, and 8);
- What impact do security protection strategies of onshore pipelines have on local communities in Bayelsa state? (Chapters 2, 3, 6, and 7);
- In What ways has the construction and operationalisation of the NCTL impacted the natural environment and the host communities in Nembe, Niger Delta? (Chapters 2, 3, 4, and 8).

In answering these questions and highlighting the underlying causes of onshore pipeline vandalism, conflicts, threats, and political tensions, the book takes "five holistic approaches". The first involved adopting NVivo 12- a professional computer-based data analysis software (Hai-Jew, 2016; Seale, 2004) followed by coding which drew on the intensive reading of the text from the transcribed interviews (Berg, 2007; Gibbs, 2018). The second data analysis approach was the comparison of emerging themes derived from the professional and community stakeholders to determine similarities and dissimilarities in patterns. The third approach developed two comprehensive thematic categorised datasets that was further broken down into seven smaller thematic categories for in-depth analysis. The fourth approach combined and synthesised the discourse and findings from the professional and community samples to develop new knowledge (see above) while addressing the central book question, aim and objectives. The final approach involved using Critical Discourse Analysis (CDA) to describe, interpret, and explain how the discourses presented by various perspectives on vandalism and insecurity construct, maintain, legitimise, and highlight the socio-economic disequilibrium in Bayelsa and many petrostates in the Global South. It examined the oil and gas regulatory policymaking and implementation processes, security architecture in Nigeria as it applies to the historic Niger Delta region, activities of oil and gas corporations, and their impacts as well as the response of the host communities.

## FIELDWORK AND DATA COLLECTION METHODOLOGY

The background, aims and purpose of this book enabled the author to adopt a case study research design, qualitative data-gathering method, and critical discourse analytical technique. Policy documents, expert think tank reviews, and legislative reports, such as the Petroleum Industry Act (PIA, 2021); Land Use Act (LUA); Transparency International (TI); oil operators, and security operations documents were accessed online and through official visit to organisation's libraries. These documentary data were triangulated with empirical semi-structured interviews. All the interview participants recruited from the professional and community groups linked with the case study were given pseudonyms to maintain their anonymity and confidentiality (Creswell, 2015). Forty-one (41) participants took part including directors and managers from Department of Petroleum Resources (DPR), now the Nigerian Upstream Regulatory Commission, -NURC, and executives at the Nigeria National Petroleum Corporation (NNPC) offices in Lagos, Port Harcourt, Abuja, Belemaoil, Seplat Oil and Gas, and Aiteo Exploration and Production.

As well as senior security officers, Navy, police, Army, State Security, and Civil Defense, that constituted Operation Delta Safe (OPDS) Joint Security Task Force including country managers of international civil society. Given that this book is a case study of Bayelsa state in the historic Niger Delta area meant recruiting community leaders, high-profile members of the communities, and environmental stakeholders to share their views on the issues. This methodological approach enabled the researcher to gain insight into the professional experience and expert opinions that created a clearer picture of the issues raised by the stakeholders. They shared their views on vandalism, the structural resilience of oil pipelines, and the impact of instrumental policies on the local communities and operators (Igbinovia, 2014; Onuoha, 2007).

## The Book and its Background

This book focuses mainly on onshore oil and gas pipeline infrastructure insecurity; vandalism, threats, and conflicts. All of these forms the issues of insecurity of oil and gas resources, infrastructure, and personnel in the Niger Delta and the wider Global South. These influenced the aims, objectives, and questions raised and answered in this book. The host communities in Bayelsa react aggressively because they are unable to access legitimate sources of livelihood to provide for their daily needs. Activities of the oil and gas industry threaten their sources of livelihood leading to civil dissent and resistance that contributes to the factors of insecurity. In the context of this book, insecurity is a state of being exposed to danger and threats due to a lack of protection. Many studies adopted a global view of what insecurity means prompting different definitions. This study adopts a more local and national perspective to defining what insecurity is. *Insecurity is where local and national security architecture is overwhelmed by incompatible demands of ethnic, socio-economic, and religious forces that are sufficient enough to disrupt the safety and activities of people and infrastructure.* However, George noted that sources of insecurity or international insecurity, are not restricted to hydrocarbon shortages, threat of global climate change, or the unintended effects of Genetically Modified Organisms (George, 2009).

Human insecurity in the Niger Delta is a direct consequence of oil and gas activities and its poor infrastructure resilience. This book aligns with Gopakumar, Leuven, Faust, and Aktan's description of infrastructure. It is a range of support facilities and services including skills and expertise that support a system or industry, the ecosystem, the social and cultural life of communities as well as finance and installations (Faust & Aktan, 2003; Gopakumar, 2012; Leuven, 2011). Oil and gas infrastructure consists of a wide range of interdependences such as stovepipes; pipelines; refineries; storage tanks; distribution networks; personnel; roads; and transportation systems (Grigg, 2010; Lesar, 2001; Lewis, 2015). Including onshore and offshore rigs/platforms; electric power; information and telecommunication technology; and oil tankers and barges. Oil and gas infrastructure insecurity issues are the totality of human and natural resources divided into three primary, secondary, and tertiary sub-sets to cover the wide range of issues associated with it. The primary, secondary, and tertiary oil and gas infrastructure insecurity problems and how they are managed determine the extent the natural resources can be accessed, explored, and developed within the host community (Devold, 2013), see Fig. 1.1. The three-phase pipeline life cycle of planning, implementation, and operationalisation resolves the primary, secondary, and tertiary infrastructure insecurity problems (Mathias, 2015; Onuoha, 2007; see Chapter 8). These primary oil and gas insecurity problems include:

1. The extent of negotiations with the host communities (contracts and MOUs)
2. Hydrocarbon feasibility studies
3. Exploration
4. Environmental vulnerabilities
5. Exploration risks
6. Equipment deployment and
7. Soil chemical composition and acidity.

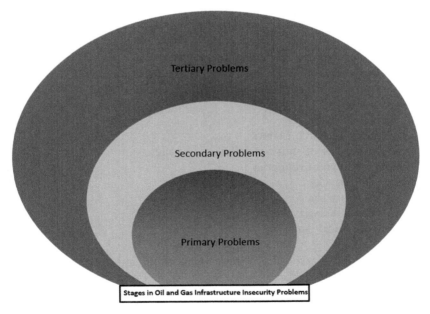

**Fig. 1.1**   Stages in oil and gas infrastructure insecurity problems (*Source* Author [2023])

The secondary oil and gas infrastructure insecurity problems are issues that could disrupt the business but do not have an immediate impact such as:

- Mapping oilfields
- Drilling oil wells
- Materiality
- Design codes
- Christmas tree construction
- Construction of flowlines, pipelines, storage tanks and networking
- Production
- Regulatory violations and
- Mechanical/technical blowouts.

However, the tertiary oil and gas infrastructure insecurity problems have a direct impact on both the government and the oil corporations because it is the stage when money and resources exchange hands. This tertiary oil and gas infrastructure insecurity includes:

    i. Threats (human and non-human)
   ii. Operational risks
  iii. Infrastructure terrorism
   iv. Vandalism
    v. Oil bunkering
   vi. Declaring Force Majure
  vii. Onshore or offshore transportation issues
 viii. Breakdown of refineries
   ix. Cyber-attacks
    x. Drone attacks
   xi. Natural disasters and
  xii. Geopolitical dynamics

This book focuses on the tertiary stage of oil and gas infrastructure insecurity which is onshore pipeline vandalism because it is central to the research question. In the context of this book, oil and gas infrastructure insecurity means pipeline vandalism, cyberattacks, threats, kidnapping of oil personnel; depletion in oil and gas reserves; lack of investment in oil and gas industries; weak structures; and price volatility (Omand, 2011;

Talus, 2011). This onshore oil and gas pipeline infrastructure insecurity is related to concern about the stability, safety, and protection of pipelines that transport oil and gas fluid over land. Thus, its increased exposure to physical attacks, terrorism, sabotage, illegal bunkering, theft, cyberattacks, technological vulnerabilities, regulatory policy challenges, environmental pollution, and climate change, in Nigeria and the Global South is a cause for worry. This has become the central focus in the geopolitical, religious, ethnic, and economic debates across Nigeria, and West Africa, and has been reflected in many resource-rich countries in the Global South.

The vandalism of the NCTL pipeline entails physical human disruptions and sabotage against the pipelines. Some scholars argued that the vandalism of the NCTL pipelines is partly motivated by the deplorable state of human security in the Niger Delta (Aluko, 2015; Ekpenyong, 2010; Madubuko, 2017; Owen, 2004; Chapter 3). However, Alabi traced other problems to poor governance (in terms of policy conflicts, legislative tensions, and lack of investment in R and D), and incompetent leadership structures created by the British colonialists (Alabi, 2013). The processes of oil and gas production, pipeline operation, vandalism, oil bunkering, and oil spills have killed many people including pipeline vandals, oil thieves, and bystanders (Goodman et al., 2016; Igbenovia, 2014). These incidences have also caused substantial damage to the ecosystem, especially marine life, and increased greenhouse gas emissions in Bayelsa and the fishing rivers of the wider historic Niger Delta region, as it has in many countries in the Global South like Sudan, Equatorial Guinea, and Venezuela (Alabi, 2013). However, Kuwait, Qatar, and Brazil appear to have reasonably managed to share and use benefits from oil and gas to trigger some measure of socio-economic and infrastructural development (Rizzo, 2016). Unfortunately, the same cannot be said in Nigeria where for instance, over 260 people were killed in Ilado, and about 269 others at Abule Egba between May and December of 2016 due to corruption, vandalism, oil spills, and operational failures (Igbinovia, 2014; Mathias, 2015).

A technical failure also killed three people in Bayelsa during the repairs of the ENI oil pipelines in 2016 (Owolabi, 2016) on top of stagnated infrastructural development (Avwunudiogba, 2023; Onolememen, 2020). Other threats and risks to oil and gas activities and infrastructure are natural disasters, climate change, and corrosion all of which have had devastating effects on the local communities and the environment (BTC Corporation, 2014; Ubong et al., 2010; Watchet, 2012). It is worth noting that continued vandalism has contributed to preventing Nigeria from achieving the Organisation of Petroleum Exporting Countries (OPEC) production quota for many years. A fluctuation in oil and gas production in Nigeria has hovered between 700,000 and 2.7 million barrels per day over the last 21 years, putting Nigeria at a considerable disadvantage in terms of oil and gas revenue (Esiedesa, 2021; NBS Report, 2017; NEITI, 2015; NNPC Report, 2017, 2018). Since 2007, it is believed there have been almost 15,000 acts of vandalism across the Niger Delta, with vandalism markedly increasing since 2017 (Adejoh, 2014; Oki, 2017; NBS, 2017; NEITI, 2015). Although there is no reliable standardised model for calculating the level of damages and gathering different views on the impact of oil and gas activities on local communities. However, a caveat in the Petroleum Act No.35 (353) set out the framework mechanism for the protection of oil and gas pipeline infrastructure against vandalism, sabotage, and illegal bunkering (Igbinovia, 2014; Onuoha, 2008).

The Criminal Justice Decree of 1975 re-visited the sabotage, and illegal bunkering law and changed same to the Anti-Sabotage law, in Section 1 of the Petroleum Production and Distribution Act of 1990 (Act 353). In practice, oil and gas laws and policies have done little to protect the onshore and offshore pipeline infrastructure in for about 64 years (see Chapters 5, 6, and 7; Okonofua, 2016; Onuoha, 2008). A crucial gap in these laws is the repeated failure to articulate guidelines for sanctioning unwholesome, unethical behaviours, and bad practices by both the oil and gas firms and their leadership for damages done to the environment (Olawuyi, 2012; Sinden, 2009; UNEP, 2012). Little has been done to ensure that oil and gas companies protect the local communities and the environment, something that has had a devasting impact on the lives of the people. Civil society and community activists have been calling for a change in the way oil companies conduct their activities in the Niger Delta for many decades now (Binuomoyo et al., 2012; Olawuyi, 2012; UNEP, 2012).

The activities of militants like the Movement for the Emancipation of the Niger Delta (MEND) and recently the Niger Delta Avengers (NDA), at various times, exposed the poor infrastructure resilience as well as demonstrated the capacity to reduce global crude oil supply and threaten peace and security (Kulungu, 2021; Moody, 2016). This book argues that security should be structured around effective regulations and strategies that transparently address internal and external threats and risks. As well as conflicts between nations, and social and environmental tensions arising from human interactions. This way, security would be seen as a process of mutual trust, benefit, and equality (Larus, 2005: 208). These elements are omitted in the business and security architecture between oil-bearing communities, security architecture, and oil firms in Bayelsa state. Neglecting the socio-economic well-being of the local communities creates a gap that insecurity feeds on (Bergstresser, 2017; Onuoha, 2008).

The book further identified historic and ongoing structural and institutional corruption as responsible for criminal vandalism, organised crimes, and infrastructure insecurity in the Niger Delta. It is problematic to blur the dividing lines between corruption and criminality in Nigeria. Corruption and organised crime are socially constructed concepts evidenced in social and economic realities. Although not all corrupt practices translate to criminality or vice versa, some corrupt practices have criminal characteristics. The anti-sabotage and vandalism laws of Nigeria make pipeline vandalism a criminal act. Some scholars broadly see organised crime as the activities of highly centralised local, national, or transnational groups of a criminal enterprise that are involved in illegal and illegitimate activities to make a profit (Neumann & Elsenbroich, 2017). The concept of organised crime in law varies between an emphasis on criminal activities and criminal organisations. A typical example of organised crime is found in the nature, and structured processes of vandalism, oil theft, and illegal bunkering. This also includes artisanal refining, siphoning oil, loading onto boats, tugboats, and transportation logistics to ocean liners on the high sea as well as sale in the international oil market in Europe. It will not be wrong to describe such a disciplined approach with which illegal oil and gas activities occur in the Niger Delta as organised crimes.

Illegal activities also include the disruption of pipelines with minimal casualties and the selling of stolen crude in the international oil market demonstrates the sophistication of organised criminals in the Niger Delta (Asuni, 2009). Politicians and high-profile private corporations complicate the process by manipulating regulatory policymaking and implementation processes in Nigeria. This is what Amundsen described as "political corruption" which he noted takes place at the highest levels of the political system involving political decision-makers (2019). Political and private corruption thrives where deviant behaviours are normalised, socialised, and rationalised (Anand & Ashforth, 2003). Corruption is when "behaviour deviates from the formal duties of a public role because of private (private clique) pecuniary or status gain" (Nye, 1967: 419). Political corruption is a central factor responsible for the socio-economic, infrastructure, and political underdevelopment of Nigeria (Amundsen, 2019; Ogbeidi, 2012).

The findings show that a lack of transparency and insincerity of the political and security stakeholders facilitate oil theft, bunkering, and underdevelopment of social amenities in the Niger Delta. Ugo and Njoku estimated that Nigeria loses about 400,000 barrels of crude oil per day due to a lack of transparency (2017; 2016). These figures were recently alluded to by Nuhu Ribadu, the current National Security Adviser—NSA, "Nigeria is still losing 400,000 barrels of crude oil daily to local and international thieves…", he stated (The Guardian Editor, 2023). At the same time, NBS and NEITI reports estimate that Nigeria lost over $80 billion in revenue due in part to corruption within the oil and gas industry value chain (NBS, 2017; NEITI, 2015; Ughamadu, 2017). The lack of transparency in the oil and gas sector led the Nigerian government to bring litigation against Chevron and Eni. Both companies were accused of withholding from the Nigerian government about USD$ 12.7 billion worth of crude and natural gas exports (Bergstresser, 2017; Okafor & Olaniyan, 2017; Transparency International, 2020). A classic example of political and private corrupt interest working to truncate the "common good" is the aborted Niger Delta gas processing plant by Process and Industrial Development (P&ID) (Hughes & Sengupta, 2020). It is argued that compromise of the criminal justice system is characteristic evidence of disregard for the "common good" (Phelippeau & Mendilow, 2019). Given the difficulty of prosecuting corrupt officials and pipeline vandals (Umar et al., 2017).

Frustration and anger have arisen in Bayelsa partly because the polluted and degraded ecosystem has impacted the socio-economic well-being and health of the people. For instance, Okumagba observed that natural water pollution is 360 times higher than allowed in Europe (2012). Only about 25 percent of the population can access proper sanitation and on top of that marine life, mangrove, and rain forest including cash crops have been destroyed (Olawuyi, 2012; Umar et al., 2017). Closely linked to that are the decades of environmental pollution resulting in years of injustice. For instance, the pollution of mangrove creeks in Bodo, Ogoniland, Ikarama, Ewelesuo, and Bonga communities and the irreversibility of such damages, trigger resentment (Linden & Palsson, 2013; Okumagba, 2012).

Tensions rose further when residents realised that blood samples from a cross-sectional study of oil spill workers were infected. Holdway (2002) stressed that the results imply impairment of the hepatic and hematopoietic systems. Findings from a study by the Colorado School of Public Health showed that people who live within 152 metres (500 feet) of oil and gas facilities are at a higher risk of suffering from neurological, haematological, and developmental health problems (McKenzie et al., 2018). This is due to exposure and inhalation of benzene and other air pollutant concentrates (McKenzie et al., 2018). The fear of death caused by diseases contracted from hydrocarbon exposure is one of the sources of frustration. There is a dearth of primary healthcare facilities in the communities. Existing local healthcare facilities are either nonfunctional or staffed with unqualified healthcare professionals or both. This further frustrates the people and increases resentment against local healthcare facilities built by the government (Edoni et al., 2012).

The NBS report reveals that difficulties in accessing skilled workers intensified socio-economic problems in Bayelsa (NBS, 2017). The difficulty of coming to terms with a dearth of social housing and social safety net for the displaced, indigent youths, individuals, and poor families creates anger and frustration. About 94 percent of Bayelsa households have one or more unemployed defendants. Dokpesi and Ibiezugbe noted that while poverty in the region is hovering at just over 18 percent, however, in some parts of Bayelsa this increases to more than 80 percent of the population living in poverty (2012). A refusal to include local communities in the development of socio-economic and regulatory policies isolates them from participating in the ownership of oil blocks/wells which worsens their economic plights (Oriola, 2016). The Traditional Rulers of Oil Mineral Producing Communities of Nigeria (TROMPCON) advocated for the redistribution of marginal oil fields between Niger Delta people and others (Oriola, 2016). It is frustrating to observe that about 97 percent of marginal oil fields are in the hands of individuals from the Northern and Southwestern regions, which in itself causes tensions (Momah, 2013: 121; Ugo, 2017: 96).

The Henry Willinks Commission Report was the first proactive approach taken to address the socio-economic development of Niger Delta minority communities aimed at providing security to the people (1958). Sections 27–30 highlighted the "Development of Special Areas" within the oil-rich lower Niger area (Boro, 1982; Umukoro, 2009). Political tensions and intrigues destroyed the implementation agendas that were set by the Henry Willinks Commission Report. The Federal Board Willinks advocated should be created to coordinate infrastructure development, but this was neglected. This marked the systemic isolation of the lower Niger leading to the build-up of conflicts and tensions. The Willinks report, however, did not set out the methodology for gauging the views of different sectors of the communities, which has remained an existential gap. As noted in Chapter 3, it is not enough to appoint a Niger Delta indigene as head of an intervention agency (Umukoro, 2009). Like the defunct Oil Mineral Producing Area Development Commission (OMPADEC) and the current Niger Delta Development Commission (NDDC). Alamieyeseigha noted that lopsided local government areas and senatorial zones reinforced the geopolitical opposition against oil and gas legislation (2005; see section 8). For instance, Bayelsa state which contributes about 40 percent to the national revenue, and is the main foreign exchange earner to Nigeria, has only eight local government areas (Idemudia, 2014). Kano state, in contrast, which contributes significantly far less to Nigeria's GDP and foreign exchange earnings has 44 local governments, with more money allocated. Etowah and Effiong noted that Bayelsa's political participation is further limited with only five members in the Federal House of Representatives compared to 15 members from Kano (2012).

The different forms of compensation schemes and memoranda constitute sources of tension and insecurity problems. This research divides compensation awards into three distinctive categories. Compensation for land acquired/leased for exploration, compensation for damages caused by either structural failure or vandalism, and the distribution of royalties to communities (see details in Chapter 3). The findings show that these compensations are problematic as most community respondents are either angry with the process or frustrated by the lack of transparency which sometimes leads to aggression (Chapters 6 and 7). The Niger Delta compensation schemes derive their powers from legislative acts, and policies of oil and gas firms and regulatory agencies, as well as the Memorandum of Understanding. The subsisting acts and policy instruments fail to clarify the structure and method of calculating compensation awards to deserving individuals and local communities. These formal documents do not differentiate or decouple between compensation awards for exploration, production processes, and the impact of the oil and gas activities. The processes of acquiring land for seismic testing, exploration, and mechanical activities, damages, displacement, deforestation caused by oil and gas activities, and distribution of royalties are entangled together (Odudu, 2017). Regardless of the compensation scheme adopted, the gravity of human, natural, and environmental damage the Niger Delta has experienced would either be impossible or take decades to reverse.

The two common sources of compensation framework in the Niger Delta are the Memorandum of Understanding and the Global Memorandum of Understanding. An MOU is a social contract document drawn up between a firm, like an oil corporation, and a specific host community stipulating intervention projects, social amenities, and infrastructure they may benefit from the oil company. GMOU on the other hand is a social contract signed between an oil and gas firm and a cluster of oil and gas communities. It serves as the guideline and principles for undertaking and duplicating compensatory projects across a cluster of communities (usually between 10 and 25) where the oil firm operates. Niger Delta MOUs and GMOUs focus mainly on the compensation for damages caused by either structural failure or vandalism which is the second category of compensation. (Not all GMOUs focus on compensation).

To protect the status quo, the Nigerian government continues to approach security from the traditional neorealist perspective (Baldwin, 1998; Jones et al., 2014). Given the reality that the heightened possibility of internal and external aggression motivates nation-states to act in their defense. Literature shows an evolving trend in security discussion amongst scholars, the political class, and social commentators. This notes that security should extend beyond the traditional narrow political and institutional perspectives to non-conventional issues like human and environmental rights, and infrastructure development (Owen, 2004). It was argued elsewhere in this study that security should take the form of "responsibility" and "concern for" something and the interest of the state and citizens should occupy the central referent point. The protection of the status quo is counter-productive and increases the threats to the nation-state. But entrenches corruption, poor governance, poverty, and inequality. This book notes that Nigeria's Niger Delta security is intricately strategic to West Africa, Africa, and the larger global economy. Failure of the government to focus on factors that enhance human security in the historic Niger Delta, particularly in Bayelsa triggers tensions and insecurity problems. Tensions and conflicts in the Bayelsa state and the disruption of oil and gas production have implications that reverberate across the socio-economic and security landscape of many resource-rich nations in the Global South (Ikelegbe, 2005).

## THE BOOK CONTEXT

The context for this book is set around the neglect of the views of different stakeholders, particularly the Bayelsa host community stakeholders and the wider historic Niger Delta, in the exploration and management of Nigeria's oil and gas businesses. The book argued that (1) the instrumental policies of the government and their implementation (2); the non-adoption of best international practices and some unethical behaviours, adopted by oil and gas multinationals, and (3); and the already devastating impact of oil activities on the environment, being suffered by the host communities is the cause of the tensions between individuals, communities, oil companies, and the government. However, the collective host community's aggressive behaviour, in turn, worsens socio-economic disequilibrium and environmental damage thus heightening the problems of insecurity for the communities in Bayelsa and the wider historic Niger Delta case study area. Whatever the reason, pipeline vandalism continues to erode economic and environmental security in Nigeria. This is supported by several civil society reports (Mathias, 2015; Transparency International, 2019, 2020; UNEP, 2012). Over 6000 km of oil and gas pipelines operated by Shell Petroleum Development Company alone are connected to about 275 flow stations and 600 onshore oil fields, 5284 onshore and offshore oil wells (Bahadori, 2017; Devold, 2013; NNPC Report, 2013, 2016, 2017, 2018; Onuoha, 2016). Oil fields are areas where a geological seismic survey shows an exploitable commercial quantity of hydrocarbon deposits. While oil wells are holes dug into the soil or sea bed through which crude oil is pumped up from underground reserves (Paki & Ebienfa, 2011; Shoewu et al., 2013).

This book makes the point that the Niger Delta pipeline network which is connected to 10 export terminals controlled by seven oil and gas multinationals including Nigeria National Petroleum Corporation-NNPC lacks adequate resilience infrastructure security and the threat is heightened by the deliberate neglect of host communities. Plenty of abandoned, unclamped, and unsecured pipelines and oil wells in Bayelsa State facilitate oil bunkering and oil theft as well as provide crude oil to artisanal refineries. Unchecked and abandoned oil and gas infrastructure encourages some illegal activities that worsen the problems of environmental pollution in the area (Mathias, 2015; Onuoha, 2016). Inactive pipelines that have never been correctly decommissioned even pose a greater risk to the public and prevent farmers from returning safely to their farmland. These onshore pipelines, sometimes, blow out and cause crude oil spills and fires when unsuspecting farmers burn their bushes (Sayne & Katsourisa, 2015). This book finding align with Mathias, Igbinovia, UNDP, and Onuoha's argument that oil spills and pipeline networks in Bayelsa and Nembe and the wider historic Niger Delta constitute sources of threats (2015; 2014; 2012; 2008). Over the years, oil and gas spills have destroyed rainforests, mangrove forests, rivers, and fishing settlements, and have displaced large populations from host communities worsening the socio-economic divide and increasing tensions and insecurity. This has caused anger, frustration, and tensions that lead to a breakdown in law and order which also triggers vandalism, which has, in turn, escalated the problem of environmental damages (Mathias, 2015; Numbere, 2018; Onuoha, 2016). This damage negatively impacts the national budget and community intervention projects (NBS, 2017; NNPC Report, 2016).

The data analysed in this book shows that the NNPC and about 18 other oil and gas operators lost over 27 million barrels of crude oil to vandalism, oil theft, and illegal refining activities between 2006 and 2015 (Akpomera, 2015; Mickolus, 2018; UNEP, 2012). It is clear that there have been about 227 vandalism incidences on the Nembe Creek Trunk Line 1, 2, and 3, the object of study, since it began operation in 2010 (NEITI, 2015; NNPC Report, 2016). Poor security architecture made it easier for the Niger Delta Avengers militant group to vandalised the 48-inch Shell giant underwater export pipeline at Forcados Export Terminal in 2016 (Mickolus, 2018). The NNPC 2016 report reveals that between January to October 2016, Nigeria lost over US$7 billion which represented over 30 percent of the National Budget (NNPC Report, 2016). The International Centre for Reconciliation (ICR) estimated the monetary value lost to pipeline vandalism and illegal oil bunkering activities between 2003 and 2008 at over US$100 billion (Paki & Ebienfa, 2011: 142). Vandalism has significantly affected Nigeria's oil production levels, such as the reduction in Nigeria's oil production in 2016 which averaged between 1.3 and 1.8 million barrels, down from its target of 2.2 million barrels per day (NBS, 2017; NEITI, 2015).

## THE BOOK STRUCTURE

Aspects of this book have been revised from my original Ph.D. thesis. However, the empirical data, and interpretation of the result, which is the core of the research, are the same because they were derived from Bayelsa State in the historic Niger Delta case study area. The book establishes that the "curse" of leadership is also a contributory factor that triggers pipeline vandalism and insecurity problems. It coined the word "Infrastructure Insecurity Nexus" (IIN) to represent factors that cause onshore oil and gas pipeline vandalism. Arguing that the underlying micro-foundational variables that trigger these factors are found in "Community Neglect Aggression Displacement Theory" (CNADT). By applying the Frustration Aggression Displacement Theory (FADT) and CNADT the book looks beyond symptomatic issues of insecurity in Nigeria and focuses on the underlying factors. All of these highlight the hindrances to achieving the UNSDGs in the Niger Delta and the Global South. Therefore, the book will represent a comprehensive and detailed guide for oil and gas students, academics, and oil and gas industry professionals (Fig. 1.2).

Chapter 2 creates the context by focusing on the infrastructural resilience of oil and gas pipelines in Nigeria and the Global South. Especially those endowed with hydrocarbon whose economy thrives on the effectiveness and efficiency or otherwise of onshore oil and gas pipeline structural resilience. Due in part to aging infrastructure, poor governance, extensive institutional corruption, disruptive and compromised security architecture, slow response to third-party disruption and operational blowouts, compromised regulatory oversights, and a dearth of technological advancement (Mathias, 2015; Ogbeidi, 2012; Tarallo, 2019; Theodoropoulos, 2011; Transparency International, 2019).

Chapter 3 draws on different perspectives on the historic Niger Delta and explores different aspects of pipeline insecurity focusing on the impact the operation of the NCTL has on Nembe communities. Using the research context to evaluate the socio-economic, geographic, and cultural diversity in Bayelsa reveals why the state is a business destination for multinational oil and gas firms. In Chapter 3, the study also explored the context of Nembe-Ewelesuo communities and the operation of the NCTL. It looked at colonial and imperialist interests as well as the critical examination of the 1895 British Nembe-Brass war. Linking it with the history of oil and exploring in the lower Niger Delta, pipeline components, and as well as oil and gas infrastructure insecurity.

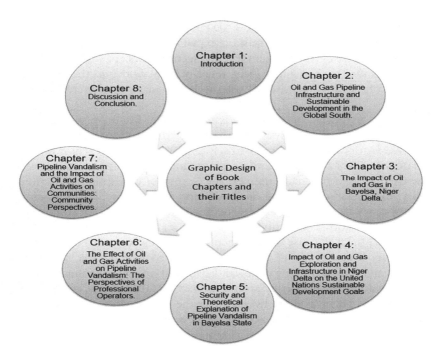

**Fig. 1.2** Graphic design and layout of book chapters and titles (*Source* Author [2023])

It gave the background to understanding their impact, and the challenges of the changing climate. It explored why historic, contemporary, recent, and emerging debates on vandalism, and pipeline insecurity, and compensation issues are escalating the tensions in Bayelsa.

Chapter 4 further contextualises the book by drilling further down into the impact of onshore oil and gas pipeline infrastructure in Bayelsa, Niger Delta on the United Nations Sustainable Development Goals (UNSDG). It focused on two key UNSDG agenda – decent employment and climate change whilst also analysing conflicts in aligning with the UN framework. As well as identify different oil and gas regulatory policy frameworks. It drew on relevant literature in addressing the research objective and strategies employed against pipeline vandalism. Including the security of pipelines, response to oil spillages, and impact of the NCTL on local communities. Chapter 5 uses the FADT hypothesis to analyse the underlying local factors that trigger onshore pipeline vandalism. It discussed the various perspectives to understanding the security concept while contextualising them within the Niger Delta security framework and the militancy problem. It also summarise the methods and data analysis techniques adopted.

Chapter 6 revisits some of the issues already discussed surrounding pipeline vandalism by analysing the views of the professionals. This was achieved by drawing on 20 semi-structured interviews with senior oil and gas policymakers as well as senior military and security officials. This was discussed around five main themes: the impact of corruption and criminality; the impact of reducing oil production and revenue, environmental pollution, conflicts over pipeline structurality, and community compensation. As well as other social and economic issues that trigger the vandalism of the NCTL which cause wider insecurity problems were also considered.

Chapter 7 discussed the exploration of the socio-economic and environmental issues causing pipeline vandalism and oil and gas infrastructure insecurity and their impact by analysing the views of different community stakeholders. This was done by analysing the perspectives of 21 community members such as civil society professional representatives, NGO workers, environmental activists, community leaders, and high-profile members of the communities. They narrated their stories around four major themes: corruption, and criminality, lack of socio-economic, and political resources, environmental pollution, social injustice, and community compensation problems. They shared their views on how these impacted their daily lives and intensified the frustration and anger leading to vandalism. Analyses of the professional and community perspectives in Chapters 6 and 7 gave a comprehensive account and insight into the underlying factors that frustrate the people leading to pipeline vandalism and insecurity.

Chapter 8 evaluates the findings and draws the research to a close. It begins by comparing the professional and community findings from chapters 6 and 7. Thus giving a more concise summary of the causes of pipeline vandalism while addressing the central research question. It explains the causes of vandalism and oil and gas infrastructure insecurity in Bayelsa and the wider Niger Delta region from two perspectives as seen reflected in many states in the Global South. From the perspective of a range of underlying social, economic, political, and environmental factors that create tensions, frustration, and anger. It was discovered that the underlying issues that facilitate and influence the above factors also impact the structural operation and management of onshore pipelines, for example, the NCTL. Secondly, from the perspective of how these factors conversely intensify the outlined causes of vandalism. Implying that the factors go beyond underlying social issues alone. The forward and backward links between the factors and the underlying micro-foundational variables create what this book coined the *onshore oil and gas pipeline infrastructure insecurity nexus*.

## References

Adejoh, O. F. (2014). Petroleum Pipelines Spillages and the Environment of the Niger Delta Region of Nigeria. *World Environment Journal, 4*(3), 93–100.

Akpomera, E. (2015). International Crude Oil Theft: Elite Predatory Tendencies in Nigeria. *Review of African Political Economy Journal, 42*(143), 156–165.

Alabi, J. O. (2013). Resource Conflicts: Energy Worth Fighting for? In M. J. Trombetta & H. Dyer (Eds.), *International Handbook on Energy Security* (pp. 70–92). Edward Elgar.

Alagoa, E. J. (2005). *A History of the Niger Delta*. Onyema Research Publications.

Alamieyeseigha, D. S. P. (2005). *Thoughts on Federalism, South–South and Resource Control, on Federalism*. Treasure Books.

Alamieyeseigha, D. S. P. (2008a). The Environmental Challenge of Developing the Niger Delta. In S. S. Azaiki, D. S. P. Alamieyeseigha, & A. A. Ikein (Eds.), *Oil, Democracy and the Promise of True Federalism in Nigeria* (pp. 249–260). University Press of America.

Alamieyeseigha, D. S. P. (2008b). The Niger Delta: Treasure Base of Energies. In S. Azaika, A. A. Ikein, & D. S. P. Alamieyeseigha (Eds.), *Oil Democracy and the Promise of True Federalism in Nigeria* (pp. 290–310). University Press of America.

Aluko, M. A. O. (2015). Social Dimensions and Consequences of Environmental Degradation in the Niger Delta of Nigeria: Suggestions for the Next Millennium. In N. P. Nchoji & P. N. Nkwi (Eds.), *The Anthropology of Africa: Challenges for the 21st Century* (pp. 199–208). Langaa Research and Publishing.

Amundsen, I. (2019). Extractive and Power-Preserving Political Corruption. In I. Amundsen (Ed.), *Political Corruption in Africa: An Extraction and Power Preservation* (pp. 1–28). Elgar.

Anand, V., & Ashforth, B. E. (2003). The Normalization of Corruption in Organisations. In *Research in Organisational Behaviour* (Vol. 25, pp. 1–52). Elsevier.

Anderson, C. A., & Dill, J. C. (1995). Effects of Frustration Justification on Hostile Aggression. *Aggressive Behaviour, 21*(5), 359–369.

Asuni, B. J. (2009). *Special Report: Blood Oil in the Niger Delta* (pp. 2–19). United States Institute of Peace. https://www.usip.org/sites/default/files/blood_oil_nigerdelta_0.pdf. Accessed 3 March 2019.

Avwunudiogba, A. (2023). Environmental Degradation and Community Poverty: Lessons from the Niger Delta of Nigeria. In B. I. Gill & G. K. Danns (Eds.), *Comparative Assessment of Social Issues in Africa, Latin America, and the Caribbean* (pp. 97–114). Rowman and Littlefield.

Bahadori, A. (2017). *Oil and Gas Pipelines and Piping Systems: Design, Construction, Management, and Inspection.* Elsevier.

Baku-Tbilisi-Ceyhan Corporation. (2014). *Protecting Pipelines-BTC as a Case Study.* In M. Edwards (Ed.), *Critical Infrastructure Protection* (pp. 55–58). IOS.

Baldwin, D. A. (1998). The Concept of Security. *Review of International Studies, 23*(1), 5–26.

Berg, L. B. (2007). *Qualitative Research Methods for the Social Sciences* (6th ed.). Pearson Education.

Bergstresser, H. (2017). *A Decade of Nigeria: Politics, Economy and Society 2004–2016,* Leiden, Brill.

Berkowitz, L. (2011). A Cognitive-No Association Theory of Aggression. In A. W. Kruglanski, P. A. M. Van Lange, & E. T. Higgins (Eds.), *The Handbook of Theories of Social Psychology* (pp. 90–120). Sage.

Binuomoyo, Y. K., Ogbewo, J. B., Okoro, E. A., & Ukaga, O. (2012). Land Reforms, Land Rights, and Development Challenges. In U. U. Ibaba & O. Ukaga (Eds.), *Natural Resources, Conflicts, and Sustainable Development: Lessons from the Niger Delta* (pp. 115–131). Routledge.

Boro, I. (1982). *The Twelve-day Revolution.* Idodo Umeh.

Buzan, B. (1984a). Peace, Power, and Security: Contending Concepts in the Study of International Relations. *Journal of Peace Research, 21*(2), 109–125.

Buzan, B. (1984b). *People, States, and Fear: The National Security Problems in International Relations.* University of North Carolina.

Cordesman, A. H. (2016). *The Underlying Causes of Stability and Instability in the Middle East and North Africa (MENA) Region.* Center for Strategic and International Studies.

Coleman, J. S. (2015). The Politics of Sub-Saharan Africa. In A. G. Almond & J. S. Coleman (Eds.), *The Politics of the Developing Areas* (pp. 247–354). Princeton University Press.

Collier, P. (2007). *The Bottom Billion* (pp. 39–52). Oxford University Press.

Creswell, J. W. (2015). *A Concise Introduction to Mixed Methods Research.* Sage.

Devold, H. (2013). *Oil and Gas Production Handbook: An Introduction to Oil and Gas Production* (pp. 6–146). ABB. https://library.e.abb.com/public/34d5b70e18f7d6c8c1257be500438ac3/Oil%20and%20gas%20production%20handbook%20ed3x0_web.pdf. Accessed 12 December 2017.

Dodd, N., & Merwe, J. V. D. (2019). *The Political Economy of Underdevelopment in the Global South: The Government-Business-Media Complex.* Palgrave Macmillan.

Dokpesi, A. O., & Ibiezugbe, M. I. (2012). Assessment the Human Development Efforts of the Niger Delta Development Commission. In O. Ukaga, U. O. Ukiwo, & I. S. Ibaba (Eds.), *Natural Resources, Conflict, and Sustainable Development: Lessons from the Niger Delta* (pp. 60–78). Routledge.

Dollard, J., Miller, N. E., Doob, L. W., Mowrer, O. H., & Sears, R. R. (1939). *Frustration and Aggression.* Yale University Press.

Douglas, O., & Okonta, I. (2003). *Where Vultures Feast: Shell, Human Rights, and Oil in the Niger Delta.* Verso.

Edoni, E. R., McFubara, K. G., & Akwagbe, R. E. E. (2012, November). Health Manpower Development in Bayelsa State, Nigeria. *Risk Management and Healthcare Policy Journal, 5,* 127–135.

Egbe, R. E., & Thompson, D. (2010, December). Environmental Challenges of Oil Spillage for Families in Oil Producing Communities of the Niger Delta Region. *Journal of Home Economics Research, (13).*

Ekpenyong, A. S. (2010). The Oil Economy, Environmental Laws, and Human Rights Violations in Niger Delta Region: Implications and Suggested Solutions. *International Journal of Social Policy Research and Development, 1(2).*

Emmer, R. (2016). Securitisation. In A. Collins (Ed.), *Contemporary Security Studies* (4th ed., pp. 168–182). Oxford University Press.

Esiedesa, O. (2021). Nigeria Earned $418.5bn in 10 Years from Petroleum, NEITI Reveals. *Vanguard News.* https://www.vanguardngr.com/2021/06/nigeria-earned-418-5bn-in-10yrs-from-petroleum-neiti-reveals/. Accessed 19 June 2021.

Etemire, U. (2016). *Law and Practice on Public Participation in Environmental Matters: The Nigerian Example in Transnational Comparative Perspective.* Routledge.

Etete, E. (2017, July 7). Ovom in Yenagoa City: A Cradle of Development but Shadow of itself. *Headline News Nigeria.* http://headlinenewsnigeria.com/ovom-yenagoa-city-cradle-development-shadow/. Accessed 2 March 2018.

Etowah, U. E., & Effiong, S. A. (2012). Oil Spillage Cost Gas Flaring Cost, and Life Expectancy Rate of the Niger Delta People of Nigeria. *Advances in Management and Applied Economics Journal, 2(2),* 211–228.

Faust, D., & Aktan, A. E. (2003). A Holistic Integrated Systems Approach to assure the Mobility, Efficiency, Safety, and Integrity of Highways Transportation. In Z. Wu & M. Abe (Eds.), *Structural Health Monitoring and Intelligent Infrastructure: Structures and Infrastructure Sustainability* (Vol. 1, pp. 7–18). Balkema.

George, L. N. (2009). American Insecurities and the on politics of the US Pharmacotic Wars. In F. Debrix & M. J. Lacy (Eds.), *The Geopolitics of American Insecurity: Terror* (pp. 34–53). Routledge.

Gibbs, G. (2018). *Analysing Qualitative Data: The Sage Qualitative Research Kit* (2nd ed.). Sage.

Goodman, A., Moynihan, D., & Goodman, D. (2016). *Democracy Now!: Twenty Years Covering the Movements Changing America*. Simon and Schuster.

Gopakumar, G. (2012). *Transforming Urban Water Supply in India: The Role of Reform and Partnerships in Globalisation*. Routledge.

Grigg, N. S. (2010). *Infrastructure Finance: The Business of Infrastructure for a Sustainable Future*. Wiley.

Hai-Jew, S. (2016). Conducting Sentiment Analysis and Post-Sentiment Data Exploration through Automated Means. In S. Hai-Jew (Ed.), *Social Media Data Extraction, and Content Analysis* (pp. 202–241). IGI Global.

Hammond, J. L. (2011). The Resource Curse and Oil Revenues in Angola and Venezuela. *Science and Society Journal, 75*(3), 348–378.

Haq, U. M. (1995). *Reflections on Human Development*. Oxford University Press.

Holdway, D. A. (2002). The Acute and Chronic Effects of Wastes Associated with Offshore Oil and Gas Production on Temperate and Tropical Marine Ecological Processes. *Marin Pollution Bulletin, 44*(3), 185–203.

Hudson, N. F. (2010). *Gender, Human Security and the United Nations: Security Language as a Political Platform for Women*. Routledge.

Hughes, S., & Sengupta, K. (2020). Priti Patel Repeatedly Backed Company Accused of Obtaining Nigerian Gas Contract through Corruption. *Independent News*. https://www.independent.co.uk/news/uk/politics/priti-patel-gas-contract-corruption-nigeria-process-industrial-development-b1759441.html. Accessed 21 November 2020.

Ibaba, I. S. (2012). Introduction: Interrogating Development Deficits in the Niger Delta. In S. I. Ibaba (Ed.), *Niger Delta: Constraints and Pathways to Development* (pp. 1–9). Newcastle upon Tyne.

Idemudia, U. (2014). Oil Multinational Companies as Money Makers and Peace Makers: Lessons from Nigeria. In G. Eweje (Ed.), *Corporate Social Responsibility and Sustainability: Emerging Trends in Developing Economies* (pp. 191–214). Emerald.

Igbinovia, P. E. (2014). *Oil Thefts and Pipeline Vandalisation in Nigeria*. African Books.

Ikelegbe, A. (2005). The Economy of Conflict in the Oil Rich Niger Delta Region of Nigeria. *Nordic Journal of African Studies, 14*(2), 207–235.

Irvine, M. (2018). *A Practical Guide to Vicarious Liability.* Law Briefs Publication.

Jones, S. R., Torres, V., & Arminio, J. (2014). *Negotiating the Complexities of Qualitative Research in Higher Education: Fundamental Elements and Issues* (2nd ed.). Routledge.

Krueger, I. J. (1996). Probabilistic National Stereotypes. *European Journal of Social Psychology, 26,* 960–985.

Kulungu, M. (2021). Movement for the "Emancipation of the Niger Delta" (MEND) Constitutes a Threat to the U.S National Security. *Open Access Library Journal, 8,* 1–17.

Larus, E. F. (2005). China's New Security Concept and Peaceful Rise: Trustful Cooperation or Deceptive Diplomacy? *American Journal of Chinese Studies, 12*(2), 218–241.

Lazarus, R. S. (1994). *Emotion and Adaptation.* Oxford University Press.

Lesar, D. J. (2001). *Securing Oil and Natural Gas Infrastructures in the New Economy.* Diane.

Leuven, L. J. V. (2011). Chapter 2: Water/Wastewater Infrastructure Security: Threats and Vulnerabilities. In R. M. Clark, S. Hakim, & A. Ostfeld (Eds.), *Handbook of Water and Wastewater Systems Protection* (pp. 27–46). Springer.

Lewis, T. G. (2015). *Critical Infrastructure Protection in Homeland Security: Defending a Networked Nation* (2nd ed.). Wiley.

Linden, O., & Palsson, J. (2013). Oil Contamination in Ogoniland Niger Delta, Stockholm. *The Royal Swedish Academy of Sciences Journal, 42*(6), 685–701.

Loft, P., & Brien, P. (2023, September). Halfway to 2023: The Sustainable Development Goals. *UK House of Commons Library.* https://commonsli brary.parliament.uk/halfway-to-2030-the-sustainable-development-goals/. 31 October 2023.

Madubuko, C. C. (2017). Oiling the Guns and Gunning for Oil: The Youths and Niger Delta Oil Conflicts in Nigeria. In E. M. Mbah & T. Falola (Eds.), *Dissent, Protest and Dispute in Africa* (pp. 260–289). Routledge.

Mathias, Z. (2015). Providing All-Round Security against Oil and Gas Infrastructure Sabotage and Physical Attacks on the Staff of NNPC and Multinational Oil Companies in Nigeria as a Critical Article of Her National Security Efforts. *International Journal of Social Science and Humanities Research, 3*(2), 45–59.

McKenzie, L. M., Blair, B., Hughes, J., Allshouse, W. B., Blake, N. J., Helmig, D., Milmoe, P., Halliday, H., Blake, D. R., & Adgate, J. L. (2018). Ambient Nonmethane Hydrocarbon Levels Along Colorado's Northern Front Range: Acute and Chronic Health Risk. *Journal of Environmental Science and Technology, 52*(8), 4514–4525.

Mickolus, E. (2018). *Terrorism Worldwide, 2016.* McFarland and Company.

Momah, S. (2013). *Nigeria: Beyond Divorce: Amalgamation in Perspective*. Safari.

Moody, J. (2016). The Niger Delta Avengers: A New Threat to Oil Producers in Nigeria. *James Foundation Journal of Terrorism Monitor, 14*(12). https://jamestown.org/program/the-niger-delta-avengers-a-new-threat-to-oil-producers-in-nigeria/. 13 November 2021.

Moyo, D. (2011). *Dead Aid: Why Aid is Not Working and How There is Another Way for Africa*. Penguin.

National Bureau of Statistics. (2017). *Social Statistics Report December 2016*. National Bureau of Statistics.

Neocleous, M. (2007). Security Liberty and the Myth of Balance: Towards a Critique of Security Politics. *Contemporary Political Theory Journal, 6*, 131–149.

Neumann, M., & Elsenbroich, C. (2017). Introduction: The Societal Dimensions of Organised Crime. *Trends in Organised Crime, 20*, 1–15.

Nigeria Extractive Industries Transparency Initiative. (2015). *Highlights of the 2015 Oil and Gas Audit Report*. NEITI.

Nigerian National Petroleum Corporation. (2013). *NNPC Annual Statistical Bulletin* (1st ed.), *Corporate Planning and Strategy*. https://www.nnpcgroup.com/NNPCDocuments/Annual%20Statistics%20Bulletin%E2%80%8B/2013%20ASB%201st%20edition.pdf. Accessed 24 September 2020.

Nigerian National Petroleum Corporation. (2016). *Monthly Financial and Operations Report September 2016* (pp. 2–9). Nigerian National Petroleum Corporation.

Nigerian National Petroleum Corporation. (2017). *Monthly Financial and Operations Report October 2017* (pp. 4–37). Nigerian National Petroleum Corporation.

Nigerian National Petroleum Corporation. (2018). *Annual Statistical Bulletin 2018*. https://www.nnpcgroup.com/NNPCDocuments/Annual%20Statistics%20Bulletin%E2%80%8B/ASB%202018%201st%20Edition.pdf. Accessed 24 September 2020.

Njoku, A. O. (2016). Oil Pipelines Vandalism and its Effects on the Socio-Economic Development in Nigerian Society. *International Journal of Multidisciplinary Academic Research, 4*(7), 45–57.

Numbere, A. O. (2018). The Impact of Oil and Gas Exploration: Invasive Nypa Palm Species and Urbanisation on Mangroves in the Niger River Delta, Nigeria. In C. Makowski & C. W. Finkl (Eds.), *Threats to Mangrove Forests: Hazards, Vulnerability, and Management* (pp. 247–266). Springer.

Nye, S. J. (1967). Corruption and Political Development: A Cost-Benefit Analysis. *American Political Science Review, 61*(2), 417–427.

Odudu, C. O. (2017). Compensation Issues in the Niger Delta-A Case Study of Boboroku Jesse, Delta State, Nigeria. *International Journal of Civil Engineering, Construction and Estate Management, 5*(4), 21–43.

Ogbeidi, M. M. (2012). Political Leadership and Corruption in Nigeria since 1960: A Socio-economics Analysis. *Journal of Nigerian Studies, 1*(2), 1–24.

Okafor, A., & Olaniyan, A. (2017). Legal and Institutional Framework for Promoting Oil Pipeline Security in Nigeria. *Journal of Sustainable Development Law and Policy, 8*(2), pp.210-224

Oki, R. A. (2017). *Barbarism to Decadence: Nigeria and Foreign Complicity.* Author Solutions.

Okonofua, B. A. (2016). The Niger Delta Amnesty Program: The Challenges of Transitioning from Peace Settlements to Long-Term Peace. *Sage Open Journals, 6*(2), 1–16.

Okonta, I. (2016). Policy Incoherence and the Challenge of Energy Security. In A. Goldthau (Ed.), *The Handbook of Global Energy Policy* (pp. 501–520). Wiley.

Okumagba, P. (2012). Oil Exploration and Crisis in the Niger Delta: The Response of the Militia Groups. *Journal of Sustainable Society, 1*(3), 78–83.

Okumagba, P. (2013). Ethnic Militia and Criminality in the Niger Delta. *International Review of Social Sciences and Humanities, 5*(1), 239–246.

Olawuyi, D. S. (2012). Legal and Sustainable Development Impacts of Major Oil Spills. *The Journal of Sustainable Development, 9*(1), 1–15.

Omand, D. (2011). *Securing the State.* C. Hurst, and Co.

Omoweh, D. (2008). Governance, Democratization and Development of the Niger Delta. In S. S. Azaiki, D. S. P. Alamieyeseigha, & A. A. Ikein (Eds.), *Oil, Democracy and the Promise of True Federalism in Nigeria* (pp. 167–186). University Press of America.

Onolememen, M. O. (2020). *Infrastructure Development in Nigeria: A Political and Economic History.* Routledge.

Onuoha, C. F. (2007). Oil Pipeline Sabotage in Nigeria: Dimensions, Actors and Implications for National Security. *African Security Review, 17*(3), 100–115.

Onuoha, C. F. (2008). Oil Pipeline Sabotage in Nigeria: Dimensions, Actors and Implications for National Security. *African Security Review, 17*(3), 100–115.

Onuoha, C. F. (2016). *The Resurgence of Militancy in Nigeria's Oil-Rich Niger Delta and the Dangers of Militarisation.* Al Jazeera Centre for Studies.

Oriola, B. T. (2016). *Criminal Resistance: The Politics of Kidnapping Oil Workers.* Routledge.

Owen, T. (2004). Challenges and Opportunities for Defining and Measuring Human Security. *Disarmament Forum Journal, 3*, 15–23.

Owolabi, T. (2016, March 29). Three Killed in Oil Pipeline Explosion in Nigeria's Delta: Environment Group. *Reuters News.* https://www.reuters.com/article/us-nigeria-oil/three-killed-in-oil-pipeline-explosion-in-nigerias-delta-environment-group-idUSKCN0WV1HR. Accessed 11 April 2018.

Paki, F. A. E., & Ebienfa, K. I. (2011). Militant Oil Agitations in Nigeria's Niger Delta and the Economy. *International Journal of Humanities and Social Sciences, 1*(5), 140–144.

Petroleum Industry Act, (2021). PIA: Explanatory Memorandum. Available from https://eproofing.springer.com/ePb/books/pnXXkMoim97Z_a_r MD9rZeEbrTrRUQmOXjtKXvfLWedcljNJBuXmZZBNYj-SztuHljv8yt2gL-1Cc-g7hvQhrTojgqtjLQ2jAUWQdwYTjfbm05PWXyArOed10ZI9Y9nrG YFRl5Bl8liyVB1qXexaAf17alFTrZ7252zWyo2Ivrw=. [Accessed 04/05/2024].

Phelippeau, J., & Mendilow, E. (2019). Introduction: Political Corruption in a World in Transition. In J. Phelippeau & E. Phelippeau (Eds.), *Political Corruption in a World in Transition* (pp. 1–17). Vernon.

Rizzo, A. (2016). From Petro-urbanism to Knowledge Megaprojects in the Persian Gulf: Qatar Foundation's Education City. In A. Shaban & A. Datta (Eds.), *Mega-urbanisation in the Global South: Fast Cities and the New Urban Utopias of the Postcolonial State* (pp. 101–115). Routledge.

Rodney, W. (2012). *How Europe Underdeveloped Africa*. Pambazuka.

Ross, M. L. (2012). *The Oil Curse: How Petroleum Wealth Shape the Development of Nations*. Princeton.

Ross, M. L. (2015). What Have We Learned about the Resource Curse? *Annual Review of Political Science Journal, 18*, 239–259.

Rutten, M., & Mwangi, M. (2014). How Natural is Natural? Seeking Conceptual Clarity over Natural Resources and Conflicts. In M. Bavinck, L. Pellegrini, & E. Mostert (Eds.), *Conflicts Over Natural Resources in the Global South* (pp. 51–69). CRC Routledge.

Sanderson, C. A. (2010). *Social Psychology*. Wiley.

Sayne, A., & Katsouris, C. (2015). *Nigeria's Criminal Crude: International Options to Combat the Export of Stolen Oil*. Chatham House.

Schwegler, V. (2017). The Disposable Nature: The Case of Ecocide and Corporate Accountability. *Amsterdam Law Reform Journal, 9*(3), 72–99.

Seale, C. (2004). *Research Society and Culture* (2nd ed.). Saga.

Shoewu, O., Akinyemi, L. A., Ayanlowo, K. A., Olatinwo, S. O., & Makanjuola, N. T. (2013). Mechatronics System: Spying and Reporting Vandalism. *Journal of Science and Engineering, 1*(2), 134–142.

Sinden, A. (2009). An Emerging Human Rights to Security from Climate Change: The Case Against Gas Flaring in Nigeria. In W. C. G. Burns & H. M. Osofsky (Eds.), *Adjudicating Climate Change: State, National, and International Approaches* (pp. 173–192). Cambridge University Press.

Talus, K. (2011). *Vertical Natural Gas Transportation Capacity, Upstream Commodity Contracts, and EU Competition Law*. Kluwer.

Tarallo, M. (2019, October Issue). Is Pipeline Security Adequate? *ASIS International Security Management Magazine*.

The Guardian Editor. (2023, August 28). Nigeria Still Losing 400,000 Barrels of Crude Oil Daily, Says Ribadu. *The Guardian News*. https://guardian.ng/news/nigeria-still-losing-400000-barrels-of-crude-oil-daily-says-ribadu/. Accessed 6 September 2023.

Theodoropoulos, T. E. (2011). *Oil-Gas Exploration and Drilling*. Book Baby.

Timashev, S., & Bushinskaya, A. (2016a). *Diagnostic and Reliability of Pipeline Systems*. Springer International Publishing.

Timashev, S., & Bushinskaya, A. (2016b). Methods of Assessing Integrity of Pipeline Systems with Different Types of Defects. In S. Timashev & A. Bushinskaya (Eds.), *Diagnostics and Reliability of Pipeline Systems* (Vol. 30, pp. 9–43). Springer.

Transparency International. (2019). Military Involvement in Oil Theft in the Niger Delta. https://ti-defence.org/publications/military-involvement-in-oil-theft-in-the-niger-delta/. Accessed 25 November 2020.

Transparency International. (2020). Corruption Perception Index 2020. https://www.transparency.org/en/cpi/2021. Accessed 24 November 2020.

Ubong, U. I., Chibuogwu, E., Aroh, K. N., Umo-Otong, J. C., Harry, I. M., & Gobo, A. E. (2010). Oil Spill Incidents and Pipeline Vandalisation in Nigeria: Impact on Public Health and Negation to Attainment of Millennium Development Goals: The Ishiagu Example. *Disaster Prevention, and Management International Journal, 19*(1), 70–87.

Ughamadu, N. (2017). *Nigeria Defers 700,000bpd of Crude Oil Due to Pipeline Vandalism*. Nigeria National Petroleum Corporation.

Ugo, P. (2017). Oil Capitalism, Precarity, and Youths Resistance to Slow Violence in Nigeria's Oil Delta. In P. Ugo & L. M. Yevugah (Eds.), *African Youths Cultures in a Globalised World: Challenges* (pp. 96–110). Routledge.

Umar, A. T., & Othman, M. S. H. (2017). Causes and Consequences of Crude oil Pipeline Vandalism in the Niger Delta of Nigeria: A Confirmatory Factor Analysis Approach. *Cogent Economics and Finance Journal, 5*(1), 1–15.

Umukoro, B. (2009). Gas Flaring, Environmental Corporate Responsibility and the Right to a Healthy Environment: Case of the Niger Delta. In F. Emiri & G. Deinduomo (Eds.), *Law and Petroleum Industry in Nigeria: Current Challenges* (pp. 36–49). Malthouse.

United Nations Development Programme. (1994). *Human Development Report 1994: New Dimensions of Human Security*. Oxford University Press.

United Nations Environment Programme Report. (2012). Environmental Assessment of Ogoniland: Assessment of Vegetation, Aquatic and Public Health Issues. http://hdl.handle.net/20.500.11822/25286. Accessed 9 May 2018.

United Nations Sustainable Development Goals. (2016). The Sustainable Development Agenda. https://www.un.org/sustainabledevelopment/development-agenda-retired/#:~:text=%E2%97%8F,future%20for%20people%20and%20planet. Accessed 31 October 2023.

Waever, O. (1998). Security, Insecurity and Asecurity in the West-European Non-War Community. In E. Adler & M. Barnett (Eds.), *Security Communities* (pp. 70–118). Cambridge University Press.

Willink Commission Report. (1958). *Nigeria: Report of the Commission Appointed to Inquire into the Fears of Minorities and the Means of Allaying them*. Her Majesty's Stationary Office.

# CHAPTER 2

# Oil and Gas Pipeline Infrastructure and Sustainable Development in the Global South

## THE GLOBAL SOUTH, EVASIVE AND PROBLEMATIC TO DISCUSS

The concept found its way into the academic, political, civil societies, and institutional lexicon after the collapse of the Soviet Union. Its usage keeps evolving. The term "Global South" describes countries that experience socio-economic and infrastructural underdevelopment, despite their endowment in natural resources including oil and gas. Thus, extends beyond mere geographical expression used to describe countries in the geographical South, such as South Africa and others. Wolvers et al. (2015) argue that the term Global South is a "complex and Subjective matter". It means countries with global economic, infrastructural, and geopolitical disparities (Westermeier & Goede, 2022). Mignolo says it is not simply the land below the equator, but an ideological concept highlighting the economic, political, and epistemic dependence (Mignolo, 2011: 165–167). Others say the term homogenises non-Western countries (Mpofu,

Unless we act now, the 2030 Agenda could become an epitaph for a world that might have been
(Antonio Guterres, UN Secretary-General, 2023)

© The Author(s), under exclusive license to Springer Nature Switzerland AG 2024
A. L. A. Jatto, *Oil and Gas Pipeline Infrastructure Insecurity*, New Security Challenges,
https://doi.org/10.1007/978-3-031-56932-6_2

2021). Global South does not only describe countries endowed with hydrocarbon.

The term is interchangeably used to describe political and economic disparities. For instance, advanced democracies vs illiberal democracies, and technologically and infrastructurally advanced vs underdevelopment. This book has a different intention for its usage. *The book, therefore, argues from the lens of political economy and international relations. The "Global South" is mostly illiberal democratic countries endowed with extractive natural resources, especially petroleum, that have failed to convert their petrodollar into a socio-economic and infrastructural transformation that benefits majority of their citizens through constructive governance.* The neglect of the local communities creates tensions and insecurity that cascade into aggression and pipeline vandalism in the Niger Delta. This forms the context for this book which interrogates the views of different stakeholders, particularly the Bayelsa community stakeholders and by analysing their stories closes the gaps in the literature. Most Global South countries are socio-economically and culturally trapped in the historical shadows of colonialism by the Global North and have been negatively impacted by capitalist globalisation (Riggs, 2015; Rodney, 2012).

They also share complex socio-economic, political, and developmental similarities and challenges (Majid, 2013; Riggs, 2015). Oil and gas producing countries within the rubric of the Global South are widely regarded as the "poorer world" spread across Africa, Asia, the Arab region, and Latin America (Dodd & Merwe, 2019; Riggs, 2015: 1). Some of these countries include Nigeria, Angola, Algeria, Libya, Egypt, Venezuela, Brazil, Mexico, Indonesia, Malaysia, Kuwait, Oman, Qatar, Iraq, Iran, Sudan, South Sudan, Ghana, Uganda, The Gambia, Zimbabwe, Sao Tome El Principe, and Mozambique (Omeje, 2017a, 2017b, 2017c; Shepard, 2015). While some of these countries have produced oil and gas for many decades, a few like Zimbabwe and Mozambique are fresh starters, but are less likely to avoid the "leadership curse" (see Chapter 4). Ferabolli (2021) disagree whether Saudi Arabia which produces crude oil, should be classified as part of the Global South, because the idea has remains contentious.

Given that is a high-income economy, a member of G20, developed infrastructure, is a regional powerhouse, and has a higher standard of living for many of its citizens. It is critical to note that these classifications, however, can be fluid and context-dependent. Global South countries are generally at an economic disadvantage with weak democratic institutions; institutionalised corruption; multiple failures at industrialisation; and increased levels of illiteracy and semi-skilled unemployed youth workforce. They suffer from aging infrastructure, poor governance, extensive institutional corruption, and disruptive and compromised security architecture. Also, they have slow response to third-party disruption and operational blowouts, compromised regulatory oversights, and a dearth of technological advancement (Mathias, 2015; Ogbeidi, 2012; Tarallo, 2019; Theodoropoulos, 2011; Transparency International, 2019). The context should determine where best suits a country, South or North. The geopolitical problems in the Global South are evasive and threaten the oil and gas infrastructure security in the regions.

## Geopolitical Threats and Insecurity Affecting Oil and Gas Infrastructure

It was Immanuel Kant, 1724–1804, who said "War is the easiest thing in the world to decide upon because war does not require of the ruler …the least sacrifice of the pleasures of his table…if the consent of the citizens is to be required…they would be very cautious in commencing such a poor game" (Kant, 2018: 100). The above statement holds true for the different geopolitical threats and insecurity dynamics emerging in the contemporary Global South. It suffices that, were these insecurity problems taking a direct and commensurate toll on the lives and properties of politicians, rulers, and business leaders, as they impact the masses, the issues would have been "desecuritised" and resolved. Just as the citizens would have been cautious in commencing a war described by Kant as a "poor game" (Kant, 2018). This book argues that subregional threats and insecurity problems do have a significant negative impact on onshore oil and gas infrastructure, particularly pipeline operations and management in Africa, Asia, the Arab region, and Latin America regions. It asserts that neglecting the United Nations Sustainability framework heightens the tensions that give impetus to the collective community aggression displacement against oil pipelines. Neglecting to gauge the views of different community stakeholders before invading their local communities to explore and exploit hydrocarbon resources bridges the fundamental principle of social contract in most petrostates in the Global South.

Onuoha (2007) and Igbinovia (2014) state that, despite country-to-country differences, the oil and gas infrastructure in Nigeria and other petrostates in Africa like Niger, Mozambique, Zimbabwe, Sudan, and South Sudan, have the same threat characteristics (Mhlanga & Chirisa, 2023). This includes political instability, terrorism, piracy, pervasive/institutional corruption, and structured/organsied oil bunkering. Others are infrastructure vulnerability-susceptibility of critical oil and gas physical and digital facilities to a range of threats, risks, mechanical, and third-party human disruptions as well as transnational conflicts (Igbinovia, 2014; Mhlanga & Chirisa, 2023). Cybersecurity threats, water scarcity, climate change, energy security, regulatory policy concerns, militancy/insurgency, and natural disasters, economic and fiscal issues, supply chain disruption, unstable taxation regimes, community conflicts, challenges to sustainability, and resource nationalism are also included (Bordoff & O'Sullivan, 2023; Kaldor, 2020). These threats are also the cause of insecurity in countries such as Algeria, Libya, and Egypt including Iran's threat to Saudi's critical oil infrastructure, and other internal tensions between the Gulf countries (GCC) Middle East/Arab region (Bollier, 2013; Harrington et al., 2019; Hussain & Al-Marri, 2017).

Asian countries (Southeast/west and Central) also face threats like geo-economic competition in the context of the "Great Game" between regional players over potential customers and suppliers. These are common in Iran, Iraq, Afghani, India, Pakistan, and Turkey (Arteaga, 2010; Bordoff & O'Sullivan, 2023). Dragos Incorporated in its report, *Oil and Natural Gas Cyber Threat Perspective for the Gulf Cooperation Council Region* 2021, suggests an increased threat of cyberattacks against oil and gas infrastructure in the Arab region (Dragos, 2021). Latin America's Brazil, Mexico, and Venezuela have their share of these complex insecurity problems (Bordoff & O'Sullivan, 2023; Oliveira, 2010).

Contemporary unfolding geopolitical insecurity trends and patterns heighten this insecurity affecting oil pipeline infrastructure. Geopolitical insecurity issues like the increased drug trade, ethno-religion conflicts, border disputes, the proliferation of small arms and light weapons, and regional power struggles. Including human rights abuses, foreign interventions, Sahel tensions, human trafficking, refugees and IDP crisis, xenophobia, and land reforms in the West, East, North, and South Africa reinforce most of the oil and gas infrastructure problems (Bordoff & O'Sullivan, 2023; Khan et al., 2023). For instance, coups and counter-coups are a threat to oil and gas assets, especially critical onshore pipeline infrastructure. The current tensions in West Africa following recent coups in Burkina Faso, Niger, and others are cases in point. This seismic power shift unfolding in the Sahara could enable Niger to monetise its own recoverable gas and gold reserves previously monopolised by France for a century (Ben, 2023; Goumandakoye, 2016). The new military regime is a direct threat to the USD13 billion project that will guarantee Europe's access to cheap Nigeria's Niger Delta oil and gas supplies through Algeria (Aris, 2023). The coup specifically threatens the Trans Saharan Gas Pipeline (TSGP), also called the Nigeria-Algeria (NIGAL) pipeline project, and disrupts the geo-economic calculation of Nigeria, particularly its long-term national economic plans (Mitchell, 2023). The wider implication of the Niger coup is that it has heightening the geoeconomic, geosecurity, and geopolitical tensions between Morocco and Algeria. It also disrupts the US$25 billion, Nigeria-Lagos to Morocco, West African, Gas pipeline linked to the existing West African Gas Pipeline. Europe might face disruptions resulting from heightened geosecurity and geopolitical tensions in West Africa. This new geo-insecurity realities feeds the tensions where geopolitical powers continue to assess politics and international relations from a myopic, selfish, and even imperialist perspectives (Nuttall, 2023).

These geopolitical and geo-economic interplay has implications on the geosecurity dynamics- protection, and management of a geographical region such as the unpredictability of North Korea, the rise of China, nontraditional threats, and the rise of popularism and nationalism (Arteaga, 2010; Bordoff & O'Sullivan, 2023); in Latin America, international economic sanctions, environmental protest and activism, organised crime, and climate change (Oliveira, 2010); as well as sovereignty disputes, cyberattacks, Strait of Hormuz, regional rivalries and proxy conflicts in the Arab region (Dragos, 2021; Harrington et al., 2019; Hussain & Al-Marri, 2017) further exposes oil and gas pipeline infrastructure to extreme vulnerabilities. "Geosecurity", in itself, reviews strategies, policies, and measures aimed at safeguarding territories, borders, and critical infrastructure against a wide range of threats, tensions, risks, terrorism, and territorial disputes peculiar to a geographical region (Nuttall, 2023). The Arab region is a critical axis for global petroleum production and transportation. Analysed evidence supports the conclusion made in this book that tensions, threats, and many other insecurities including geo-political and geo-economic dynamics threatening the onshore oil and gas infrastructure and the broader extractive industry are the same in many petrostates in the Global South. There is convergence in the proposed solutions anchored resilient infrastructure and assets combined with smarter operational and management strategies and approaches, like Artificial and or Augmented Intelligence (see Chapter 8 which proposes the solutions).

Bento et al. (2021) describe resilience infrastructure as the ability of an infrastructure system, like oil and gas infrastructure and assets, to resist natural and unnatural disruptions and kinetic impact, through changes in conditions, rapid bounce back, and abording impacts whilst sustaining functionality. Resilient infrastructure principles and guidelines create a net national scale that sets resilient values, designed to gain and improve the continuity of critical assets and services, like oil and gas, transport, and digital communication systems (Sarte, 2010; Smith, 2022). Resilient infrastructure principles set out by the United Nations Disaster Risk Reduction (UNDRR Report, 2022) are

1. Ability to adaptively transform (secure failure, suitable beyond primary purpose, operate beyond unpredictable human intervention, and withstand changing environment).
2. Integrate with the environment
3. Design protected
4. Conducive to social engagement
5. Responsibility must be shared
6. There must be continuous learning

Change in design code and materiality are components of delivering a resilient infrastructure in the oil and gas industry, delivering a sustainable environment, and reducing insecurity. The resilience and robustness in the physical structurality of the onshore oil and gas pipeline, and indeed offshore, empowers the infrastructure with the capacity of continued operation, despite a certain number of stressors like human and natural disasters, cyberattacks, and climate change.

Oil and Gas Infrastructure Insecurity (OGII) means the ability of various pipeline networks to withstand attacks, physical and cyber, and the capacity to recover from impact from external forces such as natural disasters, sabotage, vandalism, and terrorism while maintaining their functionality and minimizing negative impacts on the collective community, environment, and the larger ecosystem (Olawuyi, 2012; Sinden, 2009; UNEP, 2012). Structural resilience is relevant in contemporary Nigeria, and other oil and gas-producing countries in the Global South. Given that onshore and offshore oil and gas pipelines form significant aspects of some of the strategic and critical infrastructures that determine effective hydrocarbon production, and economic development as well as contribute to the socio-economic lives of host communities.

OGII will help oil and gas corporations to increase output by cutting unplanned shutdowns/force majuro, 100 percent reliability, and secure production, storage, transportation plants, and industrial assets (Veolia, 2016). Delivering resilient industrial assets through materiality and adopting pipeline design code that extends the life of matured assets and infrastructure partly tackle three challenges. Cost reduction; maximises industrial assets performance; and importantly the environmental footprint where these oil companies operate (Bollier, 2013; CSIS, 2021; Veolia, 2016; see Chapter 8 for new pipeline life cycle). An improved environmental footprint entails Zero Liquid Discharge (ZLD)-innovative and efficient liquid waste, sewage effluent, and industrial water management cycle including mechanical/operational blowouts and gas flaring meets the UNSDGs (Oliveira, 2010; Veolia, 2016). These targets have a ripple effect on the lives and socio-economy of communities by returning natural habitats to their natural state, delivering a sustainable environment, and mitigating tensions, and insecurity problems.

## Sustainable Development and Oil and Gas Infrastructure

It is often assumed what sustainability and sustainable development means. The concept of "sustainability" is not new, it is historical. Indigenous local communities in Nigeria and the Global South practiced different forms of sustainable living for generations, connecting with their natural habitats, and being in tune with its limits, changes, and cycles (McGill University, 2020). Sustainability, from a policy context, prevents the depletion of natural and physical resources, green spaces, forests, and rivers for long-term access (Pfister et al., 2016). Others say sustainability is the ability to exist and develop in the present without depleting and or polluting natural resources for the future, soil, water, air, and semi-natural habitats (Bergkamp, 2021; Sun et al., 2023). Whereas the key word here is "resources". It does not replace the centrality of environment, equity, and economy (McGill University, 2020). Most resources are finite, the UN and others argued that conservative, calculated, and structured usage of natural resources, by the present generation, will not compromise the ability of the future generation to access natural resources. Sustainability has been diluted and is now used to describe a plethora of associated subjects like sustainable living, sustainable cities, and sustainable energies.

However, "Sustainable Development" (SD), means meeting the development needs of the present generation without compromising the chances and abilities of future generations to meet their own development needs (Sun et al., 2023; UN). This definition has been broadly accepted as authoritative given that it overarches the principles of equity, economy, and environment, addressed in the Brundtland Commission's Report, released in 1987 (McGill University, 2020). The definition also aligns with the UN definition of the concept. Other scholars and organisations such as Lencucha et al. (2023), UNDESA (2016), Mensah and Casadevall (2019), Eisenmenger et al. (2020), and Holden et al. (2014) sometimes conceptualised sustainable development as:

a. The Brundtland Report
b. Three Pillars of Sustainability
c. Ecological Footprint
d. Resilience and Adaptive Capacity
e. Cultural and Indigenous Perspectives
f. Planetary Boundaries
g. Doughnut Economics
h. Human Development Index, and
i. Corporate Social Responsibility.

Sustainable development, as a concept, overarches the central theme of this book by exploring issues that trigger insecurity problems, both in Nigeria and in other countries in the Global South. Neglecting to resolve many of these issues has led to tensions and conflicts in many nations endowed with natural resources, especially petrostates. Some argued that the present generation has degraded the soil, and extensively polluted the waters, and air, thus, the present generation has "clearly prejudiced the ability of future generations" due to the build-up of greenhouse gases and the depletion of the ozone layer, Valance and Best argued (2013: 110). This has heightened the tensions and conflicts. This sustainable development initiative aims to advance growth whilst preserving the earth's natural resources through quantifiable, disciplined, and sustainable exploitation that will reduce the above problematic issues. Mensah and

Casadevall (2019) and the UNSDG (2016; UNDESA, 2016) outlined four key sustainable development principles, which are

- Environmental Sustainability
- Social Equity
- Economic Viability, and
- Intergenerational Equity

The UN associates itself with this sustainable development idea through the UNSDG initiatives by creating a framework that sets out target goals ranging from poverty, and hunger, to sustainable energy, and consumption (UNSDG, 2016). These UNSDGs, referred to as Global Goals, are 17 interconnected global objectives adopted in September 2015 by member states of the UN as part of the 2030 Sustainable Development Agenda. Nigeria and most countries in the Global South lack a structured and coherent policy approach toward Sustainable development goals. The Global North has not delivered on its SDG objectives which challenges its commitments toward achieving the UNSDG 2030 targets (Lencucha et al., 2023; Loft & Brien, 2023). The United Kingdom's Parliament alluded that progress on UNSDG has stalled (2023). This was observed during the 2023 United Nations General Assembly deliberations in New York. There are divergent views about the 17 Global Goals, 2030 SDG targets, or agenda are and what they are not. To restate the facts Agenda 2030 goals are;

1. No Poverty
2. Zero Hunger
3. Good Health and Well-Being
4. Quality Education
5. Gender Equality
6. Clean Water and Sanitation
7. Affordable and Clean Energy
8. Decent Work and Economic Growth
9. Industry, Innovation and Infrastructure
10. Reduced Inequalities
11. Sustainable Cities and Communities
12. Responsible Consumption and Production
13. Climate Action

14. Life Below Water
15. Life on Land
16. Peace, Justice, and Strong Institutions
17. Partnerships for the Goals

This book argues that neglecting these UNSDGs (2016) reinforces multidimensional forms of insecurity problems that continue to plague most oil and gas countries in the Global South such as Nigeria. Evidence suggests that UN sustainable development goals are harder to achieve given how hydrocarbon and other extractive resources are been aggressively extracted in Nigeria and the Global South, with disregard for social equity (Mensah & Casadevall, 2019). Due to poor cooperation between government, corporate entities, local communities, and individuals. This impacts the choices of policies and practices that balance socio-economic growth, and environmental, and natural habitat protection that create an equitable and sustainable world for the majority. Social equity concerns itself with ensuring that most individuals have access to opportunities to succeed through fair and equitable distribution of all resources, benefits, and justice within a society (Lencucha et al., 2023; Mensah & Casadevall, 2019; UNSDG, 2016). This underpins plenty of political and philosophical ideologies and explains the principles of justice, socialism, and liberalism. This book argues that oil and gas infrastructure security is facilitated when Nigeria and many petrostates in the Global South focus on sustainability principles and goals by designing policies and practices with the aim of achieving and sustaining the UN target. This defines the core criteria of Environmental, Social, and Governance (ESG) corporations are expected to adopt.

Although there have been a few achievements, these have not impacted the majority of lives in local communities across petrostates with extractive resources such as Colombia, the Democratic Republic of Congo, Niger, and Nigeria, in the Global South to name a few (Dodd & Merwe, 2019; Majid, 2013; Omeje, 2017a, 2017b, 2017c; Riggs, 2015; Shepard, 2015). The UN and most member states agree appreciable progress has been made in the Global Goal Agenda 2030 in poverty reduction, education, gender equality, health and well-being, clean water and sanitation, climate change, life below water, and life on land, technology, and innovation, and partnerships. Within the context of discussion, available evidence does not support the claims of SDG progress and, therefore deconstructs the UN conclusion on progress made (Loft & Brien, 2023).

For instance, the NBS in Nigeria, in 2022 reported that over 133 million Nigerians have fallen into multidimensional poverty (NBS, 2022, OPHI, 2022). The report revealed that in terms of education, 20 million children are out of school, implying that 29 percent of school-age children are not attending school. While some countries like Saudi appears to lift some of their citizens from poverty the same cannot be said about Ghana, DRC, or Niger (see OPHI, 2022). Citizens of some countries in the Global North like the UK recently protested in London because they are experiencing a high cost of living crisis (Townsend & Lawson, 2023).

A lack of standardisation in the SDG framework policy processes in many countries in the Global North and South is partly responsible for poor outcomes. Also, the science of some 2030 agendas, like climate change, is still contested by some government regimes such as China, and India, during President Trump's regime in the United States as well as many countries in the Global South which slowed down global action (Maizland, 2023). These countries often define their own pace rather than follow the UN framework. This suggests that some of their joint statements of commitment are mere rhetoric. Their actions heighten the very underlying socio-economic issues that lead to tensions that cascade to varying insecurity issues in the Global South. There is palpable fear that by 2030 the world will be able to achieve only 12 percent of the SDG targets given the way nations design and implement their policy thrust. Indeed, Loft and Brien argued elsewhere in this book that the whole process of achieving the 17 SDG targets has been stalled. Integrating the viewpoints of most world leaders at the recently completed 78th United Nations General Assembly progress review against the UNSDGs meeting in New York indicted the world leaders. Its scorecard showed that the world was far away and nowhere close to achieving half of the UNSDGs (Loft & Brien, 2023). Their conclusion aligns with the findings of the UNSDG progress review which revealed that headway on over 50 percent of the targets is weak with indications that 30 percent of the targets have either gone into reverse or stalled. There is a collective dearth and failure to address climate change, widening inequality gaps, and natural crises.

This failure is more of a crisis of poor governance, greed, corruption, and a mix of incompetence and "cursed" leadership, rather than that of the planet. This is also due to compromised national and global economic frameworks and "crisis" in the global financial systems, such as the 2007/2008 global financial crisis, and the dot-com bubble burst in the early 2000s. Oil and gas infrastructure security interconnects with the

UNSDGs, and vice versa. These challenges heighten the insecurity of the oil and gas infrastructure given that the collective community takes laws into their hands by engaging in oil bunkering and vandalism. Conversely, innovation, industry, and financing in secured oil and gas infrastructure would contribute to the process of achieving some UN 2030 targets. The effective functioning of the oil and gas infrastructure depressurises the water bodies and the physical environment, protecting the legitimate sources of livelihood of most local communities.

It is important to note that the oil and gas industry, in itself, seriously impacts the UNSDGs in the Global South. Many works of the literature analysed in this book suggest the relationship between the oil and gas industry, precisely onshore pipeline infrastructure, and the UNSDGs are difficult to explore, depending on the management, development, and utilisation of these natural resources. Explaining the impact that the oil and gas industry has on SDGs policy framework and implementation in Nigeria and the Global South is complex. Many countries in the Global South endowed with crude oil see the resource that could transform their economies, and upgrade their infrastructure. They forget hydro-carbon poses massive environmental and social challenges that must be addressed in order for them to align with the SDG 2030 targets that would better the lives of the rural majority. This is the dilemma. The major impact of the oil and gas industry across most of these countries lies in environmental hazards associated with the industry.

## CONCLUSION

This chapter discussed oil and gas pipeline infrastructure, its security, and the UN SDGs in the Global South. Oil and gas continue to impact the ability of nations to transition to cleaner and affordable energy; innovation, industry, and infrastructure, climate action, life below water and on land, responsible consumption and production, and formidable partnerships toward achieving the goals (Mensah & Casadevall, 2019; UNSDG, 2016). It is usually the Global North, the more powerful, and advanced, also rich in natural resources, who are able to describe the actions of the less powerful oil and gas producing countries in the Global South as the biggest polluters. This pattern of thought is reinforced by socio-cultural norms by a dominant global media that supports these countries to manufacture content and consent, thereby legalising and shaping the common frame that influences public perception who nuancedly or overtly agree that the oil and gas industry in the Global South does the biggest harms the SDGs. This frame creates a mirror opposite of reality, which is unnatural and can be reconstructed. It concluded that the perceived differences between the implementation of the SDGs-2030 targets in focus, and the operationalisation of the oil and gas industry are unreal but created by a degree of viewpoint. The book aligns with the view of some scholars who pointed out that "a frame gives structure to both an object and the way the object is perceived" (Sauer & Ensink, 2003: 3). The industrialised countries in the Global North, producing oil and gas resources, should take most blame for ozone layer depletion and its cascading impact on the environment, the SDGs, and the Global South.

## References

Aris, B. (2023). Niger Coupe Threatens Nigeria-Morocco 30bcm Gas Pipeline Project. *Intelli News*. https://intellinews.com/niger-coup-threatens-nigeria-morocco-30bcm-gas-pipeline-project-286426/. Accessed 27 October 2023.

Arteaga, F. (2010). *International Security: Energy Security in Central Asia: Infrastructure and Risks*. Elcano Royal Institute.

Bento, F., Mercado, M. P., & Garotti, M. (2021). Organisational Resilience in Oil and Gas Industry: A Scoping Review. *Safety Science Journal, 133*, 1–11.

Bergkamp, L. (2021). *Liability and Environment: Private and Public Law Aspects of Civil Liability for environmental Harm in an International Context*. Brill.

Bollier, S. (2013). All is Not Well in Northern Iraq's Oilfields. *Global Policy Forum*. https://archive.globalpolicy.org/the-dark-side-of-natural-resources-st/oil-and-natural-gas-in-conflict/middle-east/52194-all-is-not-well-in-nor thern-iraqs-oilfields.html%3Fitemid=id.html#40291. Accessed 27 October 2023.

Bordoff, J., & O'Sullivan, M. L. (2023, May/June). The Age of Energy Insecurity: How the Fight for Resources Is Upending Geopolitics, *Foreign Affairs Journal*. https://www.foreignaffairs.com/world/energy-insecurity-cli mate-change-geopolitics-resources. Accessed 27 October 2023.

Centre for Strategic and International Studies. (2021). *A New Revolution in the Middle East*. CSIS. https://www.csis.org/analysis/new-revolution-mid dle-east. Accessed 27 October 2023.

Dodd, N., & Merwe, J. V. D. (2019). *The Political Economy of Underdevelopment in the Global South: The Government-Business-Media Complex*. Palgrave Macmillan.

Dragos Incorporated Report. (2021). Oil and Natural Gas Cyber Threat Perspective for the GCC 2021. https://www.dragos.com/resource/gcc-ong-cyber-threat-perspective/. Accessed 26 October 2023.

Eisenmenger, N., Pichler, M., Krenmayer, N., Noll, D., Plank, B., Schalmann, K., Wandl, M. T., & Gingrich, S. (2020). The Sustainable Development Goals Prioritized Economic Growth Over Sustainable Resource Use: A Critical Reflection on the SDGs from Socio-ecological Perspective. *Journal of Sustainable Science, 15*, 1101–1110.

Ferabolli, S. (2021). Space Making in the Global South: Lessons from the GCC-Mercosur Agreement. *Contexto International, 43*(1).

Goumandakoye, H. (2016). Oil in Niger: A Foundation for Promise or a New Resource Curse? *The Extractive Industries and Society Journal, 3*(2), 361–366.

Harrington, N., Jones, S. G., Bermudez, J. S., & Newlee, D. (2019). *Iran's Threat to Saudi's Critical Infrastructure: The Implications of U.S.–Iranian Escalation.* Centre for Strategic and International Studies.

Holden, E., Linnerud, K., & Banister, D. (2014). Sustainable Development: Our Common Future Revisited. *Journal of Global Environmental Change, 26*, 130–139.

Hussain, F., & Al-Marri, M. A. (2017, November). *The Impact of the Oil Crisis on Security and Foreign Policy in GCC Countries: Case Studies of Qatar, KSA and UAE.* Arab Centre for Research and Policy Studies.

Igbinovia, P. E. (2014). *Oil Thefts and Pipeline Vandalisation in Nigeria.* African Books.

Kaldor, M. (2020). *Cities at War: Global Insecurity and Urban Resistance.* Colombia University Press.

Kant, I. (2018). *Project for Perpetual Peace: A Philosophical Essay.* Creative Media.

Khan, K., Faura, J. C., & Khurshid, A. (2023, June). Energy Security Analysis in a Geopolitically Volatile World: A Causal Study. *Resources Policy Journal, 83.*

Lencucha, R., Thow, A. M., & Kulenova, A. (2023). Framing Policy Objectives in the Sustainable Development Goals: Hierarchy, Balance, or Transformation? *Journal of Globalisation and Health, 19*(5).

Loft, P., & Brien, P. (2023, September). Halfway to 2023: The Sustainable Development Goals. *UK House of Commons Library.* https://commonsli brary.parliament.uk/halfway-to-2030-the-sustainable-development-goals/. 31 October 2023.

Maizland, L. (2023, September). Global Climate Agreements: Successes and Failures. *Council on Foreign Relations.* https://www.cfr.org/backgrounder/paris-global-climate-change-agreements. Accessed 2 November 2023.

Mathias, Z. (2015). Providing All-Round Security against Oil and Gas Infrastructure Sabotage and Physical Attacks on the Staff of NNPC and Multinational Oil Companies in Nigeria as a Critical Article of Her National Security Efforts. *International Journal of Social Science and Humanities Research, 3*(2), 45–59.

McGill University. (2020). *Climate and Sustainability Strategy 2020–2025.* https://www.mcgill.ca/sustainability/files/sustainability/mcgillclimat esustainability2025_-_reduced.pdf. Accessed 30 October 2023.

Mensah, J., & Casadevall, S. R. (Reviewing Editor). (2019). Sustainable Development: Meaning, History, Principles, Pillars, and Implications for Human Action: Literature Review. *Journal of Cogent Social Sciences, 51*(1).

Mhlanga, G., & Chirisa, I. (2023). Building more Sustainable and Resilient Urban Energy Infrastructures in Southern Africa. In R. Brinkmann (Ed.), *The Palgrave Handbook of Global Sustainability* (pp. 985–1005). Palgrave Macmillan.

Mignolo, W. D. (2011). The Global South and World Dis/Order. *Journal of Anthropological Research, 67*(2), 165–188.

Mitchell, C. (2023). Niger Coup, Financing Woes Rock Nigeria's Plan to Supply Gas to Europe, S and P Global Commodity Insight. https://www.spglobal.com/commodityinsights/en/market-insights/latest-news/natural-gas/090823-niger-coup-financing-woes-rock-nigerias-plan-to-supply-gas-to-europe. Accessed 27 October 2023.

Mpofu, S. (2021). *The Politics of Laughter in the Social Media Age: Perspectives from the Global South*. Springer International.

National Bureau of Statistics. (2022). *Nigeria Multidimensional Poverty Index (2022)*. National Bureau of Statistics.

Nuttall, M. (2023). *The Shaping of Greenland's Resource Spaces: Environment, Territory, and Geo-Security*. Routledge.

Ogbeidi, M. M. (2012). Political Leadership and Corruption in Nigeria since 1960: A Socio-economics Analysis. *Journal of Nigerian Studies, 1*(2), 1–24.

Olawuyi, D. S. (2012). Legal and Sustainable Development Impacts of Major Oil Spills. *The Journal of Sustainable Development, 9*(1), 1–15.

Oliveira, A. D. (2010). *Energy Security in South America: The Role of Brazil*. International Institute for Sustainable Development.

Omeje, K. (2017a). *Extractive Economies and Conflicts in the Global South: Multiregional Perspectives on Rentier Politics*. Taylor and Francis.

Omeje, K. (2017b). *High Stakes and Stakeholders: Oil Conflict and Security in Nigeria*. Routledge.

Omeje, K. (2017c). The Egbesu and Bakassi Boys: African Spiritism and Mystical Re-rationalisation of Security. In D. J. Francis (Ed.), *Civil Militia: Africa's Intractable Security Menace* (pp. 71–86). Routledge.

Onuoha, C. F. (2007). Oil Pipeline Sabotage in Nigeria: Dimensions, Actors and Implications for National Security. *African Security Review, 17*(3), 100–115.

Oxford Poverty and Human Development Initiative. (2022). *Nigeria MPI Report, 2022*. Oxford University. https://ophi.org.uk/nigeria-mpi-2022/. Accessed 3 November 2023.

Pfister, T., Reichel, A., & Schweighofer, M. (2016). *Sustainability*. Routledge.

Rodney, W. (2012). *How Europe Underdeveloped Africa*. Pambazuka.

Sarte, B. S. (2010). *Sustainable Infrastructure: The Guide to Green Engineering and Design*. Wiley.

Sauer, C., & Ensink, T. (2003). *Framing and Perspectivising in Discourse*. John Benjamin.

Shepard, B. (2015). *Oil in Uganda: International Lessons for Success*. Royal Institute for International Affairs.

Sinden, A. (2009). An Emerging Human Rights to Security from Climate Change: The Case Against Gas Flaring in Nigeria. In W. C. G. Burns & H. M. Osofsky (Eds.), *Adjudicating Climate Change: State, National, and International Approaches* (pp. 173–192). Cambridge University Press.

Smith, D. A. (2022). *The 6 Principles to Help Engineers Create Resilient Infrastructure*. Institute of Civil Engineers. https://www.ice.org.uk/news-insight/news-and-blogs/ice-blogs/the-civil-engineer-blog/principles-to-help-engineers-create-resilient-infrastructure. Accessed 29 October 2023.

Sun, Y., Zhou, K., Yi, L., & Su, X. (2023). *Environmental and Resource Protection Law*. Palgrave Macmillan.

Tarallo, M. (2019, October Issue). Is Pipeline Security Adequate? *ASIS International Security Management Magazine*.

Theodoropoulos, T. E. (2011). *Oil-Gas Exploration and Drilling*. Book Baby.

Townsend, M., & Lawson, A. (2023). 'Huge Turnouts' Reported at UK Cost of Living Protests. *The Guardian News*. https://www.theguardian.com/business/2022/oct/01/huge-turnouts-reported-at-uk-cost-of-living-protests#:~:text=Thousands%20have%20gathered%20in%20dozens,seen%20in%20Britain%20for%20years. 3 November 2023.

Transparency International. (2019). Military Involvement in Oil Theft in the Niger Delta. https://ti-defence.org/publications/military-involvement-in-oil-theft-in-the-niger-delta/. Accessed 25 November 2020.

United Nations Department of Economics and Social Affairs. (2016). *Sustainable Development: Make SDGs a Reality*. https://sdgs.un.org/. Accessed 31 October 2023.

United Nations Disaster Risk Reduction. (2022). *Principles for Resilient Infrastructure*. UNDRR. https://www.undrr.org/publication/principles-resilient-infrastructure. Accessed 29 October 2023.

United Nations Environment Programme Report. (2012). Environmental Assessment of Ogoniland: Assessment of Vegetation, Aquatic and Public Health Issues. http://hdl.handle.net/20.500.11822/25286. Accessed 9 May 2018.

United Nations Sustainable Development Goals. (2016). The Sustainable Development Agenda. https://www.un.org/sustainabledevelopment/development-agenda-retired/#:~:text=%E2%97%8F,future%20for%20people%20and%20planet. Accessed 31 October 2023.

Valance, G. D., & Best, R. (2013). *Building a Value: Pre-Design Issues*. CRC.

Veolia Resourcing the World. (2016). New Challenges of the Oil and Gas Industry. https://www.veolia.com/middleeast/our-services/our-vision/new-challenges-oil-gas-industry#:~:text=With%20rising%20global%20demand%2C%20highly,and%20improve%20its%20environmental%20footprint. Accessed 27 October 2023.

Westermeier, C., & Goede, M. D. (2022). Infrastructural Geopolitics. *International Studies Quarterly, 66*(3).

Wolvers, A., Tappe, O., Salverda, T., & Schwarz, T. (2015). *Concepts of the Global South-Voices from Around the World*. University of Cologne.

# CHAPTER 3

# Impact of Oil and Gas Infrastructure in Bayelsa, Niger Delta

## Niger Delta Geography

Most parts of the Niger Delta coastal areas are less than six metres above sea level except the Calabar highlands in the north of the Niger Delta which lies between 900 and 1500 metres above sea level (Ukpong, 2012). Bayelsa State is located in the southern part of Nigeria. It was created in 1996 from the Old Rivers state and is on average three metres below sea level (Alagoa, 1999; Brisibe & Tepple, 2018). Bayelsa is mostly riverine with nine estuaries that empty into the Atlantic Ocean. The presence of oil and gas resources has triggered intense competition between key stakeholders over who dominates the 15 percent of its dry land (Ohwo, 2015). These stakeholders are local communities, local government, state government, the federal government, and oil and gas companies. The present-day geographic Niger Delta was formed around 120 million years ago (Alamieyeseigha, 2008a). In recent years, the Niger Delta, like in Ghana, Colombia, and Zimbabwe has become a major source of oil and gas production. These activities have, and continue to have, a devastating environmental impact that has also impacted local communities (Abadom & Nwankwoala, 2018; Omeje, 2017a, 2017b, 2017c). Its topography is a major source of the environmental challenges facing Bayelsa.

A. L. A. Jatto, *Oil and Gas Pipeline Infrastructure Insecurity*, New Security Challenges, https://doi.org/10.1007/978-3-031-56932-6_3

This has also made the laying of pipelines extremely difficult. Bayelsa, Rivers, and Delta which constitute the historic Niger Delta area are situated at the peripheral axis of the Niger Delta at the bottom edge of the Atlantic Ocean (Amaiwo & Samuel, 2015). Given that most of Bayelsa's 10,773 km$^2$ landmass is riverine, some of its 1.7 million people live on lowlands that stretch from Ekeremor to Nembe (Madubuko, 2017). Bayelsa is surrounded by tropical rainforests and borders the North Atlantic in the south and west. Delta State lies in the North and borders Rivers State in the east (Petters et al., 1997). Nembe-Ewelesuo Creek, the case study area, is located in the southern part of Bayelsa. Although the three historic Niger Delta states have a combined population of around 11 million people, a large section of this population is young and unemployed (National Bureau of Statistics, 2017; Obi & Oriola, 2018). The north of Bayelsa is characterised by mangroves and thick forests with some arable farmlands for agriculture (Brisibe & Tepple, 2018). The Nun River which is the most direct distributary river in the Niger Delta area divides Bayelsa State into two parts (Alagoa, 1999, 2005). Bayelsa's topography consists of moist lowland rainforests, freshwater swamp forests, mangroves, swampy, and salt marshes as well as tidal flats (Alamieyeseigha, 2008a, 2008b). Bayelsa state receives on average about 2400 mm of rainfall annually in the southern and northern areas (Brisibe & Tepple, 2018). Bayelsa is Africa's largest delta because its accumulated sedimentary deposits cover around 75,000 km$^2$ (World Bank, 1995). It is worth noting early on that decades of oil and gas exploration have led to the pollution of large parts of Bayelsa, making many parts of the land and waters unusable (Omeje, 2017a, 2017b, 2017c).

Tensions are continuously heightened in Bayelsa, as elsewhere in the Global South, due to pollution from oil and gas extraction and the annual two-centimetre sea level rise in the area (Akuaibit, 2017). According to Udo and Akuaibit, most post-2000 conflicts in Nigeria are due to the recycling of wicked and incompetent leaders who deliver poor governance as well as the impact of climate change. Many people displaced by rising sea levels and oil and gas extraction activities relocate to Yenagoa, the state capital, which is a coastal settlement with an average height of 14 metres above sea level (Alagoa, 1999; Ohwo, 2015; see Chapter 2 UNSDGs). Climate change issues are causing a range of violent social conflicts and wars in many countries around Sub-Saharan Africa, and the Global South (Bretthauer, 2016; Welzer, 2015). For example, the shrinking of Lake Chad, the disappearance of arable farmlands due to desertification, and erosions partly account for the conflicts in Nigeria's northeastern states (Bello & Abdullahi, 2021). Literature shows that the pollution of fishing waters, farmlands, and asphyxiation of the mangrove forests has further heightened the insecurity problems in Bayelsa. This continues to impact traditional industries such as canoe carving, weaving, trading, lumbering, palm oil milling, palm wine tapping, and local gin-Ogogoro making (Cabot, 2016; Etete, 2017; Ugochukwu, 2008). Weather-related shocks and threats are extremely likely to increase in the future in Nigeria (Etete, 2017). It is estimated that Bayelsa has about 1.1 billion barrels of crude oil and about one trillion cubic feet of gas (Ecumenical Council for Corporate Responsibility, 2010). Shell describes the Gbaran-Ubie oilfield discovery as "the largest oil field from a single community in its entire West African operational history" (ECCR, 2010: 29). The discovery of the Gbaran-Ubie oil field in the Gbaran-Ekpetiama community places Bayelsa as the state with the largest oil and gas deposits in Nigeria (ECCR, 2010). Given the current levels of corruption, poor governance, poverty, and environmental damage continued oil and gas exploration and insecurity will remain a key feature in Bayelsa.

## History, Nembe Wars, and Colonialism

Before oil and gas were discovered in the historic Niger Delta area, kings, chiefs, and coastal leaders traded with the Portuguese, Germans, and later the British (Ali, 2019; Shaxson, 2008). The articles and commodities of trade were palm oil (red gold), and palm kernel produce. When the British realised that palm oil found in the area was the key ingredient needed for the mass production of soap and industrial lubricant they began to scramble for a permanent hold over the lower Niger Delta (Pakenham, 2015). To secure that foothold over the region, the British initiated the signing of trade treaties with the local kings and chiefs to guarantee some form of legitimate control over the trade of tropical palm oil plants, native to the area. The implementation of some treaties was however delayed. Because King Koko, Mingi VIII, Amayanabo Nembe-Brass (1853–1898), who was able to read, had revealed that most of the trade treaties were fraught with deceit (Douglas & Okonta, 2003). The ensuing tensions prevented the British Royal Niger Company (RNC) from the early take-over of the Nembe-Brass palm oil trading routes. King Koko had refused to sign the trade treaties which the British designed. Whereas it is unclear why the early British trade treaties were fraught with deceit against the indigenous people, it was certain that their actions marked the beginning of using instrumental mechanisms to divide the Niger Delta people. In principle, the deceit in the British trade treaties could have suggested that they had no intention of balancing trade with Nembe kings, chiefs, and merchants.

Nembe-Brass kings and merchants became infuriated when they discovered that their lands had been included within the Oil Rivers Protectorate declared by the British. This gave the British military, defence, and external affairs control which enabled them to monopolise the oil palm trade (Inengite, 2018). With the intense desire to maintain uninterrupted palm oil export to London supported by *gunboat diplomacy*, the British forcefully declared the Grand Bonny kingdom a British protectorate (Inengite, 2018; O'Grady, 2018). Gunboat diplomacy meant communities were surrounded by gunboats coercing the kings to either sign the "deceitful trade treaties" or face bombardment and forceful take-over of the entire coastal states. These heightened tensions escalated internal disputes, and communal conflicts between the inhabitants of the Lower Niger Delta people, on the one hand, and the European traders on the other (O'Grady, 2018). The use of force by the British became necessary to enable them to curtail the political and financial influence of coastal Kings like king Koko and Jaja of Opobo and to stop the French from advancing into the middle of the Niger Delta area (Meredith, 2014).

Other scholars like Gates et al. pointed out that the need to ensure full political and economic dominance and control over the oil palm trade made George Goldie form the United African Company (UAC) in 1879 (2012). By 1884, UAC had acquired about 30 trading posts (Rodney, 2012). While the British finally took direct control of the palm oil trade by 1886. The British seemingly succeeded in reinforcing their control over the local communities and manipulated the local leaders due to the harsh socio-economic realities resulting from their military and defense stranglehold (Shaxson, 2008). The fact that the British were unwilling to review their stand on the trade treaties they claimed empowered them to monopolise the oil palm trade escalated tensions. This also heightened widespread socio-economic frustration that culminated in the 1895 King Koko-led Nembe-Brass uprising. King Koko's resentment against the British was further deepened and resonated in a popular prayer: "May this evil of palm oil not get to our children" (Shaxson, 2008: 197). Therefore, it can be argued that the quest to dominate the source of Bayelsa-Nembe's economic wealth led to the 1895 *Oil Palm*

*War* (Douglas & Okonta, 2003). Once oil and gas were discovered, the problems continued and even got worse.

Tensions, the deceit of the treaties, economic and political isolation, military dominance, and forced labour, as many countries in the Global South such as Mozambique, Colombia, and Niger, coupled with poverty influenced the resentment against the British RNC which motivated King Koko to invoke "Egbesu", the Ijaw war god (Inengite, 2018). The British also imposed taxes and trade restrictions on commodities like alcohol, and isolated Nembe traders from external markets along the Orashi River, Brass Sea, Furcados, and Sombraro up to the Aboh Kingdom which they had previously dominated (Inengite, 2018). Although King Koko had hoped for a collective uprising against the British, he was disappointed by coastal chiefs like the Kings of the Okpoma Kingdom and Bonny Island (Douglas & Okonta, 2003). Frustrated by the betrayal and disappointment from such kingdoms, King Koko with an army of around 1000 men attacked and captured the British RNC headquarter at Akassa in January 1895 (Shaxson, 2008). King Koko killed around 75 British army officers, losing about 40 of his fighters (Gottsche, 2013). King Koko also seized oil palm produce, military-grade ammunition, and a maxim gun and took about 60 British men hostages. In response, a month later, the British Royal Navy, commanded by Admiral Bedford under the instructions of the British Consul-General Claude MacDonald bombarded and massacred the entire Nembe-Brass community (Alamieyeseigha, 2008a; Falola, 2009; Inengite, 2018).

The Nembe-Brass massacre Alamieyeseigha (2008a) argued, marked the beginning of uncontrolled violence, extrajudicial killings, and physical military occupation of some part of what is now known as the present-day Bayelsa and other areas in the historic Niger Delta region. The socio-economic and environmental implications of the Nembe-Brass war continue to reverberate across the wider Niger Delta region to date. Alamieyeseigha (2008a) and Boro (1982) argued that the environmental and economic stagnation of Bayelsa set the stage for self-inflicted insecurity that became the albatross of the colonialists and later the oil operators. The contemporary arbitrary and reactive oil and gas government policies from Abuja are a mirror reflection of the deceitful treaties once implemented as British trade policies and the violent response by the British against community resistance (see Chapter 8). Arbitrary policy frameworks are a series of random policy decisions that disadvantage communities which leads to tensions and violence. For instance, the implementation of guidelines on crude oil and natural gas exploration and pipeline transportation of products, storage, ownership, infrastructure, interconnection, and expansion without consideration for local communities formed the core of the problem (Douglas & Okonta, 2003; Numbere, 2018). After 45 years of direct and indirect trade in what is now known as Nigeria, Britain formally declared all of Nigeria, including the Niger Delta a British Colony. Britain took over the lower Niger businesses of the RNC because they saw Nigeria as an economic interest that must be protected given its economic resources in the south coupled with the cheap labour force from the north (Douglas & Okonta, 2003).

To Britain, an ideal colony must be a source of wealth creation in terms of raw materials and human resources (Sagay, 2008). According to Tukur (2016), the need for an uninterrupted supply of raw materials such as oil palm and cotton informed British interest in Nigeria. Colonialism Ojeleye (2016) argued transformed the lower Niger Delta into a business entity. George Thomas, a former British Commonwealth Minister once stated that "Nigeria has been structured as an economic unit, an economic satellite of the Crown, and any disruption would affect trade defining why Britain maintained Nigeria's unity" (Ejiorfor, 2012: 165). Raw materials from Nigerian territories like rubber, cotton, and oil and gas kept British industries and refineries productive. Nigeria's raw materials supplied British industries that sustained labour and livelihood for British citizens during the 1929–1939 *great depression* (Madubuko, 2017). This study argues that colonialism was driven by the economic interests of Western nations. The 1914 amalgamation of southern and northern protectorates was aimed at improving the administration of the Nigerian colony (Ojeleye, 2016). The revelation that the lower Niger Delta was rich in natural resources, by the British geologists, Collins and Harrison, in 1905 contributed to the decision to amalgamate the southern and northern Nigeria territories (Madubuko, 2017).

Since the discovery of oil and gas, local and foreign businesses have been attracted to the Niger Delta area (Oriola, 2016). The quest for crude oil-*black gold* without considering its impact on the environment and the people has pitted the government and multinational businesses against the local communities. For instance, the decision by Shell-BP Petroleum to ignore the impact of its activities on the environment, as well as ignoring the GMOUs documents signed has heightened the distrust between operators and local communities (Effiong, 2010). Also, shifting from the Community Assistance policy to Community Development and later to the Sustainable Community Development policy initiative significantly affected the trust between operators and local communities. Whereas community assistance meant giving money to oil-bearing communities, community development aimed to construct and improve access to social infrastructure. Sustainable community development meant maintaining the natural environment, and preventing pollution while developing local communities. The 1958 discovery of a commercial quantity of crude oil in Bayelsa heightened the problems between the minority ethnic groups and oil companies (Willink Commission Report, 1958). The non-implementation of the Willink Minority Commission report designed to develop minority communities shows that it was a pretext that a development template was in the offering for oil-producing communities. Nigeria gained its independence in 1960, after 63 years of British colonialism (Parsons, 2004).

Despite the decolonisation processes, beginning in the 1940s, particularly between 1957 and 1960, the impact of colonialism had already taken a difficult root in the socio-cultural, traditional, economic, political, psychological, and security architecture of Nigeria (Fisher, 2018). These are evidenced in many neo-imperialist practices across identified oil and gas business chains in Nigeria and many countries in the Global South, especially post-independence Nigerian policy framework experience (Fisher, 2018). The multinational corporations quickly replaced brute colonial dominance with nuanced influence over government policies. International oil and gas companies came to represent the neo-imperialistic interests that influenced the way and manner the Nigerian government formulated regulatory policies. In the 1950s crude oil was initially exported from the Niger Delta and refined in Britain while the finished products, petrol, and kerosene, were imported into Nigeria (Alamieyeseigha, 2008a, 2008b). Unfortunately, 40 years after, the Nigerian government in collaboration with oil and gas multinationals representing imperialistic interests has reverted back to exporting raw crude oil to be refined in Western nations.

The four oil refineries constructed between 1975 and 1985 collapsed (Ordor & Abe, 2021). Since 1995 till date, Nigeria returned to exporting raw crude and importing finished products, a business dominated by the few acquiescent class (Oshionebo, 2009). It is strange that despite Nigeria awarding over US$25 billion *Turn Around Maintenance* (TAM) contracts to different Western companies, reputed internationally in advanced oil and gas technical know-how, the four oil refineries have remained moribund (Daka et al., 2021; Otokunefor, 2017). Nigeria's self-reliance on crude oil and gas consumption has never been the top priority of Western oil and gas companies. whilst international oil firms refuse to build private refineries in Nigeria, export of raw crude oil is encouraged (Douglas & Okonta, 2003; Chapters 6 and 7).

Some scholars have also argued that Western imperialistic powers should take a large portion of the blame for the issues of community neglect. Scholars like Etemire, Olawuyi, and Alamieyeseigha (2016; 2012; 2008a, 2008b) argued that the imperialists, represented by corporations like Shell, Exxon Mobil, and others benefit from the persistent socio-economic stagnation of local communities. They benefited through a nuanced and systemic compromise by the acquiescent class that represents their interests. The slow implementation of some GMOUs signed between *clustered communities* and many oil operators, after the 1993 Ogoni protest, testifies to the fact that some of the intervention policies were indeed designed not to be implemented and hence were deceitful (Zalik, 2011). It can be argued that Nigeria and many countries in the Global South were not decolonised, rather neo-imperialism replaced colonial rule. An acquiescent class was ready to act in the interest of their past colonial masters for personal political and economic interests, which replaced the colonial administration from 1960 independence. This acquiescent class of Nigerians now represents the conduit pipeline through which to manipulate the oil and gas regulations and frustrate all processes of framing new regulations as well as implementing and operationalising them for pecuniary gains (Ogbeidi, 2012; Watson, 1992). These privileged few, largely facilitate the subjugation of the Niger Delta communities and neglect of local communities' interests. This explains their culpability in misdirecting most monies meant for CSR and intervention projects for the local communities (Osuntogun, 2020; see discussion on CSR below).

An additional dimension to the problems is the frustration and corruption of authentic representative voices like independent civil society entities and NGOs. CSOs who try to draw local and international attention to the imperialistic tendencies of the Nigerian government and the unethical behaviours of some oil firms are frustrated and corrupted by agents of the acquiescent class, making it a double tragedy (Transparency International, 2017, 2019, 2020, 2021; Zalik, 2011). Nigeria continues to be tied to the apron string of Britain, Europe, China, and the

United States government including private interests. While the destruction of the environment by oil and gas extraction continues unabated, some local voices and civil societies refuse to speak the truth to political power because they have been compromised (Zalik, 2011). This suggests that some research data on the Niger Delta may not be completely decolonised, they represent imperialistic instead of contemporary African realities. This influences data gathering, analysis, and interpretation. Such instances influence the picture presented about the impact that collective neglect has on local communities. This book triangulated interview data from the empirical fieldwork (professional and community samples), with documentary evidence, and literature sources. This way, it avoided historic colonial institutional limitations and gaps. The different subgroups within the professional and community sample populations were triangulated with different literature sources, and re-analysed documentary evidence (see Chapters 4, 5, 6, and 7).

## NEMBE CREEK TRUNK LINE AND NEMBE-EWELESUO COMMUNITY

The NCTL onshore pipeline is the object of study in this case study book research. Akpomera describes the NCTL as an extensive 97-kilometre oil pipeline, that stretches across an area of 983 km$^2$ from Nembe-Ewelesuo in Bayelsa to Bonny Crude Oil Export Terminal in Rivers state. This infrastructure traverses over 60 communities in Bayelsa which is the study area. The NCTL is the biggest infrastructural development in the Nembe local government area in recent years. It is currently producing 150,000 barrels per day but has an installed production capacity of 600,000 barrels. The pipeline was constructed and commissioned in 2010 as a Joint Venture (JV) partnership between the NNPC which owned 55 percent; Shell 30 percent; Total 10 percent, and Agip owned five percent (Royal Dutch Shell Report, 2012: 20). In 2014 however, these companies disinvested their combined 45 percent stake in the NCTL to Aiteo Eastern Exploration and Production for $USD1.7 billion (Igbinovia, 2014). Oilfields such as Santa Barbara and Okoroba fields comprise onshore oil wells that are intersected by swampy mangroves and creeks in the southeastern part of Nembe (Mickolus, 2018). Although the NCTL has a total of 11 developed oil wellheads, only four are currently producing (Akpomera, 2015).

The NCTL pipeline has frequently been disrupted by non-state actors making it an important object of study. The rough topography poses a difficult security challenge (Mathias, 2015). In the first 10 years of its operation, there were about 220 reported vandalism cases on the NCTL which disrupted the flow of oil to the Bonny Crude Oil Export Terminal in Rivers state (BCOT). Vandalism of many of the NCTL pump stations that are located between 40 and 60 miles apart may have hastened the sale of the NCTL (Igbinovia, 2014; Paravinasam, 2013). Collier has linked the level of disruption to institutional corruption (Collier, 2007). The naming of the NCTL pipeline as Nembe Creek rather than as Ewelesuo Creek Trunk Line given that the OML 29 oil field and producing well-heads are mostly located in Ewelesuo is a classic example of how political interference pit communities against each other (Akpomera, 2015; Mick-olus, 2018). Nembe local government area was chosen as the subject of this study because it includes creeks in the Ewelesuo community where the Oil Mining Lease 29 is located and the NCTL pipeline begins. Many fishing communities have been displaced and turned into environmental refugees increasing poverty, anger, and frustration. A large proportion of the Nembe population of around 175,000 people relies on scarce land for subsistence agriculture combined with fishing activities. There has been little investment in local infrastructure and its residents are mostly poor. The available land in Nembe remains a source of economic growth. But not many people can access farmland due to increased population coupled with displacement that has heightened the competition over available farmlands and fishing waters (Brinkhoff, 2017; Mathias, 2015).

Nembe is divided into two peripheral clustered hinterland communities Nembe-west-Ogbolomabiri and Nembe-east-Basambiri communities (Alamieyeseigha, 2005, 2008a, 2008b). The former describes itself as the *main Nembe* receiving all the benefits meant for the entire kingdom. Basambiri and Ogbolomabiri communities, however, share a traditional monarchical system which Alagoa explained is divided into 14 Chieftaincy Groups of Houses (2005). Their established traditional leadership structure gives each group its legitimacy. They consist of the king, chiefs, elders, Youth Leaders, Women Leaders, and Family Heads who influence projects and compensations through the identification of recipients by the Group of houses they belong (Akpomera, 2015). As Tyler noted, perceiving legitimacy heightens cooperation through reliance on the belief of communal agreement and responsibility (2004). However, the historical tensions between Basambiri and Ogbolomabiri communities have not ceased despite the creation of Okoroma, Tereke, Minikese, and Okpu Nembe Rural Development Centres. Alagoa and Alamieyeseigha noted that the constant conflict between both communities has some impact on development (2005, 2005). Ewelesuo is a small fishing and farming hinterland community in the Nembe West-Ogbolomabiri area with a population of about 3000 thousand people (Akpomera, 2015; Alagoa, 2005). There are 160 developed wellheads scattered around Ewelesuo creeks and uplands communities with only 17 currently producing as partly evidenced (Akpomera, 2015). The collective neglect of the Ewelesuo local community Akpomera noted was in part due to the local conflicts (2015).

## Oil and Gas Exploration in Nigeria

It is unclear when oil and gas exploration began in Nigeria. Some argue that oil and gas exploration began with the issuance of a mineral exploration license to D'Archy Exploration and Whitehall Petroleum by the British colonial administration (Franks & Nunnally, 2011). Others claim that oil exploration started as early as 1903 with the Joint Venture exploration for bitumen between Nigerian West African Development Syndicate Limited and Nigerian Properties Limited (Madubuko, 2017). This is supported by a geological survey conducted in the lower Niger area in 1905 which confirmed the existence of oil and gas deposits in the lower Niger area. Frynas argued that oil exploration was started by the Nigerian Bitumen Corporation, a German subsidiary, between 1907 and 1914 (2000). These conflicting accounts suggest that onshore geological exploration activities in Nigeria could have begun anytime between 1901 and 1907 with the active participation of German and British companies (Frynas, 2000; Madubuko, 2017).

The importance of oil and gas resources Franks and Nunnally (2011) argued influenced the re-issuance of an exploration license to a consortium of British Petroleum and Royal Dutch Shell in 1937. Scholars argue that commercial reserves of crude oil were discovered in Oloibiri in 1956, Ogbia Local Government Area of present-day Bayelsa state, 60 miles west of Port Harcourt. Nigeria's oil and gas sector has not witnessed significant infrastructural development in the last 63 years (Franks & Nunnally, 2011; Otokunefor, 2017). Oil and gas production significantly contributes to Nigeria's Gross Domestic Product making up over 90 percent of its foreign exchange and over 80 percent of the national and state budgets (Ministry of Budget & National Planning, 2016; NBS, 2017). The International Monetary Fund and Ogundajo et al. point out that Nigeria has the lowest global non-oil revenue mobilisation index placed amongst producing nations, put at over three percent of its GDP (2019; 2019).

Oil and gas exploration activities are divided into upstream, midstream, and downstream components. Whereas the upstream component produces crude oil from onshore and or offshore oil fields and production rigs (Devold, 2013; Otokunefor, 2017). The midstream component is responsible for the transportation of crude oil and other refined products from onshore and offshore rigs and platforms. While the downstream component is focused on the issue of refining, processing, and purification of the crude oil as well as marketing and distribution of the products (Devold, 2013; Onuoha, 2016). Oil and gas companies transport their oil and gas products through onshore and offshore distribution networks, pipeline networks, railways, tankers, ships, large Ocean liners, and barges until it gets into the open market and the final consumer (Offu, 2013; Otokunefor, 2017). Much of this research focuses on the midstream component-the vandalism of transportation pipelines. Activities in these areas directly impact local communities as the infrastructure situated on the land and the operational blowouts during drilling and production impact the local communities (Mathias, 2015; Olawuyi, 2012; Sinden, 2009). This proximity also increases the risk of environmental harm to local communities, something that is exacerbated by vandalism. The proximity of the oil and gas infrastructure and the lack of infrastructure and human security in local communities make the facilities easy targets for vandalism.

Oil and gas insecurity problems in Bayelsa are traced to fragile relationships and mistrust which Onuoha (2016) and Collier & Hoeffler (2004) stated is responsible for the vandalism and violent civil rebellion such as militancy (see next chapter for a detailed discussion on militancy). Falola and Genova (2005) argued that the displacement of residents from their homes and failure to create new socio-economic opportunities heightened tensions and vandalism. The day-to-day operation of oil and gas companies appears to have a detrimental effect on the local community. It is these activities and the constant reminder of being left behind that led to the aggression spoken of by Segall (2016) and Walters (2012). Mickolus and Duda & Wardin noted that deceit by operators and regulators encouraged militancy that has developed the capacity to disrupt onshore and offshore oil production infrastructures like pipelines, platforms, support vessels, and wellheads (2018; 2013). The deceit of oil and gas and government means failure to keep to the agreement of employing youths and developing the communities. These were some of the agreements reached either while the land was been acquired or before the pipelines were deployed. For instance, Niger Delta militants demonstrated their capacity to attack any oil and gas infrastructure when they attacked and blew up Shell's underwater pipelines 120 nautical miles offshore in 2018 (Mickolus, 2018). Although some writers like Timashev and Bushinskaya and Liu recommended strong and improved pipelines (2017; 2016), the real problems are the lack of attention on the socio-economic, environmental and political issues that lead to anger and aggression culminating in vandalism in the first place. While there are some merits in upgrading and improving the current infrastructure, this will have a limited impact on the insecurity in the region (Gates & Akyeampong 2012; Segall, 2016).

## OIL AND GAS EXPLORATION INFRASTRUCTURE IN THE NIGER DELTA

To demonstrate the marked difference in oil and gas exploration between local communities in the Global South, and to emphasise the robust depth that this case study gives this book, it is important to thoroughly explore "oil and gas exploration infrastructure in the Niger Delta". Exploration in Nigeria began in some parts of the present-day southeast while explorers also focused on the historic Niger Delta region (Alamieyeseigha, 2008a, 2008b; Madubuko, 2017). Oil and gas pipeline infrastructure operated by Shell Petroleum operates in an area of over 31,000 km$^2$ where it produces about 39 percent of Nigeria's oil output (Akemu et al., 2018; Ghosh & Prelas, 2009; Usman, 2017;). This oil exploration activity is accompanied by significant infrastructure, and specialised services to support the infrastructure used to extract, transport, and refine the oil and gas fluid. This sector can attract economic and developmental benefits to local communities (Gopakumar, 2012). The infrastructure goes beyond physical pipelines and storage facilities, it includes services such as security, human resources, and engineering services (Bahadori, 2017; Lesar, 2001; Theodoropoulos, 2011). Wellhead also called Christmas tree, and Flowlines are an important aspect of understanding the exploration of onshore oil and gas resources and the dynamics of insecurity in Bayelsa State. The reason is that both components, wellheads, and flowlines, which are vital infrastructures in oil and gas transportation are exposed to insecurity problems. Igbinovia explained that low speed, pressure gauge, and small flowlines were particularly vulnerable to vandalism (2014).

There are two types of wellheads, the *surface wellhead* which is connected and cemented on the onshore or offshore production platform, and the subsea *wellhead* or *mudline wellhead*, if it is located under the water (Fang & Duan, 2014). Wellheads are probably the most vital or important structural and technical component that is installed at the surface of a producing oil or gas well (Devold, 2013: 27). Wellheads are connected to four types of pipelines. These pipelines are; Crude Oil (CR), Liquified petroleum gases (LPG), Liquified natural gases (LNG), and High volatile liquids (HVL) (Bahadori, 2017; Devold, 2013; Lewis, 2015; Onuoha, 2016). These pipelines transit and traverse many local communities. The wellhead regulates and monitors the fluid and gas extraction, and maintains the interface for drilling and producing technical and mechanical equipment including leakages of oil or natural gas (Devold, 2013; Williams & Fenske, 2004). Wellheads run deep down from the surface pressure control equipment that connects to the storage tank into the bottom of the hole (Williams & Fenske, 2004). All wellhead infrastructure is fitted with isolation valves and choke equipment which controls the flow of well fluid either oil or liquified natural gas up into the separation tank (Fang & Duan, 2014). Wellheads mainly provide the suspension point and pressure seals for the *casing head/strings-* a welded metal used to control blowouts either during oil well drilling or oil well production (Devold, 2013). The point here is that it is not just the pipeline infrastructure that is exposed to disruptions and insecurity.

The wellhead infrastructure has been attacked and blown up at different times by militants in their efforts to stop oil and gas production while inflicting serious economic and psychological damage and pains on Nigeria and the oil firms. Few CR, LPG, LNG, and HVL pipelines are underground, therefore displacing residents which makes them an easy soft target for the displacement of aggression. This has and continues to lead to tensions, anger, and an increase in poverty levels. These social conditions lead to vandalism of the pipeline and other oil and gas infrastructure (Sanderson, 2010). Persistent vandalism of pipelines contributes to environmental pollution that underlines the causes of various respiratory illnesses in Bayelsa state and the wider region (Ite et al., 2018;

Sinden, 2009). Udofia and Joel point out that attacks and risks of attacks are common on crude oil pipelines in the Niger Delta region because crude oil is easily sold on the black market (2012). According to Etemire and Alamieyeseigha, corruption and criminality as well as widespread socio-economic stagnation cannot be decoupled from the underlying causes of vandalism (2016). Poverty and lack of access to basic services heighten tensions and put pressure on the few social infrastructures leading to anger and aggression that boil over to vandalism (Ambituuni et al., 2015).

For instance, many of Shell's operated wellheads have experienced militant attacks across the historic Niger Delta states for the above reasons (Human Rights Watch, 2002; UNEP, 2012). This forced Shell to declare *force majure* and abandoned operations and production at the five pumping stations in Ogoniland from 1993 to date (Obi, 2016). Some of the Shell's pipeline network indicates why there is a high level of pollution both on drylands, creeks, and swamps in the Bayelsa (Ross, 2012; Sunday & Chukwuma, 2013). Some of these pipelines include the NCTL now owned by Aiteo Exploration and Production. Evidence shows that underground pipelines were more secure as they do not obstruct the daily lives of local communities, therefore, were less likely to be attacked. Zecheru et al. (2018) noted that pipeline operators in Bayelsa and the wider Niger Delta rarely adhere to these principles to save costs due to poor regulations.

As much of the oil and gas infrastructure is above ground level, they are easier to target. The entire 7000–10,000 kilometres of pipeline network and 4315 marketing and distribution product lines that are connected to over 5284 onshore and offshore producing oil wells are vulnerable to vandalism (Adedeji & Elegbede 2018; Okafor & Olaniyan 2017). Shell Petroleum operates about 6000 functional pipelines which are connected to over 1000 producing oil wells, 110 oil fields, 87 flow stations, and eight gas plants spread across the entire Niger Delta region (Adedeji & Elegbede, 2018; Akemu et al., 2018). These pipelines connect Bonny and Escravos offshore terminals as well as Atlas Cove, Calabar, and Okirika Jetties from where crude oil is exported out of Nigeria. The pipelines also transport Nigerian crude to 22 petroleum storage depots across the country and are connected to four refining facilities in Port Harcourt, Warri, and Kaduna State (Okafor & Olaniyan, 2017).

## IMPACT OF THE NCTL ON NEMBE
## AND NIGER DELTA COMMUNITIES

As outlined above and in the introduction of the book, this research focuses on the NCTL in Bayelsa. The main reason for the construction of the NCTL was to transport crude oil from OML 29 in Bayelsa to the Bonny Export Terminal in Rivers. The infrastructure runs over lowland creeks and highlands in Nembe-Ewelesuo becoming an easy target for vandalism and illegal oil bunkering. The local communities expected the operation of the NCTL to create skilled and unskilled jobs for them, but it has failed to do so. The NCTL has caused pollution and displaced many local communities. Numbere (2018) stated that vandalism of the NCTL results in oil spillages into the ecosystem destroying living organisms, and contaminating soil quality, and the swamps. A major impact of the construction and operationalisation of the NCTL is that it prevents local communities from safely accessing their farmlands causing frustration that sometimes spills over to violent aggression (Fentiman, 2014; Mathias, 2015; Sanderson, 2010). The presence of the NCTL has done little to improve the livelihoods of the local communities affected by its construction.

At the same time, it has increased Nigeria's ability to export more crude oil, economic stagnations, poverty, a lack of local infrastructure, corruption, and poor governance, continue to beset Bayelsa-Nembe and the wider Niger Delta communities (Alagoa, 2005; Igbinovia, 2014). According to Visser (2017), the construction of the NCTL has made the situation worse. Haken & Taft (2015) and Olawuyi (2012) draw a direct link between environmental damage to the construction and operation of oil and gas infrastructure like the NCTL in Nembe. Ikelegbe (2013) and Dambo (2006) argued that the NCTL construction and the anticipation of potential benefits have reignited historical disputes between the Nembe Council of Chiefs with Paramount rulers, heads of ruling houses, as well as regulators, and operators. Nwobueze and Osemene (2018) explained that the relational gaps and mistrust between internal and external stakeholders have extended vandalism to smaller arteries and shorelines such as those transporting crude oil from Isoko to Eriemu manifolds. For instance, the local communities struggled to renegotiate new terms with Aiteo oil and gas when the NCTL changed its ownership from Shell. The unsuccessful negotiations impeded a smooth relationship between Aiteo, the new operators, and community stakeholders. The aggressive reaction of the people against the NCTL pipelines operated by Shell and later Aiteo is a classic case of self-inflicted frustration on both operators.

Omeje (2017a, 2017b, 2017c) stated that the sale of OML 29 and the NCTL pipeline infrastructure to AITEO Group for US$1.7 billion in 2014 was due to an escalation in vandalism and violent protests by local communities that have suffered a wide range of negative impacts. Boris (2015) says the change of ownership has not benefited AITEO because of a lack of agreement with local communities leading to more illegal bunkering. This has resulted in several shutdowns. A report by Africa Oil and Gas Monitor (2018) associated economic losses with the constant disruptions of the NCTL. Such losses are some of the factors motivating the decision to construct an alternative route to transport oil. If this is realised it means that the current NCTL infrastructure will be abandoned. Experts have also suggested that oil can be directly pumped from Nembe to the Floating Production Storage and Offloading Vessels on the Atlantic coast, meaning the interference with the NCTL will become less of an issue (Africa Oil and Gas Report, 2018). According to Mathias (2015) and Onuoha (2008) constructing an alternative pipeline route suggests that oil and gas regulators and operators were either unable to address the underlying causes of vandalism and pipeline sabotage or they are unwilling to do so.

Operators failed to understand that economically empowered communities tend to pose fewer threats and risks to the NCTL pipeline infrastructure. Igbinovia (2014) and Alagoa (1999) stress the importance of consulting with local communities before designing community-oriented intervention projects either in Nembe or in the wider Niger Delta area. The Africa Oil and Gas report concluded that displacing local communities and refusing to listen to them and include their views in policy agenda-setting and regulatory formulation processes will not help to achieve security for any proposed alternative pipeline to OML 29 (2018). The solution to insecurity, however, would be collective community involvement that produces a political solution. These structural and operational pitfalls Bergstresser (2017) noted could have been mitigated if the regulators and operators transparently implemented their promise of creating around 20,000 direct and indirect jobs through the location of their corporate offices in Nembe.

## Conclusion

This chapter further contextualised this book study by exploring a wide range of literature. It focused on the Bayelsa geography and historical context that underpinned tensions and human insecurity that later cascaded into infrastructure insecurity in Bayelsa and the wider Niger Delta. It observed that part of the issues that leads to tension is the topographical contours and scarceness of resources. This was made worse by the activities of the oil and gas corporations particularly onshore pipeline networking. This explains why the impact of the NCTL on the communities it traverses in Nembe extreme. This chapter reviewed oil and gas exploration in Nigeria as a mirror to what is largely obtained in most petrostates in the Global South. It also discovered that the OML 29 oilfield from where the NCTL Christmas Tree is situated in found in Nembe-Ewelesuo. Nembe-Ewelesuo remained largely underdeveloped. The name of the "Bonny Light" comes from Nembe. These issues underpin the reasons for collective community tensions leading to conflict in the insecurity of oil and gas assets (Gurr, 2015). The chapter found that though there might be country-to-country variations in terms of severity of socio-economic issues, what Ewelesuo and the larger Nembe communities faces in replicated across many local communities that produce any form of natural resources especially oil and gas. The corporations and government fail to realise that it is way cheaper to develop natural resource producing communities than deploying hard power or physical security round the clock to secure assets.

## References

Abadom, D. C., & Nwankwoala, H. O. (2018). Investigations of Physio-Chemical Composition of Groundwater in Otuoke and Environs, Bayelsa State, Nigeria. *International Journal of Environmental Sciences and Natural Resources, 9*(1), 1–9.

Adedeji, H. O., & Elegbede, I. O. (2018). Mapping and Modeling Ecosystem Services in Petroleum Producing Areas in Nigeria. In P. E. Ndimele (Ed.), *The Political Economy of Oil and Gas Activities in the Nigerian Aquatic Ecosystem* (pp. 159–170). Academic Press.

Africa Oil and Gas Report. (2018). *In 24 Months Nembe Creek Trunk Line Will be Running Empty* (Vol. 19(8), pp. 1–10). Africa Oil and Gas Report.

Akemu, O., Comiteau, L., & Mes, A. (2018). Shell Nigeria: Changing the Community Engagement Model. In N. C. Smith & G. G. Lenssen (Eds.),

*Managing Sustainable Business: An Executive Education Case and Textbook* (pp. 273–297). Springer.

Akpomera, E. (2015). International Crude Oil Theft: Elite Predatory Tendencies in Nigeria. *Review of African Political Economy Journal, 42*(143), 156–165.

Akuaibit, S. P. U. (2017). Sea Level Rise and Coastal Submergence Along the South East Coast of Nigeria. *Journal of Oceanography and Marine Research,* Vol.5 (4), pp.2–8

Alagoa, E. J. (1999). *The Land and People of Bayelsa State: Central Niger Delta.* Onyema Research Publications.

Alagoa, E. J. (2005). *A History of the Niger Delta.* Onyema Research Publications.

Alamieyeseigha, D. S. P. (2005). *Thoughts on Federalism, South–South and Resource Control.* Treasure Books.

Alamieyeseigha, D. S. P. (2008a). The Environmental Challenge of Developing the Niger Delta. In S. S. Azaiki, D. S. P. Alamieyeseigha, & A. A. Ikein (Eds.), *Oil, Democracy and the Promise of True Federalism in Nigeria* (pp. 249–260). University Press of America.

Alamieyeseigha, D. S. P. (2008b). The Niger Delta: Treasure Base of Energies. In S. Azaika, A. A. Ikein, & D. S. P. Alamieyeseigha (Eds.), *Oil Democracy and the Promise of True Federalism in Nigeria* (pp. 290–310). University Press of America.

Ali, D. A. (2019). The Dilemma of Colonial Transportation on the Lower Niger and Benue Rivers 1879–1960. *Jebat: Malaysian Journal of History Politics & Strategy, 46*(1), 155–171.

Amaiwo, S., & Samuel, C. Z. (2015, May 20). Niger Delta Indigenes Petitions UNO, Demands the Niger Delta Republic. *Urhobo Today.* http://urhobotoday.com/niger-delta-indigenes-petition-uno-demands-niger-delta-republic/. Accessed 2 March 2018.

Ambituuni, A., Hopkins, P., Amezaga, J. M., Werner, D., & Wood, J. M. (2015). Risk Assessment of a Petroleum Product Pipeline in Nigeria: The Realities of Managing Problems of theft/Sabotage. In C. A. Brebbia, F. Garzia, & D. Poljak (Eds.), *Safety and Security Engineering* (pp. 49–60). WIT Press.

Bahadori, A. (2017). *Oil and Gas Pipelines and Piping Systems: Design, Construction, Management, and Inspection.* Elsevier.

Bello, B., & Abdullahi, M. M. (2021, October–December). Farmers-Herdsmen Conflict, Cattle Rustling, and Banditry: The Dialectics of Insecurity in Anka and Maradun Local Government Area of Zamfara State, Nigeria. *Sage Open Journal,* 1–12.

Bergstresser, H. (2017). *A Decade of Nigeria: Politics, Economy and Society 2004–2016.* Brill.

Boris, O. H. (2015). The Upsurge of Oil Theft and Illegal Bunkering in the Niger Delta Region of Nigeria: Is there a Way Out? *Mediterranean Journal of Social Sciences, 6*(3), 563–571.

Boro, I. (1982). *The Twelve-day Revolution*. Idodo Umeh.

Bretthauer, J. M. (2016). *Climate Change and Resource Conflicts: The Role of Scarcity*. Routledge.

Brinkhoff, T. (2017). City Population: Nembe Population. https://www.citypopulation.de/php/nigeria-admin.php?adm2id=NGA006004. Accessed 3 January 2019.

Brisibe, W. G., & Tepple, D. T. (2018). Lessons Learnt from the 2012 Flood Disaster: Implications for Post-Flood Building Design and Construction in Yenagoa Nigeria. *Journal of Civil Engineering and Architecture, 6*(3), 171–180.

Cabot, C. (2016). *Climate Change, Security Risks and Conflict Reduction in Africa: A Case of Farmer-Header Conflicts over Natural Resources in Cote d'Ivoire, Ghana and Burkina Faso 1960–2000*. Springer.

Collier, P. (2007). *The Bottom Billion* (pp. 39–52). Oxford University Press.

Collier, P., & Hoeffler, A. E. (2004). *Greed and Grievance in Civil War*. World Bank Development Research Group.

Dambo, L. B. (2006). *Nembe: The Divided Kingdom*. Paragraphs.

Daka, T., Abuh, A., & Jeremiah, K. (2021, March 18). After $25b on Maintenance, FEC Approves New $1.5b for PH Refinery. *The Guardian News*. https://guardian.ng/news/after-25b-on-maintenance-fec-approves-new-1-5b-for-ph-refinery/. Accessed 18 July 2022.

Devold, H. (2013). *Oil and Gas Production Handbook: An Introduction to Oil and Gas Production* (pp. 6–146). ABB. https://library.e.abb.com/public/34d5b70e18f7d6c8c1257be500438ac3/Oil%20and%20gas%20production%20handbook%20ed3x0_web.pdf. Accessed 12 December 2017.

Douglas, O., & Okonta, I. (2003). *Where Vultures Feast: Shell, Human Rights, and Oil in the Niger Delta*. Verso.

Duda, D., & Wardin, K. (2013). Characteristics of Piracy in the Gulf of Guinea and its Influence on International Maritime Transport in the Region. In A. Weintrit & T. Neumann (Eds.), *Marine Navigation and Safety Transportation* (pp. 177–185). CRC Publication.

Ecumenical Council for Corporate Responsibility (ECCR). (2010). *Shell in the Niger Delta: A Framework for Change*. Cordaid.

Effiong, J. (2010). Oil and Gas Industry in Nigeria: The Paradox of the Black Gold. In D. E. Taylor (Eds.), *Environmental and Social Justice: An International Perspective* (Vol. 18, pp. 323–352). Emerald.

Etemire, U. (2016). *Law and Practice on Public Participation in Environmental Matters: The Nigerian Example in Transnational Comparative Perspective*. Routledge.

Etete, E. (2017, July 7). Ovom in Yenagoa City: A Cradle of Development but Shadow of itself. *Headline News Nigeria*. http://headlinenewsnigeria.com/ovom-yenagoa-city-cradle-development-shadow/. Accessed 2 March 2018.

Ejiofor, C. (2012). *Biafra's Struggle for Survival*. Catholic Institution for Development Justice and Peace.

Falola, T. (2009). *Colonialism and Violence in Nigeria*. Indiana University Press.

Falola, T., & Genova, A. (2005). *The Politics of the Global Oil Industry: An Introduction*. Praeger.

Fang, H., & Duan, M. (2014). *Offshore Operation Facilities: Equipment and Procedures*. Elsevier.

Fentiman, A. (2014). The Anthropology of Oil: The Impact of the Oil Industry on a Fishing Community in the Niger Delta. In C. Williams (Ed.), *Environmental Victims* (pp. 75–87). Routledge.

Fisher, J. J. (2018). Decolonizing Nigeria, 1945–1960: Politics, Power, and Personalities by Toyin Falola and Bola Dauda (review). *Journal of Global South Studies, 35*(1), 174–174.

Franks, S., & Nunnally, S. (2011). *Barbarians of Oil: How the World's Oil Addiction Threatens Global Prosperity and Four Investments to protect Your Wealth*. Wiley.

Frynas, G. J. (2000). *Oil in Nigeria: Conflicts and Litigation Between Oil Companies and Village Communities* (pp. 8–50). LIT Verlag.

Gates, H. L., & Akyeampong. (2012). *Dictionary of African Biography*. Oxford University Press.

Ghosh, T. K., & Prelas, M. A. (2009). *Energy Resources and Systems: Fundamentals and Non-Renewable Resources* (Vol. 1). Springer.

Gopakumar, G. (2012). *Transforming Urban Water Supply in India: The Role of Reform and Partnerships in Globalisation*. Routledge.

Gurr, R. T. (2015), *Political Rebellion: Causes, Outcomes and Alternatives*. Routledge.

Haken, N., & Taft, P. (2015). *Violence in Nigeria: Patterns and Trends*. Springer.

Human Rights Watch. (2002). *The Niger Delta: No Democratic Dividend* (Vol. 14(7), pp. 30–41). Human Rights Watch.

Igbinovia, P. E. (2014). *Oil Thefts and Pipeline Vandalisation in Nigeria*. African Books.

Ikelegbe, A. (2013). The Crisis in Relations: Multinational Oil Companies and Host Communities in the Niger Delta. In A. Ikelegbe (Ed.), *Oil, Environment and Resource Conflicts in Nigeria*. Lit Verglag.

Inengite, P. (2018). The 1914 Amalgamation of North and South: A Historic Misadventure: A History of the Niger Delta Question...-Part 2. https://patnengii.blogspot.com/20/16/06/amalgamation-of-northsouth-historical14.html. Accessed 16 December 2021.

International Monetary Fund. (2019). Nigeria: Mobilizing Resources to Invest in People. https://www.imf.org/en/News/Articles/2019/04/01/na040219-nigeria-mobilizing-resources-to-invest-in-people. Accessed 19 June 2021.

Ite, A. E., Harry, T. A., Obadimu, C. O., & Inim, I. J. (2018). Petroleum Hydrocarbons Contaminations of Surface Water and Ground Water in the Niger Delta Region of Nigeria. *Journal of Environment Pollution and Human Health, 6*(2), 51–61.

Lesar, D. J. (2001). *Securing Oil and Natural Gas Infrastructures in the New Economy.* Diane.

Lewis, T. G. (2015). *Critical Infrastructure Protection in Homeland Security: Defending a Networked Nation* (2nd ed.). Wiley.

Liu, H. (2017). *Pipeline Engineering.* CRC Press.

Madubuko, C. C. (2017). Oiling the Guns and Gunning for Oil: The Youths and Niger Delta Oil Conflicts in Nigeria. In E. M. Mbah & T. Falola (Eds.), *Dissent, Protest and Dispute in Africa* (pp. 260–289). Routledge.

Mathias, Z. (2015). Providing All-Round Security against Oil and Gas Infrastructure Sabotage and Physical Attacks on the Staff of NNPC and Multinational Oil Companies in Nigeria as a Critical Article of Her National Security Efforts. *International Journal of Social Science and Humanities Research, 3*(2), 45–59.

Meredith, M. (2014). *Fortunes of Africa: A 5,000 Year History of Wealth, Greed and Endeavour.* Simon and Schuster.

Mickolus, E. (2018). *Terrorism Worldwide, 2016.* McFarland and Company.

Ministry of Budget and National Planning. (2016). *Strategic Implementation Plan for the 2016 Budget of Change.* Ministry of Budget and National Planning.

National Bureau of Statistics. (2017). *Social Statistics Report December 2016.* National Bureau of Statistics.

Numbere, A. O. (2018). The Impact of Oil and Gas Exploration: Invasive Nypa Palm Species and Urbanisation on Mangroves in the Niger River Delta, Nigeria. In C. Makowski & C. W. Finkl (Eds.), *Threats to Mangrove Forests: Hazards, Vulnerability, and Management* (pp. 247–266). Springer.

Nwobueze, C. C., & Osemene, O. J. (2018). The Resurgence of Militant Groups in the Niger Delta: A Study of Security Threats and the Prospects for Peace in Nigeria. In C. Obi & T. B. Oriola (Eds.), *The Unfinished Revolution in Nigeria's Niger Delta: Prospects for Environmental Justice and Peace* (pp. 120–135). Routledge.

O'Grady, R. (2018). *The Passionate Imperialists: The True Story of Sir Frederick Lugard, Anti-slavery, Adventurer and the Founder of Nigeria, and Flora Shaw, Renowned Journalist for the Times.* Conrad Press.

Obi, C., & Oriola, T. B. (2018). Introduction: The Unfinished Revolution, the Niger Delta Struggle since 1995. In C. Obi & T. B. Oriola (Eds.), *The Unfinished Revolution in Nigeria's Niger Delta: Prospects for Environmental Justice and Peace*. Routledge.

Obi, C. I. (2016). From Homeland to Hopeland? Economic Globalisation and Ogoni Migration in the 1990s. In S. Gupta & T. Omoniyi (Eds.), *The Culture of Economic Migration: International Perspectives* (pp. 116–127). Routledge.

Offu, K. A. (2013). *The Nigerian Dependent Management and Leadership Development in the Postwar II Colonial Nigeria*. Author House.

Ogbeidi, M. M. (2012). Political Leadership and Corruption in Nigeria since 1960: A Socio-economics Analysis. *Journal of Nigerian Studies, 1*(2), 1–24.

Ogundajo, G. O., Akintoye, I. R., & Olayinka, I. M. (2019). Taxing Informal Sector and Revenue Generation in Nigeria. *International Journal of Commerce and Management Research, 5*(4), 81–87.

Ohwo, O. (2015). Public Perception on Climate Change in Yenagoa. *Geography Journal, 2015,* 1–10.

Ojeleye, O. (2016). *The Politics of Post-War Demobilisation and Reintegration in Nigeria*. Routledge.

Okafor, A. and Olaniyan, A. (2017), Legal and Institutional Framework for Promoting Oil Pipeline Security in Nigeria, *Journal of Sustainable Development Law and*

Olawuyi, D. S. (2012). Legal and Sustainable Development Impacts of Major Oil Spills. *The Journal of Sustainable Development, 9*(1), 1–15.

Omeje, K. (2017a). *Extractive Economies and Conflicts in the Global South: Multi-regional Perspectives on Rentier Politics*. Taylor and Francis.

Omeje, K. (2017b). *High Stakes and Stakeholders: Oil Conflict and Security in Nigeria*. Routledge.

Omeje, K. (2017c). The Egbesu and Bakassi Boys: African Spiritism and Mystical Re-rationalisation of Security. In D. J. Francis (Ed.), *Civil Militia: Africa's Intractable Security Menace* (pp. 71–86). Routledge.

Onuoha, C. F. (2008). Oil Pipeline Sabotage in Nigeria: Dimensions, Actors and Implications for National Security. *African Security Review, 17*(3), 100–115.

Onuoha, C. F. (2016). *The Resurgence of Militancy in Nigeria's Oil-Rich Niger Delta and the Dangers of Militarisation*. Al Jazeera Centre for Studies.

Ordor, A., & Abe, O. (2021). Local Content Requirements and Social Inclusion in Global Energy Markets: Towards Business and Human Rights Content. In D. S. Olawuyi (Eds.), *Local Contents, and Sustainable Development in Global Energy Markets* (pp. 392–412). Cambridge University Press.

Oriola, B. T. (2016). *Criminal Resistance: The Politics of Kidnapping Oil Workers*. Routledge.

Oshionebo, E. (2009). *Regulating Transnational Corporations in Domestic and International Regimes: An African Case Studies*. University of Toronto Press.

Osuntogun, A. J. (2020). Rights to Development of Indigenous Peoples of Africa: A Quest for the Adoption of Resource Control Mechanism for Effective Protection. In C. C. Ngang & S. D. Kamga (Eds.), *Insights into Policies and Practices on the Right to Develop* (pp. 133–161). Rowman and Littlefield.

Otokunefor, H. O. C. (2017). *Nigerian Petroleum Industry, Policies, and Conflicts Relations* (Vol. 2). Malthouse.

Pakenham, T. (2015). *The Scramble for Africa*. Hachette.

Papavinasam, S. (2013). *Corrosion Control in the Oil and Gas Industry*. Elsevier.

Parsons, T. H. (2004). *Race, Resistance, and the Boy Scout Movement in British Colonial Africa*. Ohio University Press Fisher.

Petters, S. W., Nwajide, C. S., & Reijers, T. J. A. (1997). The Niger Delta Basin. In R. C. Selley (Ed.), *Sedimentary Basins of the World: African Basins* (Vol. 3, pp. 151–172). Elsevier.

Rodney, W. (2012). *How Europe Underdeveloped Africa*. Pambazuka.

Ross, M. L. (2012). *The Oil Curse: How Petroleum Wealth Shape the Development of Nations*. Princeton University Press.

Royal Dutch Shell Report. (2012). *Royal Dutch Shell PLC: Shell in Nigeria*. Royal Dutch Shell.

Sagay, I. (2008). Nigeria: Federalism, the Constitution and Resource Control. In S. S. Azaiki, D. S. P. Alamieyeseigha, & A. A. Ikein (Eds.), *Oil, Democracy and the Promise of True Federalism in Nigeria* (pp. 370–379). University Press of America.

Sanderson, C. A. (2010). *Social Psychology*. Wiley.

Segall, M. H. (2016). *Human Behaviour and Public Policy: A Political Psychology*. Pergamon Press.

Shaxson, N. (2008). *The Poisoned Wells: The Dirty Politics of African Oil*. Palgrave Macmillan.

Sinden, A. (2009). An Emerging Human Rights to Security from Climate Change: The Case Against Gas Flaring in Nigeria. In W. C. G. Burns & H. M. Osofsky (Eds.), *Adjudicating Climate Change: State, National, and International Approaches* (pp. 173–192). Cambridge University Press.

Sunday, O., & Chukwuma, O. A. (2013). Oil Pipeline Vandalism and Nigerian National Security. *Global Journal of Human Social Science, 13*(5), 67–74.

Theodoropoulos, T. E. (2011). *Oil-Gas Exploration and Drilling*. Book Baby.

Timashev, S., & Bushinskaya, A. (2016). Methods of Assessing Integrity of Pipeline Systems with Different Types of Defects. In S. Timashev & A. Bushinskaya (Eds.), *Diagnostics and Reliability of Pipeline Systems* (Vol. 30, pp. 9–43). Springer.

Transparency International. (2017). Corruption Perception Index: What is Happening in Regions of the World. https://www.transparency.org/en/cpi/2017. Accessed 19 April 2022.

Transparency International. (2019). Military Involvement in Oil Theft in the Niger Delta. https://ti-defence.org/publications/military-involvement-in-oil-theft-in-the-niger-delta/. Accessed 25 November 2020.

Transparency International. (2020). Corruption Perception Index 2020. https://www.transparency.org/en/cpi/2021. Accessed 24 November 2020.

Transparency International. (2021). Corruption Perception Index 2021: Sub-Saharan Africa: How does your Country Measure Up?. https://images.transparencycdn.org/images/CPI2021_Report_EN-web.pdf. Accessed 19 April 2022.

Tukur, M. M. (2016). *British Colonialisation of Northern Nigeria 1897–1914: A Reinterpretation of Colonial Sources*. Amalion.

Tyler, T. R. (2004). Enhancing Police Legitimacy. *The Annals of the American Academy of Political and Social Science, 593*(1), 84–99.

Udofia, O. O., & Joel, O. F. (2012). *Pipeline Vandalism in Nigeria: Recommended Best Practice of Checking the Menace* (pp. 1–8). Society of Petroleum Engineers. https://onepetro.org/SPENAIC/proceedings-abstract/12NAICE/All-12NAICE/SPE-162980-MS/159279. Accessed 2 August 2018.

Udoh, E. W. (2015). Insecurity in Nigeria: Political, Religious and Cultural Implications, Journal of Philosophy, Culture and Religion, Vol.5, pp. 1–7.

Ugochukwu, O. (2008). The Conceptual Framework and Strategy for Niger Delta Development: A Niger Delta Development Commission Perspective. In A. A. Ikein, D. S. P. Alamiesegha, & S. Azaika (Eds.), *Oil Democracy and the Promise of True Federalism in Nigeria* (pp. 95–101). University Press of America.

Ukpong, I. G. (2012). *Nature Under Siege: Portrait of Environmental Crisis in the Niger Delta*. Author House.

United Nations Environment Programme Report. (2012). Environmental Assessment of Ogoniland: Assessment of Vegetation, Aquatic and Public Health Issues. http://hdl.handle.net/20.500.11822/25286. Accessed 9 May 2018.

Usman, A. K. (2017). *Nigerian Oil and Gas Industry Laws, Policies, and Institutions* (pp. 52–54). Malthouse.

Visser, W. (2017). *The Quest for Sustainable Business: An Epic Journey in Search of Corporate Responsibility*. Routledge.

Walters, G. D. (2012). Criminal Predatory Behaviour in the Federal Bureau of Prisons. In M. Delisi & P. J. Conis (Eds.), *Violent Offenders: Theory, Research, Policy, and Practice* (pp. 369–382). Jones and Bartlett.

Watson, D. (1992). Correcting for Acquiescent Response Bias in the Absence of a Balance: An Application to Class Consciousness. *Journal of Sociological Methods and Research, 21*(1), 52–88.

Welzer, H. (2015). *Climate Wars: What People Will be Killed for in the 21st Century*. Polity Press.

Williams, M. B., & Fenske, B. A. (2004). *Demonstrating Benefits of Wellhead Protections Programs*. AWWA Research Foundation Publication.

Willink Commission Report. (1958). *Nigeria: Report of the Commission Appointed to Inquire into the Fears of Minorities and the Means of Allaying them*. Her Majesty's Stationary Office.

World Bank Report. (1995). *Nigeria-Defining an Environmental Development Strategy for the Niger Delta* (Vol. 2). World Bank.

Zalik, A. (2011). Labelling Oil, Contesting Governance: The GMoU and Profiteering in the Niger Delta. In C. Obi & S. A. Rustad (Eds.), *Oil and Insurgency in the Niger Delta: Managing the Complex Politics of Petro Violence* (pp. 200–252). Zed Books.

Zecheru, G., Dumitrescu, A., & Dinita, A. (2018). Characterisation of Volumetric Surface Defects. In E. N. Barkanow, A. Dumitrescu, & I. A. Parinov (Eds.), *Non-destructive Testing and Repair of Pipelines* (pp. 117–136). Springer.

# CHAPTER 4

# Impact of Oil and Gas Exploration and Infrastructure in Niger Delta on the United Nations Sustainable Development Goals

## THE NIGER DELTA CLIMATE PROBLEM

Some African leaders argue that climate justice should precede climate change and adaptation initiatives for Africa. Whilst this is a valid demand, considering the socio-economic and environmental impact of the colonial past, African leaders and businesses should perhaps re-evaluate their approach. The widespread environmental devastation that is ongoing in the Niger Delta, as in many petrostates in the Global South, is mainly due to the government's failure to regulate the unethical behaviours of the oil and gas industry, lack of policy alignment with the UNSDG framework, and political misdirection (also see Chapter 2). This questions Nigeria's sincerity in implementing the adaptation principles developed at the Cancun Mexico climate summit in 2010. There is the impression that by ignoring the unprofessional practices of oil and gas corporations in the Niger Delta like uncleaned oil spills on rivers and farmlands, pollution, and not replacing old pipelines, Nigeria as in other petrostates in the Global South, pays lip service to the entire UNSDGs, particularly the climate action. The objective of the Cancun Adaptation Framework under the Cancun Agreement reached in Mexico is to enhance actions on adaptation in developing countries through international cooperation and

A. L. A. Jatto, *Oil and Gas Pipeline Infrastructure Insecurity*, New Security Challenges, https://doi.org/10.1007/978-3-031-56932-6_4

coherent considerations (Kuwornu, 2019; UNFCCC, 2010). Nigeria's commitment to the implementation of this agreement remains unclear when one juxtaposes the objective with the scale of environmental degradation allowed to happen in the Niger Delta. Some literature argue that the localised tensions and some insecurity problems in the Niger Delta are tied to climate change problems (Etemire, 2016; Olawuyi, 2012). The policy thrust of the Ministry of Petroleum suggests Nigeria intends to exhaust the use of its natural gas before transiting to renewable energies (Izuaka, 2021).

Current operational track records of most oil and gas corporations in the Niger Delta give the impression that the Nigerian Federal, State, and Local government continues to permit ecocide and environmental terrorism as well as opposed to the UNSDG 2030 agenda. Section 9 of the Petroleum Industry Act (2021) proposed that the Petroleum Ministry will dedicate 30 percent of its annual oil profit to crude oil exploration in some frontier states in the north, increasing methane gases in the atmosphere (Baiyewu & Akinkuotu, 2021). The impact of methane gases on global warming leads to sea level rise which increases flash floods that have washed away farmlands and crops and increased hunger and poverty (Loucks, 2021; UNEP, 2012). Partain says that methane hydrates are one of the most dangerous gaseous polluters causing climate change (2017). 70–90 percent of the natural gas that is flared in the Niger Delta contains methane gas which releases $CO_2$ that worsens negative climatic conditions, pollutes the mangrove, fishing waters, and the entire ecosystem provoking anger (Olawuyi, 2012; Loucks, 2021). It is unclear how bothered Nigeria is about the IPCC projections that the net damage costs of climate change are more likely to increase significantly over time (2022).

Since relevant actions are not been taken or the political will and/or political action taken to change the status quo. Therefore, it is proper to argue that Nigeria's debate on climate change and its mitigation policies could best be described as rhetorical and contradictory (Izuaka, 2021). The lack of political will, corruption, and lack of political action exacerbates issues around climate change in the Niger Delta region (Olawuyi, 2012). Oil and gas exploration in Nigeria coupled with the construction and operation of the NCTL in the Niger Delta region have negatively impacted the climatic conditions of the region, particularly local communities. Increases in structural blowouts due to natural disasters and vandalism as well as the slow pace of response to oil spills in the Niger

Delta worsen the physical safety of the pipeline infrastructure (Igbinovia, 2014; Izuaka, 2021).

The destruction of the mangrove means the destruction of the natural barriers and defence mechanisms of the coastal states and riverine communities in the Niger Delta. Defoliated mangrove forests cannot soak up the carbon and methane gases released. When these gases are left longer in the atmosphere it worsens the climate change impact on everything including the acidification of fishing waters and the ocean. The destroyed Niger Delta mangrove forests and green shrubs unbalance the atmospheric and environmental challenges faced in the coastal communities and the wider historic Niger Delta area. Numbere (2018) observed that the historic Niger Delta region is home to the largest number of mangroves in Africa. Mangroves protect water quality; their peat absorbs water during heavy rains through this way the mangrove helps check erosions. It is a natural habitat for diverse types of fish, shellfish, and oysters which form a major element of the commercial and nutrition source for the people. The mangrove forest and trees also help mitigate climate problems by pulling out about four times as much hydrocarbon pollution and many greenhouse gases such as methane away from the atmosphere and storing the same in their soils (Numbere, 2018).

Etowah and Effiong, Etekpe, Etemire, Etete, and Sinden noted that vandals and oil firms are driven by money and not bothered about the long-term consequences of their actions such as depletion of the ozone layer, deforestation, extinction of aquatic species, and bushes (2012; 2018; 2016; 2017; 2009). The destruction of these natural vegetation worsens the effect of climate change, increases poverty, conflicts, and criminality, and destroys traditional cultural values. The worsening climatic conditions kill off the green vegetation due to the atmosphere filled with hydrocarbon releases. This is motivating people to turn towards the pipelines for a livelihood by vandalising them. The amount of methane in the atmosphere worsens the atmospheric heat, asphyxiates plants, and marine animals, as well as impacts their yield. Reduced farm and marine harvest impact household incomes, finances, and traditional sources of employment and economic production. Also, a reduction in farm and marine harvest impacts household incomes and finances which directly encourages pipeline vandalism to steal oil to eke out a living. Wiebo Ludwig, a Canadian environmentalist argued in 1997 that if oil and gas companies completely ignore the rights, feelings, and opinions of the local communities, and their wellbeing the residents have to deploy necessary defensive actions against such companies (Dawson, 2021). Although Ludwig was unclear about the type of action communities should take, most Niger Delta communities impacted by oil and gas activities take to vandalism due to frustration.

Poverty and an increase in the cost of cooking gas are making people turn to charcoal, and fuelwood, as an alternative for cooking in Nigeria and the Niger Delta (Ramsay, 2021). Returning to fuelwood exacerbates the problem of deforestation if not checked by a national afforestation policy. The loss of trees and mangroves means the destruction of natural carbon absorbers in the Niger Delta and the acceleration of desertification in the Sahel. One outcome is increased migration of displaced communities from the coastal Niger Delta and the northern Sahel regions into the urban and metropolitan cities creating more social tensions. The need to survive feeds human anger leading to insecurity problems like the herder/farmer clashes that have assumed an alarming scale in Nigeria between 2014 and 2023 (Ramsay, 2021). Pipeline vandalism occurs as a result of collective frustration and the struggle for scarce amenities, and land resources. The politicians seem to pay lip service to climate change more as a conduit pipe to siphon public funds like the abandonment of many public projects in Nigeria (see Chapters 5 and 6). They are refusing to use the opportunity to invest in sustainable sources of energy management such as Hydroelectric, Geoelectric, Waste to Energy, and Biomass in Nigeria and the Niger Delta. The Nigerian political class feels that the worsening climate problems in the Niger Delta do not matter, as long as they and their families are not affected.

## Impact of Unemployment on the Niger Delta

Not only are communities deprived of their lands, but there are also few employment opportunities for the local population (Visser, 2017). This increases poverty and inequality which makes the mostly young population restive (Okumagba, 2012). The operation of the NCTL has specifically heightened the issues of unemployment because many youths who eke out a living in various fishing settlements have been displaced. After all, the NCTL traversed their fishing waters (Alagoa, 2005). Also, many families became unemployed because they were prevented from accessing the land where they practiced subsistence farming. Economic displacement of Nembe and many Niger Delta communities due to oil and gas activities and pipeline connectivity created rural–urban migration that affected other communities and cities such as Yenagoa and Nembe town as well as other suburbs further afield (Douglas & Okonta, 2003). This accounts for the widespread socio-economic pressure central to the frustration experienced in these cities. Socio-economic development theory is defined as the ability to adequately produce and grow the supply of goods and services efficiently and productively, build capital, and fairly and equitably distribute the fruits of production (Jaffee, 1998; Lanoszka, 2018).

The widespread unemployment caused by the construction and operation of the NCTL pipeline has resulted in scrambling for scarce resources, educational facilities, and income-paying jobs leading to pressure. It has made socio-economic development impossible to achieve. The economic dislocation of people became the precursor to heightened inequalities, frustration, and anger that drove many young persons to aggressive reactions. The vandalism of pipelines and the operation of illegal refining facilities became viable options for survival. It could be argued that the different insecurity problems across the historic Niger Delta state are a result of the unemployment caused by the NCTL. While many governments use unemployment figures to explain economic (in)stability, it is also used to analyse the causes of poverty, social tensions, and crimes (NBS, 2020). Physical and monetary policies, regulations, recession, and market competition to name a few, can create structural unemployment problems (Janoski et al., 2014). In the context of Nembe and the wider historic Niger Delta area, the implementation of a forceful or voluntary land acquisition stipulated in the oil and gas regulations has worsened unemployment problems (Visser, 2017; Land Use Act, 2004).

The persistence of poor monetary, and market competition create an extremely negative impact on individuals. Bejakovic and Mrnjavac argue that when such circumstances persist coupled with recession and poor regulatory policy frameworks individuals and the larger society are affected (2018). Long-term unemployment and the feeling of deprivation from their natural and traditional means of livelihood lowered their confidence to search for legitimate work. Spermann and Nicholas et al. point out that loss of confidence leads to ill health, decreases wage-earning potentials, and increases exposure to psychological and financial difficulties (2015; 2013). The accumulation of the negative impact of unemployment and deprivation might trigger physical and mental issues (Bejakovic & Mrnjavac, 2018), as witnessed by the displacement from traditional employment due to the NCTL operation. The unskilled labour force in the Bayelsa-Nembe area suffers from seasonal unemployment either due to decommissioning of an oil well or the movement of operations out of the state. Vetter et al. stated that these conditions, including income deficiency and restricted standard of living, can cause mental and psychological impact and damage to individuals (2006). The most prevalent type of unemployment in the Bayelsa-Nembe case study area is structural unemployment demonstrated by the mismatch in workers' demography and the types of jobs available. Most of the workers lack the competence and skills to work in the oil and gas industry which is the principal industry in the state.

Aside from criminality, structural and seasonal unemployment— recruitment of locals to clean spilled oil due to the NCTL vandalism or structural failure, partly triggered the violent aggressive behaviours against oil pipelines in the area. Bejakovic and Mrnjavac pointed out that gainful employment is the glue that holds society together (2018). Aligning with the claims by economic and sociological studies that employment determines social status and human well-being, but also vital in creating the feeling of "mining to life and social stability". The long-term consequences of widespread unemployment and continued deprivation in the Bayelsa-Nembe communities and the wider historic Niger Delta region result in the fear of the unknown. This is what is responsible for a rise in the demand and preference for monetary handouts, as preferred compensation, rather than tangible infrastructural development that will serve the collective good. This appears to be the cause of the mental effect of long-term unemployment and socio-economic deprivation from traditional sources of livelihood in Nembe (Vetter et al., 2006).

The people think that the best way of benefiting from oil and gas, particularly the operation of the NCTL pipeline that traverses their communities is to demand monetary pay-out or by vandalising the pipeline. Although they want infrastructure projects, they fear such projects might never see the light of day. Historical facts show that whatever project is proposed will either remain uncompleted or completely abandoned. The mistrust of Bayelsa-Nembe communities is well-founded due to the many years of "betrayal" by both the political class, government, and private institutions (Philp, 2015). The lack of transparency, secrecy, and probity in governance and those in esteemed positions in Nigeria worsen the collective socio-economic and psychological impact of the NCTL on communities.

## Oil and Gas Infrastructure Insecurity and how Pipelines can be Secured

The insecurity of oil and gas infrastructure extends to physical disruptions and vandalism of pipelines, transmission routes, oil and gas product supply chains, and attacks on oil and gas workers (Grigg, 2010; Lewis, 2015). Defective pipelines, as well as overreliance on external help for industrial and technical support, can sometimes jeopardise operations because of a lack of manpower that can resolve related issues (NBS, 2017; Chapter 7). These issues are further compounded by corruption and poor governance structure on state, regional and local levels (Collier, 2007; Hendriksz et al., 2017). Given That Nigeria derives over 80 percent of its revenue from the oil and gas sector, its infrastructure is acutely important to the country (Devold, 2013; Douglas & Okonta, 2003). It appears the Nigerian government does not see the vulnerability of the oil and gas infrastructure and the need to develop a more sustainable protective security measure that should encompass the development of the local communities.

Some scholars observed that the United States and many European countries categorise their oil and gas sector as a part of their critical national infrastructure. The European Union incorporated the Norwegian oil and gas infrastructure into its strategic critical infrastructure network to protect its geopolitical security from any vulnerabilities (Johnsen, 2016). Given that much of Nigeria's oil and gas is produced in the Niger Delta region, this area remains critically important to the security of Nigeria. At the same time, this area is replete with evidence of poor governance, corruption, poverty, and environmental damage from oil and gas extraction. For instance, the attack on the Alakiri gas flow station, the Escravos Gas Utilisation, and Oluasiri Gas Transmission Pipelines crippled gas supply to Transcorp Ughelli, Egbin, and Olokola Electric Grids (Ikelegbe, 2013; Ogunleye, 2017). The overlapping vulnerabilities of oil and gas infrastructure are exacerbated due to the outcome of implementing the instrumental policies of extractive capitalism (Mickolus, 2018).

The security of pipelines draws on two ideological debates. One talks about socio-economic development and empowerment while the other talks about the deployment of technological mechanisms. Extreme poverty, socio-economic stagnation and inequalities, educational deprivation, environmental degradation, lack of economic opportunities, and political exclusion are sources of insecurity problems in Bayelsa (Alagoa, 2005; Alamieyeseigha, 2008; Douglas & Okonta, 2003). The presence of these social phenomena caused oil and gas infrastructure insecurity ranging from pipeline vandalism and sabotage to illegal oil bunkering and operation of artisanal refineries to mention a few (Igbinovia, 2014; Mathias, 2015; Onuoha, 2008). Department of Petroleum Resources stated that the first stage in their pipeline security strategy is for operators to abide by the relevant laws of their operating licenses (Oil Pipeline Act, 2004). According to DPR, pipelines are secured if oil firms follow licensing provisions such as design code, methods of operation of the pipeline, life span of the line, pressure, integrity checks, and inspections as well as intelligence/operational pigging. Omagu (2012) pointed out that focusing on licensing alone shows that regulators were more interested in the operators' successes than the safety of the local communities.

Other scholars advocate for a technical solution. Sullivant (2007) argued that to resolve the insecurity problems, a Security Assessment Methodology framework that identifies inhibitors and threats to operational assessment should be designed. Shoewu et al. pointed out that using innovative technological systems to monitor human activities around pipelines and transmitting real-time images to Control Command Centre would positively improve pipeline security (2013). Warren et al. and Baku-Tbilisi-Ceyhan Corporation suggested that technological system innovations would suffice in securing oil and gas pipelines (2016; 2014). To these commentators, the infrastructural development of local communities does not add value or is less critical to ensuring the achievement of a pipeline security framework. Hashim et al. and Timashev & Bushinskaya pointed out that there are some limited benefits of using only technological mechanisms to secure (2018; 2016). Even though oil and gas companies are some of the wealthiest companies, some technological software takes years through formulation and deployment. Sometimes it is problematic for some oil companies to buy protective technologies directly from inventors and manufacturers.

Though technological innovations might temporarily secure pipelines in the short term, it does not guarantee their safety in the long term. If the suggestion of the oil and gas regulator on using technology is right, it questions why there is an increase in vandalism of the NCTL to the extent that Shell and other JV partners had to sell their shares. Pipeline security is related to local community development because evidence shows where there is poverty, corruption, and evidence of poor governance, there is also pipeline insecurity. Tohan (2019) stated that an insecure way of life and a degraded environment are directly connected to the (in)security of pipelines. Scheffran & BenDor (2018) and Spellman (2016) argued that the best way to secure oil and gas infrastructure is to adopt a collective stakeholders' approach.

## Strategies Nigeria Uses in Preventing Pipeline Vandalism

While it may be difficult to analyse the country-by-country approach to preventing onshore pipeline vandalism, Nigeria's approach has a global appeal across countries in the Global South. Due to geopolitical and geoeconomic similarities between Nigeria and most petrostates in the Global South. Nigeria has designed its pipeline security around institutional security and community development strategies which Okonofua classified as *hard* and *soft* strategies (2016; See Chapter 2). The *security strategy* used for the prevention of pipeline vandalism draws on its security architecture or/and what Balogun referred to as "force structure" (2018). Nigeria's security architecture or force structure is statist-militarist and is influenced by the political and constitutional authority of Nigeria. On the other hand, the *community development strategy*-inclusive capacity building and infrastructural development are used *as* a strategy to prevent pipeline vandalism. The government created the Ministry of the Niger Delta (MNDA), Niger Delta Development Commission (NDDC), 13 percent deprivation, Niger Delta Presidential Amnesty Program (NDPAP), and the newly proposed Niger Delta Development Trust Fund (NDDTF) to cater to this. Except for the yet-to-be-implemented proposed NDDTF in the new PIA Act (2021), the implementation of other Acts has failed to prevent pipeline vandalism.

This is due to poor governance, institutional corruption, and unclear policy directions that are designed to operationalise each of the Acts. Igbinovia (2014) believes that the lack of developmental policy directions and confusing wording of many Niger Delta developmental intervention Acts continue to deprive and alienate local communities. This has escalated oil theft, bunkering, and vandalism. This section is not to prove or disprove the success or failure of institutional security or/and community development Acts. It is to outline some community developmental strategies the government has created to engage and develop local communities and distract them from vandalism. The Nigerian Military and the Nigerian Police Force have operational bases in the Niger Delta region. These security bodies are supported by statutory paramilitary security structures. They include the Nigerian Immigration Service (NIS), Nigeria Customs (NC), the Nigeria Drug Law Enforcement Agency (NDLEA), and the Nigerian Security and Civil Defence Corps (NSCDC) (Balogun, 2018; Suberu, 2019). These Nigerian security agencies are supported by a layer of statutory investigation and intelligence agencies. They include the Directorate of Military Intelligence (DMI), Nigerian Intelligence Agency (NIA), Department of State Security (DSS), Economic and Financial Crimes Commission (EFCC), Federal Intelligence and Investigation Bureau (FIIB), and Independent Corrupt Practices Commission (ICPC).

The Nigeria security approach is designed to focus on the defence of Nigeria's territorial integrity. Drawing on the summary of the agencies, the following structural overview reflects the operationalisation of Nigeria's security architecture. The Nigerian President is the Commander in Chief of the Armed Forces to whom all the heads of the security agencies report (Aghedo & Thomas, 2015; Nigeria Constitution, 1999, third amendment). The National Security Adviser (NSA), the Chief of Defence Staff (CDS), and the Inspector General of Police (IGP) are the highest-ranking officers within the security architecture and operational command structure in Nigeria (Balogun, 2018; Iwuoha, 2021; Suberu, 2019). The Director Generals of all civil intelligence services like the NIA and DSS report to the President through the office of the NSA. Including the National Security Council, the Intelligence Coordinating Committees, Heads of the Paramilitary Services like Customs and Immigrations, and State Directors of National Security Agencies (Aghedo & Thomas, 2015).

Whereas the CDS heads the Armed Forces Council of the army, airforce, and Navy. The IGP is responsible for civil policing across the six geopolitical zones of Nigeria including the State Commissioner of Police (Balogun, 2018; Suberu, 2019). The CDS and the IGP report and take command directly from the President. The NSA coordinates the largest number of security agencies and paramilitary services which includes the structure and deployment of protective security personnel to critical oil and gas infrastructure, except the President makes a specific request. The architecture outlined above is supported by decentralized regional paramilitaries (Iwuoha, 2021). Much of the oil and gas infrastructure is protected by the Joint Military Task Force. In the case of the

Niger Delta, Operation Delta Safe-OPDS is supported by private security firms contracted by the state and the oil and gas companies. Some oil and gas companies usually support this architecture with their internal security structure equipped to interface with state security forces to respond to criminal attacks on their infrastructures (Igbinovia, 2014; Ordor & Abe, 2021). Such proactive security architecture suggests in principle that a rapid response to security threats to the oil and gas pipeline infrastructure should be possible. This has not been the case in reality.

The private security actors are subject to state approval, licensing, and training by the NSCDC before they can operate (Okafor, 2016). Private security operators are limited by law and operate within the guidelines set by the NSCDC. The rules of engagement of private security companies are determined by the NSCDC and their employers. Nigeria's security infrastructure is structured to interface with all layers of security agencies and private security firms as well as private local security operatives to maintain central command. The government has refused to yield to the clamour of many Nigerian scholars and public opinions to decentralise the Nigerian security structure (Iwuoha, 2021; Suberu, 2019). Many have argued that the over-centralisation of the security structure is directly responsible for the slow response by state security agencies to crimes which heightens threat levels (Mathias, 2015; Onuoha, 2008; Suberu, 2019). Edigin and Okonmah say the government keeps making unending mistakes in issues of the provision of effective security for oil and gas infrastructure and the functions of statutory developmental agencies established by Acts of the National Asembly (2010). The Nigerian government designed a Joint Security taskforce policy called Operation Delta Safe (OPDS) bringing together security agencies to protect critical infrastructure in the Niger Delta (Oluyemi, 2020; Sayne, 2013). They are mandated to prevent pipeline vandalism and threats to other oil and gas infrastructure in the area. OPDS is supported by Private Pipeline Security Contractors-PPSC who are tasked with recognisance and monitoring of the pipeline infrastructure (Iwuoha, 2021).

This is because they have detailed knowledge of the pipeline networks with the capacity to navigate deep into the creek terrain. Other details of how the PPSC operates are classified and not made public for security reasons. It has been pointed out that the *security nature* of the PPSC contractors exempts them from competition, transparency, and in-depth legislative oversight as required by the Public Procurement Act 2007 (Iwuoha, 2021). Hence, they are exposed to political influence and manipulations, and corruption. To address corruption, and political influence as well as yielding to pressure from many stakeholders the new Petroleum Industry Act created the Community Pipeline Surveillance (CPS) to replace PPSC (2021). Despite the intelligence-gathering by former militants to support state security actors, the OPDS oil and gas infrastructure and pipeline vandalism prevention joint task force has been unable to eliminate the threat (Micholus, 2018). According to John (2017) and Onuoha (2008), the OPDS security strategy in operation in Bayelsa has resulted in indiscriminate arrests and extrajudicial killings. The security action also left many negative physical and psychological scars in the minds of residents. Community leaders have continued to oppose the military approach, which has further stoked the discontentment and opposition of local leaders.

In effect, security in the Niger Delta is controlled by the central government operating from Abuja. The incompetent, corrupt, and nepotistic leadership nature of many of Nigeria's security agencies impact negatively on their effectiveness (Balogun, 2018). The problem of ineffectiveness of the security structure is linked to the poor categorisation of Nigeria's critical national infrastructures and threats. Omand pointed out that if critical national infrastructures and vulnerabilities are not accurately categorised it weakens and negatively impacts national resolve to design effective security response strategies (2011). Corruption is also responsible for the abysmal performance of OPDS and private sector security partners. According to Transparency International, members of the various security agencies as well as private security firms are involved in oil bunkering and theft in the Niger Delta (2019). Niger Delta pipeline security architecture is a product of security policy decisions with a mandate to violently respond to civil protests and threats to oil and gas infrastructure in the area. Yet, such policies have failed to prevent vandalism (Franks & Nunnally, 2011).

The government also uses a *community development* strategy to prevent pipeline vandalism. This is designed from the various subsisting economic and infrastructural developmental frameworks such as MNDA, NDDC, the NDPAP, the NDDTF, and the 13 percent derivation formula (PIA Act, 2021). The 13 percent establishment Act was designed to give 13 of oil revenue back to oil-producing states as a way of royalties benefits or/ and compensation. The combined statutory responsibilities of these socio-economic and infrastructural development agencies are to ensure that the human and infrastructural developmental gaps manifest in the Niger Delta region due to oil and gas activities are addressed. many decades after, they have neither succeeded in developing the infrastructure of local communities or/and build the capacity of many unemployed youths. These agencies have been unable to prevent or discourage pipeline vandalism. As Ambassador Mbu rightly stated, it was not just creating a ministry for the Niger Delta that is important, what mattered is the character of the person that carried out the responsibilities that will make all the difference (2018: 124). The MNDA was created in 2008 to develop and lead a coordinated development framework that will deliver human and infrastructural development to all communities in the Niger Delta (Mbu, 2018). The ministry is mandated to focus its attention on the infrastructure development of oil-producing states like Bayelsa and address all underlying issues such as youth unemployment and pollution that lead to agitations and vandalism. The MNDA was also set up to interface with oil corporations to control oil pollution, encourage the private sector to invest in the region, advice the federal government on security-related matters as well as formulate policies for youth mobilisation to name a few (Mbu, 2018). It is unclear how far the MNDA has achieved its mandate.

Furthermore, the NDDC was created in 2000, section 7(1–3) of the establishment Act to support the MNDA and the commission is mandated to resolve all lingering socio-economic issues while facilitating rapid sustainable development of the Niger Delta (NDDC Act, 2000). It was expected that an economically prosperous and infrastructurally stable, and ecologically regenerated Niger Delta region will be achieved (NDDC Act, 2000). Again, available evidence suggests that this has not been achieved, 20 years after the creation of the agency. It is the only agency directly under the supervision and management of the MNDA. Also, in 2009 the Nigerian government developed the Niger Delta Presidential Amnesty Program for militant agitators—NDPAP. This was divided into four stages Disarmament, Demobilisation, Reintegration, and Development (Aderogba, 2016; Ajibola, 2015; Okonofua, 2016). The NDPAP was established by the Presidential Program on Rehabilitation and Reintegration for the Implementation of the Presidential Amnesty Program in the Niger Delta Act in 2016 (Aderogba, 2016). It provides for the disarming, training, and retraining of agitators who have submitted their weapons and renounced violence (Aderogba, 2016). The program initially placed over 30,000 Niger Delta agitators on a monthly wage to address the problem of lack of household income. As well as enrolled and trained and retrained restive youths and agitators to become self-employed to prevent pipeline vandalism. According to Okonofua, the amnesty program was designed as a humanitarian and socio-economic development strategy (2016). While the disarm and demobilise phases of the program were partly been implemented, the reintegration and development, the third and fourth stages, were never implemented by the government (Abidde, 2017; Ukiwo, 2011).

The NDPAP is considered the most important soft or development strategy designed to prevent vandalism. The NDPAP policy has not yielded the desired result although it encouraged many militants to vacate the creeks and surrounded their weapons. Acts of vandalism are still an ongoing insecurity issue in the region. Sometimes, vandalism has increased because of competition amongst local youths to access government handouts. Rather than give out money for no work done, these monies would have been used to establish different industries that would employ young people. It is worth pointing out that young people did not take up arms because they wanted financial handouts from the government. One reason why they took up arms is to force the government to create legitimate sources of employment and economic empowerment such as small, medium, and large-scale industries to employ those who want to work. It was also to make case for community participation in some aspects of the oil and gas business chain as well as environmental regeneration, reclamation, and development of infrastructure (Douglas & Okonta, 2003).

Furthermore, the 13 percent derivation fund to oil-producing states enabled the governors of those states to leverage direct royalty from the sale of oil. This has not percolated the grassroots and so the tensions and frustration remain and the anger is displaced against the pipelines. Although most of these agencies and intervention initiatives have added value and helped to develop some areas in the Niger Delta. The problem is that all the Niger Delta agencies are divided between the Presidency, the Office of the Secretary of the Federation, and only the MNDA. Political and regional interests, and sometimes, ethnicity influences how Niger Delta issues are handled by those in positions while the region continues to suffer underdevelopment and vandalism continues. The underperformance, may not be entirely due to multiple overlapping mandates between the agencies in terms of socio-economic and infrastructural development. It can be argued that the developmental impact is hardly felt

because of the extensive level of degradation, deprivation, economic alien-
ation, and infrastructure decay in the region. These reasons are directly
linked to lingering anger, frustration, and aggression against pipelines.
By examining the security and economic strategies designed to prevent
vandalism this thesis addresses research question three which evaluates
the strategies the Nigerian government deploys to protect pipelines.

The entire programs, security, and economic development, designed
to improve the Niger Delta are beset by corruption, poor governance,
and compromised leadership and not only failed to deliver on their statutory mandates and promised security but made the security situation
worse (Mathias, 2015; Omeni, 2018). It was revealed that in 2014 oil
and gas regulators, operators, and security agencies combined lost about
USD$ 14 billion due to ineffective implementation of various pipeline
security strategies (Kyuka, 2017; Okonjo-Iweala, 2018). This research
explores why there is a constant failure in security, using the framework of
the frustration-aggression displacement theory. This thesis will continue
to highlight that it is only through addressing the underlying issues of
poverty, corruption, poor governance, environmental damage, and political engagement with local communities that security can be re-established
in the region. Oriola (2016; Igbinovia 2014; Mathias, 2015) agrees that
Bayelsa has witnessed an increase in pipeline vandalism and illegal crude
oil refining, and oil theft. While Delta and Rivers states have experienced
the highest level of kidnappings and oil bunkering. Akwa Ibom, Edo, and
Ondo states have become the epicentre of sabotage.

## OIL AND GAS REGULATORY FRAMEWORKS
## AND CAUSES OF VANDALISM

This section explores some of the regulatory frameworks governing the
oil and gas industry which draw their relevance from the 1999 Constitution of the Federal Republic of Nigeria (third amendment) (Nwuke,
2021; Odudu, 2017). The Nigerian 1999 Constitution stipulates the
importance of improving and protecting the environment (Nwuke,
2021; Odudu, 2017). It explains how these regulations link to pipeline
vandalism. The main oil and gas regulatory frameworks are the Land Use
Act (1978, 2004), Oil Pipeline Act (OPA, 2004), Nigeria Mineral and
Mining Act (NMM Act, 2011), Petroleum Industry Act (2021), Climate
Change Act (2021), and Environmental Impact Assessment Act (EIA Act,

1992, 2004). As well as Nigeria's Flare-Gas-Prevention of Waste-and-Pollution-Regulation Act (2018). These regulatory frameworks are used to explore the historical, contemporary, recent, and emerging schools of thought about factors that are responsible for oil and gas pipeline vandalism. The Nigerian oil and gas and mining regulatory framework gives control and ownership of oil and gas found anywhere in Nigeria to the Federal government which has triggered anger and protests due to the increase in poverty levels.

For instance, the Oil Pipelines Act (2004, Chapter 338, Cap 07 LFN 1999; 2015) stipulates that individuals and corporations who want to operate and maintain pipelines linked to oil fields and oil mining must apply and comply with the licensing processes. The oil and gas license focuses on the holder and or agents rather than the ancestral landowners. The Acts stipulates that the licensee, subject to the provisions of sections 14, 15, and 16 of the OPA, can enter and take possession of a stripe of the land of a width not exceeding two hundred feet with any necessary equipment or vehicle (Oil Pipeline Act, 2004). Also, the Climate Change Act does not consider the various environmental violations caused by oil and gas activities in the Niger Delta. Although, it demonstrates Nigeria's commitment to net-zero GHG emissions between 2050 and 2070 through environmental and economic accountability (Climate Change Act, 2021; National Climate Change Policy, 2021). Section I(1–6) outlines the emission target, a five-year carbon budget within the context of a National Climate Change Action Plan, and a climate fund to help mitigate climate change and support adaptation. However, the implementation policy does not highlight how Nigeria will achieve these objectives within the context of environmental damage in the Niger Delta.

Furthermore, the Environmental Impact Assessment Act (EIA Act, 2004) originally conceptualised social, health, and environmental impact assessments to be carried out before any development project is done in Nigeria. The oil and gas regulatory agencies adopted it to set Environmental Guidelines and Standards (EGAS) that outlines general principles, procedures, and methods of environmental impact assessment in the oil and gas industry (1992, 1999, 2004, Cap E12 LFN 2015). The EIA Act makes provisions for oil and gas field development, construction of onshore and offshore as well as overland pipelines including the construction of oil and gas separation, processing, and loading and storage infrastructure to name a few. Oil firms are legally required to undertake an environmental assessment to determine how to minimise various forms of the social and environmental impact of their activities on communities. The EIA Act mandates oil firms to protect and preserve the Niger Delta and Nigerian environment while exploring for oil (EIA, 2004). But the functions and responsibilities overlap and are duplicated like the processes that guide the issues of impact assessment confusing oil operators and local communities.

The Land Use Act (LUA) empowers people to own lands. But such powers do not include federal government lands or lands belonging to its agencies (1978, 2004, Chapter 202 LFN 2015). The Nigerian government is vested with the power to seize any land along with any landed property thus nobody has a freehold over land in Nigeria. The LUA empowers the state government to hold state lands in trust for the people and issue a *Certificate of Occupancy* when land is leased. By giving sweeping powers to the government the land use Act sets the local communities on a collision course with different levels of the Nigerian government structure for many decades (Ako, 2011). The government in Nigeria, drawing on relevant LUA clauses, can seize any private land without paying compensation and this has heightened disputes between government and communities over lands especially lands with mineral deposits. The Land Use Act which also stipulates that all lands where mineral oil and gas are found in commercial quantity are automatically acquired by the federal government, gives impetus to the PIA (2021; Section 115(1)).

Furthermore, the Petroleum Industry Act provides for the legal, governance, regulatory, and fiscal framework for the Nigerian petroleum industry. It also provides the central framework that guides and governs the exploration, production, and use of petroleum resources in Nigeria. The PIA provides for the exploration of petroleum from territorial waters and the continental shelf of Nigeria and vests the ownership of, and all onshore and offshore revenue from petroleum sources derivable in the federal government of Nigeria (Nwuke, 2021). However, the Act prohibits oil and gas pollution of watercourses and the atmosphere and regulates the construction, maintenance, operations, and transportation of petroleum products and flammable oils and liquids. The PIA Act also exercises dual regulatory control over the petroleum industry through the Nigerian Upstream Petroleum Regulatory Commission (NUPRC) responsible for the technical and commercial regulation of the upstream petroleum operation. As well as the Nigerian Midstream and Downstream Petroleum Authority (NMDPA) is responsible for the technical and commercial regulation of the midstream and downstream petroleum operation (PIA, 2021; Section 29(3)).

Section 257 of the PIA Act imposes duty and responsibility for the protection of the oil and gas assets on host communities. This sets the stage for tensions and resentment. The clause stipulates that any host community that fails to protect oil assets in its community from vandalism will be accountable for the repairs (Olalere, 2021; PIA Act, 2021). This section of the PIA Act is extremely complex and complicated given that the local communities cannot physically prevent pipeline vandalism. It opens a gap for vandalism to continue. However, the communities thought their local vigilante groups and neighborhood watch already partner with statutory state security forces, but this has not yielded substantive results (the next section discusses Nigeria's security architecture and its operations). These petroleum Acts have relevance to the Nigerian Mineral and Mining Act (2011). NMM Act regulates the exploration and exploitation of solid materials in Nigeria. It vests control of all properties and minerals in Nigeria in the Federal Government and prohibits unauthorised exploration or exploitation of minerals. All lands where commercial quantities of minerals are found are automatically acquired by the Federal Government. Failure to set out and explain the procedures for achieving the principles set out in these Acts leaves them open to multiple interpretations by oil and gas companies. This is partly why the oil and gas exploration laws are flouted by relevant oil and gas corporations (Olawuyi, 2012; Ukiwo, 2020). Therefore, it is safe to argue that oil and gas infrastructure insecurity problems are not due to the absence of oil and gas laws in Nigeria. However, the lack of political will and political action to implement subsisting oil and gas laws.

Drawing on some of the provisions contained in some oil and gas regulatory frameworks above, vandalism and oil and gas infrastructure insecurity problems can be traced to five main schools of thought. These are historical, contemporary, recent, community neglect, and leadership curse. Political historians like Alamieyeseigha, Doughlas, Okonta, Alagoa, and Saro-Wiwa argued that policy deceit and arbitrary and reactive implementation of extractive minerals laws set the stage for vandalism (2008; 2005; 2003; 1992). The implementation of the British pre-colonial trade treaties did support the inclusive growth of the oil palm trade with the local communities (Alamieyeseigha, 2008; Saro-Wiwa, 1992). Contemporary Niger Delta commentators argue that the unprofessional and unethical practices of oil firms, like the failure to clean polluted waters and farmlands, are facilitated and reinforced by the gaps in the LUA, EIA, and OPA legislations leading to resentment and vandalism (Okonofua, 2016; Okumagba, 2012, 2013). While recent Niger Delta security experts like Onuoha and Matthias believe the reasons for vandalism and oil and gas infrastructure insecurity in Bayelsa are a combination of deceitful historic policies and contemporary factors (2015; 2008). It is noteworthy, to state that deceit and policy inconsistencies began far back as during the days of the British Royal Niger Trading Company between 1850-and 1895 (Madubuko, 2017).

What Madubuko is pointing out here is that the Nigerian government may have inherited the behaviour of using policy to deceive Niger Delta local communities. As reflected in many oil and gas regulatory policies above. For instance, the Land Use Act allows the federal government to take control of any land with oil and gas natural resources. This continues to create resentment, anger, and frustration. The implementation of Nigeria's oil and gas regulations and policies like EIA, LUA, and Minerals and Mining Acts discussed above continue to undermine the security situation in the Niger Delta based on their contents. Some scholars believe that social conflicts and perhaps resentment in local communities would have been less if the government took its responsibilities more seriously (Douglas & Okonta, 2003; Umukoro, 2009). Although some companies have invested in community schools, hospitals, roads, and industries, but this remains inadequate. The government has created new laws to focus on the social, economic, environmental, and infrastructure development of the area such as MNDA, NDDC, and others. This is what Environment, Social, and Governance framework is proposing.

According to contemporary commentators, unprofessional and unethical practices in the oil and gas sectors like failure to respond appropriately to the continued degradation and contamination of the mangrove forests and water bodies by oil spills and gas flaring make people angry (Omeje, 2017a, 2017b, 2017c; Oriola, 2016; Otokunefor, 2017). The oil firms have found it easier to operate because the numerous regulations, some of which have been discussed above, do not stipulate appropriate punitive measures to deter relevant regulatory violations. There are instances where intervention projects like community health centres have been located where they have less impact (Tuodolo, 2009; Umar & Othman,

2017). Although the number of intervention projects oil firms give to communities is nothing compared to their profits and the environmental damage they have caused. Frustration arises due to the general lack of investment in the local communities despite the high level of profits the oil and gas firms make (Okumagba, 2013). The nature of the projects and the way they are spread across communities continue to pit communities against each other, and between communities with the oil operators (Dambo, 2006; Olawuyi, 2012; Ukiwo, 2020).

Scholars like Mickolus (2018), Mathias (2015); Onuoha (2008), and Alamieyeseigha (2008) blame the problem of pipeline vandalism and oil and gas infrastructure insecurity on historic and contemporary factors. They argued that various issues bothering on Niger Delta environment and lack of regulatory clarity or consistencies have frustrated residents for many years. This suggests that the issues and problems around the Niger Delta oil and gas infrastructure insecurity are receiving inappropriate attention given the persistence of pipeline vandalism. Mallin (2016) and Wight & Morton (2007) linked vandalism to the moral aspect of corporate governance. They pointed out that regulators and multinational corporations failed to balance the interest of the local community with their business interests. Some unethical business practices like ignoring the impact of gas flaring and oil spills on the environment, Wetzel noted are directly responsible for the underdevelopment of communities (2016). Corporate capitalists design their policy objectives towards the pursuit of profit and the interest of the members they serve before any consideration is given to the impact of their activities on the local communities (Idemudia, 2014).

According to Schwab, capitalism is an economic system with little government presence and control where monetary goods and capital assets such as industries are owned and controlled by private individuals or companies (2021). Corporate capitalism is an economic system or society where large private shareholder-owned corporations dominate the marketplace (Bruland, 1998). Corporate capitalism is privately funded by an individual or collective that operates in a hierarchical and bureaucratic marketplace where they dominate and control the factors of production and determine the number of profits they generate for their investors. One could argue that the likes of Royal Dutch Shell Petroleum and Aiteo Exploration and Production or Belemaoil Producing Company operating in the Niger Delta are corporate capitalists. Johnson noted that the 2008 global economic crisis occurred because those in charge of capitalist corporations went a little deeper and beyond core principles by putting personal gains before financial prudence, and shareholder interests thereby taking the advantage of regulatory complacency (2010).

Friedman's statement of *profit first* business approach supports the behaviour of some of the oil and gas firms operating in Nigeria because his argument is influenced by corporate capitalism principles (1993). While the sole purpose and social responsibility of a corporate business are to make profits for its shareholders. Friedman stated pointed out that the activities of the corporation must not be deceptive, or fraudulent and the corporation should operate within set regulations. Analysis of some oil and gas regulatory regimes in Nigeria shows that oil firms may exactly be operating within the best regulatory regimes. They might be completely exonerated because evidence shows that oil and gas multinationals have failed in some of their obligations like caring for the environment which is a core element of international best practice (UNEP, 2012). Their failure to meet this moral responsibility to local communities Leipziger (2017) and Wight et al. (2007) pointed out means they may have failed in some aspects of their fiduciary responsibilities. Although corporate capitalism reinforces the right of individuals to determine their labour to improve their social and economic wellbeing which is not widespread in Bayelsa. Corporate entities have other moral obligations such as obedience to the laws of the land, protection of personnel and local people from obvious harm, and well as building trust by keeping to agreements and promises.

The moral responsibilities of corporations are broadly judged within the limits of those responsibilities reflected and encapsulated within the oil and gas regulatory frameworks. The regulatory frameworks are designed to ensure ethical behaviour and define the expectations that communities should have from oil firms. They appear to have failed in their moral duties in Bayelsa because the Nigerian government's oil and gas regulations have been designed with the needs of the oil companies in mind. The needs of local communities are secondary and broadly neglected. Although the oil and gas corporations operating in the Niger Delta should not entirely take the blame for all the underlying issues causing vandalism and insecurity in Bayelsa. They should however take the blame for their failure to uphold some moral duties despite operating within the principles of corporate capitalism. Oil and gas corporations have to blur the lines between the flaws in extant oil and gas regulations and their corporate capitalism rights to achieve their mid and long-term business objectives. Shaw (2016) and Shaw & Barry (2015) make the point that if the Nigerian government adopts *Galbraith's visible moral force of governance model* there would be a progressive relationship between the government, local communities, civil societies, and oil corporations. The Nigerian government shares a substantial part of the blame due to the high level of incompetence, political corruption, criminality, and badly designed and implemented oil and gas regulatory frameworks. If the government takes appropriate political action, it would be seen to complement the developmental contributions made by oil and gas corporations.

The intention of this book is not to prove or disprove historic deceit, lack of transparency, problematic and often arbitrary and reactive regulatory frameworks, and issues of environmental degradation. The book points out that the Nigerian government is aware of the many underlying issues causing vandalism and oil and gas infrastructure insecurity. This book agrees with the pioneers of the *community neglect hypothesis.* The emerging school of thought argues that various forms of neglect motivate pipeline vandalism (Bergstresser, 2017; Coleman, 2015; Ekpenyong, 2010; Etowah & Effiong, 2012; Igbinovia, 2014; Okonta, 2016; Okumagba, 2012, 2013, Saro-Wiwa, 1992). They pointed out that the government and oil and gas firms have taken advantage of the gaps created by the oil and gas regulations to the detriment of the local communities. There are no clear penalties for environmental violations and communities have to wait on the court to give directives on compensation. This shows the interest of communities is secondary. In some other instances, they have deliberately violated some provisions in the EIA Act, LUA Act, and OPA Acts, due to regulatory complacency.

The government, oil and gas multinationals and regulatory agencies have collectively neglected to address issues of corruption and criminality that continue to permeate the oil and gas industry. The government has done little to encourage alternative sources of employment to help local economies and communities thrive. Knowing fully well that oil and gas activities have dislocated many people from their traditional sources of livelihood and created economic disequilibrium that has increased household poverty and hunger leading to anger and frustration that has led to vandalism. Both the government and oil firms have ignored appropriate actions to correct issues of environmental neglect such as pollution and gas flaring which has increased the amount of methane and impacted Niger Delta communities and worsened climate change issues. They have neglected the infrastructural underdevelopment of the area intensifying poverty, inequality, and lack of human security leading to anger, frustration, tensions, and resentment that leads to vandalism. They also agree that the current handling of the government and multinational oil and gas companies is increasing insecurity in the region (Onuoha, 2008, 2016). The literature further highlights that neglecting local communities triggers frustration due to their current plight which increases anger against the government and oil and gas companies. The frustration leads tome youths and local communities to vent their anger and aggression against softer targets through acts of vandalism.

This book argues that neglecting to integrate local communities in finding a political solution to the problems caused by oil and gas activities heightens tensions, anger, and frustration that trigger vandalism. Since all these forms of deliberate neglect are inherently linked, the government needs to address all of them to stand a chance at resolving oil and gas infrastructure insecurity in Bayelsa state. The evidence that this book presents aligns with Etekpe and Akpomera's assertion that the voices of the local communities that make them take to vandalism should be heard (2018; 2015). Hermans agrees with Jane Goodall's statement that "change happens by listening and starting a dialogue with people who are doing something you do not believe is right" (2010-no page number). Okumagba and Okonta also argue that neglecting to aggregate diverse perspectives of different sectors of the community has aggravated frustration that has led to different forms of violence and insecurity situations in Bayelsa (2016; 2012; 2013).

Therefore, this book expands the community neglect hypothesis debate by proposing the Community Neglect Aggression Displacement theoretical framework. The CNADT explains that the collective neglect of critical issues concerning local communities leads to anger and frustration that triggers the displacement of aggression against onshore pipelines. This supports the FADT discussed in Chapter 3. This insecurity dilemma can only be solved if the government, and oil and gas companies work with local communities to solve poverty, inequality, poor access to government services, poor governance, and corruption problems. As outlined above, oil and gas exploration continues to have a detrimental effect on the local communities and the local environment. This partly explains why communities are angry and frustrated and some of them engage in vandalism of pipelines as well as the attack on oil and gas infrastructure. This thesis proposes the "leadership curse" phenomenon in addition to the *community neglect hypothesis,* the emerging school of thought, as responsible for tensions and vandalism in the case study area.

## THE TROUBLING PHENOMENON OF LEADERSHIP "CURSE" IN NIGERIA

Leadership, particularly, social and political leadership has assumed the toga of a curse, in Nigeria. Each time an individual assumes socio-political elevation they turn against Nigeria and the people, no matter how morally and socially upright they must have been. The Oxford Dictionary describes a curse as a solemn utterance intended to invoke a supernatural power to inflict harm or punishment on someone (2016). A curse is a negative situation that defiles all sense of logic where its persistence seemingly appears to be influenced by a nuanced, subtle, and unexplained supernatural force. This paper describes the *leadership curse* as a phenomenon of an unbroken cycle of bad leaders in Nigeria leading to tensions, infrastructure insecurity, and pipeline vandalism. Such leaders persistently fail to develop Nigeria and rather steal away all of Nigeria's commonwealth to foreign lands (Jatto et al., 2023). Given that this attitude has defiled common sense and logic over many decades, the author correctly coined it as the "leadership curse phenomenon".

Peter Obi, the Presidential candidate of the Labour Party in the 2023 Presidential election in Nigeria, described the same Nigeria's leadership scenario as a "curse of missed opportunities and squandered hopes". Interpreted to mean either consistent misplacement of numerous opportunities to transform Nigeria's socio-economic woes for the benefit of the greater good; each circle of leadership in Nigeria is consistently characterized by misplacement of priorities and opportunities thus sinking Nigeria deeper into underdevelopment; or Nigerians consistently chose to miss (directly or by default) opportunities to elect good leaders and select bad once. Furthermore, Obadiah Mailafia termed this same leadership problem in Nigeria as "leadership misrule strangulation" (Vanguard, 2021). Explaining that it depicts an unbroken cycle of politicians consistently exhibiting bad leadership character, and intentions, and lacking competence and capacity to translate natural resource wealth into collective socio-economic gains. When the three descriptions are taken together, it clearly shows that the underdevelopment of the

Bayelsa and Nembe communities leading to tensions, vandalism, and insecurity is more accurately and correctly termed as a *leadership curse*. Given the cyclical appointment, promotion, and elevation of leaders with bad characters to leadership responsibilities. Many leaders and oil and gas companies can be directly tied to criminal behaviours and corruption that are responsible for the prolonged problems of insecurity in the Niger Delta (Jatto et al., 2023; Okonofua, 2016) which this book refers to as a "leadership curse". This book describes the *leadership curse hypothesis* as the unbroken pattern in the recycling of "short-sighted", "corrupt", and "incompetent" leaders.

The positions of Obadiah and Obi confirms that the author is right to assert that "leadership curse phenomenon" is responsible for tensions and vandalism. Therefore, describing the problem as a "curse of missed opportunities", "leadership misrule strangulation" or a "leadership curse", the three scenarios describe an unnatural situation consistently susceptible to internal and external variables that harms Nigerians. The leader(ship) is characterised by "selfishness", "(in)competence", "wickedness", "short-sightedness", and "corruption". Laundering of stolen monies to oversee banks" (Jatto et al. 2023), and "unpragmatic". These few privileged Nigerian leaders, indeed African political leaders, quickly transform into totalitarianism due to paranoia, uncontrolled access to natural resources, and a nuanced sense of eternal entitlement. Despite when some of them may have ascended to political power through popular support. The unbroken cycle of leaders with the above character appears jinxed and 'cursed', who are controlled by a supernatural force that ensures they stagnate the system, de-develop the country, and harm the Nigerian people. The author has appropriately coined this as the *leadership curse* phenomenon. The emergence of such leaders, over many decades has stagnated Nigeria's oil and gas industry and heightened its infrastructure insecurity problems.

The triangulated data revealed that the leadership curse phenomenon, taken together with other factors, has the greatest adverse impact on the oil and gas industry in Nigeria. This is responsible for the poor delivery of public goods. Analysing the character of individuals in government representing the people reveals a deeper insight into the extent of poor governance and poor delivery of public goods. The unbroken culture of appointing, promoting, and nominating people with bad and questionable characters whose overtly or nuanced actions cause harm and pain, and punish Nigerians has become a jinx- curse. This unbroken paradigm is seemingly influenced by a nuanced, subtle, and unexplained supernatural power that has jinxed Nigeria's leadership trajectory is what Obi correctly described as the "curse of missed opportunities". The consistent emergence of incapable individuals who have failed to weld their political and private powers, as leaders, to trigger infrastructural development demonstrates how "leadership became a curse" to crude oil resource-rich Nembe communities, Bayelsa state, the Niger Delta region, and Nigeria.

The neglect suffered by local communities is frustrating the people leading to anger and aggression. As Luong and Weinthal pointed out, oil resources are not a curse (2010). The economic stagnation of oil-rich nations like Nigeria is based on the direct effect that export windfalls have on the real exchange rate and the influence of political leadership. Quoting Emperor Caesar, "Men, at sometimes, are masters of their fates. The fault, dear Brutus, is not in our stars, but ourselves, that we are underlings" (Shakespeare, 1807: 16, Act 1, scene 2). The January 1966 Nigerian coup speech of Major Nzeogwu focused on corrupt individuals. Achebe emphasised that; "it is bad leadership and not the climate, land, water, air or anything else, that is the root cause of the troubles and predicament with Nigeria" (Achebe, 1984: 1). The underdevelopment of resource-rich communities and countries like Nigeria, Bayelsa and Nembe and the plethora of infrastructure and human insecurity problems that follows rests squarely and tied to the foot of the "leadership curse".

## Government and Operators' Response to Oil Spillages

There is a range of factors that cause oil spills across Bayelsa communities and other crude oil-producing communities of the wider Niger Delta. Some of these are structural failures, operational blowouts, vandalism, oil theft, bunkering, and natural disasters. Whereas the PIA (2021) and OPA Acts (2004) stipulate that oil and gas firms should report any oil or gas spills and leaks to the Ministry of Environment and National Oil Spill Detection and Response Agency (NOSDRA). The oil companies are legally liable to clean up and/or pay NOSDRA to clean oil spills caused by structural failure and operational blowouts. However, oil companies are exempt from taking any responsibility if the oil spill is caused by third-party vandalism or acts of natural disasters like an earthquake (NOSDRA Act, 2006; OPA Act, 2021). The unfair regulatory frameworks allow oil and gas companies to get away with many cases of oil spills. NOSDRA estimated over 3203 oil spills occurred in the Niger Delta between 2006 and 2010, suggesting that within this time frame, there were at least two oil spills per day (Oriola, 2013). About 23 percent of oil spills during this time was due to equipment failure, corrosion, erosion, operation, and maintenance issues while over 45 percent was due to vandalism and sabotage.

The remaining 32 percent of oil spill cases were due to oil theft and bunkering (Oriola, 2013). NOSDRA is the federal government agency with statutory responsibility to monitor and respond to spillages and keep track of spills. It also undertakes surveillance and ensures oil and gas firms comply with extant environmental regulations (Okonkwo, 2020). It interfaces between local communities, oil firms, and members of the Joint Investigation Team of oil spill sites. NOSDRA has fewer offices in states where the most pollution occurs suggesting that it has a limited operational reach. It is severely understaffed and exposed to political interference and corruption (Okonkwo, 2020). This is partly why oil spill cleanup is either not properly done or in many instances neglected in the Niger Delta. An effective response to oil spillage and gas leaks is a critical phase in the pipeline life cycle. Doing so helps to sustain the socio-economic and environmental life of the community. Oil spills have caused untold environmental damages in Bayelsa state. Ong (2017) and Sinden (2009) argued that these have caused significant destruction of farmlands, fishing rivers, and ponds as well as pollution of the atmosphere as illustrated in Fig. 4.1.

The images in the figure above only illustrate a snapshot of the damage that has been caused over many decades. NOSDRA does not have helicopters and boats and relies on the goodwill of oil and gas multinationals to ferry them to oil spill sites that cannot be easily reached (Ukiwo, 2020). A lack of equipment and a dearth of accurate information and data hinders the effective cleanup of oil spills and gas leaks in Bayelsa. According to Folorunsho and Awosika (2014), inaccurate information about the location and difficulties in accessing oil spill areas has made responses difficult. Where the spillage sites are easily identifiable and accessible, the responses have been better. Omeje (2017a, 2017b, 2017c) argued that lack of accurate data jeopardises as well as impedes environmental agencies and oil operators from locating oil spills. The nature and structure of the government influence the responses of the agencies responsible for environmental and pollution issues. Delays in responding to oil spills and gas leaks could sometimes reflect a lack of technical expertise and

Crude oil spillage on farmland in Nembe

Impact of crude oil pollution on plants in Nembe

Atmospheric pollution with hydrocarbon

Bust underwater oil pipeline polluting fishing water

**Fig. 4.1** Oil spillage in Nembe-Ewelesuo communities (*Source* Photographed and Compiled by Author [2019])

inadequate equipment which are what Rukeh (2015) and Ukiwo (2011) argued influenced the nature and type of responses seen in the Niger Delta.

According to Oriola (2016), oil operators respond quicker to spillages caused by mechanical, structural, and operational failures than those suspected to have been a result of vandalism or sabotage. In the eyes of the enabling Acts such as the OPA and PIA Acts discussed elsewhere in this thesis, oil and gas companies are not necessarily wrong to ignore oil spills that occurred due to vandalism, although it is in their interest to fix vandalised pipelines otherwise, they lose money. However, they are statutorily mandated to report any oil spills and clamp the facility to enable NOSDRA to move and effect cleanup. Douglas and Okonta (2003) stated that sometimes NOSDRA allows political consideration to influence their response to pipeline damages to avoid investigations and possible government sanctions. This type of behaviour and excuses by some oil firms infuriate local communities which leads some of them to attack pipelines, which further damages the environment (Okumagba, 2012; UNEP, 2012). Wright (2003) and Saro-Wiwa (1992) believe that Shell's delay in responding to oil spills resulted in the extensive pollution of Ogoniland destroying farmlands, fishing ponds and rivers, underground water table, and natural habitats in 1991. This provoked the collective violent protest led by Ken Saro-Wiwa against Shell Nigeria. For example, Doerffer (2013) argued that delaying response to oil spills on water surfaces, rivers, and fishing ponds enables the wind to dissolve oil slicks into discontinuous stripes and patches that make it more difficult to later cleanup.

About 42,500 Niger Delta farmers, fishermen, and women from Ogale and Bille communities in Ogoniland won a Supreme Court appeal in the United Kingdom. The court ruled that local communities can bring litigations against Royal Dutch Shell in England (Khalid, 2021). The UK Supreme Court noted that Royal Dutch Shell has a vicarious liability to local communities who have suffered many decades of environmental degradation by Shell subsidiary in Nigeria. Also, Bayelsa's Oruma, River's Goi, and Akwa-Ibom's Ikot Ada communities won an appeal at the International Court of Justice against Shell in Hague, the Netherlands (Azubuike, 2021). The various communities that brought litigations against Shell were able to prove that Shell Nigeria systematically damaged its natural environment in its operation in Nigeria. This explains why the UK Supreme Court and the International Criminal Court in the Hague ordered Shell to cleanup polluted areas, restore their livelihood, and compensate victims whose livelihoods were lost. The Courts pointed out that Shell's activities have made fishing rivers and ponds inaccessible, destroyed traditional sources of income for the communities, destroyed fishing nets, and failed to put preventative measures in place to stop aged pipelines from structural failure and blowouts.

As noted by the UNEP (2012) and supported by Loucks (2021), there was evidence of 8 cm layers of refined oil floating on top of the waters, rivers, and creeks supplying local communities with drinking water. NOSDRA and Shell are aware that oil spillages on the water are extremely difficult to clean up and the impact can be felt for up to three decades which is why they should respond faster irrespective of what caused an oil spill. Shell often argues, without evidence from Joint Investigation Team, that vandalism was the cause of many oil spillages in the Niger Delta, which is why most of their claims are rejected by civil society groups. Azubuike stated that oil and gas companies must build preventative warning systems on pipelines, conduct regular structural tests, and update old oil pipeline infrastructure (2021). Shell's culpability in the Niger Delta environmental pollution is what Irvine (2018) describes as a failure in its *vicarious liability* responsibilities. These court rulings achieve two things, first, they compel extractive industries to implement relevant environmental policies to demonstrate commitment to global emissions targets signed in the Paris Climate Agreement (UNCC, 2010). Secondly, after losing their appeal cases in their home country Courts, the UK, and the Hague, Shell is aware that it can no longer argue that they are not liable for cleaning up oil spills and compensating affected communities, even if the oil spills are caused by vandals (Azubuike, 2021; Khalid, 2021). Given these legal victories, oil and gas companies should put an increased focus on health and safety-keeping communities safe from the devastating impact of oil spills. Further, oil and gas companies must engage with communities to clean up the environmental damages that they have caused over the last five decades or so in the historic Niger Delta, as well as not wait for affected communities to win court cases before compensating them. This would be one step toward creating a more sustainable and secure business environment, without the need for military interventions.

Corruption and poor governance have made Nigeria's oil and gas regulatory laws turn a blind eye to the facts of environmental damage and an increase in household poverty. Sayne and Katsouris point out that Nigerian crude oil is being stolen on an industrial scale (2015). This research argues that the oil and gas infrastructure insecurity problems go beyond corruption and poor governance. It extends to the quality and character of leadership in governance who cannot continue to hide under the *concept of government* to escape taking responsibility for the decades of socio-economic stagnation in Bayelsa state. This study believes the behaviour and character of individuals that represent *the government* should be analysed to give deeper insight into why there is poor delivery of public good.

# The Issues with Compensations

## Corporate Social Responsibility to Environmental, Social, and Governance

This book outlined three categories of compensation. These are:

1. Compensation for land acquisition used for oil and gas extraction;
2. Compensation for environmental damages caused by oil and gas companies through oil spills; and
3. Non-mandatory compensation through royalties, Corporate Social Responsibility, and investment in local communities.

The procedure for compensation for land acquired or leased for oil and gas exploration and exploitation and pipeline route are contained in the LUA (2004) and OPA (2004). Tensions, resentment, and anger steam from the fact that Part II Section 4(1) of the OPA stipulates that anybody can apply to the Minister of Petroleum for a permit to survey potential land for an oil and gas pipeline route subject to payment of the required fees stipulated in Section 31 of the OPA. Section 20(1–4) of the OPA stipulates that compensation could either be total/ and or periodical or even both dependent on court pronouncement. Sub-section 4 consistent with the provisions in the LUA (2004) stipulates that anyone who gets approval from the Minister of Petroleum to survey land for an oil and gas pipeline route is not legally mandated to pay compensation for unoccupied lands. Payment of compensation is subject to the condition the land was met. If it is an unoccupied land, the community or individual who lays claims to it can only get compensation based on the pronouncement of the courts. Ibagere noted that there is forceful dispossession of landed property against the will and consent of the owner (2012).

The government and oil firms do not always pay adequate compensation for compulsorily acquired lands which leads to tensions (Odudu, 2017). Oil firms who lease lands from individuals, families, and communities are liable to pay some compensation and if there is a dispute the court pronouncement will suffice (Ibagere, 2012). Therefore, neither the government nor the oil firm has any legal obligation to pay local communities, if their lands are acquired for the public interest, particularly those with resources. This thesis argues that leaving compensation for acquired lands to judicial interpretation harms the natural rights of the local community because it removes their power over their ancestral lands, exacerbating poverty that leads to anger. Local communities whose lands are forcefully acquired may not be able to afford legal representatives and the OPA Act expects them to pay the legal cost of the defenders if they lose the case. Communities feel their rights are neglected. Odudu observed that the productivity of economic crops and trees is not considered nor were compensation claims based on market values (2017: 21). This is a source of instrumental aggression by the Nigerian government against the community. The issue is that most lands with oil and gas deposits in the Niger Delta are claimed as the properties of the federal government. Therefore, communities who may have farmed on such lands lose their rights, leading to anger and resentment.

In sharp contrast, Sections (I) and 7 of the NMM Act talked about the land occupier as reserving rights of ownership and payment of surface rent to local communities as well as constant assessment of various compensation schemes. It mandates community development agreements; the preparation and submission of environmental impact assessment statements as part of the environmental obligations of companies. This contradicts the Oil Pipeline Act (1956, 2004) which states that the communities and individuals under the OPA Act are expected to claim compensation and not for damages caused by pipeline operation or oil spills. The Act does not provide relief for the damage to properties such as fishing nets, fishing ponds, waters, or economic trees to name a few. Section 11 of the OPA Act states that individuals and communities who are aggrieved about the damages or injuries caused by oil and gas exploration, production, oil pipeline installation, and operation can only be compensated (Oil Pipeline Act, 1956). They cannot claim damages for destroyed properties.

Furthermore, compensation for damages caused by oil and gas extraction is based on regulatory guidelines on structural failure and vandalism. On the one hand, oil and gas regulations say oil companies have a legal responsibility to respond to oil spills and environmental remediation irrespective of the cause of the spill (EIA Act, 1992, 2004). At the same time, regulatory agencies ignore oil firms when they neglect damages they assume were caused by vandalism. Section 102 of the PIA (2021) provides for the environment. It stipulates that any oil and gas exploration license holder operating in the upstream or downstream petroleum sector is required, between six months to one year, to grant the license or lease, submit an Environmental Management Plan in respect of projects that require Environmental Impact Assessment to the PIA for consideration and approval (Nwuke, 2021; Olalere, 2021). The National Environmental Standards and Regulation Enforcement Agency (NESREA Act, 2007) defines the environment as air, water, and all human beings who inhabit these places. This Act prohibits the discharge of any hazardous substance into the environment. It stipulates that oil and gas operators should take responsibility and bear the cost of the cleanup by government agencies. While Section 27(1–5) mandates oil firms to restore, and compensate third parties as determined by the NOSDRA Act (2006), except if the oil spill is caused by a natural disaster like an earthquake. The NESREA Act is silent about who takes responsibility for environmental damages caused by vandalism.

The Nigerian Mineral and Mining Act talks about penalties for offences that border on smuggling and unlawful obstruction of infrastructure. It does not state penalties for environmental degradation and pollution perpetrated by oil and gas companies which is a major gap. Although the new PIA penalises oil and gas companies for flaring gas and mandates the use of revenue from penalties for environmental remediation and relief for impacted communities. The PIA Act misses the point by not setting out what should be the penalties for oil spillages caused by vandalism or operational failure. This seemingly explains why many structural failures are blamed on vandalism to avoid liability and penalties stipulated in sections 35 and 36 of the Act. Therefore, oil spills caused by vandalism or third-party human interference are left to the discretion of the government and oil firms. The UK Supreme Court and the International Criminal Court in the Hague judgment ordered Shell to cleanup polluted areas and compensate victims whose livelihoods were lost because it is the responsibility of the oil firm to put preventative mechanisms in place to prevent vandalism and structural failures (Azubuike, 2021; Khalid, 2021).

In 2008 and 2009, two massive oil spills had a catastrophic impact on the fishing towns of Bodo (Amnesty International Report, 2018). The report pointed out that thick black oil leaked into rivers and creeks for many weeks killing fish and robbing people of their livelihoods and incomes. Shell, operators of the leaking oil pipeline repeatedly underestimated the volume of oil spilled and offered the community a paltry sum of ($4000) as compensation. Amnesty International backed the legal action of the Bodo community before Shell finally admitted to having made a false statement about the volume and size of the spill and agreed to settle out of court, paying £55 million in compensation (Amnesty International Report, 2018). This shows that the regulatory environment is not clear enough about oil spill damages and vandalism. Although NOSDRA guidelines say they should visit within 24 hours, this is rarely followed which explains why there are hectres of land covered with oil spills for many decades. Institutional corruption and deliberate negligence by both the regulatory authorities and the oil companies are responsible for this. The regulators have historically underdelivered on their mandate living oil firms to do whatever they like which explains the high level of pollution and environmental degradation in the area leading to unending anger and frustration. It suffices to say that the various government agencies and the legislature are accountable for the confusion in the wording and omissions in most of the regulatory Acts. These Acts tend to encourage criminal manipulations of environmental policies of oil firms to the detriment of the local communities which leads to tensions and more vandalism.

Although all the oil and gas Acts mandate oil and gas operators to pay a percentage of royalty to the federal government of Nigeria PIA Act (2021; OPA Act, 2004). Royalties from oil and gas are shared between the federal, state, and local governments according to the laws of Nigeria (Osuntogun, 2020). Violent agitations for resource control by oil-producing communities compelled the government to make statutory provisions that allocate 13 percent derived from the royalty to oil-producing states for the development of oil-producing communities (Constitution of Nigeria, 1999-third amendment, Section 162(2). Although a new bill is been debated seeking the allocation of the 13 percent derivation royalty payment directly to impacted communities because the state government has corruptly prevented such payment from percolating into the communities (Ako, 2014: 165). He pointed out that the local communities are pushing for a 50 percent increase in the allocation before environmental justice is seen to have been done. A dearth of socio-economic opportunities and uneven spread of infrastructure, corruption, poor governance, and a leadership curse is why oil-producing communities agitate for resource control.

Section 234 of the new PIA Act provides for the Petroleum Host Community Development (PHCD) (Nwuke, 2021). The central objective is to foster sustainable prosperity within host communities, by providing direct social and economic benefits from petroleum operations to support the development of the host communities. Although the PIA

Act provides for a structured compensation scheme for host communities by mandating the incorporation of a Host Community Development Trust (HCDT). Section 29(4a–c) of the Land Use Act 2004 stipulates that compensation should only be paid for crops, buildings, and farms contradicting the PIA Act 2021. Yet this clause has not been expunged from the LUA. Sections 240–244 of the PIA Act sets out the sources of the allocation using a matrix system to set out the board of trustees of HCDT (Nwuke, 2021; Olalere, 2021). Both the PIA and NMMA (2011) failed to set out a matrix for calculating compensation payment for oil spillages and gas leaks. This thesis argues that although the new PIA Act (2021) attempts to resolve the historic oil and gas infrastructure insecurity problems, it is advertently or inadvertently creating new problems. The issue of compensation is a political matter because the oil firms rely on and use their political influence to either avoid paying accurate compensation to the communities, delay the process or underpay communities leading to anger that triggers frustration and aggression, and vandalism.

It must be noted that no aspect of the oil and gas regulatory guidelines discussed here suggests operating firms should enter into a social contract in the form of a Memorandum of Understanding (MOU) or General Memorandum of Understanding (GMOU) with any local community. This is why the MOU and GMOU documents have become the easiest way to contain community anger by giving them the impression of an expected trickle-down benefits, promises that are often unimplemented. MOU is an agreement with a specific local community about areas the oil firm is willing to compensate and support their development, in return for their full support. While GMOU is an agreement with a cluster of communities on socio-infrastructure, an oil firm is willing to contribute to a cluster of communities (10–25) in return for full support of the communities (Akemu et al., 2018). Although these social contracts compensation models have achieved some level of success in communities. They have failed to make a tangible impact in the lives of communities; hence vandalism has continued. The frustration is beyond the fact that the MOUs and GMOUs are not enforceable by law or legally binding on oil companies and the Nigerian government. The frustration is found in their exposure to political manipulation, deceit, and corruption which leads to anger, tension, and insecurity. The next chapter discusses security concepts and Frustration-Aggression-Displacement Theory. Explaining the aggression of local communities against oil and gas infrastructure and vandalism in the context area.

In response to heightening climate change challenges, businesses are encouraged to shift their corporate governance paradigm. Environmental, Social, and corporate Governance (ESG), designed to replace Corporate Social Responsibility (CSR), is more encompassing and encapsulates issues beyond social responsibility of businesses to communities (Hill, 2020; O'Connor, 2022; Shastry, 2023). ESG sets out criteria and behaviour that addresses environmental sustainability, and pollution matters. CSR is an instrument for impacting social good in local communities while making profits and promoting the corporate brand of the company (Alshbili et al., 2020). Social good focuses on providing varying forms of benefits such as access to education, cleaner water, cleaner air, accessible healthcare, and a sustainable environment to the largest number of people (Ablo, 2020). Although CSR plays a central role in achieving the Millenium Development Goals which seek to eradicate poverty, hunger, and diseases, and create a sustainable environment (Eneh & Enuoh, 2015). These global aspirations have hardly been met in the Niger Delta. Environmental damage is separate from CSR. The nexus is found in the fact that responsible environmental activities mitigate against environmental damages, that not only worsen health conditions but also increase poverty, displacement, and decreased incomes (Etekpe, 2018). There is some evidence that some oil and gas corporations operating in the Niger Delta render some form of social good to local communities through skills acquisition and healthcare centres (Etete, 2017).

Many local communities consider such gestures obsolete as they rarely met the aspirations of the people (Eneh & Enuoh, 2015; Etete, 2017). Plenty of evidence abounds suggesting that communities have been neglected and most oil firms do not centralise CSR as a core value as they do to ethics and professionalism in their activities in the Niger Delta (Agudelo et al., 2019). In theory, the published CSR policy frameworks of most oil and gas firms look robust but they are not reflective of the contemporary socio-economic and environmental realities in oil-producing nations like Nigeria (Ablo, 2020). The implementation processes of the CSR policies of oil and gas firms do not keep to global best practices in terms of oil and gas exploration and production, compliance with extant laws, community interface, and ensuring environmental sustainability. This has further compounded the issues of compensation, and the accusation of community neglect which in turn worsened tensions, anger, and aggression against pipelines (Okumagba, 2012; Sanderson, 2010). Ablo says that the lack of understanding between stakeholders on interest and strategy, coupled with restricted alliance-building on value co-creation affected the content and strategies that contributed to the failure of CSR in resource-rich communities across Africa (2020).

On the other hand, ESG focuses on the interest of the environment, the world we live in, the social lives of the people, and government regulatory laws streamlined into processes of corporate policy drafting and implementation. Despite its "existential defect" seen in its two conflicting meanings from inception which makes it relatively challenging to decipher and implement (Shastry, 2023: 138). The framework gives the impression to be harmonising the UNSDG Agenda 2030 goals as contemporary business behaviours. But lacks a clear time frame to businesses to self-regulate and transition to ESG. This is a critical underbelly of the concept that might lead to delays in its deliverables. Shastry, O'Connor and Hill (2023, 2022; 2020) broke down the ESG criteria into three central pillars which are:

1. Environmental

    a. Energy usage and efficiency
    b. Climate change strategy
    c. Waste reduction
    d. Biodiversity loss
    e. Greenhouse gas emissions
    f. Carbon footprint reduction

2. Social

    a. Fair pay and living Wages
    b. Equal Employment opportunity
    c. Employee benefits
    d. Work place health and safety
    e. Community engagement
    f. Responsible supply chain partnerships
    g. Adherence to labour laws

3. Governance

    a. Corporate governance
    b. Risk management
    c. Compliance

d. Ethical business practices
e. Avioding conflicts of interest
f. Accounting integrity and transparency

Available evidence and published climate change data about Nigeria and across many countries in the Global South do not support the governments claims of adopting a structured process in measuring a company's overall sustainability within the context of ESG criteria. Giving that the stark realities on ground in Niger Delta clearly contradicts the claims of a paradigm shift to ESG. Many communities remain polluted while the people are displaced from their legitimate sources of socio-economic livelihood. Critical analysis of the ESG criteria shows that they align with the UNSDG and Agenda 2030 which compels oil and gas corporations to drive a sustainable environment through corporate governance whilst investing in renewables (Hills, 2020; O'Connor, 2022; Shastry, 2023). The marked difference between CSR and ESG is in their criteria, objectives, and expectations. The drafters of ESG give the impression that it ties in with human and infrastructure security in both the Global South and Global North. The integration of ESG criteria with UNSDG partly demonstrates the desire of the government to tackle the lingering socio-economic and environmental issues that underpin tensions and conflicts. It remains to be the extent that oil and gas companies operating in the Niger Delta will implement these emerging global environmental and social resolutions.

## CONCLUSION

Pipeline vandalism and insecurity of oil and gas infrastructures are threats that have defined the Nigerian oil and gas industry in the last 20 years. This section has stated many factors that facilitate and intensify vandalism and oil bunkering in Bayelsa and the wider Niger Delta region of Nigeria. The response of the government and the oil and gas industry has largely remained the same and the outcome has led to more cases of vandalism and oil theft. There have been decades of socio-economic and infrastructural stagnation in the Niger Delta. Early refusals to implement mutually agreed trade treaties and policies as well as the use of military force by the British, sowed the seed of distrust between residents and the British State. Nigerian institutions and structures have adopted these behaviours and continued to govern local communities in similar terms.

For instance, the Petroleum Degree of 1969 and the Land Use Decree of 1978 Alamieyeseigha (2008) and Douglas and Okonta (2003) argued are mirror evidence of pre-1895 oil palm trade treaties as well as the Mineral Ordinance Act of 1914 and 1946. This is why Ejiofor concluded that Shell and other oil and gas multinationals are neo-imperialistic representatives of the British and other western governments. Thus, persistency in mistrust and mutual suspicions, socio-economic stagnation, and political exclusion as well as the diverse problems caused by the construction of the NCTL are the sources of frustration leading to vandalism.

## References

Abidde, S. O. (2017). *Nigeria's Niger Delta: Militancy, Amnesty, and the Post Amnesty Environment*. Lexington.

Ablo, D. A. (2020). Enterprise Development? Local Content, Corporate Social Responsibility, and Disjunctive Linkages in Ghana's Oil and Gas Industry. *Extractive Industry and Society Journal, 7*(2), 321–327.

Achebe, C. (1984). *The Trouble with Nigeria*. Heinemann Educational Publishers.

Aderogba, A. (2016). Government Amnesty Programme and Peace Efforts in the Niger Delta Region: An Analysis of Newspaper Coverage. *European Scientific Journal, 12*(20), 1–12.

Aghedo, I., & Thomas, A. N. (2015). Security Architecture and Insecurity Management: Context, Content, and Challenges in Nigeria. *Sokoto Journal of the Social Sciences, 1*(4), 22–36.

Agudelo, M. A. L., Johannsdottir, L., & Davidsdottir, B. (2019). A Literature Review of the History and Evolution of Corporate Social Responsibility. *International Journal of Corporate Social Responsibility, 4*(1).

Ajibola, I. O. (2015). Nigeria's Amnesty Program: The Role of Empowerment in Achieving Peace and Development in Post-Conflict Niger Delta. *Sage Open*, 1–11. https://doi.org/10.1177/2158244015589996

Akemu, O., Comiteau, L. & Mes, A. (2018). Shell Nigeria: Changing the Community Engagement Model. In N. C. Smith & G. G. Lenssen, *Managing Sustainable Business: An Executive Education Case and Textbook*, pp. 273–297. Dordrecht: Springer.

Ako, R. (2011). Resource Exploitation and Environmental Justice: The Nigerian Experience. In F. N. Botchway (Ed.), *Natural Resource Investment, and Africa's Development* (pp. 50–72). Edward Elgar.

Ako, R. (2014). Environmental Justice in Nigeria's Oil Industry: Recognising and Embracing Contemporary Legal Developments. In R. V. Percival, J.

Lin, & W. Piermattei (Eds.), *Global Environmental Law at a Crossroads* (pp. 160–176). Edward Edger Publication.

Akpomera, E. (2015). International Crude Oil Theft: Elite Predatory Tendencies in Nigeria. *Review of African Political Economy Journal, 42*(143), 156–165.

Alagoa, E. J. (1999). *The Land and People of Bayelsa State: Central Niger Delta.* Onyema Research Publications.

Alagoa, E. J. (2005). *A History of the Niger Delta.* Onyema Research Publications.

Alamieyeseigha, D. S. P. (2008). The Environmental Challenge of Developing the Niger Delta. In S. S. Azaiki, D. S. P. Alamieyeseigha, & A. A. Ikein (Eds.), *Oil, Democracy and the Promise of True Federalism in Nigeria* (pp. 249–260). University Press of America.

Alshbili, I., Elamer, A. A., & Beddewela, E. (2020). Ownership Types Corporate Governance, and Corporate Social Responsibility Disclosures: Empirical Evidence from Developing Country. *Accounting Research Journal, 33*(1), 148–166.

Amnesty International Report. (2018). Amnesty International Report 2017/18: The State of the World's Human Rights, Available from https://www.amn esty.org/en/documents/pol10/6700/2018/en/. Accessed 7 May 2024.

Azubuike, V. (2021). International Court Orders Shell to Compensate Niger-Delta Communities over Oil Spillage. *Daily Post News.* https://dailypost.ng/ 2021/01/29/breaking-international-court-orders-shell-to-compensate-niger-delta-communities-over-oil-spillage/. Accessed 30 January 2021.

Baiyewu, L., & Akinkuotu, E. (2021, July 5). PIB: North, Ogun's Quest for Oil get Boost, Exploration Receives 30%. *The Punch News Paper.* https:// punchng.com/pib-north-oguns-quests-for-oil-get-boost-exploration-receiv es-30/. Accessed 8 July 2021.

Baku-Tbilisi-Ceyhan Corporation. (2014). *Protecting Pipelines-BTC as a Case Study.* In M. Edwards (Ed.), *Critical Infrastructure Protection* (pp. 55–58). IOS.

Balogun, A. O. (2018). Muhammed Chris Ali and the Politics in the Nigerian Army: A Philosophical Approach. In M. Dukor (Ed.), *Muhammed Chris Ali's The Federal Republic of Nigerian Army Symposium on Sage Philosophy* (pp. 24–57). Malthouse.

Bejakovic, P., & Mrnjavac, Z. (2018). The Dangers of Long-Term Unemployment and Measures for its Reduction: The Case of Croatia. *Economic Research Journal, 31*(1), 1837–1850.

Bergstresser, H. (2017). *A Decade of Nigeria: Politics, Economy and Society 2004–2016.* Brill.

Bruland, K. (1998). The Era of Corporate Capitalism. In K. Bruland & P. O'Brien (Eds.), *From Family Firms to Corporate Capitalism* (pp. 219–247). Claredon Press.

Coleman, J. S. (2015). The Politics of Sub-Saharan Africa. In A. G. Almond & J. S. Coleman (Eds.), *The Politics of the Developing Areas* (pp. 247–354). Princeton University Press.

Collier, P. (2007). *The Bottom Billion* (pp. 39–52). Oxford University Press.

Constitution of the Federal Republic of Nigeria. (1999). Third Amendment, Section 43(3). https://publicofficialsfinancialdisclosure.worldbank.org/sites/fdl/files/assets/law-library-files/Nigeria_Constitution_1999_en.pdf. Accessed 5 August 2020.

Dambo, L. B. (2006). *Nembe: The Divided Kingdom*. Paragraphs.

Dawson, T. (2021, November 25). Pipelines Will Be Blown Up, Says David Suzuki, If Leaders Don't Act on Climate Change. *National Post*. https://nationalpost.com/news/canada/pipelines-will-be-blown-up-says-david-suzuki-if-leaders-dont-act-on-climate-change. Accessed 25 November 2021.

Department of Petroleum Resources Flare-Gas-Prevention-of-Waste-and-Pollution-Regulations-Gazette. (2018, July 9). *Federal Republic of Nigeria Official* Gazette (Vol. 105(88)). https://ngfcp.dpr.gov.ng/media/1120/flare-gas-prevention-of-waste-and-pollution-regulations-2018-gazette-cleaner-copy-1.pdf. Accessed 10 August 2020.

Devold, H. (2013). *Oil and Gas Production Handbook: An Introduction to Oil and Gas Production* (pp. 6–146). ABB. https://library.e.abb.com/public/34d5b70e18f7d6c8c1257be500438ac3/Oil%20and%20gas%20production%20handbook%20ed3x0_web.pdf. Accessed 12 December 2017.

Doerffer, J. W. (2013). *Oil Spill Response in the Marine Environment*. Elsevier.

Douglas, O. (2008). A Community Guide to Understanding Resource Control. In A. Ikein, D. S. P. Alamieyeseigha & S. Azaiki, Oil, *Democracy, and the Promise of True Federalism* (pp.331–340). Maryland, University Press of America.

Douglas, O., & Okonta, I. (2003). *Where Vultures Feast: Shell, Human Rights, and Oil in the Niger Delta*. Verso.

Edigin, L., & Okonmah, I. E. (2010). Mystifying Development Policy Strategies in the Niger Delta: The Unending Mistake. *Journal of Research in National Development, 8*(2).

Ekpenyong, A. S. (2010). The Oil Economy, Environmental Laws, and Human Rights Violations in Niger Delta Region: Implications and Suggested Solutions. *International Journal of Social Policy Research and Development, 1*(2).

Eneh, S., & Enuoh, R. (2015). Corporate Social Responsibility in the Niger Delta Region of Nigeria: In Who's Interest? *Journal of Management and Sustainability, 5*(3), 74–82.

Environmental Impact Assessment Act. (1992). Environmental Impact Assessment Degree No. 86 (1992). https://faolex.fao.org/docs/pdf/nig18378.pdf. Accessed 7 May 2024.

Etekpe, A. (2018). The Challenges of Climate Change on the Livelihood and Sustainable Development of Selected Coastal Communities in Nigeria's Niger Delta (1990–2015). In V. U. James (Ed.), *Capacity Building for Sustainable Development* (pp. 254–264). CAB International.

Etemire, U. (2016). *Law and Practice on Public Participation in Environmental Matters: The Nigerian Example in Transnational Comparative Perspective.* Routledge.

Etete, E. (2017, July 7). Ovom in Yenagoa City: A Cradle of Development but Shadow of itself. *Headline News Nigeria.* http://headlinenewsnigeria.com/ovom-yenagoa-city-cradle-development-shadow/. Accessed 2 March 2018.

Etowah, U. E., & Effiong, S. A. (2012). Oil Spillage Cost Gas Flaring Cost, and Life Expectancy Rate of the Niger Delta People of Nigeria. *Advances in Management and Applied Economics Journal, 2*(2), 211–228.

Folorunsho, R., & Awosika, L. (2014). Estuaries and Ocean Circulation Dynamics in the Niger Delta, Nigeria: Implication for Oil Spill and Pollution Management. In S. Diop & J. P. Barusseau (Eds.), *The Land/Ocean Interactions in the Coastal Zone of West and Central Africa* (pp. 77–86). Springer.

Franks, S., & Nunnally, S. (2011). *Barbarians of Oil: How the World's Oil Addiction Threatens Global Prosperity and Four Investments to protect Your Wealth.* Wiley.

Friedman, M. (1993). The Social Responsibility of Business is to Increase its Profits. In G. D. Chryssides & J. H. Kaler (Eds.), *An Introduction to Business Ethics* (pp. 249–265). Thomson.

Goodall, J. (2010). *In the Shadow of Man.* Orion.

Grigg, N. S. (2010). *Infrastructure Finance: The Business of Infrastructure for a Sustainable Future.* Wiley.

Hashim, A. S., Gramescu, B., & Nitu, C. (2018). Pipe Leakage Detection Using Humidity and Microphones Sensors—A Review. In G. I. Gheorghe (Eds.), *Proceedings of the International Conference of Mechatronics and Cyber-Mix Mechatronics—2018* (pp. 129–137). Springer.

Hendriksz, M., Chetty, M., & Teljeur, E. (2017). Africa's Prospect for Infrastructure Development and Regional Integration: Energy Sector. In N. Ncube & C. L. Lufumpa (Eds.), *Infrastructure in Africa: Lessons for Development* (pp. 185–256). Policy Press.

Hill, J. (2020). *Environmental, Social, and Governance (ESG) Investing: A Balanced Analysis of the Theory and Practice of a Sustainable Portfolio.* Academic Press.

Idemudia, U. (2014), Oil Multinational Companies as Money Makers and Peace Makers: Lessons from Nigeria, In G. Eweje (eds.), *Corporate Social Responsibility and Sustainability: Emerging Trends in Developing Economies* (pp. 191–214). London, Emerald

Igbinovia, P. E. (2014). *Oil Thefts and Pipeline Vandalisation in Nigeria*. African Books.

Ikelegbe, A. (2013). The Crisis in Relations: Multinational Oil Companies and Host Communities in the Niger Delta. In A. Ikelegbe (Ed.), *Oil, Environment and Resource Conflicts in Nigeria*. Lit Verglag.

Intergovernmental Panel on Climate Change. (2022). *The Ocean and Cryosphere in a Changing Climate: Special Report of the Intergovernmental Panel on Climate Change*. Cambridge University Press.

Iwuoha, V. C. (2021). Strategic Security Planning and Protection of Multinational Oil Pipeline Assets in the Niger Delta International. *Journal of Intelligence, Security, and Public Affairs, 23*(3), 343–366. https://doi.org/10.1080/2300992.2021.2005933

Izuaka, M. (2021, March 29). Nigeria Will Continue to Rely on Natural Gas as a Transitional Fuel. *Premium Times*. https://www.premiumtimesng.com/business/business-news/451981-nigeria-will-continue-to-rely-on-natural-gas-as-a-transition-fuel-sylva.html. Accessed 8 July 2021.

Jaffee, D. (1998). *Levels of Socio-economic Development Theory* (2nd ed.). Praeger.

Janoski, T., Luke, D., & Oliver, C. (2014). *The Causes of Structural Unemployment: Four Factors that Keeps People from the Job they Deserve*. Polity Press.

Jatto, A. A., Skoczylis, J., & Horner, G. (2023). UK Anti-Money Laundering and Counter-Terrorist Financing Measures. In S. N. Romaniuk, C. Kaunert, & A. P. H. Fabe (Eds.), *Countering Terrorist and Criminal Financing* (1st ed.). Routledge & CRC Press. https://doi.org/10.4324/9781003092216. Accessed 18 November 2023.

John, M. (2017). *Al-Shabaab and Boko Haram: Guerrilla Insurgency or Strategic Terrorism*. World Scientific.

Johnsen, S. (2016). Mitigating Vulnerabilities in Oil and Gas Assets via Resilience. In M. Rice & S. Shenoi (Eds.), *Critical Infrastructure Protection X* (pp. 43–62). Springer.

Johnson, P. (2010). *Making the Market: Victorian Origins of Corporate Capitalism*. Cambridge University Press.

Khalid, I. (2021). Shell in Nigeria: Polluted Communities Can Sue in English Supreme Courts. *BBC News*. https://www.bbc.co.uk/news/world-africa-56041189. Accessed 13 February 2021.

Kuwornu, J. K. M. (2019). *Climate Change and Sub-Saharan Africa: The Vulnerability and Adaptation of Food Supply Chain Actors*. Vernon Art and Science Incorporated.

Kyuka, U. A. (2017). *Nigerian Oil and Gas Industry Law: Policies and Institutions*. Malthouse.

Land Use Act. (1978). Vesting of all land in the State; Control and management of land; advisory bodies; Designation of urban areas; Applicable law for the interim management of land. https://faolex.fao.org/docs/pdf/nig67625. pdf. Accessed 7 May 2024.

Land Use Act. (2004). *The Complete Laws of Nigeria, a Searchable Compendium.* Land Use Act. https://lawsofnigeria.placng.org/view2.php?sn=228. Accessed 20 February 2022.

Loucks, D. P. (2021). Impacts of Climate Change on Economies, Ecosystems, Energy, Environments, and Human Equity: A Systems Perspective. In T. M. Letcher (Ed.), *The Impacts of Climate Change: A Comprehensive Study of Physical, Biophysical, Social, and Political Issues* (pp. 20–39). Elsevier.

Leipziger, D. (2017). *The Corporate Responsibility Code Book.* Routledge.

Lewis, T. G. (2015). *Critical Infrastructure Protection in Homeland Security: Defending a Networked Nation* (2nd ed.). Wiley.

Lanoszka, A. (2018). *International Development: Socio-Economic Theories, Legacies, and Strategies.* Routledge.

Luong, P. J., & Weinthal, E. (2010). *Oil is Not a Curse.* Cambridge University Press.

Madubuko, C. C. (2017). Oiling the Guns and Gunning for Oil: The Youths and Niger Delta Oil Conflicts in Nigeria. In E. M. Mbah & T. Falola (Eds.), *Dissent, Protest and Dispute in Africa* (pp. 260–289). Routledge.

Mallin, C. (2016). *Corporate Governance* (5th ed.). Oxford University Press.

Mathias, B. A. (2011). The Social Effects of Oil Production in Gbaran Ubie, Bayelsa State, Nigeria. *International Journal of Development and Management Review*, Vol.6, 151–159.

Mathias, Z. (2015). Providing All-Round Security against Oil and Gas Infrastructure Sabotage and Physical Attacks on the Staff of NNPC and Multinational Oil Companies in Nigeria as a Critical Article of Her National Security Efforts. *International Journal of Social Science and Humanities Research, 3*(2), 45–59.

Mbu, M. T. (2018). *Dignity in Service.* Safari Books.

Mickolus, E. (2018). *Terrorism Worldwide, 2016.* McFarland and Company.

National Bureau of Statistics. (2017). *Social Statistics Report December 2016.* National Bureau of Statistics.

National Bureau of Statistics. (2020). *Labour Force Statistics: Unemployment and Underemployment Report: Abridged Labour Force Survey Under COVID-19.* National Bureau of Statistics. https://www.nigerianstat.gov.ng/pdfuploads/ Q2_2020_Unemployment_Report.pdf. Accessed 26 May 2021.

National Climate Change Policy. (2021). Federal Ministry of Environment, Department of Climate Change: Climate Change Policy for Nigeria 2021–2030. https://climatechange.gov.ng/wp-content/uploads/2021/08/ NCCP_NIGERIA_REVISED_2-JUNE-2021.pdf. Accessed 22 February 2022.

National Environmental Standards and Regulation Enforcement Agency Act. (2007). Discharge of Hazardous Substance and Related Offences. http://lawsofnigeria.placng.org/laws/nesrea.pdf. Accessed 22 February 2022.

National Oil Spill Detection and Response Agency (Establishment) Act. (2006). As Amended. http://extwprlegs1.fao.org/docs/pdf/nig124170A.pdf. Accessed 5 August 2020.

Nicholas, A., Mitchell, J., & Lindner, S. (2013). *Consequences of Long-Term Unemployment*. The Urban Institute.

Niger Delta Development Commission Act. (2000). Functions and Powers of the Commission. https://www.chr.up.ac.za/images/researchunits/bhr/files/extractive_industries_database/nigeria/laws/Niger-Delta%20Development%20Commission.pdf. Accessed 22nd February 2022.

Nigeria Climate Change Act. (2021). Climate Change Act 2021, An Act to provide for the mainstreaming of climate change actions, establish the National Council on Climate Change; and for related matters. https://cdn.climatepolicyradar.org/navigator/NGA/2021/nigerias-climate-change-act_6c83884695bbf609fcd795a49d196e89.pdf. Accessed 7 May 2024.

Nigeria Mineral and Mining Act. (2011). Administration of the Act. http://admin.theiguides.org/Media/Documents/Nigeruian%20Minerals%20and%20Mining%20Act,%202007.pdf. Accessed 5 October 2022.

Numbere, A. O. (2018). The Impact of Oil and Gas Exploration: Invasive Nypa Palm Species and Urbanisation on Mangroves in the Niger River Delta, Nigeria, In C. Makowski & C. W. Finkl, *Threats to Mangrove Forests: Hazards, Vulnerability, and Management* (pp. 247–266). London, Springer.

Nwuke, K. (2021). *Nigeria's Petroleum Industry Act: Addressing Old Problems, Creating New Ones*. Africa in Focus. https://www.brookings.edu/blog/africa-in-focus/2021/11/24/nigerias-petroleum-industry-act-addressing-old-problems-creating-new-ones/. Accessed 19 February 2022.

Odudu, C. O. (2017). Compensation Issues in the Niger Delta-A Case Study of Boboroku Jesse, Delta State, Nigeria. *International Journal of Civil Engineering, Construction and Estate Management, 5*(4), 21–43.

Ogunleye, E. K. (2017). Political Economy of Nigerian Power Sector Reform. In D. Arent, C, Arndt, M. Miller, F. Tarp, & O. Zinaman (Eds.), *The Political Economy of Clean Energy Transitions* (pp. 391–409). Oxford University Press.

Oil Pipeline Act. (1956). An Act to make provision for licenses to be granted for the establishment and maintenance of pipelines incidental and supplementary to oil fields and oil mining, and for purposes ancillary to such pipelines- No. 31.1965 No. 24, https://faolex.fao.org/docs/pdf/nig44569.pdf. Accessed 7 May 2024.

Oil Pipeline Act. (2004). Chapter 338: Laws of the Federal Republic of Nigeria. https://www.chr.up.ac.za/images/researchunits/bhr/files/extractive_industries_database/nigeria/laws/Oil%20Pipelines%20Act.pdf. Accessed 28 March 2020.

Okafor, N. (2016). *Reconstructing Law and Justice in a Postcolony*. Routledge.

Okonjo-Iweala, N. (2018). *Fighting Corruption is Dangerous: The Story Behind the Headlines*. MIT Press.

Okonkwo, E. C. (2020). *Environmental Justice and Oil Pollution Laws: Comparing Enforcement in the United States and Nigeria* (1st ed.). Routledge.

Okonofua, B. A. (2016). The Niger Delta Amnesty Program: The Challenges of Transitioning from Peace Settlements to Long-Term Peace. *Sage Open Journals, 6*(2), 1–16.

Okonta, I. (2016). Policy Incoherence and the Challenge of Energy Security. In A. Goldthau (Ed.), *The Handbook of Global Energy Policy* (pp. 501–520). Wiley.

Okumagba, P. (2012). Oil Exploration and Crisis in the Niger Delta: The Response of the Militia Groups. *Journal of Sustainable Society, 1*(3), 78–83.

Okumagba, P. (2013). Ethnic Militia and Criminality in the Niger Delta. *International Review of Social Sciences and Humanities, 5*(1), 239–246.

Olalere, O. P. (2021, August 19 Monday). Nigeria: Behold the Brand-New Nigerian Petroleum Industry Act, 2021. https://www.mondaq.com/nigeria/oil-gas-electricity/1103114/behold-the-brand-new-nigerian-petroleum-industry-act-2021. Accessed 19 February 2022.

Olawuyi, D. S. (2012). Legal and Sustainable Development Impacts of Major Oil Spills. *The Journal of Sustainable Development, 9*(1), 1–15.

Oluyemi, A. O. (2020). The Military Dimension of Niger Delta Crisis and its Implications on Nigeria National Security. *Sage Open Journal*. https://doi.org/10.1177/2158244020922895

Omagu, D. O. (2012). Oil Multinationals: 'Environmental Genocide' and Socioeconomic Development in Nigeria's Niger Delta. In T. Falola & A. Paddock (Eds.), *Environment and Economics in Nigeria* (pp. 107–124). Routledge.

Omand, D. (2011). *Securing the State*. C. Hurst, and Co.

Omeje, K. (2017a). *Extractive Economies and Conflicts in the Global South: Multi-regional Perspectives on Rentier Politics*. Taylor and Francis.

Omeje, K. (2017b). *High Stakes and Stakeholders: Oil Conflict and Security in Nigeria*. Routledge.

Omeje, K. (2017c). The Egbesu and Bakassi Boys: African Spiritism and Mystical Re-rationalisation of Security. In D. J. Francis (Ed.), *Civil Militia: Africa's Intractable Security Menace* (pp. 71–86). Routledge.

Omeni, A. (2018). *Counterinsurgency in Nigeria: The Military and Operations against Boko Haram, 2011–2017*. Routledge.

Ong, D. (2017). Litigation against Multinational Oil Companies in their Home State Jurisdictions: An Alternative Legal Response to Pollution Damage in Foreign Jurisdictions? In C. Tan & J. Faundez (Eds.), *Natural Resources and Sustainable Development: International Economic Law Perspectives* (pp. 278–297). Edward Elgar.

Onuoha, C. F. (2008). Oil Pipeline Sabotage in Nigeria: Dimensions, Actors and Implications for National Security. *African Security Review, 17*(3), 100–115.

Onuoha, C. F. (2016). *The Resurgence of Militancy in Nigeria's Oil-Rich Niger Delta and the Dangers of Militarisation*. Al Jazeera Centre for Studies.

Ordor, A., & Abe, O. (2021). Local Content Requirements and Social Inclusion in Global Energy Markets: Towards Business and Human Rights Content. In D. S. Olawuyi (Eds.), *Local Contents, and Sustainable Development in Global Energy Markets* (pp. 392–412). Cambridge University Press.

Oriola, B. T. (2016). *Criminal Resistance: The Politics of Kidnapping Oil Workers*. Routledge.

Oriola, T. B. (2013). *Criminal Resistance?: The Politics of Kidnapping Oil Workers*. Ashgate publication.

O'Connor, B. (2022). *The ESG Investment Handbook: Insights and Developments in Environmental, Social and Governance Investment*. Harriman House.

Osuntogun, A. J. (2020). Rights to Development of Indigenous Peoples of Africa: A Quest for the Adoption of Resource Control Mechanism for Effective Protection. In C. C. Ngang & S. D. Kamga (Eds.), *Insights into Policies and Practices on the Right to Develop* (pp. 133–161). Rowman and Littlefield.

Otokunefor, H. O. C. (2017). *Nigerian Petroleum Industry, Policies, and Conflicts Relations* (Vol. 2). Malthouse.

Oxford English Dictionary. (2016). Oxford Dictionary of English, (Stevenson, A. eds.), https://www.oxfordreference.com/display/10.1093/acref/978019 9571123.001.0001/acref-9780199571123. Accessed 7 May 2024.

Partain, A. (2017). *Environmental Hazards from Offshore Methane Hydrates Operations: Civil Liberties and Regulations for Efficient Governance*. Kluwer.

Petroleum Industry Act. (2021). PIA: Explanatory Memorandum, https://eproofing.springer.com/ePb/books/pnXXkMoim97Z_a_rMD9rZeEbrTrR UQmOXjtKXvfLWedcljNJBuXmZZBNYj-SztuHljv8yt2gL-1Cc-g7hvQhrTo jgqtjLQ2jAUWQdwYTjfbm05PWXyArOed10ZI9Y9nrGYFRl5Bl8liyVB1q XexaAf17alFTrZ7252zWyo2Ivrw=. Accessed 4 May 2024.

Philp, M. (2015). The Definition of Political Corruption. In P. M. Heywood (Ed.), *Routledge Handbook of Political Corruption* (pp. 17–30). Routledge.

Ramsay, A. (2021). Climate Action is Nigeria's Chance to Free Itself from the Tyranny of Oil. *Open Democracy.* https://www.opendemocracy.net/en/climate-action-is-nigerias-chance-to-free-itself-from-the-tyranny-of-oil/. Accessed 24 November 2021.

Rukeh, R. A. (2015). Oil Spill Management in Nigeria: SWOT Analysis of the Joint Investigation Visit (JIV) Process. *Journal of Environmental Protection,* 6, 259–267.

Sanderson, C. A. (2010). *Social Psychology.* Wiley.

Saro-Wiwa, K. (1992). *Genocide in Nigeria: The Ogoni Tragedy.* African Books.

Sayne, A. (2013). *Special Report: What's Next for the Security in the Niger Delta?* United States Institute of Peace.

Sayne, A., & Katsouris, C. (2015). *Nigeria's Criminal Crude: International Options to Combat the Export of Stolen Oil.* Chatham House.

Scheffran, J. & BenDor, T. K. (2018). Agent-Based Modeling of Environmental Conflict and Cooperation, London, CRC Press.

Spellman, F. R. (2016). *Energy Infrastructure Protection and Homeland Security.* Bernan Press.

Shastry, V. (2023). *The Notorious ESG: Business, Climate, and the Race to Save the Planet.* Emerald.

Schwab, K. (2021). *Stakeholder Capitalism: A Global Economy that Works for Progress, People, and Planet.* Wiley.

Shakespeare, W. (1807). *Julius Caesar.* John Cawthorn.

Shaw, W. H. (2016). *Business Ethics: A Textbook with Cases* (9th ed.). Cengage.

Shaw, W. H. & Barry, V. (2015). Moral Issues in Business, (13th Eds.), London, Cengage.

Shoewu, O., Akinyemi, L. A., Ayanlowo, K. A., Olatinwo, So. O. & Makanjuola, N. T. (2013). Mechatronics System: Spying and Reporting Vandalism, *Journal of Science and Engineering,* 1(2), pp. 134–142.

Sinden, A. (2009). An Emerging Human Rights to Security from Climate Change: The Case Against Gas Flaring in Nigeria. In W. C. G. Burns & H. M. Osofsky (Eds.), *Adjudicating Climate Change: State, National, and International Approaches* (pp. 173–192). Cambridge University Press.

Spermann, A. (2015). How to Fight Long-Term Unemployment: Lessons from Germany. *IZA Journal of Labour Policy,* 4(1), 4–15.

Suberu, R. T. (2019). Constitutional Infidelity and Federalism in Nigeria. In C. M. Fombad & N. Steytler (Eds.), *Decentralisation and Constitutionalism in Africa* (pp. 101–132). Oxford Press.

Sullivant, J. (2007). *Strategies for Protecting National Critical Infrastructure Assets: A Focus on Problem-Solving.* Wiley.

Timashev, S. & Bushinskaya, A. (2016). Methods of Assessing Integrity of Pipeline Systems with Different Types of Defects. In S. Timashev and A.

*Bushinskaya, Diagnostics and Reliability of Pipeline Systems*, Vol.30 (pp. 9–43), Cham, Springer.

Transparency International. (2019). Military Involvement in Oil Theft in the Niger Delta. https://ti-defence.org/publications/military-involvement-in-oil-theft-in-the-niger-delta/. Accessed 25 November 2020.

Tyler, T. R. (2004). Enhancing Police Legitimacy. *The ANNALS of the American Academy of Political and Social Science, 593*(1), 84–99.

Ukiwo, U. (2011). The Nigerian State, Oil, and the Niger Delta Crisis. In C. Obi & S. A. Rustad (Eds.), *Oil and Insecurity in the Niger Delta* (pp. 2–15). Zed Books.

Ukiwo, U. (2020). Nigeria's Oil Governance Regime: Challenges and Policies. In A. Langer, U. Ukiwo, & P. Mbabazi (Eds.), *Oil Wealth and Development in Uganda and Beyond: Prospects, Opportunities and Challenges* (pp. 309–331). Leuven University Press.

Umar, A. T., & Othman, M. S. H. (2017). Causes and Consequences of Crude oil Pipeline Vandalism in the Niger Delta of Nigeria: A Confirmatory Factor Analysis Approach. *Cogent Economics and Finance Journal, 5*(1), 1–15.

Umukoro, B. (2009). Gas Flaring, Environmental Corporate Responsibility and the Right to a Healthy Environment: Case of the Niger Delta. In F. Emiri & G. Deinduomo (Eds.), *Law and Petroleum Industry in Nigeria: Current Challenges* (pp. 36–49). Malthouse.

United Nations Environment Programme Report. (2012). Environmental Assessment of Ogoniland: Assessment of Vegetation, Aquatic and Public Health Issues. http://hdl.handle.net/20.500.11822/25286. Accessed 9 May 2018.

United Nations Framework Convention on Climate Change. (2010). Report of the Conference of the Parties on its Sixteenth Session, held in Cancun from 29 November to 10 December 2010. https://unfccc.int/sites/default/files/resource/docs/2010/cop16/eng/07a01.pdf. Accessed 16 February 2022.

Utebor, S. (2021). Shell, Bayelsa Communities at Loggerheads over Oil Spillages, The Nations. https://thenationonlineng.net/. Accessed 02 November 2021.

Vanguard News. (2021). State of the Nation: Nigeria No Longer Working-Obadiah, Utomi, Henshaw, Ademolekun, others, Vanguard News, 21 February. Available from https://www.vanguardngr.com/2021/02/state-of-the-nation-nigeria-nolonger-working-obadiah-utomi-henshaw-adamolekun-others/. Accessed 14th February 2022.

Vetter, S., Endrass, J., Schweizer, I., Teng, H. M., Rossler, W., & Gallo, W. T. (2006). The Effects of Economic Deprivation on Psychological Well-being Amongst the Working Population of Switzerland. *BMC Public Health, 6*(223), 1–10.

Visser, W. (2017). *The Quest for Sustainable Business: An Epic Journey in Search of Corporate Responsibility*. Routledge.

Warren, D., Biringer, B., & Vugrin, E. D. (2016). *Critical Infrastructure System Security and Resilience*. CRC.

Wetzel, J. R. M. (2016). *Human Rights in Transnational Business: Translating Human Rights Obligations into Compliance Procedures*. Springer.

Wight, J. B., & Morton, J. S. (2007). Teaching the Ethical Foundations of Economics, New York, Council of Economic Education.

Wright, B. (2003). Race, Politics and Pollution: Environmental Justice in the Mississippi River Chemical Corridor. In J. Agyeman, R. D. Bullard, & B. Evans (Eds.), *Just Sustainabilities: Development in an Unequal World* (pp. 125–145). MIT Press.

# CHAPTER 5

# Security and Theoretical Explanation of Pipeline Vandalism in Bayelsa State, Nigeria

They have sown the wind, and they shall reap the whirlwind…
(Hosea, 8:7a; King James Version)

## UNDERSTANDING SECURITY CONCEPTS

This section discusses security concepts around international, national, and human security approaches. The practice of security has continuously been dominated by "moral and ethical" debates. According to Heurlin and Kristensen security was conceptualised as a national object and military power by Lippmann after the Second World War (2010). While rejecting the hierarchical, androcentric, and exclusionary undertone with which states describe security. Oswald suggested that to do justice to the concept, we must understand the origin of security (2009). As social issues evolved, nation-states are shifting their focus away from confrontation. Often, states now seek to cooperate to overcome their *security dilemmas*. Nation-states are conceptualising security practice as a source of mutual trust, benefit, and cooperation rather than the traditional position of strength, military might, and force (Wang & Deng, 2005). The dynamics and process of achieving security are changing from a *zero-sum* game to a *win–win* relationship (Zhao, 2011). A functional security system is increasingly been tied to the socio-economic development of a community. The socio-economic development of communities

A. L. A. Jatto, *Oil and Gas Pipeline Infrastructure Insecurity*, New Security Challenges, https://doi.org/10.1007/978-3-031-56932-6_5

131

is now integral to the practice of contemporary security. Schechter points out that the declining use of military force and the expanding scope of security muddle the academic role of security (2016).

Spring defines security as the state, feeling, or means of being secured. That is protection from attacks, theft, and a surety or defence against attacks as well as freedom from fear and danger (2009). Others argued that security is a state where human beings should not worry over social insecurities (Oswald, 2009). This study argues that security should be viewed from the lens of "responsibility" and "concern for" something. It is difficult to study security from a limited perspective because of its complex connotations. From another perspective, some scholars have extended security studies to socio-economic, political, and environmental justice (Emmers, 2016; Hudson, 2010). The capacity to deliver socio-economic and political goods lay mostly with the political authorities. At times, some politicians however are motivated by selfish interests to depoliticise crucial social issues under the pretext of providing more security. It is possible that integrating some social demands into political debate could mitigate tensions that degenerate into insecurity because the collective masses can participate in the process of resolving some of the issues that matters to them.

Booth and Jones believe that the expansion of the security concept relegates Machiavellian and Hobbesian realism that focuses on state-centric security (2007, 2014). Given that excessive expansion of security away from its traditional sense could spell danger for the subject (Curley & Pettiford, 1999). The gains of globalisation support expanding security concepts to nonphysical and social objects (Cha, 2011). After decades of dominating international relations, theorists like Buzan and Hansen as well as Hough believe that security should be studied from the stability or instability of the state (2009, 2004). They stressed that the citizens are only secured when the state is secured. Machiavellian and Hobbesian realism is corroborated by Booth and Jones who insisted that realism should influence the referent point of security, determine threat characteristics, and suggest experts that will interpret the concept (2007, 2014). Although the security of the state that protects citizens from external attacks may be a necessary condition for the security of individuals, a secured state might not necessarily translate automatically into a secured people (Human Security Report Project, 2013; Poku & Therkelsen, 2016). While Mills says security and liberty are synonymous because the security of persons and properties are the first needs of society

(1863). To Baldwin (1998) and Buzan (1984a, b), the whole concept of security should be reconceptualised. Given that most definitions focus on the security policy agenda of nation-states rather than focusing on the concept of security.

It is important to understand the extent of a constructivist influence that an actor has over what is security and what security issues are as objects of analysis (Krahmann, 2008). The expected outcomes of security influenced its division into three meanings, conceptually distinguished across levels of analysis and threats. Krahmann says security is first seen as the "absence of a threat. Existing threats that are suspended in the realm of possibilities, and the third meaning defines security as the survival of a threat that does become a reality" (2008: 382). Irrespective of the complexities and controversies surrounding its scope, meaning, and practice security continues to occupy the central part of geopolitics, geoeconomics, and international relations between countries in the Global South and the Global North. "No other concept in international relations packs the metaphysical punch and commands than the disciplinary power of security" (James, 1995: 24). Security should identify existential threats, emerging responses, and outcomes of inter-unit relations (Buzan & Hansen, 2009). This way everything does not become a security issue in practice. Wolfers describes security as objective; absence of threats to acquired values, and subjective; absence of fear that acquired values would be attacked (1952). Baldwin (1998) describes this as a "low probability of damage to acquired value". Macy and Fierke further conceptualised security into traditional and non-conventional or non-traditional security. They identified military, political, diplomatic, as well as human, climate, and civil liberty as non-conventional forms of security-political security (2016, 2015). The non-conventional approach to security is supported by the United Nations Development Program Report (1994) and Pirates (2013: 139). Given its fluidity and protection of individual's safety and wellbeing, as itemised in the 1994 UNDP human security benchmark or/ and index. Kashubsky (2016) Herbst and Ndlangisa (2010), and Waltz (2000) also divide security into traditional, security as a public good, and security in a universal sense. The marked difference between traditional and non-traditional perspectives of security lay in the debates and postulations about domestic and world views (Baldwin, 1998).

Buzan and Hansen (2009) raised four questions that should refocus and address the concept of security:

(1) Should states be the central referent object of security
(2) Should internal and external threats be included in the security concept? They also questioned
(3) Whether security should be expanded beyond the traditional sector and the deployment of force and finally
(4) Whether security should be viewed as inextricably tied to a dynamic of threats, danger, and urgency.

Hough points out that *Understanding Global Security,* the defining paradigm of international relations, provided a different conceptual framework (2004). Various international political intricacies, in many ways, directed the thinking about security issues in international relations. Booth explained that the ability of individuals, small groups, and human society to inflict destructive damage on each other and the natural world constitutes the biggest threat to human existence (2007). His views are grounded in Emmer and Hudson's statements that the conceptualisation of security should include complex political dynamics and international diplomatic conflicts (2016, 2021). To the inalienable rights of citizens, security should not be restricted to its traditional purview of freedom from obvious and implied fear. By the very nature of the concept, security is not expected to protect the inalienable rights of citizens rather Emmer and Hudson stated that security seeks political powers to curtail the inalienable rights of citizens. Hence, security should be tied to the existence of the state because security by itself without the state and the state without security is meaningless. If only public protests are allowed to reinforce civil liberties in societies as Thoreau noted (2016) raises the question of what security is.

This book argues that security cannot simply be the absence of insecurity, which cannot be achieved. A concrete and absolute security situation could only be experienced in a state of "Utopia"-which is an ideal nation-state that provides near-perfect quality of life for its citizens (More, 2020, 1516). The socio-political tensions and conflicts that trigger insecurity situations in Bayelsa are inherent miscommunication and misrepresentation between the government, the local communities, and the oil and gas firms. Whether human beings can thrive and achieve social and psychological satisfaction in a state where everything is near perfect is not guaranteed. From the foregoing, it makes sense to point out that the insecurity situation remains fluid and dynamic across different climes as experienced in the Niger Delta. Cordesman noted that it takes many years for the best regimes to meet popular demands, hopes, and expectations due to the universality of struggles and challenges (2016). Creating institutions that support, protect, and transparently settle conflicts between citizens and the state where the hopes and aspirations of citizens clash with the policy direction of the state is more proactive- which is what political security should be. Rather than creating laws that take away the fundamental human rights of citizens in the name of providing *more* security which is the practice in the historic Niger Delta.

Security is therefore defined in this thesis as the creation of effective structures and instruments designed to transparently address external threats as well as internal tensions and conflicts that arise from human interactions. Attention should be given to both human security which is the defense of the inalienable rights of citizens (political security) and the state as central referent points. This study believes security should be practiced as a sense of responsibility to citizens while demonstrating "concern for" the territorial integrity of the nation-state. The fact that no nation has fully achieved security is a pitfall of security in representative capitalist democracies. This is an outcome (poor security) of capitalist representative democracies Brennan points out have not been good enough partly because human needs are ignored (2016). Therefore, security may also involve the politics of securitisation and desecuritisation. Securitisation theory advocates that security is a speech act that when altered suggests something has been done by the securitising actor (Neocleous, 2007). Desecuritisation is when something is removed from the security framework and introduced into political debate.

Nigeria adopts and practices more of the traditional state-centric security principles rather than the Copenhagen nonconventional approaches. Securing Nigeria should be intricately tied to the protection of the socio-economic as well as human and environmental values and identities of its citizens and local communities across the country (see Huq above on human security). This is the core of political security. As Richards says a secured nation-state protects itself from internal and external threats while creating a conducive environment for its citizens to aspire for the greater good and individual prosperity (2015). Conventional and non-conventional divisions of security created non-conventional critiques attempting to re-conceptualise security based on emerging contemporary international realities. Owen and Brennan suggest that it does little justice to define security from the close perspective of military reality (2004, 2016). Since it completely overlooks and eliminates threats, social issues, and risks. The insecurity in Nembe and Bayelsa state demonstrates this point. Newman and Mclean say the demise of conventional wars has been replaced by emerging tensions and violent intra-state wars due to gains in globalisation, identity, and global politics (2004, 2000).

State security practice draws upon the wider conceptualisation of security. It focuses on the protection of oil workers, pipelines, oil fields, oil wells, export terminals, refineries, and transportation facilities like ships from threats of vandalism, bunkering, and illegal refining. Many scholars say the protection of the citizens and their institutions is the core function of the state. Stressing that, security is supposed to draw on national contexts and ontological meaning to create and/or trigger an interesting collective. They noted that civil liberties such as freedom of expression and assembly, which are some of the defining principles of democracies, have been eroded by enhanced executive powers. As demonstrated in the failure of the Nigerian government and oil firms to resolve the underlying issues that cause pipeline vandalism. An open discussion about the impact of oil and gas extraction and related state policies on oil and gas infrastructure insecurity in the Niger Delta region is necessary. The implementation of policies that enable oil corporations to continue to destroy the environment and impoverish communities without any consequences is how oil and gas infrastructure insecurity is been manufactured in the Niger Delta. Thus, a deeper understanding of the process of manufacturing environments and poverty problems would be a rational precursor for conceptualising a security model for Nigeria. According to Neocleous depoliticisation of social issues and wrapping them with a security blanket reduces and exposes the citizens to the mercy of government and corporate powers (2007). In Nigeria and as in many countries in the Global South, the practice of security centres on protecting the status quo. The Nigerian government's security mechanisms focus on sideling local communities at the expense of alienating human rights and the abuse of civil liberties.

Current security practices in Nigeria, Zimbabwe, Venezuela, Colombia, are many other petrostates in the Global South erode civil liberties at different levels. States assets are deployed for the protection of those engaging in poor governance, particularly the few corruptly benefiting from oil and gas resources. Such practices do little to change the underlying causes of pipeline vandalism, oil and gas infrastructure insecurity, and the wider problem of insecurity across Nigeria but rather exacerbate the problem. According to Xiaofeng and Jia (2016) and

Masys (2016) integrating conventional and non-conventional security models proposes the best approach to achieving national security. The reality is that the Nigerian state does not seem to have any interest in developing the prevention, protection, and resilience security model. The security architecture in Nigeria, as elsewhere, is mainly about the protection of a small group of political and corporate personalities. State security philosophy should go beyond the traditional approach which is the focus of Nigeria as demonstrated in their security operations to Bayelsa-protection. It should include the prevention and resilience elements as well as extend through the whole non-conventional spectrum of security (Lawrence, 2013; Owen, 2004). The Nigerian government deploys military power to protect the oil and gas infrastructure, even when it means a violation of collective community liberty. Security in the Niger Delta cannot improve without addressing the underlying issues that cause the vandalism of the NCTL oil and gas pipeline infrastructure, in the first place. Implying that political security is the appropriate way forward. This links with the *prevention* element of the three-security approach developed by the Spanish (Lawrence, 2013). Focusing on the traditional approach alone explains why nothing changes but explains little about why the state is not bothered or interested in addressing the underlying causes of the problem.

The traditional state security approach Nigeria adopts means neglecting the provision of socio-economic needs for the citizens (Thurston, 2019). This leads to the worsening of its insecurity problems, demonstrated by way of Community-Neglect- Aggression-Displacement. This behaviour is consistent in the Niger Delta and across other regions of Nigeria and in tandem with what is observed in local communities in the Global South. Transparency International emphasised that Nigeria's security strategy is complex, unclear, and riddled with corruption, and internal conflict (2019). The lack of depth and content in Nigeria's security architecture especially policies, processes, empirical research-based databases, and relevant knowledge is traced to corruption, a dearth of expertise, and funding (Otobo, 2016; see Chapter 8). Therefore, Ikelegbe and Oshita argued that Nigeria's state security is essentially reactive (2019). Worsened by the inadequacy of its intelligence, reconnaissance, surveillance driven security management. Thereby exposing Nigeria's security to extensive corrupt political manipulations and interference. The Nigerian government consistently made the flawed assumption that the deployment of more security in the Niger Delta, at the expense of addressing the extreme socio-economic devastations in the area, would provide increased security for oil and gas infrastructure, particularly onshore pipelines. But it has not worked out that way. An agonising Bayelsa woman accurately summed this up by stating that: "If we had known that this is what oil exploration would turn into, we would have told the white people right from the onset to hold it, for not long after they started, our suffering began…" (Abah, 2011: 4).

The reality of her expression is that there are increased conflicts and militancy, pollution, multiplication of widows, increased number of out of school children, displacement, traumatised people who have suffered continued injustice by the state. Exclusion and brutality on top of the frustration suffered from oil activities and not mere criminality drive militancy in the case study area. Mickolus (2018), Onuoha (2016) and Linden and Palsson (2013) stated that the insecurity problems in Bayelsa and the historic Niger Delta region are tied to the outcome of the human impacts of oil and gas activities. The use of raw state power or what Neocleous described as *prerogative powers* to quell agitations in the Niger Delta violates fundamental principles of executive prerogative (2007). The insecurity in the Niger Delta is a combination of the activities of the state, national elites, and the multinational oil corporations combined with the locals that are reacting to the situation. Nigerian citizens should not tolerate the use of such *prerogative powers* nor accept the use of brute force for civil and conventional policing duties, as witnessed during the 2020 *EndSars* national protest, as normal (BBC News, 2021; Osawaru, 2020).

The general fear in Bayelsa and indeed the concerns expressed by Alagoa, Okumagba, Onuoha, Olawuyi, and Igbinovia is the frequency of the deployment of military assets to the area. The deployment of the Nigerian military and security agencies to the historic Niger Delta continues to aggravate the insecurity situation. Although military deployment might be sometimes necessary during an emergency, the problem lies in the frequency at which the function of civil policing is suspended. The danger is that when the police return to the communities they often carry on their duties with military tactics as though they too are responding to an emergency that threatens the national territorial integrity, thus the community perceives them as hostile. The idea of "policing in military" guise gradually legitimises the use of brute force and normalisation of force which soon becomes the rule of law tipping the balance of security against and over civil liberty. This can erode some core democratic principles leading to the gradual re-introduction of absolutism and authoritarianism.

## Human Security

The concept of human security is an upshot of reflections on *individual security* theory by Blatz (1966). According to Haq, "human security encapsulates everything about human dignity"-part of the human security agenda called "political security" (Haq, 1995: 116; UNDR, 1994). While crafting the UNDP Human Development Report Haq articulates a universal, preventative, people-centred approach that focused on freedom from fear and wants thereby setting the tone for the futuristic definitions of human security. Although the core characteristics of human security are "people-centred, multi-sectoral, comprehensive, context-specific, and prevention-oriented" (UNOCHA, 2009: 7). Other scholars like Jatto and Stanislas argued that it is difficult to align human security principles with Nigeria and other Sub-Saharan African conventional security practices, realities, and frameworks (2017). Particularly the military deployment in the Niger Delta (Jatto & Stanislas, 2017). The neglect of creating socio-economic well-being without bothering about human and material resources Jatto and Stanislas noted leaves a gap in the practice of security (2017). That gap is where the tensions and conflicts that trigger Community Neglect-Aggression Displacement feed upon.

The friction lay in the difficulty of integrating the expectations of international agencies like the United Nations with the security approaches promoted by Nigeria and other Sub-Saharan African countries. Particularly in *hybrid security governance* which Ahram, Bagayoko say is the interaction and integration of state security practices with those of different armed non-state actors in policing and provision of security (2021, 2016). The United Nations Human Development Report (UNHDR) defines human security as people's "safety from chronic threats and protection from sudden hurtful disruptions in the patterns of daily life" (1994: 116). Human security definition draws on freedom from chronic threats such as hunger, diseases, and repression as well as protection from sudden calamities for individuals and communities which are the two dimensions of the 1994 UNHDR.

The human security approach requires institutions to be preventive and protective in providing institutionalised responses to tensions and threats rather than being rigid and arbitrary. Alkire pointed out that the human security approach parallels the movement in economic development and international law to shift the focus of emphasis from instrumental policy objectives like growth, or state rights, to human development and human rights (2003). Although universally applicable, Human security is limited by the scope of protection of fundamental human rights such as survival, livelihood, and dignity regardless of ideology, race social preference, creed, religion, or nationality. It does not entirely cover all important and expanded aspects of human life. The prioritisation of human rights and capability which is seen by some to be fundamental is a difficult value judgment that is however worthy of consideration if human security is to be achieved. Human security does not isolate state security practice rather it encapsulates all forms and agendas of security which includes the defence of the territorial integrity of the state which is a precursor to achieving core human security values.

These days the most severe forms of tensions and conflicts that lead to insecurity arise from local conflicts over common interests like the environment. This book aligns with the claim by Cordesman that security must be developed based on meeting human needs such as food, shelter, and health while countering violence because repression of dissenting voices alone cannot bring stability to any nation (2016). This suggests that the individual is the *irreducible base unit* for discussing security. Human security realities in Bayelsa and the historic Niger Delta lack the core principles of human security advocated by UNDP (1994, 2017) and Owen (2004). Buzan argues that the individual should attract the centre focus in the national security debate which links to human security (Buzan, 1984a, b). The crafters of human security are acutely aware that insecurities, tensions, and social disorders vary considerably across different settings. The activities of oil and gas firms on the Nembe environment and the lack of regulatory implementation impact the natural human security architecture (accessing the fishing waters and farmlands to meet the economic and cultural needs) in Bayelsa state. The distortion of these natural socio-economic security arrangements in Nembe communities and Bayelsa state is responsible for some of the underlying socio-economic factors that trigger anger and frustration which leads to vandalism. Owen and the UNDP described the provision of socio-economic and environmental well-being of communities as human security or political security (2004, 1994). The next section uses FADT to explain how the combined anger and frustration lead to vandalism and insecurity situations.

## Frustration-Aggression-Displacement Theory

The security and peace of the Niger Delta are tied to the sustenance of the natural habitat and the socio-economic and cultural wellbeing of the residents. Interference with this structure has triggered aggressive reactions leading to violent social conflicts and insecurity in the region. Anger, frustration, and tensions do not cause insecurity problems, on their own. Insecurity problems are caused by underlying issues like the government's failure to tackle poverty, refusal to acknowledge socio-economic and political policy conflicts, or bridging the inequality gap. The political isolation and environmental devastation which disrupt the daily lives of Bayelsa communities also cause insecurity problems. Law and order breakdown where numerous issues of frustration, tensions, and anger remain unresolved. The tensions and insecurity problems in Bayelsa are not restricted to socio-economic and political issues alone (see Chapter 8). FADT explains the aggression of local communities against government security forces, pipelines and other oil and gas infrastructure, and oil and gas operators. It does not examine aspects of Nigeria's institutional and structural policy gaps in which the structural-functionalism and greed versus grievance models suggest triggers aggression.

The Structural Functionalism theory is a sociological model that explains the interdependence between society drilling down on why society functions the way it does. SF was developed in the 19th Century by Auguste Comte who noted that studying "societal science is the same as a natural science" (Scott, 2014: 19). The SF theory reveals that the whole structure of society is interconnected and accountable for the maintenance of societal balance, solidarity, stability, and equilibrium (Holborn & Haralambos, 2021). The function of one structure of the society oftentimes does have a direct or indirect impact on the remaining structure thereby disrupting the entire societal functions. Many scholars have redefined structural functionalism theory from various perspectives as an explicative or explanatory theory. Durkheim defines structural-functionalism or functionalism theory as a framework for understanding social differentiation, social order, and the social evolution of society (1956). Human nature and interaction are the fundamental sources of societal tensions and conflicts (Shimko, 2015). Structural function-alism acknowledges that culture, institutions-from the family level to the economy, and structures have to be socially and rationally organised through institutional rules and norms to provide solutions and prevent people and communities from destroying themselves. Expanding the structural-functionalism theory Almond demonstrated his quest to understand the strains and intensity of interactions between institutions in a political system (2015). Almond drilled down on institutional policy initiatives, functionality, and dysfunctionality. He used the structural-functionalism theory to explain how the statutory functions of legislative, executive, and judicial institutions including political parties influence social outcomes. Institutions and their policy frameworks are configured and affected by social relationships (Smith, 2013).

That is why the model advocates for institutional collaboration in policy formulation and implementation, it believes utilising institutional differences could resolve tensions. The disjointedness in policy trajectory between oil and gas companies, pipeline regulators, and oil and gas regulators in Nigeria affects policy agenda-setting. Thus, policy implementation assumes instrumental aggression because the policy outcome and guidelines are different from the collective realities in the Niger Delta area (Berkowitz, 1993; Okumagba, 2012). These policy gaps in resource-rich countries like Nigeria create the perfect conditions for political and corporate corruption that enables a few privileged people to enrich themselves, at the expense of the greater majority, and provoke the grievance of the majority (Collier, 2007; see Chapter 7). FADT and SF models lend explanatory relevance to the central research question of this thesis. The central relevance of both models is found in the way they converge to explain inequalities and corruption, violent civil protests, rebellion, and armed conflicts. Adedeji observed that conflicts and their sources continue to intrigue scholars and create intense anxiety in the minds of humanity (1999).

The greed versus grievance theory is sometimes called politics of resentment or grievance politics. The theory advocates that the quest for economic profitability by a few and socio-economic isolation of the majority leads to tensions and conflicts. It points out that while greed may focus on private gains, grievance expressed in form of rebellion can produce public good. The theory states that where "economic greed or grievance" is acutely present in institutional policy formulation and implementation there was bound to be tensions and conflicts (Collier &

Hoeffler, 2004; see Chapter 7). The pains from a grievance or the reaction against the greed of a few privileged elites who loot the resources of their victims due to unusual opportunities Collier and Hoeffler noted trigger violent rebellion and aggression (2004). Grossman points out that greed motivates rebellious aggression in the quest to generate profits from looting where profitable opportunities from rebellion would not normally be passed up (1999).

This can be seen in the interactions between the Federal Ministry of Petroleum Resources, DPR, and the NNPC which should interface and combine to set common standards for the oil and gas industry, particularly oil pipeline operations. Oftentimes, however, this is not happening. Oil and gas companies exploit these gaps to increase their private profitability margins at the expense of the government and local communities. This creates the conditions for aggression to suffice. Murshed and Cuesta (2013) stated that institutions, policies, power, and economic opportunities are the marked differences between structural functionalism and greed versus grievance theories. The inability of SF and greed versus grievance theories to elicit a deeper understanding of the insecurity situation and vandalism in Bayelsa points out why frustration-aggression theory is adopted as the most appropriate theoretical underpinning for this study.

Freud (2015) and Burlton (2007) stated that the actions of humans were driven by their instincts, particularly, self-preservation, acquisition, and pleasure instincts. Upon critical analysis of Freud's hypothesis, Langford stated that the frustration of man's instincts would usually drive aggressive reactive behaviour (1986). Expanding this hypothesis Dollard et al. realised that preventing an individual driven by instinct from attaining their goal can lead to frustration (1939). While Dollard and Sears et al. tried to reframe aggressive behaviour, a person demonstrates when prevented from attaining objectives set by instinct, they invented FADT (1939). They argued that obstructing an individual from attaining instinctively set objectives would frustrate the individual and lead to either *overt* or *non-overt* aggression. Bushman et al.'s General Aggression Model (GAM) contribute to the FADT hypothesis (2018). GAM is an integrative framework that considers how social, cognitive, personal, and developmental factors contribute to the understanding of aggression. While analysing aggression and its causes Bushman et al. discovered that a person's situational factors affect arousal, thoughts, and feelings. They observed that these elements influence appraisal and decision-making processes that affect aggressive and non-aggressive behaviours just as environmental, and biological factors also influence aggressive tendencies (Bushman et al., 2018). Nigeria's oil and gas regulatory processes and the numerous unresolved environmental issues are sufficient to trigger displaced aggression against pipelines.

FADT divides aggression into two distinctive typologies. Instrumental or institutional aggression and reactive or hostile aggression. Berkowitz says instrumental and reactive aggression are the ingredients that lead to frustration (1993). Instrumental aggression is usually deliberate, conscious, planned, and unprovoked specifically targeted at achieving either profit, information, or gratification, and it is goal-driven (Anderson & Dill, 1995; Segall, 2016). On the other hand, reactive aggression is unplanned, emotional, driven by instinct infused with passion, and provoked (Walters, 2012). This is demonstrated when people fight back against an obstructor or resist, and counteract those preventing them from achieving their set goals (Shaw, 2019). When an individual's set goals are intercepted, it unsettles their self-preservation making it difficult to satisfy their pleasure which instinctively triggers the aggressive instinct to counteract and fight to destroy the source of that frustration. The counteraction caused by instrumental aggression inflicts frustration on the original obstructor. This outcome is described as "self-triggered" or "self-inflicted" frustration. Given that it was the unprovoked and deliberate actions of the instrumental aggressor that provoked reactive aggressive resistance and counteraction from the individual or community (Bushman et al., 2018). This behaviour is replete in the various dimensions of insecurity in Bayelsa and the wider Niger Delta region.

The implementation of various oil and gas legislation and policies of oil and gas companies premediated to achieve set objectives through a proactive framework constitutes sources of instrumental aggression (Bushman & Anderson, 2002; Dollard et al., 1939). Although the legislation and policy instruments were set to enable oil and gas regulators and operators to engage in hydrocarbon extraction and production not to harm communities. The implementation of the guidelines impacts the socio-economic lives of the local communities which provokes an aggressive reaction against oil and gas infrastructure such as vandalism. Instrumental policies may not necessarily be aggressive. It is their implementation that makes them instrumental aggression because oftentimes they do not meet the realities in local communities which leads to resistance. Therefore, community neglect and devastating socio-economic and environmental conditions are the instrumental aggression that assumes the original provocateur that triggers community tensions. The breakdown of law and order resulting from unresolved tensions, anger, and frustration, occasioned by instrumental aggression of the government, triggers several insecurity problems such as pipeline vandalism.

Reactive aggression of this nature is what FADT is developed to explain. Political and economic decision-making processes and their implementation by the Nigerian government are examples of instrumental aggression that is directly responsible for the provoked and instinctive aggressive reaction in Bayelsa state. Aggression occurs when, and only where, there is frustration. One reason for using this model as the theoretical underpinning for this research is because it explains the complex counteractive aggressive behavioral nature of oil and gas local communities. Aggression Berkowitz (1993) and Bulhan (1985) noted is a relationship imposed by an actor that leads to devastating consequences on the physical and psychological wellbeing of others. Berkowitz (2011) argued that the changes in contextual factors were enough to modulate the strength and severity of aggression. An individual's mental experience upon provocation Krueger (1996) observed is thought to be a state of frustration which is a sufficient and a necessary trigger for aggression. Stone sees the actions of human agents, individuals, and or collectives as responsible for aggressive outcomes (2007). Aggression occurs when there is a threat to the *ego* or when an individual's *self-esteem* is affected by arousal, thoughts, and feelings (Bushman et al., 2018; Lazarus, 1994). They noted that something or situational factors must have happened to challenge or unsettle a person's sense of self-image or esteem. This model aligns with Langford's observation that FADT explains aggressive human behaviors and reactive tendencies (Langford, 1986).

The fact that Dollard and Sear et al.'s frustration-aggression hypothesis resonates extensively across contemporary western environments, it influences how aggression is perceived (Berkowitz, 2011; Krueger, 1996; Lazarus, 1994). Given that the FADT model is structured, articulated, and uncomplicated, the hypothesis remains a guide to experimentation in human aggression (Anderson & Dill, 1995; Bandura, 1973). At times, Bushman and Baumeister noted that this theory appears to justify the occurrence and acceptance of aggressive behaviour occasioned by frustration, for instance, "I did it because I was in a bad mood and distraught" (2018: 324). As well as the government-sponsored Janjaweed militia genocide against Darfur or the Serbs genocide against Bosnian Muslims.

They stressed that experimental research has shown that not all aggression was tied to frustration. Walters (2012) gives an example of the aggressive reaction of a collective group of people against a government's national immunisation policy under the assumption that the immunisation was directly responsible for the outbreak of diseases. The reactive aggression of the people is due to the dislike for the outbreak of diseases and what they have suffered not necessarily because of frustration from the instrumental policy of national immunisation. Although the impact of implementing instrumental policies can trigger aggressive and non-aggressive behaviours as well.

The foundations of instrumental aggressions are traced to the implementation of the Mineral Ordinance Act of 1914 as well as the Oil Mineral Ordinance Act of 1946. Igbinovia noted that these Acts forcefully vested "ownership and control of the entire minerals and properties under and above the ground in Nigeria, its rivers, streams, and waters to the British Crown" (2014: 40). The Land Use Decree of 1978 moved and transferred the ownership of the land and its resources to the Nigerian government (Alamieyeseigha, 2008; Etikerentse, 1985). The implementation of these intimidating policies compelled local communities to forcefully vacate their resource-rich ancestral farmlands for crude oil exploitation and production without adequate compensation, most times (Segall, 2016; Walters, 2012). Communities in Nembe and Bayelsa states are only too aware of the socio-economic cost of oil and gas exploration on their communities and the environment. The implementation of the very policies that empowered oil and gas companies failed to empower local communities but affected their self-esteem leading to frustration (Okumagba, 2012).

Kee states that aggressive policies trigger frustration, hostilities, and insecurity (2012). The outcomes invariably become self-inflicted frustration against the Nigerian government which inadvertently created those frustrating circumstances by implementing their instrumental policies. Gurr (2015) and Heleta (2009) believe that a common source of anger and popular discontent or relative deprivation can result in frustration which could trigger collective mobilization and rebellion. Unprovoked aggression by the Nigerian government gave rise to militant groups such as the Movement for the Emancipation of the Niger Delta (MEND) as well as the Niger Delta Avengers (NDA) (Okonofua, 2016; Olusanya, 2014). The inability of the regulators and oil and gas companies to address environmental pollution is responsible for worsening socio-economic and environmental conditions (Olawuyi, 2012; UNEP, 2012).

Huesmann (2013) argues that aggression was an aspect of leaned social behaviour in human beings, stressing that it is not an innate characteristic. What does not reconcile expressly in Dollard et al.'s FADT hypothesis is found in Krueger's variant (1939; Krueger, 1996). Huesmann describes aggression from the point of proactive-rational perspective where a frustrated person was more inclined to lean toward the hilarity of the source of provocation rather than reactive aggression (Krueger, 1996). Although FADT does justice in explaining the direct attacks by frustrated Bayelsan on government security forces, oil operators, and oil and gas infrastructure. This explanation misses out on the overt or reactive-inexpressive aggressive behaviour provoked by the activities of the same government and oil and gas operators. FADT recognises the contradictions which greed-grievance has over one another. Despite being mutually dependent, they disconnect in local and national structural–functional policy in explaining conflicts and insecurity problems (Sanderson, 2010; Webb, 2016).

Fukuyama (2018) and Collier (2007) believe that a large percentage of conflicts and wars in regions across the world reflect a lack of national policy collaboration and integration. Not explaining the internal and external triggers for the patterns of reactive-aggressive behaviours of communities due to oil and gas activities form the basis for rejecting SF and greed versus grievance theoretical models. Fifty-four-person experimentation done by Anderson and Dill (1995) found the effect that frustration has on reactive aggression. Anderson and Dill's work supports Dollard et al.'s proposition that frustration triggers aggression (1939). In the Bayelsa context, this suggests that it is socio-economic stagnation caused by the types of policies the government implement, corruption, and oil and gas companies' exploitation that define the underlying causes that trigger aggression against pipelines. Rather than the production of oil and gas by itself. Whereas unprovoked frustration Berkowitz (2011) says would result in aggression, unprovoked frustration might not necessarily eliminate some level of aggression. According to Krueger aggression will occur, when and only when there is frustration (1996). What Anderson and Dill's experimentation proves is that where an individual or a collective are convinced that their survival is threatened for no just cause or put at risk from eternal forces, they are inclined towards reactive aggression.

## APPLYING FRUSTRATION-AGGRESSION-DISPLACEMENT THEORY TO NIGERIA NIGER DELTA

FADT hypothesis appropriately completes the explanation for the *overt aggressive* behaviour of some militant youths and some local communities in Bayelsa to do justice to the central research question which explores the causes of pipeline vandalism in Bayelsa state. The vandalism of pipelines is an outcome of the implementation of the Land Use Decree of 1978 as an instrumental policy of the government (Alamieyeseigha, 2008). It explains how and why residents *displace* or exhibit *non-overt* expressions of aggression by engaging in vandalism, attacking wellhead manifolds, kidnapping, and oil theft. The by-product and outcome of this translate into increased regional insecurity. Berkowitz describes all of these insecurity actions as an outcome of *reactive-inexpressive* aggressive behaviour which is the defence of local communities from sources of frustration (2011). Engaging the FADT hypothesis from the perspective of *overt* aggression alone overlooked the model's wider picture. This thesis engaged in a detailed review of Dollard et al.'s FADT (1939) and observed that their suggestions and contributions to the causes of violent conflicts and aggression were, in some cases, completely misunderstood or misapplied. They were simply clarifying and deepening the understanding of their hypothesis in the explanation that conflicts and wars can be caused by *overt* and *non-overt* aggression.

Many scholars identify overt aggression as the main definition of aggression neglecting the hidden non-overt aggressive behavioural tendencies of a frustrated person, often misrepresented as non-aggression (Dollard et al., 1939). They noted that it is the unexpressed, non-overt, or inhibited aggression that would normally become apparent as *transferred* or *reactive-inexpressive aggression*. Displacement of aggression occurs, when the provocateur cannot be attacked as the source of frustration, or for whatever reason, become the target of the aggression. Aggression is displaced to other less fortified or less hostile targets (Dollard et al., 1939; Sanderson, 2010). Such displacement can, of course, become counter-productive by making the situation worse like vandalism which results in re-pollution of the environment already polluted by oil extraction and gas flaring. Faleti drilled deeper into the displacement of aggression by pointing out that in such situations the target of attacks would normally be physical infrastructure and individuals with significant links to the provocateur (2006). Sanderson was guided by the social conflict aspect of this model suggesting that social learning, learning from the environment, accounts for the prevalence of aggression displacement behavior (2010). All these formed significant bases for why the FADT model is the best theory for analysing pipeline vandalism, kidnappings, and crude oil bunkering in the historic Niger Delta. Okumagba says reactive or transferred aggression by some youths and some communities against pipelines were directly triggered by unjustified provocation and frustration because they are isolated from the oil and gas business processes (2012).

Aggression is therefore not triggered by local communities because they want government and oil and gas companies to vacate their land or stop oil production, far from it. By vandalising the pipelines, perpetrators demonstrate their resolve to inflict psychological and mental pain as well as economic losses on the Nigerian government and the oil and gas operators who are seen as the provocateurs. This reflects Berkowitz's (1993) and Balham's (1985) arguments that aggression is a relationship imposed by an actor to devastate the physical and psychological well-being of others. Bushman et al.'s General Aggression Model (GAM) points out the effect of arousal, thoughts, and feelings on appraisal and decision-making processes, and its effect on aggressive and/or non-aggressive behaviours (Bushman et al., 2018). Such aggression against pipelines is what Sanderson (2010) referred to as "transferred" aggression. Berkowitz (2011) described it as "inexpressive reactive aggression" while Okumagba (2012; Dollard et al., 1939) referred to it as frustration displacement. By vandalising pipelines, the local communities believed that the outcomes of their actions would challenge and re-organise the existing social order while destroying previous provocative activities obstructing their self-esteem and preservation (Tausch et al., 2011). Huesmann noted that social learning behaviour means that a frustrated person might adopt one or several behavioural tendencies towards a frustrating situation (2013), like trying to solve a problem by taking drugs and alcohol. Pipeline vandalism and seizure of vessels or piracy by militant agitators are a demonstration of aggressive behaviour. Although, frustration might be one ingredient that triggers aggression and social violence Sanderson (2010), and Gurr (2015) were quick to point out that it did not always result in collective violent responses or tendencies.

Despite the formation of a structured and organised Operation Delta Safe (OPDS)-a joint military and security task force established to secure and protect oil and gas infrastructure, some angry and frustrated youths and some communities still aggress against the government and oil and gas pipelines. This shows that development cannot be replaced with security deployment. OPDS is comprised of the Army, Navy, Police, Department of State Security, and Nigerian Security and Civil Defence Corps. They constitute the sources of frustration. The angry and frustrated communities cannot sustain direct attacks against the OPDS and hence transfer their aggression to softer targets such as the pipelines because these infrastructures are connected to the oil companies and the government which frustrates the local communities. The 1999 Kaiama declaration is an upshoot of frustration. The young people resolved to retreat into the creeks and displace their anger against pipelines, kidnap oil personnel, hijack oil vessels as well as engage in oil bunkering (Alamieyeseigha, 2008; Douglas & Okonta, 2003; Okumagba, 2012). They were acutely aware that their reactive transferred aggressive tactics would cause extensive damage and harm as well as inflict maximum psychological pain, financial loss, and economic downturn to the Nigerian government while also crumbling the oil and gas operators. This changed the social order in Bayelsa and the wider historic Niger Delta region by creating a new generic community of power brokers in the former militant groups. The government and oil operators could no longer ignore the destruction caused by the militants hence sorting their views and collaborating on how to develop the neglected region.

This aligns with the claim that aggressive action can sometimes bring about new conditions that re-order society or trigger future social changes (Tausch et al., 2011). To counteract the oil firms and the Nigerian government who are the sources of frustration to the Niger Delta people, the militants adopted a *non-overt* or indirectly *transferred aggressive* approach to the vandalism of pipelines. The Nigerian Bureau of Statistics (2017) and Oki (2017: 115) noted that about 10,000 pipelines have been destroyed in the 15 years up to 2019 in the region. Okumagba contended that militants transferred their aggression against softer targets such as pipeline vandalism and kidnapping because it was much more lucrative and because they are unable to sustain the military power of the Nigerian state (2012). Kidnapping revealed the extent transferred aggression strategy rewarded the militants. For instance, in 2006 MEND carried out the high-profile kidnapping of about nine oil workers (William, 2012). Between 2008 and 2010 another seven workers were seized from Exxon-Mobil, STEMCO, and China Civil Engineering Construction Company which escalated the problems of oil and gas infrastructure insecurity in the region (Akpan, 2021; Oriola, 2016).

The kidnapping of oil and gas expatriates increased in 2016 contributing to the plummeting of oil production and the declaration of *Force Majeure*-rejecting liabilities for the interruption and unavoidable catastrophes by ExxonMobil-operators of Qua Iboe Terminal (Oki, 2017). Sea piracy is another transferred aggression strategy adopted to express the frustration felt from oil and gas activities, economic and infrastructure neglect of the local communities as well as human rights abuses by security agencies. Cases of sea piracy in Niger Delta waters, especially Forcados, Nun River, and Tungbo creeks have increased since 2011 (Allen, 2011; Duda & Wardin, 2013; Duquet, 2011). The outcome of various variants of transferred or reactive aggression displaced by militants on infrastructure and persons with close affinities to sources of their frustration reverberates across the global oil market. Particularly the kidnapping of expatriates and the near stoppage of oil production in Nigeria (Chapter 7). A critical review of the strategies deployed by some militant groups showed that the majority of them did not engage in kidnapping just to collect ransom (Mickolus, 2018; Ibaba, 2012). Groups like Niger Delta People Volunteer Force led by Melford Dokubo Goodhead Jr., popularly called Mujahid Dokubo-Asari, and the Niger Delta Vigilante led by Ateke Tom did not engage in kidnapping. Also, the emergent Niger Delta Avengers led by a self-acclaimed Brigadier-General Murdoch Agbinibo were into kidnapping.

These groups used their structures to refocus national and international attention on the collective suffering of the Niger Delta people due to the deliberate socio-economic and infrastructural neglect of local communities. Hence, what peaceful agitators like Ken Saro-Wiwa could not achieve in death, the militants believe they achieved alive with brute force, with honour. This has led to a national and global focus on the Niger Delta. This thesis agrees with Horowitz's (1985) position that there is no sense in applying a bloodless model to a bloody social phenomenon. The Nigerian government now discusses with militants directly to mitigate the numerous incidences of aggression and vandalism against the onshore and offshore oil and gas pipelines and related infrastructure (Bergstresser, 2017). The priority of Niger Delta militants is not stealing oil or engaging in illegal artisanal refining of petroleum products. It is fundamentally to shut down Nigeria's crude oil export to draw international attention to the socio-economic and infrastructure neglect of local communities (Egbe & Thompson, 2010).

Onuoha (2016) believes that the insecurity problems were tied to prevailing socio-economic struggles between oil operators, regulators, and the entire Niger Delta region. It will not be wrong to argue that civil protesters could be senseless in making the mistake of applying a peaceful approach to the extremely bloody Niger Delta oil and gas phenomenon. Given that Saro-Wiwa and his four colleagues applied bloodless civil protest but paid with their lives without achieving anything, the collective community neglect continued (Agbonifo, 2019; Don Pedro, 2006; Douglas & Okonta, 2003). At this point, this research supports the FADT with *Community Neglect Aggression-Displacement Theoretical framework*. CNADT explains why some youths and some communities get angry and transfer their aggression against pipelines. The frustrated local communities lack constructive avenues to vent the anger triggered by infrastructure and socio-economic neglect they have suffered for many years. The exclusion of their views from the policy processes worsens their frustrations and heightened insecurity problems. This is consistent with the direction of this study which agrees with the pioneers of the community neglect debate. Bergstresser, Okonta, and Coleman stated that the neglect of the perspectives of different sectors of the communities along with their socio-economic predicaments is some of the critical factors that trigger frustration and aggression against softer targets like the pipelines (2017, 2016, 2015; see Chapter 3). This research also proposes the integration of socio-economic, infrastructure, and environmental benefits along with the planning, implementation, and operationalisation phases of the pipeline life cycle (this is discussed later).

## APPLYING
## COMMUNITY-NEGLECT-AGGRESSION-DISPLACEMENT THEORY

The Community Neglect-Aggression-Displacement Theory explains the neglect of underlying socio-economic, environmental degradation, good governance, and political issues that provoke anger and displacement of aggression against pipelines (Bergstresser, 2017; Coleman, 2015; Okonta, 2016). This proposed CNADT theory is used to explain the causes of onshore oil and gas pipeline vandalism; collective frustration-aggression;

and infrastructure insecurity problems in the Niger Delta and Nigeria. The factors that cause onshore oil and gas pipeline vandalism and infrastructure insecurity problems, are highlighted throughout this thesis, and the micro-foundational variables and triggers of those factors are found in the micro-foundational and operational variables of CNADT. Neglect means ignoring, disregarding, and overlooking without giving due attention to the socio-economic and infrastructural development of local communities (Hoeffler, 2011).

Physical neglect is the lack of access to education, health care, and psychological wellbeing of the local community (Hoeffler, 2011). This thesis defines CNADT as the ignoring and disregarding of the processes of equitable distribution of national wealth, education, income, jobs, land, finance, environmental sustainability, and other public goods to local communities. Hoeffler and Samuelson described public good in economic theory as non-rivalrous- which means the access and consumption of the public good by one person does not make the good inaccessible, unavailable, or exclude others from consuming that same good (2011, 1954). Often, the government and oil companies show little concern about unemployment and if they do it is usually lip service about increased unemployment and household poverty in the Niger Delta region; thus, they are complacent about the insecurity problems bedeviling the area (Fig. 5.1).

The CNADT figure shows that the neglect of social, economic, environmental, political, and leadership issues motivates people into aggression displacement. The factors that cause onshore oil and gas pipeline vandalism and infrastructure insecurity problems, highlighted throughout this thesis, and the micro-foundational variables and triggers of those factors are found in the micro-foundational and operational variables that underpins CNADT. The general factors and micro-foundations that influence the outcomes of the proposed CNADT theory are economic deprivation and stagnation, political isolation, social inequalities, and environmental degradation. Others are widespread poverty, socio-cultural disequilibrium, and widespread environmental refugees. Uncleaned oil spills over farmlands and fishing rivers, abandoned pipelines, neglected and unimpactful community intervention projects, and unclamped pipelines from technical blowouts are some other micro-foundational factors leading to CNADT. The outcomes of these operating variables on the CNADT theoretical framework are impoverishment, unemployment, oil theft and bunkering, lack of access to farmlands, decreased household

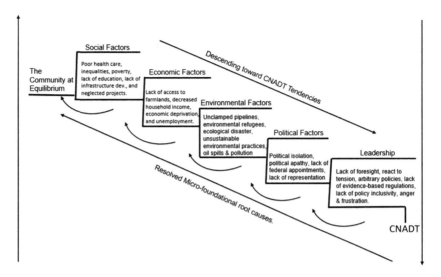

**Fig. 5.1** Community neglect-aggression displacement theory (*Source* Designed by Author)

incomes, poor health care facilities, militancy, and organised crimes (Etemire, 2016; Etete, 2017; Etowah & Effiong, 2012; Okumagba, 2012). Ravaging hunger, displacement from fishing communities, frustration, corruption, tensions, and aggression are also micro-foundation that influence the outcome of CNADT.

The CNADT also proposes that the behaviour of both the government and the oil firms regarding the upward social mobility of the greater number of Bayelsa population results in resentment and tensions. Based on these micro-foundational factors and operating variables the CNADT theoretical model can be applied in explaining how frustration and anger triggered by the highlighted factors cause the vandalism of pipelines in Bayelsa state. Given that the micro-foundational factors and operating variables are acutely present across Bayelsa communities and the wider historic Niger Delta region. The novelty of this proposed theory is that it is the first time the CNADT is been used to support FADT. CNADT builds on FADT in expanding on the motivation behind reactive aggression against the vandalism of oil and gas pipeline infrastructure in Bayelsa.

The failure of the Nigerian government and private oil corporations to resolve the variables impacts negatively on the behavior of the local communities. The outcome also impacts oil and gas production activities by way of causing the insecurity of oil and gas infrastructure. The collective community neglect by the government and private entities is the principal reason behind the tensions, anger, and frustration that pervades the local communities in Bayelsa. The data shows that any community where there are angry and frustrated people is bound to experience displacement of aggression against the sources of their frustration and neglect. In the case of the historic Niger Delta area, the government and its agencies, and the private oil and gas corporations are to be blamed for neglecting the local communities. This proposed CNADT theory views "fact" or/and "evidence" from the perspective of physical observations of the activities of the oil and gas operators, verbal, and nonverbal narratives from the professional and community participants and other stakeholders. It also views facts from the research-based publications of civil society organizations as well as analysing documentary evidence from oil and gas regulators, multinational corporations, and official government websites. Triangulating the sources of these various facts proves why the bases for why the local communities are involved in displaced aggression against pipelines. The proposed CNADT influenced the methodological choices of this study. The researcher visited the local communities and other stakeholders to conduct face-to-face interviews with those who implement regulatory guidelines and those impacted by oil and gas activities. Therefore, the research methods are designed in line with the factors that influence the CNADT.

The gradual destruction and obliteration of the once fertile Niger Delta land are visible to all including the oil and gas corporations and the government to see. The findings from *decoders-researchers* drawn from 142 countries comprising 3545 participants and analysing over 2985 documents of incidents from 2001 to 2017 show that the Niger Delta region has been neglected (Amnesty International, 2018). This research argues that community neglect triggers the same feeling of anger and frustration that instrumental and regulatory aggression arouses. Both experiences lead to reactive overt aggression that culminates in the vandalisation of the oil and gas pipelines. Langford observed that aggressive behaviour occurs when an individual's instinct is frustrated (1986). Martin Luther King noted that; "As long as people are ignored… voiceless…trampled by the iron feet of exploitation, there is the danger that they, like little children, will have their emotional outbursts which will break out in violence in the streets" (King, 1967, 2016: 16). This implies whether the Niger Delta communities are deliberately neglected, vandalism orchestrated, or socio-economic stagnation intentional, collective outburst was inevitable. The government and the respective oil and gas corporations are to be blamed for these neglects because they are the main operators of the oil and gas value chain. The failure to construct industries, accessible local health centres, and general hospitals, accessible educational facilities, and re-settle displaced fishing communities to the sand filled shallow creeks remains a persistent problem. The isolation from national politics prevents local communities and individuals from achieving their instinctively set goals and objectives. The combined neglect deprives local communities of the direct trickle-down benefits in the distribution of national resources.

Isolating many local communities from legitimately participating in different aspects of the oil and gas business chain is like preventing them from attaining their self-esteem which Bushman et al. and Lazarus says leads to aggression (2018, 1994). The implementation of the government and the oil and gas companies' policies are responsible for the negative impact of oil and gas activities in the communities leading to collective aggression (Gurr, 2015). This aligns with the views of the pioneers of the *community neglect* debate (see Chapter 3; James, 2018; Issa, 2015). Using the neglect hypothesis to explain the vandalism of pipelines in Bayelsa contributes, complements, and supports FADT. The people of the Niger Delta have suffered a profound and broad range of neglect. Bushman et al. and Dollard et al. noted that feelings, thoughts, arousal, interruption of self-esteem, and prevention from achieving instinctively set goals trigger aggressive behaviour (2018, 1939). Whereas FADT argues that frustration leads to aggression displacement. CNADT explains that different shades of neglect lead to aggression displacement and insecurity issues.

## Militancy in the Niger Delta

The concept, motivation, and practice of militancy are as fluid as understanding the concepts of terrorism and terrorist acts. Militancy is difficult to define by nation-states, institutions, political leaders, and scholars. While it may not always be easy to fully understand why some communities and individuals use confrontational and violent methods to express, support, or pursue a political or social cause. Political exigencies and the need to protect political interests shape the official perspective and understanding of states. This does not sufficiently define what militancy is in reality. Not every confrontation and public rebellion reflect the characteristics of militancy, in the same vein, not all militant activities like religious extremism represent the public good. In the theory of collective action, Olsen points out that common interests within a group are insufficient to produce a public good (1965). The economic theory defines a public good as a non-rivalrous and non-excludable good (Samuelson, 1954). Non-rivalry means that an individual's consumption of the public good does not reduce or make the good unavailable for consumption by others (Hoeffler, 2011). All militants or militancy are not alike as different variants raise a range of important moral and political questions.

The philosophy and circumstances that motivate them, sometimes interface, and infiltrate each other thus making it hard to separate militant groups from violent confrontational rebellious civil protests. As Hoeffler noted without so-called *selective incentives* to motivate participation in protests, collective action is unlikely to occur even when the groups have common interests (2011). "A riot is the language of the unheard, the language of the voiceless...I hope we avoid riots but be as militant and as determined...", Martin Luther King once observed (King, Jr., 1967: 30). Militancy is a form of social expression by the oppressed, as D'Arcy points out, militancy and public rebellion may not necessarily be a danger to democratic norms and values of consensus-building (2013). D'Arcy distinguished between provoked and justified and unprovoked and unjustified militancy. By pointing out that the crucial contrast is between democratic and undemocratic action, rather than violent and non-violent actions (2013). If violent public protests, confrontations, and militancy is the language of the unheard, as King describes above, it is imperative to identify what it is that the Nigerian state and the oil and gas companies have refused to hear.

Focusing on the identity of militants disentangles and decouples between violence and militancy, and inclusively appreciates the range and depth of practices that militancy represents (Jenkins, 2022). This way, the meaning and significance of militancy are better reflected by militants. Brown and Sessions define militancy as a favourable attitude and intentions towards the support of collective bargaining by participation in strikes-job action, meetings, or other actions (2000). Militancy is driven by *"pure democratic* principles as long as it concerns *higher-order* norm stabilisation of the general principles of norm-production... or *rights-driven* if the main accent lies in fundamental rights" (Mouffe, 2005: 63). For this study, militancy means participation and support for protests, armed violent aggression, and public dissent as means of bargaining for democratically guaranteed fundamental human rights. Militancy is a by-product of anger and frustration (Okumagba, 2012). D'Arcy says militancy normally arises in response to the patterns of persistent insensitivity to the concerns of certain classes and categories of people that are excluded, exploited, and oppressed (2013).

The government and oil firms are aware that militancy and violent resistance do not erupt out of the ordinary, as they are by-products of many unheard frustrating issues. These need to be addressed to mitigate violent confrontations. These issues centre around the continued implementation of instrumental aggression in forms of policies and collective socio-economic, environmental stagnation, and the neglect of the communities resulting in prolonged economic poverty. The Niger Delta militants were motivated by years of anger and frustration suffered from the negative impact of implementing various instrumental aggression (Okumagba, 2012). As well as many decades of socio-economic, environmental, and infrastructure neglect of their communities (Bergstresser, 2017; Coleman, 2015; Okonta, 2016). The Nigerian government and the oil companies have not paid extensive attention to agitations from the region nor constructively addressed their pains and sufferings coupled with different forms of neglect. Neglect such as the damage to the environment and source of livelihood is what FADT and CNADT exhaustively explain above (Bushman et al., 2018; Dollard et al., 1939).

Contemporary structured, organised, and weaponised militant activities started in the Niger Delta after the December 1998 Kaiama declaration which coined, popularised, and sharpened the term "resource control" as firmly reflected in Article 10 (Douglas, 2008; Douglas & Okonta, 2003). Douglas and Okonta noted that resource control as a concept started in the early eighth and nineteenth Centuries when the indigenous people of the Niger Delta struggled to participate in the palm oil trade (red gold) and the politics of self-government in the region (2008, 2003). Article 1 of the 1998 Kaiama declaration introduced the debate. They declared ownership of all "land and natural resources within the Ijaw territory as belonging to the Ijaw communities... bases of our survival" (Douglas, 2008: 332). The Kaiama declaration has its root in the founding philosophy of three previous movements.

The 1990 Ogoni Bill of rights was adopted by the Movement for the Survival of the Ogoni People, and the 1992 Izon People's Charter by the Movement for the Survival of the Izon (Ijaw) Ethnic Nationality. As well as the 1992 Charter of Demands of the Ogbia People which was adopted by the Movement for the Reparation to Ogbia (Human Rights Watch, 1999). Douglas argued that Niger Delta confrontational groups drew on the ideologies of Major Isaac Boro when he declared the Niger Delta Republic in 1965 (2008). His ideas were propelled by the pains and neglect suffered by his people despite the abundance of crude oil resources (Douglas, 2008). The militants are acutely aware that violence would not wholly resolve the issues of decades of community neglect and frustrating and aggressive policies. But they are convinced however that militancy would galvanise national and international attention to their plight.

The central motivation that drives most confrontational activities of militants is to see the restoration of socio-economic and infrastructure development justice for the Niger Delta region. While militants are not terrorists, they use terrorist propaganda such as a systematic use of fear-provoking violence, and the use of fear and violence by private groups and individuals to achieve some political goals to propagate their cause (Novotny, 2007). At times it becomes difficult to separate their actions from that of terrorists. How the militant is perceived is dependent on what the political leaders shape in the narrative and feel about their activities. Charles Tilly (2003) stated that political and normative beliefs influence how terrorism, terror, and terrorist are perceived, including militants and militancy. MEND is arguably the most formidable and strategic of all Niger Delta militant groups. It is unclear when it was formed but it started before 2006 or earlier (Kulungu, 2021). The group was founded by Government Oweizide Ekpemupolo (also known as Tompolo). A feared and revered spiritual leader believed to have magical powers, an astute negotiator, and Henry Emomotimi Okah, who is a trained marine engineer, and an expert in intelligence gathering, and weapon smuggling (Duda & Wardin, 2013; Orere, 2009). Okah's skills and training explain why MEND could blow up onshore pipelines as well as are able to launch deadly offshore attacks on oil and gas infrastructure -up to 200 nautical miles into the sea (Duda & Wardin, 2013). The marked difference between MEND and others is that their leader integrates spiritual and physical leadership believing that God has given them the mandate to free communities across the Niger Delta from historic neglect, abuse, and frustration.

The structure is such that the self-acclaimed militant *generals* with direct control over decentralised commands are below Tompolo and Okah. This discentralised leadership structure controls about 25,000 fighters across creeks spread around the Niger Delta states. Okah once admitted before a Guardian newspaper journalist that, "injustice in the land provokes even the meek" (Orere, 2009). The decentralised structure has enabled MEND to consistently demonstrate the capacity to mobilise and innovate new technologies. They can use guerilla tactics quickly across the creek without exposing its leadership hierarchy (Kulungu, 2021). They use speed boats to effect swarm-based maneuvers in the swamps that often outsmart the government's defence infrastructure. MEND leadership structure understands the theory of rebellion which points out that group size is critical in achieving collective action (Olsen, 1965). At the same time, decentralisation of the structure into cells in the creek makes the reality of private gain possible in the face of common interests as a possible determinant to encourage participation (Hoeffler, 2011). The group executed hundreds of attacks between 2005 to 2014 such as vandalism, kidnapping, war with the Nigerian Army, Piracy, and seizure of crude oil Ocean liners to mention a few. Most of their attacks were directed against Shell, Eni, ExxonMobil, Total, NNPC, and Chevron onshore and offshore infrastructure (Kulungu, 2021). MEND is the melting pot of many relevant militant groups that sprang out of the Kaiama declaration and new ones like NDA.

Although Tompolo claimed to have accepted the Federal government amnesty program in 2009, their political influence coupled with the ability to assemble fighters at short notice gives MEND a dreadful outlook (Duda & Wardin, 2013). As Hoeffler noted rebellion is anchored on two assumptions, that public rebellion produces public good, and participants make a rational choice whether to join in a rebellion (2011). Niger Delta militants are driven by agitations for socio-economic justice. They are generally considered terrorists because Hosen (2011) had earlier stated that terrorism might not necessarily be influenced by religious inclinations. Militancy also satisfies the second element (achieving some political goals) of Novotny's classification. Jomo Gbomo, the Niger Delta militants' spokesperson noted, "the aims of militancy were strictly to achieve socio-economic and political redirection" (Leonardo, 2012: 183).

Meaning the heightened levels of militancy and insecurity in the historic Niger Delta and Bayelsa state are politically motivated which is a major ingredient of terrorism. Nigeria's Description of oil and gas militancy is consistent with its characterisation of the terrorism Act. Although the description of terrorism lacks a structural or agency approach, despite taking 10 years to frame. Nigeria's terrorism Act describes terrorism as an act that is deliberately done with malice, or aforethought, and which seriously harms or damages a country or an international organisation (Ejeh et al., 2019; Terrorism Prevention Act, 2013). Its wording does qualify as the anti-terrorism law that the UN resolution 1373 mandated nation-states to enact. But Nigeria's National culture, and media perception view pipeline vandalism and infrastructure sabotage as terrorism.

According to Igbinovia (2014: 27) and aspect of the Oil Pipeline Act (2004) vandalism, kidnapping, and sea piracy are also oil and gas terrorism. Skoczylis points out that "government policies refine, reshape, and qualify the points at which aspects of human behaviour are or are not linked to terrorism" (2015: 19). The level of normative and political influences over what constitutes terror, terrorism, and terrorist acts makes analysing it difficult (Nacos, 2016; Sloan & Bunker, 2012). Nigeria's state security practice and its perception of oil and gas militancy as terrorist activities reflect on how security is practiced in the Bayelsa-Nembe case study area. The activities of international pirates operating in the Gulf of Guinea and the Bight of Benin worsen militancy and the terrorism question in Nigeria and around Nigeria's waters. They put pressure on both crude oil, and human and material infrastructure in the coastal communities. The compromised security structure around the nine Niger Delta estuaries that empty into the Atlantic Ocean makes it harder to contain oil bunkering, mitigate militancy, and resolve oil and gas terrorism (Transparency International, 2019).

## Terrorism Question and Oil and Gas Pipeline Infrastructure Vandalism

There is this blurring line separating onshore oil and gas pipeline vandalism, associated vulnerabilities and threats by militants, and outright acts of oil and gas infrastructure terrorism. As Hosen (2011) stated, terrorism is not conducted by a bunch of frustrated and irrational people experiencing mental illnesses but mostly by well-trained individuals. Terrorism narrative is extremely influential and thus provides a strategic framework on which states actions and policy responses are based. Between the Nigerian Terrorism Prevention Act (2013) and the UN Resolution 1373 documents analysed in this book, including national culture, and media perception, do not expressly view oil and gas pipeline vandalism as terrorism. A slim link between oil and gas infrastructure sabotage as terrorism is presented in the Nigerian Terrorism Prevention Act, but it does not do justice to the broader complicity of the terrorism phenomenon in the petroleum sector. The term "oil and gas infrastructure saboteur" gives the false impression that every action against the operation of the oil and industry automatically falls within the rubric of oil and gas terrorism. This is because the distinctive borderline between acts of sabotage and infrastructure terrorism has become diffused and confusing. Hiding the fact that plenty of acts of terrorism in the past, such as the bombing of pipelines that are 200 nautical miles into the sea (Duda & Wardin, 2013). Using "militancy" as a prefix to describe such acts isolate and shifts the blame of national terrorism to local oil and gas infrastructure militant saboteurs.

Political actors, the criminal justice system, and law enforcement agencies should be blamed for conveniently labelling unapproved activities or emerging formidable threat as terrorism, especially when under pressure to respond, doing so makes nonsense of the categorisation. This section explains that motivation, targets, processes, actions, and outcomes should be the focal referent points of defining terrorism, and counter-terrorism should not be defined to subjective socio-political or state security philosophical trajectory alone. A consensus definition will discourage claiming benefits for violence as against evaluating the mental, physical, and psychological impact it has on humans and society. Doing so would deconstruct the debated cliché that 'one man's terrorist is another's freedom fighter' (Ganor, 2010). Richardson (2006) reveals that terrorism appears in many different forms across many parts of the world, in pursuit of different objectives. Perpetrators of terrorist acts differ from each other in many ways as ideology and specificness of their objectives are influenced by domestic socio-economic and political dynamics and the international trajectory of global affairs. The only thing terrorism may have in common is their desire to harm innocent people often while remaining undetected.

Every other thing about perpetrators of the act is fluid as they attack democracies, authoritarian regimes, developed and underdeveloped worlds. As evidence has shown terrorists were either follower of diverse religious beliefs or followers of non. According to Richardson (2006), the search for the underlying causes of terrorism is a "complicated endeavor". It is simplistic therefore to focus on political, ideological, and or religion as fundamental motivations of terrorism even though they often appear as triggers. The difficulties of searching for an acceptable definition suggest the issues are deeper than what scholars often occupy themselves with. The search for a generally accepted definition is not going to yield a definitive solution but would be determined by the internal and external interactions between multiple risk factors (Richardson, 2006). Implying that the definition would be as complicated as the act of terrorism, involving a combination of alleviating the risk factors and stopping interactions between them. Rapport reveals three dynamic phases of terrorism from the time of modern terrorism in the 1870s such as the anarchist wave; anti-colonial waves of the 1920s to the 1960s; though this extended to the third left wave that began from 1860s and reaching its crest was sometime in the 1980s (Hosen, 2011). Deconstructing this order of arrangement Ahmed (2005) suggested that the 1949 Soviet Atomic Bomb and increasing nuclear arms race that followed should be viewed as the first waves of terrorism.

Stressing that religiously motivated and nuclear-biological–chemical terrorism should constitute the second and third waves respectively. Ahmed (2005) argued that the era of Al-Qaeda and Osama Bin Laden were the new forms of terrorism. According to Stout (2004), the international dimension of terrorist attacks should be considered new and not the act of terrorism itself. Whereas the 'deterministic', structural approach, does not give the terrorist a choice implying that one or more conditions can trigger terrorism, but the 'intentional', agency approach, gives a choice. Hain and Pisoiu (2017) stressed that whether terrorism occurs or not depends on the choice and intention of the individual or organisation. The choice, therefore, is the concept that differentiates structural, and agency approaches from deliberate and external environmental influences. Whilst the US defines terrorism as; "premeditated, politically motivated violence perpetrated against non-combatant targets by sub-national groups or clandestine agents, usually to influence an audience" (Richardson, 2006: 2; United States Department of States, 2005). The confusion in the US definition is found in the fact that it failed to recognise that religion plays a critical role in triggering terrorism. Jones et al. (2014) stated that events have shown many terrorist attacks were not restricted to sub-national and or clandestine groups only as correctly. The UK's definition states that terrorism is the; "use or threat, of action, designed to influence the government or to intimidate the public or a section of the public, and the use or threat is made to the advancement of terrorism following Lord Carlile 2006 and 2007 assessment concluded that a political, religious or ideological cause" (House of Commons, 2013: 126).

Although Lord Carlile added "racism", in his 2006/2007 review, as a motivating cause of terrorism. His conclusion is that the UK's definition is consistent with international comparators and treaties and hence fit for purpose. However, he failed to identify those countries the UK used as its "comparator". Just as it will be profoundly dangerous to assume from a preconceived list of potential countries. Gupta generally defines terrorism as a politically triggered violent act that is perpetrated by a non-state actor (Gupta, 2008). The problem with this definition which shows its defect is the assumption and deliberate omission of critical aspects like evidence of states' sponsored terrorism whose outcome reflects violent attacks driven by religious or social views. The United Nations' definition of the concept is found in the UN International Convention for the Suppression of Financing Terrorism. In Article 2, Section 1, the UN defined terrorism as.

Any behavior or act of violence designed to cause death or serious bodily injury to any person who may not have taken part in the violence during armed conflicts, when the purpose of such act is intended to intimidate a population or to compel a government or international community to either forcefully undertake or refrain from an action. (Cox, 2005; United Nations, 1999)

This definition is too broad and confusing in addressing the definitional problem of terrorism. Given that some aspects of it seemingly resonate with state and or non-state-sponsored violence designed to unjustly intimidate both combatants and the civil population. At the same time, its crafters recognise that terrorism might occur without necessarily demonstrating underlying political or religious motivation. Hosen (2011) stated that most terrorist incidences were not influenced by religious inclinations. To V. I. Lenin, former Russian communist leader, as quoted by

Weinberg (2009) terrorism is a tactic used to frighten and threaten individuals to impress in their minds as well as the government that anything could happen at any time. Attempt to make sense of the concept, Novotny (2007) argued that terrorism should be divided into three definitional perspectives.

(1) As a systematic use of fear-provoking violence
(2) As a progressive use of fear and violence by a legitimate state or private groups and individuals to achieve some political goals
(3) Perspective throws confusion into the mix by suggesting that terrorism is when individuals or groups illegally and indiscriminately direct any attacks against any non-combatants to achieve some political relevance.

The Niger Delta militancy can be classified as demonstrating this form of terrorism. The weakness in Novotny's definition lay in the fact that states and non-state-sponsored terrorist attacks were not limited to civilian non-combatants alone but sometimes these attacks are diffused against legitimate forces as well. Gultekin (2007) and Hosen (2011) believe religion is the fourth and most critical trigger of terrorism giving the example of the 1979 Iranian Islamic Revolution. The international community can respond to terrorism in five ways.

(1) Accept that international terrorism was a global problem
(2) Gather formidable opposition against the belief that one country's terrorist is NOT another's a freedom fighter, but a terrorist.
(3) Unified action, codification, and exposure of terrorists along with their states and individual sponsors (Stout, 2004).
(4) Through international multi-layered actions against nations that harbor or give haven to terrorists and
(5) Seek the full support of national citizens and deploy democratic principles (Stout, 2004).

The international community needs to go further, even though some of these approaches may have been adopted. They must look at terrorist recruitment strategies, and sources of funding including trials and sentencing (Jatto & Skoczylis, 2023). Nigeria's state security practice and its perception of oil and gas terrorist activities in the historic Niger

Delta region reflect on how the Bayelsa-Nembe host communities practice community security. The porous sea borders connecting the nine historic Niger Delta estuaries to the Atlantic Ocean make it harder to contain oil bunkering, and vandalism, or arrest militants who use that axis as escape routes. Onuoha and Mathias (2016, 2011) pointed out that the canoes-barges-tugboat that ferry stolen crude oil do so through the Niger Delta area into the Gulf of Guinea. The geopolitical maritime security threats between the estuaries and the Gulf of Guinea, advertently or inadvertently, introduce international dimensions to the issue of pipeline infrastructure vandalism and insecurity in Nigeria. Militancy, oil and gas saboteurs, disruption of production, or whatever other name it is called assume "terrorism" the moment it goes beyond civil social dissent.

## Methodology and Fieldwork

A case study research design was adopted to gather the data for this book. The case study design reveals detailed facts about the nature of social interaction across Bayelsa's local communities, a micromirror of what is obtainable in many countries in the global South rich in oil and gas. Qualitative data were gathered through face-to-face interviews and triangulated with documentary evidence like Acts of the National Assembly, official publications, and policy documents to enrich the book's findings. The result shows that a combination of poverty, inequality, lack of employment, environmental degradation, political corruption, criminality, poor governance, and leadership curse led to the frustrations experienced amongst Bayelsa host communities. Although cases of oil and gas infrastructure insecurity, particularly pipeline disruptions, are prevalent across the nine states of the Niger Delta region. These insecurity issues are more widespread and of a much higher scale within the states of Bayelsa, Delta, and Rivers (Mathias, 2015). The choice of Bayelsa case study state is informed by the fact that it has the highest number of operating oil and gas pipeline networks as well as the highest number of crude oil and gas producing fields and oil wells crisscrossing the uplands and creeks in the region (Akpomera, 2015; Onuoha, 2007). As Creswell (2015) notes, case studies are well suited to understanding a societal problem on a local and communal level. Also, Bayelsa, the epicenter of oil and gas activities in Nigeria, has the longest and most expensive crude oil trunk line-the NCTL. OML 29 oilfield stretches across some parts of the Nembe-Ewelesuo Creek community, in the Nembe

Local Government Area, where the wellhead that connects the NCTL pipeline is located (Akpomera, 2015; Madubuko, 2017; Mathias, 2015). The NCTL pipeline has been vandalised over 220 times between 2008 and 2018 which is why Nembe was chosen as subject of interest (Njoku, 2016). My central objective of offering explanations about the relationships between the communities, government, and oil and gas operators informed my choice of Bayelsa-Nembe as a local case study area (Astalin, 2013; Denscombe, 2007: 44–45).

Case studies enabled the researcher to undertake an in-depth empirical investigation of a specific situation (Yin, 2012). As part of the case study, I chose to conduct face-to-face interviews, which were audio-recorded and transcribed as well as collected and re-examined documentary data. I interviewed oil and gas policymakers, representatives from the oil and gas sector, frontline staff, security officials, civil society, and community members. I recruited my Bayelsa samples from Yenagoa and its surrounding communities such as Ayamanbele, Gbarain-Ekpetiama, Igbogene, and Amassoma in Nembe from Nembe-Ewelesuo communities, Nembe-Basambiri, which host OML 29 oilfield and the NCTL wellhead. The participants from the joint military task force, civil society, environmental activists, high-profile community members, and oil and gas personnel reside in Yenagoa, Nembe, and surrounding communities. I also interviewed senior policymakers and oil and gas executives in Lagos, Port Harcourt, and Abuja because these were the locations where they agreed to meet with me. These interviews complement the data obtained in the case study area. Given their seniority with the government and/ or with the oil and gas sector in Nigeria, the data provided by them can be more broadly generalised because of their professional position and in-depth understanding of the oil and gas sector. Onuoha and Mathias noted that policies made by senior government officials guide the operation of oil activities in Bayelsa (2016, 2015).

Gatekeepers were used to gain access to the professional (oil and gas, security, and civil society), and community (leaders, environmental activists, and high-profile members) sample population. I considered Nigeria's cultural specificity, built around social, economic, ethnic, and environmental stratification of the broader society which was discussed with the primary and secondary gatekeepers. The marked difference between the two is that whilst the primary gatekeepers, the first point of call, represent the top echelon of the socio-economic, political, traditional, and cultural leadership stratification in Nigeria's Niger Delta.

The secondary gatekeepers were those that linked me with other gate-keepers in each sector from where the sample population was selected and recruited. For instance, the primary gatekeeper from the United Niger Delta Energy Development and Security Strategy-UNDEDSS and the Department of Petroleum Resources-DPR were the most vital links between me and oil and gas executives, civil societies as well as some participants. Most of the secondary gatekeepers had access to either NGOs or relevant oil and gas corporations as well as local community leaders. This strategy was vital to my accessing the population samples in the local communities in Bayelsa.

Using "gatekeepers within gatekeepers" helped soften the ground towards selecting and recruiting the final participants. Organising meetings with important people in the Nigerian society is very difficult. These different levels of gatekeepers only had minimal influence over the processes that led to sample selecting and evidence gathering. They did not influence the process of interviewing because they had no preview of the interview questions nor were they able to influence the selection of the interview venues. The primary and secondary gatekeepers had no idea of the type of answers, stories, and narratives shared by different participants. Therefore, the gatekeeper had no access to the data collected. However, some participants may have told biased stories as they narrated what they wanted me to believe to be true. But they did it without any influence. The gatekeepers could have introduced me to former militants directly involved in vandalism, artisans, and/or top politicians, but they did not due to the insecurity problems in the area. This detailed background to gatekeeping provides an additional contribution to knowledge in terms of how to do "research studies" in Nigeria.

41 respondents were selected and recruited from oil and gas companies, security agencies, professional NGO representatives, community leaders, high-profile community members, and environmental activists. Professional interviewees included oil and gas workers, security officials, and representatives of civil societies working in communities across Bayelsa State. While the community members were community leaders-king/chiefs, high-profile community members, and environmental activists. Interviewing few respondents suffices when gathering data for qualitative research, especially when studying hidden and hard to access populations such as professionals and deviant groups (Adler & Adler, n.d.: 8). The interviews were conducted at suitable and safe locations such as hotels, private residences, university campuses, churches, a

**Table 5.1**  Categorisation of professional and community interviewees

|                                         | Professional interviewees | Community interviewees |
| --------------------------------------- | ------------------------- | ---------------------- |
| Interviews in case study area           | 18                        | 13                     |
| Interviews outside case study area      | 7                         | 3                      |
| Total number of interviews (41)         | 25                        | 16                     |

*Source* Author, 2021

palace, and workplaces that were suitable and safe for both the respondent and the researcher. The interviews sessions lasted between 45 minutes and two and a half hours. Table 5.1 shows the sample groups and number of respondents.

The table shows most of the professionals were not members of the Bayelsa communities. The professional civil society NGO representatives interface with the oil and gas sector, the government as well as the communities. It was important to group the interview questions into two distinctive categories, operationalisation of oil and gas pipelines and security and social interaction to meet my research objectives.

Respondents were selected using the purposive sampling method. Johnson and Christensen (2008) noted that selecting the appropriate number of participants that can offer insights and decisively explain the phenomenon under review is a good aspect of a purposive sampling strategy (2008; Adler & Adler, no date). I used a structured approach by distributing the "research information sheet" and "consent forms" to different categories of respondents within the sample population. However, there is the danger that the sample population could be biased. This issue was overcome by asking the same question to different participants within the two sample groups and comparing their stories and narratives. By analysing data gathered from a cross-section of professional respondents this book answered questions of *why*, *how*, and *what* issues are behind onshore oil and gas infrastructure insecurity in Bayelsa and pipeline vandalism. Selecting regulatory experts with local knowledge and policy formulation and implementation experience makes this study purpose-driven data-gathering research. Patton (2002: 236) and Jones et al. (2014) noted that purposeful sampling enables the researcher to select participants with relevant knowledge and maximises the credibility of the data collected.

This book also gathered data from a range of official sources such as Acts of Parliament and policies of government and oil and gas operators. The research involved the collection and analysis of documents as well as different photographic evidence showing the socio-infrastructural conditions in the Bayelsa-Nembe case study area. Adopting the documentary data technique enabled the researcher to identify, understand and interpret data extracted from different documents to comprehensively support and enrich the research subject (Bowen, 2009). I examined some oil and gas regulatory Acts that influenced the design of some of the operational guidelines such as the Land Use Act (2004, 1978), Oil Pipeline Act (2004), Nigeria Mineral and Mining Act (2011), Petroleum Industry Act (2021), and Climate Change Act (2021) regulations. Others are the Environmental Impact Assessment Act (2004, 1992), the National Environmental Standards and Regulation Enforcement Agency Act (NESREA Act, 2007), and Nigeria's Flare-Gas-Prevention of Waste-and-Pollution-Regulation Act (2018).

The data gathering, processing, and storage complied with the University of Lincoln's ethical guidelines and procedures. The research ethics were approved by the School of Social and Political Science's ethics committee where the initial doctoral research that served as the basis for this book was done by aligning with the agreed principles stated in the consent form and GDPR guidelines (GDPR, 2018). The details of the entire participants were anonymised during and after this research. Data anonymisation is a process Clark (2006) described as removal of all indications and identifiable information from a set of data to ensure that the real identity of the respondent is hidden and anonymous. The private information of the research participants was anonymised in dairies, field notes, interview sessions, and transcription and data reduction processes in adherence to confidentiality principles. For instance, for clarity and understanding, the oil and gas participants are codified from "OILG-01" to "OILG-10". The respondents range from the Executive Director of a regulatory agency and Managing Director of oil companies to the Security Coordinator of the NCTL. The security respondents are codified from "SEC-01" to "SEC-10" and the respondents range from Navy Commanders, Army Major to Police Inspector, and Zonal lead of DSS. On the community respondents, the professional civil society representatives are coded from "Professional NGO-01" to "Professional NGO-05" while the Kings and chiefs are codified from "Community

Leader-01" to "Community Leader-05". The local community environmental activists are codified from "Environmental Activists-01" to "Environmental Activists-05" while the high-profile community members are codified from "Community Member-01" to "Community Member-06". This enabled meaningful referencing of participants' quotations and narratives to the research question and specific theme being analysed. For the full discussion on the places of recruitment, positions held, years of experience, and ethnicity refer to Appendix D.

Although my "objectivity" and the extent of my biases regarding what I wrote down and how I interpreted my entire data were challenged based on my "insider" knowledge of the Niger Delta region, being born in one of the Niger Delta states, this was extremely small compared to what I did not know. I have never visited the Bayelsa case study area, nor do I know the people, their social issues, or sub-cultures. My interest was reinforced when I realised this fact and increased my focus on the research question and my attention to detail which enabled me to maintain objective conversations with the respondents. Although, Asselin has noted that research insiders may not necessarily understand the sub-culture of the case study (2003). Though some researchers may have preconceived notions about something, this did not influence how I selected and recruited the participants for this study. But to some extent, listening to statements and engaging in conversation with respondents created some element of sympathy and biased my views. This justified Bryman's (2016) and Creswell's (2015) statement that this could influence how the data are interpreted. At the same time, I was attentive to drawing extensive insights from participants' narratives which Dwyer and Buckle (2009) stated was the hallmark and positioning of an objective "outsider". Hence the risk of my subjectivity was substantially low and adequately mitigated.

As Gibbs (2018: 38–40) noted, data analysis starts with coding after an intensive reading of the transcribed interviews. This leads to the identification of patterns and themes which are refined to assume similarity with ideas that are linked to the main categories. Coding is a way of categorising the text that is under scrutiny to establish a framework of thematic ideas which are sometimes interlinked and grouped under a general idea. Upon establishing the relationship between emerging themes, I allocated, organised, and named the different categories which enable me to develop different sections of the data. The initial coding enabled me to sort my findings into meaningful themes. The conversion of all the interview data, oil and gas regulatory Acts and policies, photographic evidence, and field notes helped me make sense of the dataset. As Berg notes, software such as NVivo assists the researcher in the analysis process, but does not do the analysis (2007).

The five holistic approaches adopted are (1) NVivo 12 followed by coding drawing on the intensive reading of text from the transcribed interviews; (2) comparing emerging themes derived from the professional and community stakeholders; (3) developed two comprehensive thematic categorised datasets further broken into seven smaller thematic categories; (4) combined and synthesised the discoveries and findings from the professional and community samples groups to develop new knowledge (see Chapters 1 and 2) and; (5) using Critical Discourse Analysis to describe, interpret, and explain how the discourses presented by various perspectives on vandalism and insecurity construct, maintain, legitimise, and highlight the socio-economic inequalities in Bayelsa and many petro-rich communities in the broader Global South.

The data processing and analysis process also involved categorisation of emerging themes from each of the sampled population-professionals and community groups' dataset which were manually coded and compared to determine similarities and or dissimilarities in patterns. This enabled me to either include them or not include them in the two comprehensively broad thematic datasets which are; (1) Onshore Oil and Gas Pipeline Infrastructure Insecurity in Bayelsa-Nembe; (2) and Socio-economic and Political conditions in Bayelsa-Nembe. By overarching the results with the central research question enabled me to establish, analyse, and present the entire research dataset. The two comprehensive thematically categorised datasets were broken into seven smaller thematic categories for in-depth analysis. I aligned with gray's assertion that it is better to thematically reorganise and rearrange the data into different categories (2018: 636). Thematic analysis is a qualitative analytical method that involves reading through an entire transcribed dataset to identify emerging patterns from the transcript and these are further developed into themes (Clarke & Braun, 2006). The objective is to identify important, meaningful, and or interesting themes that can be used to address the central research question. Doing so was not to assume weakness or validate either of the techniques, rather, I used both to ensure robustness and comprehensiveness of the outcome which Creswell noted has a significant positive impact on the research findings (2007, 2013). Systematically and rigorously undertaking qualitative analysis of the entire dataset revealed the nexus between all phases of answering the central research question. Chapters 6 and 7 elucidate the practical application of this approach. The thematic analysis of patterns that emerged from the transcribed interview data ensured a focus and deeper analysis of what the participants narrated.

Using thematic and Critical Discourse Analysis (CDA) in presenting, interpreting, and analysing the data aligned with Bryman, Ping, and Annan Singh's statements that the combination of more than one analytical technique means *triangulation of analysis* (2016, 2015). One aim for using CDA is to show that knowledge and authority can be derived from the linguistic construct in political discourse. I used CDA analytical technique to explain the specific insecurity context in the Bayelsa-Nembe study area. Each text was relied upon as the basic unit of communication. As Wodak and Meyer stated, critical discourse analysis focuses on the relationship between language, power, and conflict (2004). I leveraged the power of literature, documentary evidence, and research strategies to explain what Wodak and Meyer described as micro-sociological and theoretical perspectives (2004). Proponents like Fairclough and Wodak (1997) argue that language and the way it is used and interpreted determines and influences power relations and social conflicts from the perspective of the oppressed and the oppressor. CDA enabled me to analyse the different perspectives of each respondent from the sample population.

Revealing a new understanding of the impact of oil and gas regulatory guidelines and the impact of oil and gas activities on local communities. As an independent researcher, I analysed the data and used the power of text to decipher all the data sources in their presentation of facts. A critical review of the text forms and languages (verbal and nonverbal) of participants suggested that the views of the government and operators were supported by some works of literature like Mathias (2015) and NNPC reports (2016). The researcher was able to reveal the conflicts between the participant perceptions and literature on why oil and gas pipelines are vandalised, and the insecurity of oil and gas infrastructure in the Bayelsa area.

## Conclusion

FADT explains how instrumental aggression is the original precursor to the transfer of aggression against onshore oil and gas infrastructure particularly onshore pipelines (Okumagba, 2012). This book extended the debate by proposing CNADT which explains that ignoring, disregarding, and overlooking various socio-economic issues in local communities arouses anger and frustration that leads to aggression against pipelines. Pipeline vandalism and its underlying root causes deserves serious policy attention. Onshore oil and gas pipeline infrastructure insecurity, security, and securitisation. Acts of oil and gas pipeline terrorism like vandalism, illegal oil bunkering, sea piracy, and militancy in the Bayelsa Niger Delta should attract debate on how to mitigate the problems through the reconceptualization of the terrorism phenomenon. Pipeline vandalism deserves serious attention in the interest of both the host communities, climate change, the environment, the government, and oil operators. However, policies aimed at establishing security around the oil and gas infrastructure must go beyond issues of security. New Experiences in terms of meeting people across diverse socio-economic classes combined with the hands-on empirical exposure and practical knowledge skills in conducting face-to-face interviews are part of the vital gains of using this case study method.

As discussed throughout the chapter, such policies and their implementation guidelines must consider every action that leads to anger, frustration, and aggression. This means the Nigerian government; local authorities and the oil and gas sector need to acknowledge the damage that the current approach is causing. Instead of focusing on the deployment of security, the government and oil and gas corporations' policies must explore solutions that solve the underlying poverty, inequality, poor governance, corruption, environmental degradation, and political exclusion and participation issues. A failure to do so will only lead to further insecurity against oil and gas infrastructure and the wider region. Co-opting the host communities and protecting civil liberties would help to change the orientation of militants and create a people-centred security ideology. This would be the best way to design state and regional security architecture.

## REFERENCES

Abah, B. (2011, January–March). Agonies of Niger Delta Women. In *Environmental Rights Action/Friends of the Earth*. https://womin.africa/wp-content/uploads/2020/09/Environmental-Rights-Action-Agonies-of-Niger-Delta-Women.pdf. Accessed 10 June 2019.

Adedeji, A. (1999). *Comprehending and Mastering African Conflicts: The Search for Sustainable Peace and Good Governance*. Zed Books.

Adler, P. A., & Adler, P. (No Date). *How Many Qualitative Interviews is Enough?*. National Centre for Research Method. https://eprints.ncrm.ac.uk/id/epr int/2273/4/how_many_interviews.pdf. Accessed 2 March 2022.

Agbonifo, J. (2019). *Environment and Conflict, the Place and Logic of Collective Action in the Niger Delta*. Routledge.

Ahmed, H. H. (2005). Palestinian Resistance and Suicide Bombing: Causes and Consequences. In T. Biorgo (Ed.), *Root Causes of Terrorism: Myths, Reality, and Ways Forward* (pp. 87–102). Routledge.

Ahram, A. I. (2021). Hybrid Security Governance and the Search for the State in the Middle East, War the Rocks. *Texas National Security Review*. https://warontherocks.com/2021/01/hybrid-security-govern ance-and-the-search-for-the-state-in-the-middle-east/. Accessed 12 February 2022.

Akpan, U. (2021). 1.1bn OML 17 Development, Operations will Boost Local Content. *Vanguard News*. https://www.vanguardngr.com/2021/01/1-1bn oml-17-development-operations-will-boost-local-content-rewane/. Accessed 22 January 2021.

Akpomera, E. (2015). International Crude Oil Theft: Elite Predatory Tendencies in Nigeria. *Review of African Political Economy Journal, 42*(143), 156–165.

Alamieyeseigha, D. S. P. (2008). The Environmental Challenge of Developing the Niger Delta. In S. S. Azaiki, D. S. P. Alamieyeseigha, & A. A. Ikein (Eds.), *Oil, Democracy and the Promise of True Federalism in Nigeria* (pp. 249–260). University Press of America.

Allen, F. (2011). *Implementation of Oil Related Environmental Policies in Nigeria: Government Inertia and Conflict in the Niger Delta*. Cambridge Scholar.

Alkire, S. (2003). *A Conceptual Framework for Human Security* (CRISE Working Paper 2). University of Oxford. https://assets.publishing.service. gov.uk/media/57a08cf740f0b652dd001694/wp2.pdf. Accessed 24 January 2022.

Almond, A. G. (2015). Introduction: A Fundamental Approach to Comparative Politics. In G. A. Almond & J. S. Coleman (Eds.), *The Politics of the Developing Ages* (pp. 3–57). Princeton University Press.

Amnesty International Report. (2018). *Amnesty International Report 2017/18: The State of the World's Human Rights*. https://www.amnesty.org/en/doc uments/pol10/6700/2018/en/. Accessed 7 May 2024.

Anderson, C. A., & Dill, J. C. (1995). Effects of Frustration Justification on Hostile Aggression. *Aggressive Behaviour, 21*(5), 359–369.

Asselin, M. E. (2003). Insider Research: Issues to Consider when Doing Qualitative Research in your Setting. *Journal for Nursing in Staff Development, 19*(2), 99–103.

Astalin, P. K. (2013). Qualitative Research Designs: A Conceptual Framework. *International Journal of Social Science and Interdisciplinary Research, 2*(1), 118–124.

Bagayoko, N., Hutchful, E., & Luckham, R. (2016). Hybrid Security Governance in Africa: Rethinking the Foundations of Security, Justice and Legitimate Public Authority. *Journal of Conflict, Security and Development, 16*(1), 1–32.

Baldwin, D. A. (1998). The Concept of Security. *Review of International Studies, 23*(1), 5–26.

Bandura, A. (1973). *Aggression: A Social Learning Analysis*. Prentice-Hall.

BBC News. (2021, November 23). EndSars Protests: Nigeria's Lekki Massacre Report Fake. *Says Minister*. https://www.bbc.co.uk/news/topics/cezwd6k5k6vt/endsars-protests. Accessed 20 January 2022.

Berg, L. B. (2007). *Qualitative Research Methods for the Social Sciences* (6th ed.). Pearson Education.

Bergstresser, H. (2017). *A Decade of Nigeria: Politics, Economy and Society 2004–2016*. Brill.

Berkowitz, L. (1993). *Aggression: Its Causes, Consequences, and Control*. McGraw-Hill.

Berkowitz, L. (2011). A Cognitive-No Association Theory of Aggression. In A. W. Kruglanski, P. A. M. Van Lange, & E. T. Higgins (Eds.), *The Handbook of Theories of Social Psychology* (pp. 90–120). Sage.

Blatz, W. E. (1966). *Human Security some Reflections*. University of Toronto Press.

Booth, K. (2007). *Theory of World Security*. Cambridge University Press.

Bowen, G. A. (2009). Document Analysis as a Qualitative Research Method. *Qualitative Research Journal, 9*(2), 27–40.

Brennan, J. (2016). *Against Democracy: New Preface*. Princeton University Press.

Brown, S., & Sessions, J. G. (2000). Employee Militancy in Britain: 1985–1990. *Applied Economics Journal, 32*, 1767–1774.

Bryman, A. (2016). *Social Research Methods* (5th ed.). Oxford University Press.

Bulhan, H. A. (1985). *Frantz Fanon and the Psychology of Oppression*. Plenum.

Burlton, A. H. A. (2007). *Pleasure and Instinct: A Study in the Psychology of Human Action*. Routledge.

Bushman, B. J., & Anderson, C. A. (2002). Human Aggression. *Annual Review Psychology Journal, 53*, 27–51.

Bushman, B. J., Anderson, C. A., & Allen, J. J. (2018). The General Aggression Model. *Current Opinions in Psychology Journal, 9*, 75–80.

Buzan, B. (1984a). Peace, Power, and Security: Contending Concepts in the Study of International Relations. *Journal of Peace Research, 21*(2), 109–125.

Buzan, B. (1984b). *People, States, and Fear: The National Security Problems in International Relations*. University of North Carolina.

Buzan, B., & Hansen, L. (2009). *The Evolution of the International Security Studies*. Cambridge University Press.

Cha, V. D. (2011). Globalisation and Security. In M. Y. Lai & C. W. Hughes (Eds.), *Security Studies*. Routledge.

Clark, A. (2006). *Anonymising Research Data* (ESRC National Centre for Research Methods Working Paper Series). https://eprints.ncrm.ac.uk/id/eprint/480/1/0706_anonymising_research_data.pdf. Accessed 3 January 2018.

Clarke, V., & Braun, V. (2006). Using Thematic Analysis in Psychology. *Qualitative Research in Psychology Journal, 3*, 77–101.

Coleman, J. S. (2015). The Politics of Sub-Saharan Africa. In A. G. Almond & J. S. Coleman (Eds.), *The Politics of the Developing Areas* (pp. 247–354). Princeton University Press.

Collier, P. (2007). *The Bottom Billion* (pp. 39–52). Oxford University Press.

Collier, P., & Hoeffler, A. E. (2004). *Greed and Grievance in Civil War*. World Bank Development Research Group.

Cordesman, A. H. (2016). *The Underlying Causes of Stability and Instability in the Middle East and North Africa (MENA) Region*. Center for Strategic and International Studies.

Cox, D. G. (2005). Political terrorism and Democratic and Economic Development in Indonesia. In W. J. Crotty (Ed.), *Democratic Development and Political Terrorism: The Global Perspective* (pp. 255–267). Northeastern University Press.

Creswell, J. W. (2007). *Qualitative Inquiry and Research Design: Choosing Among Five Approaches* (2 ed.). Sage.

Creswell, J. W. (2013). *Research Design: Qualitative, Quantitative, and Mixed Methods Approaches* (2 ed.). Sage.

Creswell, J. W. (2015). *A Concise Introduction to Mixed Methods Research*. Sage.

Curley, M., & Pettiford, L. (1999). *Changing Security Agendas and the Third World*. Pinter.

D' Arcy, S. (2013). *Languages of the Unheard: Why Militant Protests is Good for Democracy*. Zed Books.

Denscombe, M. (2007). *The Good Research Guide for Small-Scale Social Research Projects* (3rd ed.). Open University Press.

Dollard, J., Miller, N. E., Doob, L. W., Mowrer, O. H., & Sears, R. R. (1939). *Frustration and Aggression*. Yale University Press.

Don Pedro, I. (2006). *Oil in the Water, Crude Power and Militancy in the Niger Delta*. Forward Communications Limited.

Douglas, O. (2008). A Community Guide to Understanding Resource Control. In A. Ikein, D. S. P. Alamieyeseigha, & S. Azaiki (Eds.), *Oil, Democracy, and the Promise of True Federalism* (pp. 331–340). University Press of America.

Douglas, O., & Okonta, I. (2003). *Where Vultures Feast: Shell, Human Rights, and Oil in the Niger Delta*. Verso.

Duda, D., & Wardin, K. (2013). Characteristics of Piracy in the Gulf of Guinea and its Influence on International Maritime Transport in the Region. In A. Weintrit & T. Neumann (Eds.), *Marine Navigation and Safety Transportation* (pp. 177–185). CRC Publication.

Duquet, N. (2011). Swamped with Weapons: The Proliferation of illicit Small Arms and Light Weapons in the Niger Delta. In C. Obi & S. A. Rustad (Eds.), *Oil and Insurgency in the Niger Delta: Managing the Complex Politics of Petrol-Violence*. Zed Books.

Durkheim, E. (1956). *Education and Sociology*. Free Press.

Dwyer, S., & Buckle, J. (2009). The Space Between on Being an Insider-Outsider in Qualitative Research. *International Journal of Qualitative Methods, 8*(1), 54–63.

Egbe, R. E., & Thompson, D. (2010, December). Environmental Challenges of Oil Spillage for Families in Oil Producing Communities of the Niger Delta Region. *Journal of Home Economics Research*, (13).

Ejeh, E. U., Bappah, A. I., & Dankofa, Y. (2019). Nature of Terrorism and Anti-terrorism Laws in Nigeria. *Nnamdi Azikiwe University Journal of International Law and Jurisprudence, 10*(2), 186–192.

Emmer, R. (2016). Securitisation. In A. Collins (Ed.), *Contemporary Security Studies* (4th ed., pp. 168–182). Oxford University Press.

Environmental Impact Assessment Act. (1992). *Environmental Impact Assessment Degree No. 86 (1992)*. https://faolex.fao.org/docs/pdf/nig18378.pdf. Accessed 7 May 2024.

Etemire, U. (2016). *Law and Practice on Public Participation in Environmental Matters: The Nigerian Example in Transnational Comparative Perspective*. Routledge.

Etete, E. (2017, July 7). Ovom in Yenagoa City: A Cradle of Development but Shadow of itself. *Headline News Nigeria*. http://headlinenewsnigeria.com/ovom-yenagoa-city-cradle-development-shadow/. Accessed 2 March 2018.

Etikerentse, G. (1985). *Nigerian Petroleum Law*. Macmillan.

Etowah, U. E., & Effiong, S. A. (2012). Oil Spillage Cost Gas Flaring Cost, and Life Expectancy Rate of the Niger Delta People of Nigeria. *Advances in Management and Applied Economics Journal, 2*(2), 211–228.

Fairclough, N., & Wodak, R. (1997). Critical Discourse Analysis. In T. van Dijk (Ed.), *Discourse as Social Interaction* (pp. 258–284). Sage.

Faleti, A. S. (2006). *Theories of Social Conflicts*. Spectrum.

Fierke, K. M. (2015). *Critical Approaches to International Security* (2nd ed.). Polity.

Freud, S. (2015). *Beyond Pleasure Principle*. Dover.

Fukuyama, F. (2018). *Identity: The Demand for Dignity and the Politics of Resentment*. Profile Books.

Ganor, B. (2010). Defining Terrorism: Is One Man's Terrorist Another Man's Freedom Fighter? *Journal of Police Practice and Research, 3*(4), 287–304.

General Data Protection Regulation. (2018). *Guide to the General Data Protection Regulation (GDPR)*. Information Commissioner's Office. https://assets.publishing.service.gov.uk/government/uploads/system/uploads/att achment_data/file/711097/guide-to-the-general-data-protection-regulation-gdpr-1-0.pdf. Accessed 10 January 2019.

Gibbs, G. (2018). *Analysing Qualitative Data: The Sage Qualitative Research Kit* (2nd ed.). Sage.

Grossman, H. I. (1999). Kleptocracy and Revolutions. *Oxford Economic Papers Journal, 51*, 267–283.

Gultekin, K. (2007). Women Engagement in Terrorism: What Motivates Females to Join in Terrorist Organisations? In D. M. Al-Badayneh, S. Ozeren, & I. D. Gunes (Eds.), *Understanding Terrorism: Analysis of Sociological and Psychological Aspects, the NATO Science for Peace and Security Programme* (Vol. 22, pp. 169–174). IOS.

Gupta, D. K. (2008). *Understanding Terrorism and Physical Violence: The Life Cycle of Birth, Growth*. Routledge.

Gurr, R. T. (2015). *Political Rebellion: Causes*. Routledge.

Hain, D., & Pisoiu, S. (2017). *Theories of Terrorism: An Introduction*. Routledge.

Haq, U. M. (1995). *Reflections on Human Development*. Oxford University Press.

Heleta, S. (2009). *The Darfur Conflict from the Perspective of the Rebel Justice and Equality Movement*. Nelson Movement University.

Herbst, D., & Ndlangisa, M. (2010). CII Protection- Lessons for Developing Countries: South Africa as a Case Study. In R. Bloomfield & E. Rome (Eds.), *Critical Information Infrastructures Security*. Springer.

Heurlin, B., & Kristensen, K. (2010). International Security. In P. D. Williams, P. Bilgin, Sekiguchi, J. K. Galbraith, S. T. Inayatullah, J. Wiener, R. A. Schrire, & I. L. Murphy (Eds.), *Global Security, and International Political Economy* (Vol. III, pp. 65–109). EOLSS Publication.

Hoeffler, A. (2011). Greed Versus Grievance: A Useful Conceptual Distinction in the Study of Civil War? *Studies in Ethnicity and Nationalism Journal, 11*(2), 274–284.

Holborn, M., & Haralambos, M. (2021). *Sociology: Themes and Perspectives* (8th ed.). Collins.

Hosen, A. (2011). Religion and Security: What's Your Motive? In N. Hosen & R. Mohr (Eds.), *Law and Religion in Public Life: The Contemporary Debate* (pp. 137–151). Routledge.

Hough, P. (2004). *Understanding Global Security*. Routledge.

House of Commons. (2013). *Serious and Organised Crime Strategy*. Stationery Office.

Hudson, N. F. (2010). *Gender, Human Security and the United Nations: Security Language as a Political Platform for Women*. Routledge.

Huesmann, L. R. (2013). *Aggressive Behaviour: Current Perspectives*. Springer Science.

Human Rights Watch. (1999). *Nigeria: Crackdown in the Niger Delta* (Vol. 11(2)). Human Rights Watch.

Human Security Report Project. (2013). *The Decline of Global Violence: Evidence, Explanation, and Contestation*. Human Security Press. https://rel iefweb.int/sites/reliefweb.int/files/resources/HSRP_Report_2013_140226_ Web.pdf. Accessed 3 July 2020.

Ibaba, I. S. (2012). Introduction: Interrogating Development Deficits in the Niger Delta, In S. I. Ibaba (Ed.), *Niger Delta: Constraints and Pathways to Development* (pp. 1–9). Cambridge.

Igbinovia, P. E. (2014). *Oil Thefts and Pipeline Vandalisation in Nigeria*. African Books.

Ikelegbe, A., & Oshita, O. O. (2019). An Overview of Theoretical and Practical Issues in Internal Security Management in Nigeria. In O. O. Oshita, I. M. Alumona, & F. C. Onuoha (Eds.), *Internal Security Management in Nigeria: Perspectives, Challenges, and Lessons* (pp. 29–48). Palgrave.

Issa, A. (2015). *Reflections on Industrial and Economy*. Maulthouse.

James, D. D. (1995). The Value of Security: Hobbs, Marx, Nietzche, and Baudrillard. In R. D. Lipchitz (Ed.), *On Security* (p. 24). Colombia University Press.

James, U. V. (2018). *Capacity Building for Sustainable Development*. Centre for Agriculture and Bioscience International-CABI Publication.

Jatto, A. A., & Stanislas, P. (2017). Contemporary Security Challenges Facing Edo State Nigeria. *Journal of Geopolitics, History, and International Relations, 9*(2), 118–140.

Jatto, A. A., Skoczylis, J., & Horner, G. (2023). UK Anti-Money Laundering and Counter-Terrorist Financing Measures. In S. N. Romaniuk, C. Kaunert, & A. P. H. Fabe (Eds.), *Countering Terrorist and Criminal Financing* (1st ed.). Routledge & CRC Press. https://doi.org/10.4324/9781003092216. Accessed 18 November 2023.

Jenkins, L. (2022). *Sisters and Sisterhood: The Kenney Family, Class, and Suffrage 1890–1965*. Oxford University Press.

Johnson, B., & Christensen, L. (2008). *Educational Research: Qualitative*. Sage.

Jones, S. R., Torres, V., & Arminio, J. (2014). *Negotiating the Complexities of Qualitative Research in Higher Education: Fundamental Elements and Issues* (2nd ed.). Routledge.

Kashubsky, M. (2016). *Offshore Oil and Gas Installations Security: An International Perspective*. Routledge.

Kee, C. (2012). *Global Sales and Contract Law*. Oxford University Press.

King, M. L., Jr. (1967). *The Other America and Black Power*. Beacon Press.
King, S. O. (2016). Engineering Students' Approaches to Learning Mathematics. In L. Ling & P. Ling (Eds.), *Methods and Paradigms in Education Research* (pp. 167–190). Hershey, IGI.
Krahmann, E. (2008). Security: Collective Good or Commodity? *European Journal of International Relations, 14*(3), 382–383.
Krueger, I. J. (1996). Probabilistic National Stereotypes. *European Journal of Social Psychology, 26*, 960–985.
Kulungu, M. (2021). Movement for the "Emancipation of the Niger Delta" (MEND) Constitutes a Threat to the U.S National Security. *Open Access Library Journal, 8*, 1–17.
Land Use Act. (2004). *The Complete Laws of Nigeria, a Searchable Compendium*. Land Use Act. https://lawsofnigeria.placng.org/view2.php?sn=228. Accessed 20 February 2022.
Langford, P. (1986). *Modern Philosophies of Human Nature: Their Emergence from Christian Thoughts*. Lancaster.
Lawrence, M. (2013). *Three Approaches to Security: Prevention. Protection, and Resilience*. Centre for Security Governance. https://www.ssrresourcecentre.org/2013/02/04/three-approaches-to-security-prevention-protection-and-resilience/. Accessed 12 April 2020.
Lazarus, R. S. (1994). *Emotion and Adaptation*. Oxford University Press.
Leonardo, D. A. (2012). Pirates and Militants in the Niger Delta: An Overview. In S. C. Giotti (Ed.), *Piracy and Maritime Terrorism: Logistics, Strategies, Scenarios* (pp. 170–190). IOS Press.
Linden, O., & Palsson, J. (2013). Oil Contamination in Ogoniland Niger Delta, Stockholm. *The Royal Swedish Academy of Sciences Journal, 42*(6), 685–701.
Madubuko, C. C. (2017). Oiling the Guns and Gunning for Oil: The Youths and Niger Delta Oil Conflicts in Nigeria. In E. M. Mbah & T. Falola (Eds.), *Dissent, Protest and Dispute in Africa* (pp. 260–289). Routledge.
Masys, A. J. (2016). Manufactured Risk, Complexity and Non-traditional Security: From World Risk Society to a Networked Risk Model. In A. J. Masys (Ed.), *Exploring the Security Landscape: Non-Traditional Security Challenges* (pp. 313–320). Springer.
Mathias, B. A. (2011). The Social Effects of Oil Production in Gbaran Ubie, Bayelsa State, Nigeria. *International Journal of Development and Management Review, 6*, 151–159.
Mathias, Z. (2015). Providing All-Round Security against Oil and Gas Infrastructure Sabotage and Physical Attacks on the Staff of NNPC and Multinational Oil Companies in Nigeria as a Critical Article of Her National Security Efforts. *International Journal of Social Science and Humanities Research, 3*(2), 45–59.
Mickolus, E. (2018). *Terrorism Worldwide, 2016*. McFarland and Company.

Mill, S. J. (1863). *Utilitarianism, On Liberty and Considerations on Representative Government*. Parker, Son, and Bourn.

More, T. (2020). *Utopia*. Open Road Media.

Mouffe, C. (2005). *The Return of the Political*. Verso.

Murshed, S. M., & Cuesta, J. (2013). Greed, Grievance, and Globalisation. In P. Justino, T. Bruck, & P. Verwimp (Eds.), *A Micro-Level Perspective on the Dynamics of Conflict, Violence, and Development* (pp. 50–68). Oxford University Press.

Nacos, B. L. (2016). *Terrorism and Counterterrorism* (5th ed.). Routledge.

National Bureau of Statistics. (2017). *Social Statistics Report December 2016*. National Bureau of Statistics.

National Environmental Standards and Regulation Enforcement Agency Act. (2007). Discharge of Hazardous Substance and Related Offences. http://lawsofnigeria.placng.org/laws/nesrea.pdf. Accessed 22 February 2022.

Neocleous, M. (2007). Security Liberty and the Myth of Balance: Towards a Critique of Security Politics. *Contemporary Political Theory Journal, 6*, 131–149.

Newman, E. (2004). A Normatively Attractive but Analytically Weak Concept. *Journal of Security Dialogue, 35*(3), 355–360.

Nigeria Climate Change Act. (2021). *Climate Change Act 2021*. An Act to Provide for the Mainstreaming of Climate Change Actions, Establish the National Council on Climate Change; and for Related Matters. https://cdn.climatepolicyradar.org/navigator/NGA/2021/nigerias-climate-change-act_6c83884695bbf609fcd795a49d196e89.pdf. Accessed 7 May 2024.

Nigeria Mineral and Mining Act. (2011). Administration of the Act. http://admin.theiguides.org/Media/Documents/Nigeruian%20Minerals%20and%20Mining%20Act,%202007.pdf. Accessed 5 October 2022.

Nigeria's Flare-Gas-(Prevention of Waste and Pollution) Regulations. (2018). Flare Gas (Prevention of Waste Pollution) Regulations. https://ngfcp.dpr.gov.ng/media/1120/flare-gas-prevention-of-waste-and-pollution-regulations-2018-gazette-cleaner-copy-1.pdf. Accessed 19 September 2021.

Nigerian National Petroleum Corporation. (2016). *Monthly Financial and Operations Report September 2016* (pp. 2–9). Nigerian National Petroleum Corporation.

Njoku, A. O. (2016). Oil Pipelines Vandalism and its Effects on the Socio-Economic Development in Nigerian Society. *International Journal of Multidisciplinary Academic Research, 4*(7), 45–57.

Novotny, D. D. (2007). What is Terrorism. In E. V. Linden (Ed.), *Focus on Terrorism* (pp. 23–31). Nova.

Nwuke, K. (2021). *Nigeria's Petroleum Industry Act: Addressing Old Problems, Creating New Ones*. Africa in Focus. https://www.brookings.edu/blog/afr ica-in-focus/2021/11/24/nigerias-petroleum-industry-act-addressing-old-problems-creating-new-ones/. Accessed 19 February 2022.

Oil Pipeline Act. (2004). Chapter 338: Laws of the Federal Republic of Nigeria. https://www.chr.up.ac.za/images/researchunits/bhr/files/extrac tive_industries_database/nigeria/laws/Oil%20Pipelines%20Act.pdf. Accessed 28 March 2020.

Oki, R. A. (2017). *Barbarism to Decadence: Nigeria and Foreign Complicity*. Author Solutions.

Okonofua, B. A. (2016). The Niger Delta Amnesty Program: The Challenges of Transitioning from Peace Settlements to Long-Term Peace. *Sage Open Journals, 6*(2), 1–16.

Okonta, I. (2016). Policy Incoherence and the Challenge of Energy Security. In A. Goldthau (Ed.), *The Handbook of Global Energy Policy* (pp. 501–520). Wiley.

Okumagba, P. (2012). Oil Exploration and Crisis in the Niger Delta: The Response of the Militia Groups. *Journal of Sustainable Society, 1*(3), 78–83.

Olawuyi, D. S. (2012). Legal and Sustainable Development Impacts of Major Oil Spills. *The Journal of Sustainable Development, 9*(1), 1–15.

Olsen, M. (1965). *The Logic of Collective Action: Public Goods and the Theory of Groups*. Harvard University Press.

Olusanya, O. (2014). Using the Macro-Micro Integrated Theoretical Model to Understand the Dynamics of Collective Violence. In I. Bantekas & E. Mylonaki (Eds.), *Criminological Approaches to International Criminal Law* (pp. 222–239). Cambridge University Press.

Onuoha, C. F. (2007). Oil Pipeline Sabotage in Nigeria: Dimensions, Actors and Implications for National Security. *African Security Review, 17*(3), 100–115.

Onuoha, C. F. (2016). *The Resurgence of Militancy in Nigeria's Oil-Rich Niger Delta and the Dangers of Militarisation*. Al Jazeera Centre for Studies.

Orere, O. (2009). Henry Okah: The Struggle of my Life, Ijaw Monitoring Group: Niger Delta Rights Defender. https://www.ijawmonitor.org/news. php?ct=4& article=113. Accessed 4 February 2022.

Oriola, B. T. (2016). *Criminal Resistance: The Politics of Kidnapping Oil Workers*. Routledge.

Osawaru, J. A. (2020). *Endsars Protest Hidden Truth you Need to Know*. Independent Publication.

Oswald, S. E. S. (2009). The Impossibility of Securitizing Gender vis-à-vis 'Engendering' Security. In H. G. Brauch, H. Krummenacher, N. C. Behera, P. Kameri-Mbote, J. Grin, O. Spring, U. Chourou, & B. Mesjasz (Eds.), *Facing Global Environmental Change: Environmental, Human, Energy, Food, Health, and Water Security Concepts* (pp. 1143–1156). Springer.

Otobo, D. (2016). *Essentials of Labour Relations in Nigeria: Public Sector Labour and Employment Relations* (Vol. 3). Malthouse Press.

Owen, T. (2004). Challenges and Opportunities for Defining and Measuring Human Security. *Disarmament Forum Journal, 3,* 15–23.

Paes, W. C. (2003). Oil Production and National Security in sub-Saharan Africa. In *Oil Policy in the Gulf of Guinea.* Friedrich-Ebert-Stiftung.

Patton, M. Q. (2002). *Qualitative Research and Evaluation Methods.* Sage.

Ping, G. C., & Annansingh, F. (2015). *Experiences in Applying Mixed Methods Approach in Information Systems Research.* In Management Association Information Resources.

Pirates, D. C. (2013). Ecological Security: A Conceptual Framework. In R. Floyd & R. A. Matthew (Eds.), *Environmental Security: Approaches and Issues* (pp. 139–148). Routledge.

Poku, N. K., & Therkelsen, J. (2016). Globalisation, Development, and Security. In A. Collins (Ed.), *Contemporary Security Studies* (pp. 262–276). Oxford University Press.

Ray, S. N. (2004). *Modern Comparative Politics: Approaches, Methods and Issues.* Prentice-Hall.

Richards, A. (2015). *Conceptualising Terrorism.* Oxford University Press.

Richardson, L. (2006). The Roots of Terrorism: An Overview. In L. Richardson (Ed.), *The Roots of Terrorism* (pp. 1–17). Routledge.

Samuelson, P. A. (1954). The Pure Theory of Public Expenditure. *Review of Economics and Statistics Journal, 36*(4), 387–389.

Sanderson, C. A. (2010). *Social Psychology.* Wiley.

Schechter, M. G. (2016). *Future Multilateralism: The Political and Social Framework.* Springer.

Scott, J. F. (2014). The Nature of Social Research and Social Knowledge. In I. Marsh (Ed.), *Theory and Practice in Sociology* (pp. 3–25). Routledge.

Segall, M. H. (2016). *Human Behaviour and Public Policy: A Political Psychology.* Pergamon Press.

Shaw, P. (2019). *100 Great Leading through Frustration Ideas.* Marshall Cavendish.

Shimko, K. L. (2015). *International Relations: Perspectives, Controversies, and Readings.* Centage Learning.

Skoczylis, J. J. (2015). *The Local Prevention of Terrorism: Strategy and Practice in the Fight Against Terrorism.* Palgrave Macmillan.

Sloan, S., & Bunker, R. J. (2012). *Red Teams and Counterterrorism Training.* University of Oklahoma Press.

Smith, B. (2013). *Understanding Third World Politics: Theories of Political Change and Development* (4th ed.). Palgrave Macmillan.

Stone, J. (2007). *Aggression and World Order: A Critique of United Nations Theories of Aggression.* The Law Book Exchange.

Tausch, N., Becker, J., Spears, R., Christ, O., Saab, R., Singh, P., & Siddiqui, R. N. (2011). Explaining Radical group Behaviour: Developing Emotion and Efficacy Routes to Normative and non-normative Collective Action. *Journal of Personality and Social Psychology, 101,* 129–145.

Terrorism Prevention Act. (2013). *Federal Republic of Nigeria Official Gazette: Terrorism (Prevention) Amendment Act, 2013.* https://placng.org/lawsofnig eria/laws/terrorism_bill.pdf. Accessed 08 May 2024.

Thoreau, H. D. (2016). *Civil Disobedience.* Xist Publishing.

Thurston, A. (2019). *Boko Haram: The History of an African Jihadist Movement.* Princeton.

Tilly, C. (2003). *Politics of Collective Violence.* Cambridge University Press.

Transparency International. (2019). Military Involvement in Oil Theft in the Niger Delta. https://ti-defence.org/publications/military-involvement-in-oil-theft-in-the-niger-delta/. Accessed 25 November 2020.

United Nations Convention for the Suppression of the Financing of Terrorism. (1999). Special Treaty Event, 2009. https://www.unodc.org/documents/tre aties/Special/1999%20International%20Convention%20for%20the%20Supp ression%20of%20the%20Financing%20of%20Terrorism.pdf. Accessed 18 May 2020.

United Nations Development Programme. (1994). *Human Development Report 1994: New Dimensions of Human Security.* Oxford University Press.

United Nations Development Programme. (2017). *Human Development Report 2016: Human Development for Everyone.* United Nations.

United Nations Environment Programme Report. (2012). Environmental Assessment of Ogoniland: Assessment of Vegetation, Aquatic and Public Health Issues. http://hdl.handle.net/20.500.11822/25286. Accessed 9 May 2018.

United Nations Office of Coordination of Humanitarian Affairs. (2009). *Human Security in Theory and Practice.* United Nations. https://www.unocha.org/ sites/dms/HSU/Publications%20and%20Products/Human%20Security%20T ools/Human%20Security%20in%20Theory%20and%20Practice%20English. pdf. Accessed 24 January 2022.

United States Department of States. (2005). *Office of the Coordinator for Counterterrorism: Country Report on Terrorism 2004.* Government press.

Walters, G. D. (2012). Criminal Predatory Behaviour in the Federal Bureau of Prisons. In M. Delisi & P. J. Conis (Eds.), *Violent Offenders: Theory, Research, Policy, and Practice* (pp. 369–382). Jones and Bartlett.

Waltz, K. (2000). *Theory of International Politics.* McGrew Hill.

Wang, F., & Deng, Y. (2005). *China Rising: Power and Motivation in Chinese Foreign Policy.* Rowman, and Littlefield.

Webb, M. J. (2016). *Separatists Violence in South Asia: A Comparative Study.* Routledge.

Weinberg, L. (2009). *Global Terrorism.* Rosen Publishing.

Wodak, R., & Meyer, M. (2004). *Methods of Critical Discourse Analysis* (Wodak and Meyer Eds.). Sage.

Wolfers, A. (1952). National Security, as an Ambiguous Symbol. *Political Science Quarterly, 67*, 483.

Xiaofeng, Y., & Jia, L. (2016). Human Security: China's Conceptual Approaches and Policy Making Patterns. In W. T. Tow, D. Walton, & R. Kersten (Eds.), *New Approaches to Human Security in the Asia-Pacific: China, Japan, and Australia* (pp. 5–22). Routledge.

Yin, R. K. (2012). *Application of Case Study Research* (3rd ed.). Sage.

Zhao, Z. (2011). Non-Traditional Security and the New Concept of Security of China. In H. G. Brauch, J. Birkmann, U. O. Spring, J. Grin, C. Mesjasz, B. Chourou, P. Dunay, & P. K. Mbote (Eds.), *Coping with Global Environmental Change, Disasters and Security: Threats, Challenges, Vulnerabilities and Risks*. Springer.

# CHAPTER 6

# The Effect of Oil and Gas Activities on Pipeline Vandalism: The Perspectives of Professional Operators

## Insight into the Data Presentation and Analysis Process

In this chapter and the next (6 and 7), the book presents and analyses the stories narrated by different professional oil and gas and government stakeholders as well as different community and civil society stakeholders who were interrogated during the empirical fieldwork in Nigeria (see Chapters 2, 3, and 4). The structure of this book has been illuminated around two distinctive areas: (1) the analysis of oil and gas infrastructure insecurity in Nigeria and the Global South, midstream and downstream petroleum regulatory policies and operational activities of oil and gas multinational organisations coupled with the Nigerian security architecture (Mahmood et al., 2023; Oil Pipeline Act, 2004; Okonofua, 2016); and (2) the analysis of multiple literature and documentary evidence on the impact of oil and gas regulatory policies and activities of multinational oil and gas operation on host communities in Nembe, Bayelsa state, Nigeria (Alamieyeseigha, 2005, 2008; Matthias, 2015; Okumagba, 2013).

The book centres its argument around three areas (1) that the instrumental policies of the government and their implementation; (2) the non-adoption of best international practices and some unethical behaviours, by oil and gas multinationals; (3) and on top of the devastating impact

A. L. A. Jatto, *Oil and Gas Pipeline Infrastructure Insecurity*, New Security Challenges, https://doi.org/10.1007/978-3-031-56932-6_6

of oil activities on the environment, the communities have suffered, caused tensions between individuals, communities, oil companies, and the government which cascades to varying degree of insecurity problems. The book was effectively framed to raise and address some very critical and vital overarching questions which were answered across the entire Chapters focusing on the vandalism of the NCTL in Bayelsa in the historic Niger Delta region such as:

- Have socio-economic, environmental, and political issues contributed to oil and gas pipeline infrastructure vandalism and insecurity problems in Bayelsa State, Nigeria's Niger Delta? (Chapters 2, 3, 4, and 8);
- What impact have regulatory policy guidelines had on oil and gas extraction and production, and pipeline operations in terms of responses to vandalism and oil spills in Bayelsa State, Nigeria? (Chapters 2, 3, 4, and 8);
- What impact do security protection strategies of onshore pipelines have on local communities in Bayelsa state? (Chapters 2, 3, 6, and 7);
- In What ways has the construction and operationalisation of the NCTL impacted the natural environment and the host communities in Nembe, Niger Delta? (Chapters 2, 3, 4, and 8).

The book takes "five holistic approaches" in the context of the Nigerian oil and gas industry to analyse and answer these questions and highlight the underlying causes of onshore pipeline vandalism, conflicts, threats, and political tensions in the case study area.

## THE IMPACT OF CORRUPTION AND CRIMINALITY

Despite the differences between corruption and criminality, a combination of both phenomena exerts a significant level of tension on communities due to environmental damage and lack of infrastructure or its decay. Those engaged in pipeline vandalism are often labeled as criminals and sometimes even terrorists. Pipeline vandalism and oil theft by some of these youths are seen as morally repressible by society. What emerges from the interviews, however, is that the oil and gas and security professionals draw a link between corruption, criminal youths, and organised crime

(Anand & Ashforth, 2003; Neumann & Elsenbroich, 2017; Nye, 1967; Ogbeidi, 2012). More discussion on this point is further down. The fact remains that those engaging in pipeline vandalism, only have limited influence over government regulatory policymaking. Although their actions have some impact on regional security, they are unable to determine the institutions or their policies from within (Ioannides, 2017; Lynch et al., 2015).

In its broadest sense, corruption is the abuse of power by those in official positions for their gain, or the gain of those close to them (Amundsen, 2019). Corruption is not only present in the public sector but also permeates throughout the private sector and civil society. Corruption is when "the agent betrays the principal in pursuit of her interests" (Philp, 2015: 18). The political class and those who hold esteem positions "betray" public interests and trust in pursuit of their private interests with impunity. Philp noted that certain social conditions must be present that will enable the political class to have such domineering monopolistic control. Such as control of the judiciary, security, lack of accountability, and probity. This reinforces the deviant behaviours of the political class. Data from transparency International suggests that Nigeria made little or no progress in ending the perceived levels of public sector corruption. It is difficult to demarcate the essential characteristics of the corruption phenomenon.

As Theobald said, the nature of corruption is inseparable from questions of "public morality or morality in general" (1990: 1). Bellow points out, "In every community, there is a class of people profoundly dangerous to the rest. I do not mean criminals. For them, we have punitive sanctions. I mean the leaders. Invariably, the most dangerous people seek the power" (Bello, 1964: 51). Those in power can divert public money, set regulatory frameworks as well as shape policies to benefit themselves, rather than working for the good of those they serve. Such behaviour is common amongst Nigerian leadership in Abuja and the Niger Delta, and its impact can be felt across Nembe communities (Ogbeidi, 2012). Quantifying corruption in Nigeria is difficult. What is clear, however, is that public and private officials and well-connected multinational oil and gas firms have used their influence to shape oil and gas regulations and policies in the Nigerian petroleum industry which is impacting the Niger Delta.

One of many examples is the awarding of an oil and gas mining license to OML 46 to Halkin Exploration and Production, despite it lacking the technical or financial capacity to explore the oil field (Disu, 2021). Rather than the Bayelsa Oil and Gas Company who had been operating the oilfield successfully for some time. What this means is that powerful individuals are wielding political and financial powers hiding behind Halkin Exploration and Production company. Disu noted that they worked in cahoots with the powerful political and bureaucratic class to seize a state asset (2021). Participants agreed that corruption and criminality were major issues within the oil and gas sector, however, each exonerated their sectors from the problems. Pipeline regulators, security, and oil and gas producers neglect and refuse to take responsibility for the crippling impact of corruption and criminal activities that are destroying Nigeria's petroleum industry.

The 20 professional oil and gas and security respondents agree that the corruption in the oil and gas industry is causing tensions and problems. Further analysis showed that 15 out of the 20 professional respondents, seven oil and gas and eight security officials blame the extensive corruption on oil companies, regulators, and their related services. While five out of the 20 respondents believe corruption and criminality are minimal and that where it exists it is should be blamed on the community and security agencies. Just because the community and security were not mentioned in the narrative of respondents who blamed the oil and gas sector does not suggest that the community and security sector is not corrupt as well. Far from it. Five out of the 20 respondents focused on the community and the security sector. This means that corruption is manifest amongst regulators, operators, contractors, community leaders, youths, and the security sector. Although there is a general agreement amongst the participants on the issues of corruption and criminality in the Nigerian oil and gas sector, they are relaxed because the oil sector continues to attract investment.

Politicians, ministers, civil servants, and even members of the judiciary are linked to the Nigerian oil and gas industry and they appear willing to change the regulatory framework and policy guidelines and/or look the other way when laws are broken for pecuniary gains (see discussion on corruption in the introduction chapter). A general manager at an oil and gas company appears to shift the blame of corruption to local politicians. In his words,

> I have been involved in some community development projects estimated at millions of dollars yearly. But some of the influential community politicians hijack and use fake companies to collect a substantial part of the budget for some social interventions in communities and disappear. They

prevent the bulk of that money from percolating to the grassroots, which leads to tensions and increases poverty and leads to vandalism (OILG-06).

What he failed to acknowledge is that these actions are only possible because of the lack of due diligence checks, and monies the oil and gas industry pays out, although the government takes part of the blame for this. Nor is there any acknowledgment that this money is paid to these very officials to influence policies and regulations that favour the oil and gas industry. Taking money from the oil and gas industry becomes even more attractive as poverty in the area increases (Okonofua, 2016). This creates tensions within local communities and a lack of household income. The other issue is that much of the money that manages to be invested into local areas disappears offshore and so does not reflect the actual investment in the area (Okumagba, 2012, 2013).

A former Commissioner of the Environment argues that high-ranking local security officials are misusing their positions. He claimed that,

> The security task force has been accused of encouraging the vandalism of pipelines to justify the deployment of security to that area and what they are doing. Some lines are broken into if the operator refuses to expand the scope of security coverage in the area. You will be shocked and amazed by the actions of some security commanders when you speak with the pipeline department in this ministry of environment (OILG-04).

Again, the issue of corruption is heightened here. Not only does this suggest that security agencies are trying to justify their actions and why they should remain in the Niger Delta area, but it also suggests collusion between the security agencies and some criminal youths (see Chapter 3 on militancy). These claims are supported by a manager of one of the oil and gas companies who further expands the claims of security involvement in oil crimes and corruption.

> The nine estuaries patrolled by Operation Delta Safe task force serve as strategic exit routes for organised criminal gangs who steal and bunker crude oil from the Bayelsa axis since it empties itself into the Atlantic Ocean. Without connivance from high-ranking security officials and theatre commanders, it would have been practically impossible for illegal tugboats or oil badges and pipeline vandals to access and exit from that area (OILG-06).

The data and the literature suggest that not only are part of the security agency's corruption, but they are also colluding with criminal gangs and/or criminal youths in siphoning off oil to sell on the local open or black market and the international western black-market space (Transparency International, 2020). This also suggests that the security agencies in Bayelsa are compromised and that little is done about it. Arguably the impairment of integrity and legal and moral principles by Nigeria's security agencies is the hallmark of corruption (NEITI, 2015; Transparency International, 2020).

However, an OPDS Navy Lieutenant Commander shifted the blame for corruption to the oil and gas regulators, operators, and related services like the contractors. In his words,

> If you convert the dollar value of one barrel of crude oil into Nigeria Naira and multiply it by thousands of barrels of underdeclared oil per day, you will have a sense of the daily loss of the government. Even where billions have been budgeted for communities you cannot fathom where all the monies go (SEC-10).

It is worth pointing out that the respondent does not outrightly deny that the security services were/are indeed involved in collusion and corruption. Taken together, the data paints a worrying picture as corruption is highlighted across the public and private sectors, though each minimising its role while blaming others.

The Chief Operating Officer of an oil and gas company argues that the criminality and corruption situation make pipeline vandalism inevitable as everyone within the local communities wants some of the money being paid out by the oil companies. By this, he effectively blames the local communities for the criminality and corrupt tendencies that lead to tensions and insecurity. He pointed out that,

> Money is dished out from the NCTL to violent and influential groups in Bayelsa, therefore, it is natural that criminality and vandalism would be rampant in communities where oil is most available to quickly get monies from both the government and oil firms (OILG-07).

This position was supported by an OPDS Major. The high rate of unemployment, he stated has created a high population of criminal youths in Bayelsa-Nembe and the historic Niger Delta region (Janoski et al., 2014; Vetter et al., 2006). He stressed that,

> The criminal activities of a few youths have caused communities serious problems. They have destroyed whatever social and economic life that is left in the communities through piracy on waterways, oil bunkering, and artisanal refineries that do more damage to our crops and farmlands (SEC-08).

Again, collusion might be absent from the above statement, but there is clear evidence to support collusion between criminal gangs and some officials within the security services (Transparency International, 2019). The desire for money and a better life appears to be a motivating factor. Corruption and criminality have infiltrated all sections of Bayelsa society. This creates the perfect conditions for frustration and anger towards the oil and gas companies, leading to pipeline vandalism. Corruption and criminality are seen as one of the few ways of gaining some benefits of the *black gold rush-* crude oil that lies underneath communities. The odd pay-out to some sections of the community will do little to change the situation and stave off criminal activities on pipelines.

A Department of State Security officer noted that "most local inhabitants believe oil constructors use their links with approving authorities, and community surveillance contractors and government agencies to perpetrate a crime" (SEC-04). Criminality is even worse due to the absence of a standardised project evaluation framework. What comes through in the professional interviews is that a lack of socio-economic opportunities within communities is creating the perfect conditions for corruption and criminality to flourish and thrive in the case state area and the oil industry. As Dodd argues, government policies and regulations need to increase social mobility, improve education, and improve governance as well as leadership quality to reduce poverty and crime and without a reduction in poverty and crime, progress will be difficult to achieve in the area (2021). In particular, poor governance, corruption, and lack of transparency continue to affect oil and gas regulations which in turn influence and affect oil and gas policies (NEITI, 2015). In particular, poor governance, corruption, and lack of transparency continue to affect oil and gas policies in the area (NEITI, 2015, 2021).

Further, five out of the 20 professional respondents, three oil and gas and two security respondents believe that corruption is minimal and if it exists at all it should be blamed on the community and security sectors. They stated that corruption and criminality were not the issues because there seems to be a good amount of investment coming into the oil industry. For instance, they noted that "there are occasions where the country has achieved Green Flow Levels in oil and gas production" (OILG-05). The deputy general manager of an oil company pointed out that, the increase in oil production appears to suggest that corruption in the industry may have been exaggerated. What they did not say is the percentage of investment coming to the oil sector because Nigeria is the largest oil and gas producer in Africa. Secondly, they did not mention how long Nigeria sustained Green Flow Levels in oil production without experiencing one form of criminal vandalism or bunkering. According to Nigeria Extractive Industries Transparency Initiative, there was a very marginal increase of over 4 per cent in 2019 (Esiedesa, 2021). There is some skepticism about the percentage provided given that these numbers are often open to manipulation due to corruption in the oil sector (NEITI, 2021). Transparency in data collection and reporting is not guaranteed, making it difficult to verify what is going on (NEITI, 2021).

There is no doubt some sort of green flow levels may have occasionally been achieved. This is supported by a Navy Lieutenant Commander who pointed out that, "when you are given a task as a staff officer, and you don't comprise there will be results and it is the result that you are seeing now in the oil industry" (SEC-09). The point is that even if green flow levels have been achieved, the issue of corruption should not be minimised or blamed on a few sectors. Corruption continues to reverberate in the Niger Delta and is eroding the trust between the public sector, the private sector, and the local communities. Until corruption, poor governance, and poor leadership are tackled local communities will continue to agitate and grow frustrated with the government, oil regulators, and the private sector's efforts to extract oil and gas in the Niger Delta region.

A regulatory agency executive director noted that corruption is rampant across the oil and gas sector in Nigeria and amongst the regulatory agencies, including his organisation.

Things are the way they are because of a lack of transparency and corruption which has plummeted Nigeria's reputation and stagnated the oil and gas industry in the last 30 years that I have spent here. The industry is caught between two forces, powerful political and dangerous business interests (OILG-01).

When the oil and gas sector cuts costs and corners, and the regulators turn the other way is part of the problem. This means an acknowledgment of the fact that corruption is a problem across the sector not restricted to one stakeholder or another. This can be seen across the industry. Cutting costs and corners led to the issue of the Deepwater Horizon oil spill in the Gulf of Mexico a few years ago in the United States of America (Knutson, 2021). Using sub-standard pipelines and not upgrading the pipeline infrastructure as at when due continues to plague the Niger Delta. This is partly allowed to happen due to institutionalised corruption and criminality (Amundsen, 2019). A former Environment Commissioner responsible for regulating the impact of oil and gas activities argued that "pipelines are a very huge business in Nigeria from the Presidency and the National Security Advicer's Office to the National Assembly. This is partly responsible for the corruption in that sector" (OILG-04).

Poor working conditions and low pay motivate those in the security agencies to collude with criminal gangs to vandalise, bunker, steal, and illegally refine oil in the Niger Delta region. According to an army Captain in the OPDS task force,

> The security officers are largely compromised which is why there is an increase in the scale of oil theft, bunkering, sea piracy, kidnapping of oil workers, and vandalism of pipelines. I suggest that our officers and men should be neutral, as much as possible because that is the greatest problem leading to vandalism (SEC-07).

As outlined above, greed and easy access to oil pipelines, and weak infrastructure could also explain why some security personnel engages in vandalism (Transparency International, 2020).

This implies that most stakeholders compromise their integrity to have a share of the profit from oil resources. An oil and gas security coordinator blamed all the stakeholders for the menace of corruption and criminality that is troubling the oil industry, pointing out that,

> Lack of transparency between all stakeholders, deliberate cover-ups, insincerity on the part of the oil and gas operators, personnel of government agencies, greed amongst the security task force, and the deviant behaviours

amongst local people in oil-bearing communities all contributes to what triggers pipeline vandalism (OILG-09).

This result summaries that most oil and gas professional respondents agree that corruption and criminality pervading the petroleum industry should be blamed on oil and gas firms, regulators, and some contractors, due to their influence over regulations. The majority of the security respondents believe that security agencies are not corrupt because they are just following orders and regulations. However, the analysis revealed that only a few oil and gas and a few security respondents agree that the issue of corruption should be laid on the doorstep of the government, community, and security sectors. Sometimes the issue may have been overstated. It is the endemic nature of corruption and the collusion between criminal gangs and the public and private sectors that make addressing corruption so difficult. It is the very same people, those involved in corruption and collusion who would need to address their behaviour. But there are few incentives to do so in Nigeria. Failure to find solutions and/or incentives for people to change their behaviour will mean that corruption, poor governance, and poor leadership will remain endemic. This will continue to lead to frustration within local oil-bearing communities and only escalate pipeline vandalism in Bayelsa and the wider Niger Delta region. Although the petroleum industry in Nigeria is broadly ineffective and lacks transparency and accountability mechanisms, the problem is more about data secrecy (about production and vandalism) than a lack of it.

The blame game between the security, regulators, civil society, oil operators, and community will continue as everyone accuses the other, and money will continue to grease the wheels of power to water down their responsibility and loosen regulations. Corruption and criminality will continue to have a debilitating impact on Nigeria's oil and gas industry and the local communities affected by it (NEITI, 2021). The behaviour of influential and powerful public and private leaders in terms of disbursement of oil money without due diligence will continue to impact project delivery and harm local communities. Criminal activities of some youths are dangerous to communities just like the corruption of political leaders is (Transparency International, 2019; Mathias, 2015; see also Chapter 3). There are widespread corrupt practices and criminality despite some occasional increases in production. The occasional increase experienced in the oil industry is because private investors believe there is profit to be made in the industry and the investors can influence the regulatory agencies and policy guidelines. Most participants argue that endemic and institutionalised corruption and collusion with criminal gangs are major factors leading to pipeline vandalism in Bayelsa and Nembe.

## Impact of Community Projects on Vandalism

The oil companies and government appear to be using vandalism, reduction in production, and finance as a smokescreen to deny the community of necessary projects, effectively heightening vandalism (Igbinovia, 2014). A reduction in oil production is caused by multiple factors like human interference, operational blowout, policy reforms of the OPEC, and the declaration of force majeure either due to natural disasters or/and disruption of production. A cut in oil and gas production impacts Nigeria's revenues and decreases the already meagre funding available to states and oil and gas companies to execute projects in the local communities (Okumagba, 2013). Pipeline vandalism in Bayelsa State leads to a decrease in oil production, which affects the revenues of oil and gas companies and the construction of community projects. A loss of revenue affects the state, companies, and ultimately the local community, which further inflames tensions in the region. All of the respondents acknowledged a direct link between the reduction in oil production, community projects, and nexus with community tensions and the wider insecurity problem in Bayelsa. Given that oil and gas revenue represent the principal sources of income for the Nigerian State. A loss of oil revenue has severe implications for the state and delivery of community projects. This is the claim of most of the participants working for the oil and gas firms and security. This is also supported by the wider literature (NBS, 2020; NEITI, 2021; Tomlinson, 2018; NNPC Report, 2018; 2017; Makholm, 2012; Ross, 2012, 2015; Local Content Act, 2010; Collier, 2007).

As a sequel to the above, 18 out of the 20 oil and gas and security professional respondents argue that community projects are not often delivered when the Nigerian government experiences a fall in oil production as well as private oil producers. When further broken down, all the 10 security participants and eight oil and gas participants agree that the Nigerian government is impacted the most when there is a fall in oil production. This affects the delivery of community intervention projects amongst other social responsibilities by the government and the oil firms. The point is, once the government is impacted it means that the oil producers will be impacted because the oil producers only pay government royalties based on what they earn and a reduction in oil production reduces their earnings. However, the marked difference between both of them is that the government has a larger scope of social and infrastructural responsibilities which is drawn from the national budget that is financed by the proceeds from the sale of oil and gas resources.

This trickles down to the security agencies including the military and paramilitary. A deputy Superintendent of Corp and a Senior DSS intelligence Officer noted that "some of our activities are impacted in the Niger Delta and across Nigeria that I would not care to mention here, because security finances and materials are stretched" (SEC-03; SEC-05). Frustration comes not only because of a lack of benefits or community projects, but because promises made are not kept (Alamieye-seigha, 2008; Douglas & Okonta, 2003). Again, this can trigger more violence and pipeline vandalism. A combination of poor delivery of infrastructure projects, corruption, and criminality angers the community leading to frustration, poverty, and aggression that results in vandalism (Okonofua, 2016; Okumagba, 2013). For example, constant vandalism implied revenue shortfall and finances of federal and state governments and in such instances struggle to meet their financial obligations across all sectors. It affects the salaries and allowances of officers and the deployment of security logistics. Also, it reduces government capacity to finance critical infrastructure projects, meet and manage local and international debt servicing obligations, and depletes foreign reserves. Thereby influencing the value of the national currency at any material time.

The Executive Director of a regulatory agency stated that "the government losses the most when oil production is reduced and when the oil sector is unstable given that it controls about 60 per cent of all oil and gas Joint Ventures. This impacts on their ability to finance community projects" (OILG-01). The problem is the failure of the Nigerian government to calibrate a strategic development ahead of oil and gas potential disinvestment like many Middle Eastern countries are doing now. There is currently a heavy reliance of the government on oil and gas proceeds which ought not to be the case, which makes Nigeria a very volatile and vulnerable economy (NEITI, 2021; NNPC, 2018, 2016). Unlike some Middle Eastern countries like the United Arab Emirates (UAE), the Nigerian government has not shown any concrete and verifiable plans to diversify its economy or to improve the welfare of its citizens (Akintunde, 2020; Hairshine, 2021). Other parts of the economy like agriculture are largely unproductive coupled with the fact that the government seldom follows through with most of its policies. Sometimes, they speak one thing and do another. This is mostly down to poor governance, leadership curse-recycling of incompetent, failed and wicked political leaders without national vision, and corruption.

When community projects are halted and abandoned due to a dearth of oil revenue, youths who may have depended on those projects, as unskilled workers are immediately frustrated out of work leading to vandalism. An increase in household poverty, and hunger which motivates those unemployed youths to look for illegitimate sources of income such as oil bunkering and artisanal refineries. A deputy Superintendent of Corp, Nigeria Security, and Civil Defence Corp noted,

> A revenue shortfall of federal and state government affects the salaries and allowances of OPDS officials and deployment of security logistics which means we cannot effectively monitor and report pipeline vandalism and third-party interference. I would not care to mention here the several activities of the military and police that are impacted in the Niger Delta communities, securing financing and materials become extremely overstretched (SEC-05).

Wider literature argues that inadequate funds have an impact on the behaviours of security officers some of whom connive with vandals to disrupt the pipelines (Transparency International, 2019). This same funding from impacts delivery on some UNSDGs. Political and bureaucratic interference and delays in the budget appropriation by the legislature, sometimes lead to delays in security, SDGs, and humanitarian funding which cascades down to tensions and insecurity situations. This may increase acts of vandalism and other forms of oil and gas infrastructure insecurity problems. According to a deputy manager in charge of engineering standards for pipelines in a regulatory agency, he noted that;

> It is difficult to put figures to the monthly or annual volume of oil the Nigeria National Petroleum Corporation (NNPC) loses, or the revenues lost to the government. However, it is estimated at between 15, 20, and recently 80 percent of annual projections. This affects the budget of ministries, parastatals, and departments including agencies mandated to cater to one thing or another in communities (OILG-03).

Most of the professional respondents did not focus on this point but those who did point out that it is hard to find a consensus amongst oil and gas executives and the communities therefore it is unclear whether the lack of statistics in oil production validates a dearth in community projects. An oil and gas industry general manager noted that

> Oil wells are shut down to prevent oil spills due to technical failure or vandalism and to minimise the financial impact on companies. Clamping, repairs, and returning to maximum operating capacity might take days, weeks, and sometimes even months. This way government loses money in terms of taxes and royalties calculated based on production and sales (OILG-05).

As noted above, this may lead to serious long-term consequences for the Nigerian government, oil and gas companies, and in the end delivery of social infrastructure for local communities (Okonofua, 2016). This can intensify tensions as the Nigerian government is under pressure to cancel projects in affected local areas due to a shortage of funding. Also, the oil firms cannot actualise promises made in the social contracts signed with communities in their MOUs (see chapter for details on MOUs/GMOUs). As pointed out, numerous times such actions usually lead to increased frustration amongst local Bayelsa communities. An Environmental Commissioner noted,

> Disruption in oil production and sales impedes government capacity to finance critical infrastructure and intervention projects. It threatens the survival of our people themselves by shrinking many economic opportunities across communities. Making some of our people dam the consequences to engage in oil bunker, vandalism, and artisanal refineries as last resort, to make fast cash (OILG-04).

It is worthy of note that it is not necessarily just the lack of funding that makes government fail in delivering community projects but the corruption of the system that stops certain projects at the detriment of tensions and more vandalism and insecurity. An Inspector in Nigeria Security and Civil Defence Corp with vast experience in pipeline surveillance and security duties across the historic Niger Delta stated that

> The government is unable to provide employment and care for youths across many oil-bearing communities due to a lack of funds, and oil

bunkering, and vandalism of pipelines worsen an already bad and precarious situation. A direct consequence of a fall in oil production, exports, and government revenue is the dearth in the distribution of free money. We are aware that this impacts activities in the creeks and transit pipelines because the boys must look for a source of livelihood, cost of security doubles (SEC-06).

The narrative created by the government and oil and gas companies like Shell is that oil and gas production has rarely exceeded projections leading to a paucity of funds, therefore, a cut to socio-economic programs in the Niger Delta is a direct response to revenue falls and inevitable (Mickolus, 2018). This is, however, not the case. An Assistant Superintendent of police in OPDS stated that

> Nigeria loses as much as 20 percent of annual revenue to pipeline disruptions in terms of repairs and sales. It affects the image of Nigeria as a country. A situation whereby outsiders and potential investors hear about recurring incidences of pipeline vandalism will think twice before coming to invest in the Niger Delta region and the government suffers (SEC-02).

Investment in the oil and gas sector is trickling into the Niger Delta which appears to contradict the point made by the above respondent. Although, the Nigerian government has consistently mismanaged different episodes and regimes of oil windfalls and surplus revenue missing opportunities to improve and upgrade the social infrastructure of local communities (Ross, 2012, 2015; Collier, 2007; Collier & Hoeffler, 2004). A lack of these social infrastructure intensifies poverty and hunger that frustrates people leading to aggression. A small part of the frustration and tensions leading to the insecurity of oil and gas infrastructure are consequences of global dwindling finances and inconsistencies. The NBS (2017) and NEITI (2015) reports claim that disruption of pipelines remains a critical factor responsible for a cut in oil production and ultimately a fall in the national Gross Domestic Product (GDP). This has a real impact on the local communities in Bayelsa State and the wider Niger Delta.

Given that oil and gas companies operate within the communities their facilities are vandalised due to frustration from those who feel cheated out of the oil wealth. The attackers do not care and are not bothered whether their actions aggravate the production of crude oil or impact the revenue needed to finance community projects, which by all accounts are far and few between even when oil is flowing (Okonofua, 2016). Whatever factor may cause a decline in oil and gas production and depletion in revenue, the point remains, that skilled and unskilled workers often lose their jobs (Janoski et al., 2014; National Bureau of Statistics, 2020; Oki, 2017). The frustration of some former employees who worked on community projects or were employed by oil firms as unskilled laborers may lead them to collaborate with individuals who engage in pipeline vandalism (Okumagba, 2012, 2013). An increase in vandalism is an outcome of a direct aggressive displacement reaction from communities due to economic neglect (see Chapter 3 on community neglect). The oil firms lose both infrastructures, crude oil, and revenue which is why they believe they suffer more impact (Oki, 2017). Given the endemic nature of corruption, poor governance, and recycling of wicked and incompetent leadership, it comes as no surprise that little attention is paid to broader socio-economic and institutional reforms required to break the vicious cycle of continued community neglect and the *leadership curse phenomenon* (see Chapters 2 and 3). A former Environmental Commissioner observed that "the problem of pipeline breakages heightens whenever leaders fail to settle the boys-youths with free oil monies which are dependent on production and revenue" (OILG-04). Again, what is highlighted here, is the failure to diversify the economy, rather than remaining entirely reliant on revenues from oil and gas.

Only two oil and gas respondents from the regulatory agency out of the 20 professionals questioned on a dearth of community projects agreed that it is the oil firms that are impacted the most and hence are unable to deliver on community projects due to a reduction in oil production. Due to the direct presence in local communities and the reactions they experience when they are unable/unwilling to deliver on agreed community projects in MOUs and GMOUs (see Chapter 2 for more details on MOUs). These projects are outlined and agreed upon in a social contract document called the MOUs and the GMOUs. This respondent only saw poor community project delivery from the lens of poor finances available to the oil and gas firms. They did not bother to talk about the impact on government obligatory responsibilities. A managing director of an oil and gas company stated that:

> oil and gas companies are severely impacted when any of their production facilities are disrupted or when a producing oil well with just enough

pressure to keep flowing is clamped. That is usually the end of the operation of that oil well because oftentimes when you restore normalcy and return to stimulate and re-pressurise the oil well, it may never come or be re-activated, and the company stands the risk of losing hundreds if not thousands of crude oil fluid left in that oil well. It is like a double edge sword. The lack of product affects access to finance which hinders the execution of intervention projects. This exposes the infrastructure to the danger of vandalism by frustrated people or communities (OILD-04).

This is a classic case of a link between oil production, finance, and a lack of community support which exposes oil and gas infrastructure to vandalism and insecurity problems. The Chief Operating Officer of an oil and gas company said that insecurity against their pipelines escalates when they stop spending money due to a shutdown. He noted that

When the NCTL is shut down, means the crude oil produced by five oil and gas companies who evacuate their oil through the NCTL is stopped and trapped. The quantum volume of crude oil Aiteo losses daily is estimated at about 10,000 barrels You can only imagine the huge financial impact both in terms of servicing credits and loans from banks, obligations to communities, and cost of repairs (OILG-07).

This statement further agrees with the huge loss the government suffers even though the primary loser in this instance may be the oil firm. Again, it is worth highlighting, that this participant is somewhat oversimplifying the matter, as communities and infrastructure projects provided are not exactly widespread across communities, even when the oil is flowing freely. The shutdown of oil production only compounds an already poor situation rather than creating new frustrations and aggression. The irony, of course, is that oil and gas companies will report profits annually and pay dividends to shareholders while claiming poverty, and lack of funds. When oil companies make profits there seems to be an inadequate deployment of resources to communities (Mathias, 2015; Okonofua, 2016). It appears the communities do not believe that disruptions account for a lack of profitability (NBS, 2017).

A dearth of interventions and neglect triggers social tensions, frustration, and aggression leading to vandalism. Oil companies are, however, not solely to be blamed for the lack of intervention projects in the Nigeria Delta area. The political class and the government ought to complement their efforts. Therefore, the problem of lack of community projects is a combination of poor government planning, many decades of community neglect in terms of infrastructure and economic development, corruption, and conflicting regulatory frameworks. The tug of war between the public and private sector regarding who is responsible to and for local communities and lack of regulatory clarity leads to inaction on all sides. It is this inaction that translates to collective community neglect by both the government and oil firms which continues to trigger collective frustrations, inflame local tensions, and aggression and leads to pipeline vandalism, and oil bunkering. This in turn escalates the insecurity of oil and gas infrastructure in the area (Gurr, 2015; Okumagba, 2013; see Chapters 2 and 3).

The analysis shows that the 10 security and eight oil and gas respondents out of the 20 professional respondents agree that the impact of community projects on vandalism is based on extensive losses of finances and a cut in oil production. This impacts the government more than the oil firms if you look at it from the lens of broad-based social responsibility as enumerated above. This causes more poverty and frustration leading to aggression against oil and gas infrastructure like oil bunkering and vandalism. However, the two oil and gas participants who disagreed argued that the finances of oil firms are deeply impacted and overstretched with a reduction in production. The two oil and gas respondents who disagreed focused their point mainly on the need to make a profit and pay a dividend to their shareholders which is again consistent with corporate capitalism (Schwab, 2021; Idemudia, 2014; Bruland, 1998; Friedman, 1993; see Chapter 2 on corporate capitalism). A lack of funds worsens the government's ability to deal with different layers of insecurity problems. Although the NEITI audited report does not support a fall in revenue or oil production across some years. It reveals that between 2010 to 2019 the aggregate increase in financial flows from the oil and gas sector to the government amounted to USD$418.544 billion (Esiedesa, 2021).

However, the International Centre for Reconciliation estimated the amount Nigeria lost between 2003 to 2008 to pipeline vandalism, disruptions, oil theft, bunkering, and cut in production at USD$100 billion (Okonjo-Iweala, 2018; Paki & Ebienfa, 2011). As of January 2016, the Nigerian government lost around USD$7 billion (around two trillion Naira) to a combination of corrupt civil servants, politicians, private players in the oil and gas business, and organised gangs and/or criminality (NNPC, 2016). This translates to about 30 per cent of its national budget. This suggests Nigeria has lost a lot of oil revenue which impacts community projects and is partly responsible for the general neglect of oil-bearing communities. These kinds of losses are what Okumagba (2012, 2013), and Dollard et al. (1939) described as "self-inflicted aggression" (see Chapter 3). Nigeria, like many oil-producing states/countries, suffers a lack of accelerated and compelling reforms in tax-to-GDP that would have triggered an impactful change to enable Nigeria to increase its developmental expenditure (Ogundajo et al., 2019). This would have prevented the exposure of the annual budget to market volatility and internal insecurity problems.

## IMPACT OF ENVIRONMENTAL POLLUTION ON VANDALISM

The environmental impact of oil and gas extraction is well known such as the emission of methane, sulfur dioxide air pollutants, and other dangerous gases within the SDG 2030 agenda, like clean water and sanitation, and affordable and clean energy climate action (see Chapter 2). It includes the release of $CO^2$ and other greenhouse gases, the pollution of rivers, the underground water table, and the air. Governments of most petrostates in the Global South fall short of taking responsibility for environmental degradation in their domain. They are aware that a polluted environment is a critical factor that leads to tensions and contentions over scarce resources like water and land. It is unclear why most of them chose to ignore their environmental security. In addition to the *normal* environmental damage, the Niger Delta is plagued by oil spills, as outlined above. These oil spills increase environmental damage by contaminating and damaging natural aquifers, waterways, arable lands, and forests through toxic oil sludge, and excessive heat and noise (Gbobo, 2020; Rieuwerts, 2017). Much of this damage exceeds the limits set by the Nigerian Federal Environmental Protection Act and the UNSDGs (Loft & Brien, 2023; UNSDG, 2016; Mba et al., 2018; see Chapter 2, 3, and 4). This environmental pollution has significant negative impacts on the local communities across the Niger Delta. In many cases, the pollution passes into the food chain. It breeds insecurity tendencies because it deprives local communities from their legitimate sources of livelihoods. Communities' health and quality of life are decreasing, and so are mortality rates (Olawuyi, 2012; Sinden, 2009).

A UNEP report found that drinking wells scattered around the Niger Delta area had a high measure of the carcinogen benzene that was 900 times over World Health Organisation prescribed limits (2012). This questions Nigeria's sincerity towards achieving the UNSDG goal six which is clean water and sanitation (UNSDG, 2016). Higgins described the human damage to the ecosystem and socio-economic outcomes of oil and gas activities as "ecocide" (2010). The collective community's neglect of the environment and its associated disasters like pollution of waterways and gas flaring is what provokes community neglect aggression displacement against oil and gas infrastructure such as oil bunkering and vandalism. These are people who engage in the disruption of oil and gas infrastructure to make their voices heard locally, nationally, and internationally (see Chapter 5 on CNADT). Okonkwo (2020) suggested an amendment to oil and gas laws and regulations to enforce environmental justice and oil pollution penalties in Nigeria. Okonta (2016; Otokunefor, 2017), pointed out that policy incoherencies are a major challenge to energy security in Nigeria.

The damage to the local environment and the impact on communities' health further compound existing frustrations, the same frustrations that led some to engage in the vandalism of oil pipelines. Some of this vandalism is meant to encourage the government and oil and gas companies to clean up the mess that oil and gas extraction causes to the environment. The irony is that vandalism increases environmental pollution, leads to a decrease in oil production, and ultimately means less investment into the Niger Delta (Otokunefor, 2017). This vicious cycle and the collateral damage of oil and gas extraction, as well as pipeline vandalism, entrenches inequality, poverty, and further damage to the very same environment the communities and the oil and gas sector rely on. Perpetrators of pipeline vandalism are acutely aware of its impact on the environment. All the professional oil and gas and security respondents agree that the environmental situation in Bayelsa and Nembe, and indeed the Niger Delta is getting worse. It is worth noting that cleaning up oil spills and reclaiming damaged lands can take plenty of decades to complete (UNEP, 2012). The professional respondents further agreed that criminals and the oil and gas companies showed little regard for the environment.

An in-depth analysis reveals that 14 out of the 20 professional respondents, eight oil and gas and six security professionals, argued that the various damages done to the environment are due to the unethical and unprofessional behaviour of the oil and gas operators. The deviant behaviour of oil and gas companies is encouraged by the conflicting regulatory framework of the Nigerian government and operational policy guidelines of oil firms. They further stressed that the government regulations mandate the OPDS security officials to burn stolen crude into the environment tends to aggravate an already bad situation (see Chapter 2 on oil and gas regulations). In essence, they blame the oil and gas activities, the security, and combined neglect for the environmental damage in Bayelsa. A Navy Lieutenant Commander at OPDS argues that

> When we patrol the creeks, we come to appreciate the extent of the irresponsibility of the oil and gas companies to the environment. We see things like oil sludge/black sludge all over the creek waters and around the flora plants. This has significantly worsened the environmental damages for many years in the community (SEC-09).

What is worth pointing out here, is that oil and gas companies have few incentives to protect operational blowouts and effect cleanup activities, as accountability is lacking due to poor governance, neglect of extensive corruption in the oil sector, and poor leadership. The above claim is supported by the statement of a Police Deputy Superintendent who noted,

> Due to a combination of bad behaviour from the oil and gas forms and human factors, we are losing between 250,000 to one million hectares of mangrove forests yearly to environmental devastation that has hitherto provided sources of food and economic activities to indigenous people in the Bayelsa state. This has also impacted the breeding water for fish and loss of over 55 per cent of commercial fisheries in the Gulf of Guinea (SEC-02).

Climate change is further compounding the damage to the environment and biodiversity. This is yet another reason that feeds the frustration in communities (see Chapter 2 on climate impact in the Niger Delta).

A major in the Nigerian army also aligns with the claims above. He pointed out many irreparable damages oil and gas companies have caused to the entire Niger Delta environment. In his words, "the deployment of heavy-duty equipment into the hinterland forests by oil and gas companies to explore and drill deep down into the soil for crude oil and gas destabilises the natural ecosystem" (SEC-08). Oil leaks from unclamped pipelines and processes of trenching and decommissioning old pipelines heighten threats of vandalism and infrastructure insecurity problems (Devold, 2013; Sinden, 2009). A former Commissioner of the Environment noted how the extractive industries have destroyed the natural fertile land and green vegetation including trees, and fruits dotting the Bayelsa landscape. He pointed out that:

> Every inch of dry land, creeks, and farmland within our habitable natural environment that Bayelsa people hold dear has been extensively devasted. It is agonising to watch helplessly how the extractive oil companies slowly destroyed our common heritage. It is even worse to know that for many years these oil companies have failed to put corrective measures in place to either reclaim devasted farmlands or cleanup the oil spills and lost habitats. This sort of behaviour is a sin that may never be forgiven (OILG-04).

The commissioner respondent further observed that

> Environmental pollution has destroyed the natural ability of the mangrove to protect the coastal areas from storm surges and sea waves. We have lost our natural resistance and protection against climate change like a rise in sea levels, flash floods, coastal erosions, and effective carbon sink (OILG-04).

The erosion of topsoil and the release of waters from crude oil drilling sites have further dislocated over 100 coastal communities inland, all competing for scarce lands (Sinden, 2009). Also, coastal creek dwellers who fell trees destroy the natural resistance against tidal waves from the Atlantic Ocean and expose the habitable coastal lands to extreme climatic conditions (Kuwornu, 2019; Etemire, 2016; Olawuyi, 2012). These unmitigated circumstances worsen the psychological trauma the people experience provoking further frustration, tensions, and vandalism (Alagoa, 2005; see Chapter 3).

An Oil and Gas company Executive Director stated that

> aggressive political behaviours, illegal bunkering, pipeline sabotage, and militancy are tied to oil and gas activities, and all these affect the environment. Although the bad topography of the area makes it difficult for oil companies to operate, everything within the spectrum of oil and gas exploration and production activities causes one problem or the other to the environment (OILG-01).

The fact that the statement above is made by an executive director speaks volumes about the culpability of the oil and gas firms and regulatory agencies. It also means the regulatory framework is not designed to reflect the realities in oil-bearing communities. A gap in regulatory guidelines influences the policy thrust of oil and gas industries which encourages failure in their *vicarious liability* (Irvine, 2018). Vicarious liability is an aspect of the law of evidence that stipulates strict enforcement of secondary liability on entities.

Further, a Deputy Superintendent in Nigeria Security and Civil Defence Corps insisted that "you can hardly separate pipeline vandalism, insecurity of oil and gas infrastructure and tensions from the unmitigated oil and gas industry pollution and the unregulated harvesting of resources in Nembe" (SEC-05). There seems to be a lack of probity within the oil and gas business chain in Nigeria. This disregard for the environment to protect oneself is evident. A senior DSS Intelligence officer stated that

> When the security and oil and gas regulators go to arrest oil thieves and bunkering criminals, they end up blowing up the illegal refining facilities/artisanal refineries into the environment and emptying the entire crude oil content and petrol chemical fluid into the waters, forests, and farmlands. Further degrading the ecosystem which takes away the moral ground to blame vandals and oil firms (SEC-04).

There are few explanations as to why this is happening. One can only surmise that this destruction is necessary to cover up corruption and collusion and to deny those who profit from the illegality (Transparency International, 2020). Most environmental damages in Bayelsa appear to have been caused or triggered by the oil and gas extractive industry. It is unclear, however, whether all illegal refining facilities are destroyed, sources of oil bunkering are clamped, or some are left (NEITI, 2021; NBS, 2016). The speed at which these illegal activities multiply suggests that vandalism is rife in the Niger Delta. The government regulatory frameworks and policy trajectory is a source of instrumental aggression because the implementation of those regulations orchestrates environmental pollution in Bayelsa state (Transparency International, 2020; Igbinovia, 2014; Okumagba, 2013).

A Regulatory Agency Deputy Manager in charge of engineering standards stated that "from the green environmental point of view the emission of oil and gas or its carbon footprint is believed to affect Bayelsa environment and contributes to global warming" (OILG-03). He further stated that a review by scientists from Niger Delta University on the impact of crude oil extraction on the mangrove forests revealed that over 36 per cent of the global impact on mangroves occurred in the Niger Delta...In the 60 years of operating the extractive petroleum industry in Bayelsa-Nembe, the Niger Delta mangrove has become the most degraded and polluted mangrove forest and ecosystem in the world (OILG-03).

A devasted ecosystem triggers food insecurity which in turn compounds frustration and increases pipeline vandalism. In the words of a Naval Lieutenant Commander in OPDS, oil and gas companies should be classified as humans, stressing that,

the oil companies created the environmental conditions that Bayelsa has found itself through consistent disobedience of set rules. In Aberdeen in the UK humans do the same oil business yet the government does not deploy hard military power for maintaining pipeline security. There is near zero crude oil pollution in their environment (SEC-10).

The oil and gas environment in the UK is a good example because the government's oil and gas regulations set, and implement good laws from which oil companies mirror and design operational policies. In the case of Nigeria, this suggests that something is wrong with the regulatory framework and its implementation in Nigeria which is affecting the operation and oil firms and the behaviour of security agencies in the Niger Delta. It is also worth pointing out, that many of the sources of frustration, such as poor governance, corruption, and neglect that exist in the Niger Delta are not present in other countries that safely extract oil and gas. An oil and gas company General Manager notes that the "lack of preventative measures to forestall pipeline failure is an operational problem. Some pipelines may not have been designed for the Niger Delta corrosive soil type, or adequately maintained leading to hydrocarbon leakages" (OILG-06). An effective regulatory system is required to curb the instincts of oil and gas companies to cut corners and costs in order to increase profits (Okonkwo, 2020; Okonjo-Iweala, 2018; NEITI, 2015, 2021). This requires good governance, and competent leadership devoid of corruption. It also requires investment into upgrading and adding adequate oil and gas infrastructure. However, Schwegler (2017) believes oil corporations should be criminally held liable under international laws for the widespread destruction of the environment and crimes against humans and nonhuman species.

However, six out of the 20 respondents, four security and two oil and gas professional respondents stated that the community and the criminal behaviour of vandals, oil theft, and operation of artisanal refining facilities have dealt the most damage to the Niger Delta environment. To these few some of the environmental damage is a result of criminal activities such as cooking stolen crude oil fluid and bunkering. These can result in some of the oil sludges seen in most parts of the polluted Niger Delta environment especially the creek waters. These few professional respondents are saying that the implementation of the regulations and policies currently governing the Nigerian oil and gas industry is well thought out. The fact remains that some youths vandalise pipelines to draw a different layer of attention to their worsening environmental and socio-economic plight that is frustrating them daily caused by oil companies and poor governance, incompetent and corrupt leadership in Nigeria (Bergstresser, 2017; see Chapter 2). The Chief Operating Officer overseeing the security architecture of one of the Nigeria pipeline networks stated that "over 80 per cent of environmental pollution cases from crude oil spillages happen in Bayelsa because of third-party human interference and bad environmental governance and regulations" (OILG-07).

There is recognition here that it is not only criminals who are to blame, but also the implementation of inadequate environmental governance regulatory policies which influence the response and attitude to the environment. Environmental degradation particularly pollution resulting from the oil spill is caused by a combination of factors such as historical frustrations, pipeline vandalism, and an inadequate government response that are stoking violence and aggression against onshore oil pipelines (Anderson & Dill, 1995; Malici, 2007).

An army Commander in OPDS headquarters in Bayelsa further observed that:

> If human beings are thinking right the oil devastation that leads to environmental pollution and tensions will not happen. It is not about the oil industry alone. Attitude to the environment is also another problem. If you go to the waterways, they are dumping waste materials that are non-degradable into the waters which will be consumed by fish and other aquatic life and all that (SEC-09).

To some extent, he is empathising with individuals who chose to engage as criminals, as the oil and gas industry is slowly destroying the indigenous way of life as well as hope for a better future. The success of one community or criminal group over another, directly and indirectly, encourages others to further vandalise pipelines and establish artisanal refining facilities. Historical evidence suggests many communities have been suffering environmental pollution caused by the operational failure of oil companies for about 30 to 50 years, though no fault of theirs (Alagoa, 2005; Alamieyeseigha, 2008; Saro-Wiwa, 1992). Vandalism only really took off in the latter part of the 1990s and early 2000s (Mathias, 2015; Okonofua, 2016; see Chapters 3 and 4).

An Oil and Gas Company Managing Director tried to push back by shifting some blame on illegal activities and criminality. In his words,

> We have a major contaminant called the "Black Pander" which is a powdery substance released from artisanal refining activities in the creeks and parts of highlands. It comes from the Bonny light crude and other similar crude oil fluid extracts which generate light hydrocarbon residue when cooked. This pollutant results in condensed environmental particles called *soot* that is currently flying in the atmosphere and all over the air. We see it everywhere (OILG-08).

The narrative of some oil executives is quite interesting. Whereas some blame the oil and gas companies, regulatory laws and practices, poor governance, and even leadership incompetence, and criminality. Others are attracted to criminality when they see how others profit from such illegal activities without punishment. Criminals and organised gangs do contribute to environmental problems, and oil bunkering and artisanal refining appear lucrative (NEITI, 2021; Mathias, 2015).

The professional respondents have once again demonstrated a different degree of responses to the issue of environmental pollution. The result shows that the majority of the oil and gas and a majority of security respondents blame oil extraction activities and the policy guidelines for the environmental damage in Bayelsa. While a few oil and gas and security professional respondents believe that criminal vandals and community ignorance is responsible for the massive environmental damage suffered in Bayelsa. They agree that different forms of environmental challenges pervading Bayelsa state were caused by multiple factors. Chief of which are deviant social behaviour, government regulations and oil and gas policies, and pipeline disruptions. This means a combination of government and regulatory practices, community neglect, criminality, corruption, oil and gas activities, and security approach are all responsible for the devastation of the Bayelsa environment.

While no stakeholder is accused of being solely responsible for the crime against the environment, however, the issue fosters. The OPA Act (2004) regulatory mechanism is weak which is why the oil and gas policies are designed to operationalise the Act in ensuring an effective monitoring road map that creates business opportunities for all stakeholders (see Chapter 2 for details on oil and gas regulations). The failure of oil companies to adopt cleaner approaches to oil extraction feeds frustrations. This is in tandem with other factors that push some youths and some communities into pipeline vandalism and illegal oil and gas activities that are disastrous to the environment. The environmental impact of pipeline vandalism must be acknowledged; however, the evidence still suggests that the oil and gas industry remain by far the largest polluter in the area (Sinden, 2009; Okonofua, 2016; Olawuyi, 2012; Otokunefor, 2017; Oyadongha, 2020, 2021; UNEP, 2012).

## Impact of Pipeline Structural Integrity on Vandalism

It is worth noting that, weak pipeline structures on their own do not cause vandalism, but make vandalism easier to occur. Also, the failure of governments in most Global South countries to regulate the nature and physical resilience of the oil and gas pipelines deployed contributes to environmental degradation, make it easier for vandalism to occur and oil theft. Although it might be costlier to construct or manufacture stronger and more resilient oil and gas pipelines, but it is necessary if corporations and regulators want to key into the UNSDGs. When old pipelines, wellheads, and flow lines are structurally weak, they are prone to mechanical and operational blowouts which pollute the environment (Oyadongha, 2020, 2021; see UNEP, 2012 report). Structural blowouts destroy the natural habitats of local communities and dislocate people from their farmlands and lead to hunger and increased household poverty which heightens anger and frustration (Okumagba, 2012). The professional respondents argue that the pipeline infrastructure plays a significant role in understanding the causes of onshore oil and gas vandalism in Bayelsa.

Structural, mechanical, and operational oil and gas pipeline blowouts have beleaguered Bayelsa-Nembe and the entire Niger Delta region for many decades (see Chapters, 2, 3, and 6). The professional oil and gas and security respondents link increased criminal vandalism to weak pipeline structures, oil bunkering, external sales, and demand for local artisanal refineries. There is no question, that pipeline blowouts and sub-standard pipeline infrastructure have increased the problems in the area under study. Many oil companies have also cut costs by not replacing failing and leaking pipelines and oil wellheads (Linden & Palsson, 2013; Olawuyi, 2012; Oyadongha, 2020, 2021). The professional respondents deflect from the real issue of poor governance and corruption as the main reasons influencing the neglect of defective pipelines. Further exploration of the underlying causes of mechanical and operational blowouts of pipelines such as corrosion and the use of internal inspection gauge systems will give a deeper insight and comprehensive understanding of insecurity issues. However, this is not the immediate focus of this book.

The data shows that 13 out of the 20 professional respondents, 10 security and supported three oil and gas professional interviewees agree that the prevalence of old and structurally weak pipelines made it easier for vandalism to occur in the case study area. They pointed out that the lack of use of preventative technologies accounted for many operational blowouts and facilitated oil bunkering (Oyadongha, 2021). A deputy manager of a pipeline regulatory agency noted that,

> Technical and mechanical evidence revealed a nexus between the frequency of pipeline vandalism and failure of pipeline structures due to the poor designs, maintenance, and a fall below the minimum industry standard of pipeline manufacturing which increases hydrocarbon leakages and facilitates vandalism (OILG-03).

Again, leaving pipelines longer underground and allowing sub-standard pipelines to operate in the area only suggest a defective oil and gas pipeline policy made possible by the lack of implementation of the OPA Act (see Chapter 3). According to NEITI most of the oil and gas regulations in Nigeria are mere rhetoric and theoretical (). Although oil and gas pipeline regulations are scarcely implemented because of corruption, poor governance, and a lack of clarity of penalties for erring companies. The real factors here are poor or compromised security and other conditions explored above. Shell Petroleum points out that between 2019 and 2021 there have been 35 oil spills caused by mechanical and operational factors in the Niger Delta (James, 2021). It is unclear how DPR and operating companies measure, maintain and enforce pipeline integrity and structural standards. Aligning with the claims made elsewhere in this research that the causes of vandalism go beyond the underlining social issues alone. As Timashev and Bushinskaya (2016) argued oil and gas pipeline manufacturing must fulfill minimum structural standards before they are deployed. The wider literature and analysed data from the professional oil and gas and security respondents reveal that soil corrosivity, lack of pipeline integrity testing, and inadequate use of internal inspection gauging systems-*smart pig*, expose the pipeline structure to technical and operational blowouts (Oyadongha, 2021). The weak and old pipelines in Bayelsa facilitate, encourage, and heightens the scale of vandalism.

The operation of pipelines in Bayelsa is made worse by the dearth of safety technologies (Oyadongha, 2020, 2021). This causes technical and mechanical failures that increasingly facilitate vandalism. Underlying causes of structural blowouts are lack of deployment of In-line Intelligence Inspection Guage, design code, infrequent testing of fluid chemicals, soil acidity, and chemical components (Ebiye, 2000; Onuoha, 2008; Paki & Ebienfa, 2011). These impact pipeline structural integrity, resilience, functionality, and life span. When pipelines are weak, they rupture easily and pollute the environment destroying sources of livelihood which leads to poverty, anger, and frustration that triggers vandalism.

The Deputy Manager in charge of Engineering Standards in a pipeline regulatory agency stated that:

> Pipeline and oil and gas assets are exposed to frequent and constant chemical and environmental changes in Bayelsa which weakens the integrity and strength of the structure. This makes most of the oil pipelines vulnerable to either operational blowouts or vandalism. Studies have shown that some new pipelines are poorly designed or certified for use in the Niger Delta area. Other times they are not properly welded before trenching. Safety technology mechanisms are rarely adopted by operating firms (OILG-02).

Though some oil and gas participants agree on the importance of ensuring the structural safety of the pipelines, curiously the industry mostly directs the structural insecurity debate toward the local communities. A Police Deputy Superintendent recalled his experience of growing up in the Bayelsa and Nembe area. In his words, "I grew up to meet many of these pipelines that have operated for the past 50 years. Some operational blowouts are due to the corrosivity of our soil type which is why the old pipelines should have been tested and changed more frequently" (SEC-02). It is unclear whether vandals are trained by pipeline experts working in cahoots with compromised oil and gas employees. Considering that it is difficult for local criminals to know that the chemical composition of the soil weakens the structural integrity of a pipeline as well as which pipeline is weak or easier to vandalise. As stated elsewhere in this book some oil insiders recruit willing hands in the community to facilitate vandalism for pecuniary benefits in most of the petrostates in the Global South (see Chapters 2 and 4).

The planning and coordination of vandalism strategies by some oil workers and local criminals make them organised criminal gangs (Neumann & Elsenbroich, 2017). These organised criminal gangs do not operate in isolation, they seem to enjoy some element of support from the political class, and high-profile members of society (Amundsen, 2019; Ogbeidi, 2012). An Army Major and OPDS Commander claimed that "pipelines disrupted are those that the vandals perceive and know are structurally weak due to internal corrosion and other underlying factors" (SEC-08). These contribute to environmental pollution and damage to the natural habitat of indigenes leading to tensions (Akpomera, 2015; Linden & Palsson, 2013).

The gaps in the Pipeline Act (2004; see Chapter 2) encourage oil and gas firms to rely on their operational and management discretion in deciding whether to change an oil pipeline or not. The Deputy Manager in a regulatory company emphasised that:

> Regulators don't compel oil companies to replace their old pipelines because they are not statutorily required to do so. Except it becomes apparent that the pipeline is unsafe or the recommendation of the Joint Investigation Visit shows that structural weakness and operational issues expose the pipeline to frequent vandalism and/or blowouts (OILG-03).

This is one gap in the existing subsisting oil and gas pipeline operation legislation in Nigeria. Litigation cannot be brought against operators that refuse to change their old pipelines or use technologies to mitigate against frequent vandalism of such lines to protect the environment because the courts will refer to the OPA Act (2004). However, the ruling by the British Supreme Courts and the International Criminal Courts at the Hague on Bodo, Oruma, Goi and Ikot Ada communities' judgment may have changed all that perception (Azubuike, 2021; Khalid, 2021; see Chapters 3 and 4).

Furthermore, the executive director of a pipeline regulatory agency stated that oil and gas companies break DPR regulations that mandate operators to publish the proposed routes of pipeline networks in a national gazette before approval and issuance of licenses are granted. The real issue here is the extent to which the subsisting regulations are implemented. He noted that

> The Oil Pipeline Act governs the design, construction, installation, operation, and maintenance of oil and gas pipelines. Occasionally, you see some operators break these laws. They do not ensure periodic testing to evaluate the in-line conditions of their pipelines which contributes to structural failures (OILG-01).

This is self-indicting on the part of the regulatory agency. Pointing out the extent and gap in many oil and gas regulatory frameworks in Nigeria. It also suggests a dearth of prosecution and a broken criminal justice system that would have enforced whatever penalties are available. A situation such as this discourages compliance to set rules and intensifies organised criminality and other deviant behaviours that compromise infrastructure security. The executive director of a pipeline regulatory agency insisted that

> Many operators violate the three guiding principles of pipeline operations-one which mandate operators to apply for and renew oil pipeline licenses every two years. Get a Permit to Survey-PTS the route and publish the design, pipeline life span, and materiality used as well as highlight the pressure at which the pipeline will operate. Failure of which may expose the pipeline infrastructure to compromised its structural integrity, easy human interference, and operational blowouts (OILG-01).

It appears the regulators are less thorough about the implementation of oil industry rules giving room for easier political and bureaucratic influences and manipulations that are detrimental to the structural quality of the pipelines including human and environmental safety (Amundsen, 2019; Nye, 1967).

Where regulatory agencies are stringent on standards and oversight functions like ensuring pipeline thicknesses and corrosion allowances sometimes discourage investors. Defective pipeline infrastructure that facilitates vandalism might not wholly be due to a lack of laws. Other times, it might be due to deliberate steps adopted by relevant agencies to boost investment in the sector. Their lack of capacity to gauge when to either tighten or slacken the regulations to boost investment is the problem and this makes it easier for vandalism to occur. A lack of deployment of drones and Supervisory Control and Data Acquisition (SCADA) security systems exposes the pipelines to further vulnerabilities. This addresses the research objective which "evaluate the strategies deployed in protecting oil and gas pipeline infrastructure in Bayelsa".

Further, a Navy Lieutenant Commander in charge of engineering and former Intelligence Officer Joint Intelligence Fusion Centre in OPDS pointed out that, "the deployment of standard and mechanically certified pipelines is critical for the protection of both the environment and the people and mitigate against vandalism" (SEC-09). Aligning with the above point, a Superintendent of Police stated that:

> Changing and replacing oil pipelines with those that cannot be broken reduces pipeline vandalism to the barest minimum. Currently, no operator uses Horizontal Directional Drilling (HDD) that can trench pipelines without digging to save the environment and protect the infrastructure. It is done with Geographical Positioning Systems (GPS). You can be here in Nembe and be drilling in Port Harcourt and vandals will hardly know (SEC-01).

Though safety technologies might not be in wide use does not suggest oil and gas companies may not be contemplating doing so. The Intelligence Officer, Department of State Security Service stated that:

> Most oil pipeline operating companies do not deploy smart pigging systems designed to enable operators to check for structural weaknesses, defects, and internal corrosion. Intelligent pig helps to determine the line thickness, erosions, abridgment, cracks, sun cutting, or such things that could happen along the pipeline. Not using this vital mechanical equipment increases the chance of pipeline blowout (SEC-04).

African Oil and Gas report noted that a shift to a Sea Vessel Storage facility would reduce focus on pipelines and curtail structural failures (2018). Security should include the protection of the inalienable rights of the citizens which include their rights to the environment (see

Chapter 3). As Zhao stated, security should no longer be considered a "zero-sum-game" rather it should be a "win–win" relationship (2011).

However, seven out of the 20 professional respondents interviewed from the oil and gas sample population argue that many preventative technologies are been used by companies and insisted that old pipelines are been replaced. They attributed the frequent criminal acts of vandalism to the greedy criminal tendencies of some local communities and their youths. They did not provide any evidence to show where they have changed old pipelines or instances of new technologies deployed. All of the professional interviewees, in part, ignored the fact that vandalism does not occur because of the poor infrastructure, but because local communities feel left out and behind as well as neglected. Adding to this ravaging poverty, increased corruption, poor governance, and incompetent short-sighted leadership issues are left unaddressed, leading to more frustration and CNAD tendencies. The General Manager in charge of health, safety, and environment in an oil-producing firm observed that

> The regulators are deploying new types of pipelines such as flexible pipelines, and other equipment as preventative technologies to mitigate against structural failures that facilitate blowouts and vandalism (OILG-05).

The statement above is not backed up by evidence gathered on the field. Infact, its more of rhetoric. While there could be a possibility of this taking place, it might have been in principle, and not in practice. A chief Operating Officer of an oil and gas producing firm stated that official memos exchanged between strategic meetings with the DPR show that

> DPR is giving permissions and encouraging industrial usage of fibre optics cable that protects the rights of way, records human activities, and vibration, and sends signals to the control command centre. Although we are yet to explore data from the control command centre during our joint investigation of criminal sabotage (OILG-07).

The contradiction is why oil and gas security personnel not gathering data from control command centres since they claimed that DPR has approved the use of high-tech pipelines. The government agencies appear to be economical with the facts. A pipeline security coordinator in an oil firm noted that:

We are using flexible composite pipelines in the most vulnerable areas. We know an area of 4 or 5 kilometres was recently piloted and information reaching us suggests that vandals can hardly blast it even after using explosive dynamites. The pipeline is still operating and working (OILG-09).

There appears to be a lack of evidence substantiating that the composite pipelines they claimed have been deployed were responsible for protecting the lines from an explosion. What is obvious is plenty of pipeline routes that were constructed over 40 to 60 years ago are visible for all to see. Further, a technical supervisor with an oil and gas infrastructure manufacturing company stated that

Criminal saboteurs operating in the Nembe area are not relenting. You may be hearing about vandalism and the disruption of facilities on the NCTL. I am aware that oil companies are collaborating to install a 24-hour pipeline monitoring satellite. The objective is to create multi-level security and enhance response to vandalism (OILG-10).

The communities are often blamed for the lack of responsible management of the Nigerian oil sector. Although this has been convenient in the past due to a lack of cohesion amongst communities, the debate has shifted in contemporary times because many oil-bearing communities are now able to narrate their own stories and access local and international justice.

Analysis of the insightful professional narratives shows gaps and a complex approach to pipeline operations in Nigeria. Refusal to change defective pipelines or deploy modern preventative operational technologies has helped to facilitate the vandalism of the NCTL. The structural infrastructure insecurity problems persist and remain unmitigated due to ineffective regulatory framework and oversight functions ridden with corruption. This has led to the infiltration of the oil sector with substandard facilities that facilitate vandalism and operational blowouts. It seems a large proportion of the pipeline network in Bayelsa is extremely old, and the use of new technologies might not be widespread. It might be technologically difficult to deploy new oil spills and anti-vandalism technologies on old pipelines (Devold, 2013; Timashev & Bushinskaya, 2016). Radom and reactive deployment of technologies Bergstresser observed limits expected results (2017). The lack of a structured and systematic security mechanism to gather and synthesize information

Okafor and Olaniyan believe has made the deployment of security a failed approach (2017; see Chapters 3 and 4). Although Downstream Remote Monitoring Systems (DRMS) technology is designed to give accurate product inventory, enhance regulations, check criminality, and prevent product theft (Eboh, 2021). One pitfall of DRMS is the lack of graphic explanation and implementation timeline summary. Thereby defeating the anticipated objective of safety, integrity, and valuable source of data for efficient pipeline operation and management in Nigeria. The bottom line is that effective mechanical processes should be integrated with socio-economic opportunities and infrastructure development to form a strategic approach against vandalism.

## Impact of Community Compensation on Pipeline Vandalism

Many argue that local communities should be compensated for giving up their lands for crude oil exploration (Alamieyeseigha, 2008; Douglas & Okonta, 2003). But this is not the case according to the relevant oil and gas regulatory frameworks (PIA, 2021; LUA, 2004, 1978; OPA Act, 2004; see details in Chapter 2). The issue of compensation for lands, oil spills, environmental pollution, and damage as well as trickle-down benefits in form of royalty are subjected to different interpretations by relevant oil and gas Acts and regulations in Nigeria. The problem is not the oil and gas companies who are using the gaps in regulations to maximise their profits, rather it is a classic case of poor governance and neglect. Given the benefits of oil and gas resources, as well as the environmental degradation caused by the extractive industries the people have a right to share in the oil benefits (Boro, 1982; Saro-Wiwa, 1992). A refusal to adequately compensate communities for oil extraction and its attendant effects and impacts, using the land for infrastructure and the damage caused by oil spills further exacerbates tensions that cause further frustration and aggression. This is one aspect of the Community Neglect-Aggression Displacement theoretical framework explained in Chapter 3. Some have argued that communities should be entitled to their "share of the crude oil spoil" (Saro-Wiwa, 1992), after all, it is a local resource extracted from under their ground and soil (Okumagba, 2012, 2013). This section discusses the professional views on the lack of adequate compensation for the vandalism of pipelines and oil and gas infrastructure insecurity.

This book identifies three categories of compensatory schemes. They are compensation for land acquired/leased for exploration, compensation for damages caused by either structural failure or vandalism, and the distribution of royalties to communities. This is further supported by the MOU and GMOU social contracts which oil and gas firms sign with a community and/or cluster of communities. Thereby decoupling the confusion in the oil and gas regulatory compensatory frameworks (see details in PIA Act, 2021; LUA Act, 2004, 1978; OPA Act, 2004; NMM Act, 2011; Chapters 1 and 2). What is the common compensation scheme is that the regulations give more rights to the federal, state, and local government and the oil companies over the communities on issues bothering land acquisition. It is worth noting that, although all three categories of compensation are sources of tension, frustrations, and vandalism they also tie in with the factors that trigger CNADT. The main focus of the problem lay in compensating communities for oil spills and pollution damages caused by vandalism and/ or structural failure. The professionals agree that some communities and individuals have benefited more from compensation paid for damages, but not without court litigations. Given that most communities lose out from getting compensated for lands seized by the government. Compensation for pollution and oil spills have either benefited only the agitating communities, community leaders, or individuals that the companies and or government think can protect the interests in communities leading to tensions.

17 out of the 20 professional respondents, nine from the oil and gas and eight from the security samples argue that the government, oil and gas corporations, and contractors were dedicated to compensating oil-bearing communities affected by oil and gas activities. What they did not clarify is the category of compensation, payment for lands, damages, and pollution or royalties, or the three of them. Evidence and stories from the professional participants suggest that these three compensations were entangled and therefore the government or oil firms rely on the provisions of the Land Use Act (2004, 1978), and other regulations. Resource control agitations and militancy has compelled the amendment of the constitution to allow the federal government to allocate 13 per cent in derivation as royalty from oil and gas to the state to develop their communities, but this fund is embezzled by the state government (Constitution of Nigeria, 1999-third amendment, Section 162(2).

For example, oil and gas regulatory frameworks in Norway, Canada, and Russia make provisions for the state to leverage oil and gas resource for the socio-economic development of local oil-bearing communities (Tysiachniouk, 2020: 1–2). Norway has diversified its economy from fossil fuel and developed social safety net structure for its citizens- aspect of political security, and infrastructure as a way to ensure the oil money percolates to the grassroots and people are not left behind (Addison, 2018). They fund these developmental programs through the Government Pension Fund Global (GPF-G) which invested in some of the surpluses from the oil and gas sector. It is however a bit hypocritical for many Western countries though, given that they are still enriching themselves through oil and gas which partly responsible for for climate change. Alaska oil and gas regulations on the other hand stipulate a range of multiple community compensation schemes like formal trickle-down benefits and distributive equity (Tysiachniouk, 2020). This automatically reaches communities alongside development. It is ironic that although Nigeria has the same oil resources, its regulatory framework does not take the benefits oil makes to communities very seriously. It seems the difference is found in the corrupt political interaction between politics, the economy, the character of the state, and democracy versus abuse of power which are the complex mix that mostly causes tensions in Nigeria. Even when social contracts are signed with communities in form of MOUs and GMOUs are signed the regulations cannot enforce them. They easily translate into a document of deceit.

Some scholars argue that Nigeria should amend its regulatory policy framework that allows compensation schemes to include social safety net that redistributes the oil wealth to communities as well as allocation of marginal oil blocks (Dokpesi & Ibiezugbe, 2012; Oriola, 2013, 2016). Mercer-Mapstone et al. pointed out that compensation should include benefit-sharing schemes (2017). An executive director in a regulatory agency justified the compensatory scheme of the government

> The government ensures monies are paid and economic palliatives like boats and fishing nets are distributed to deserving recipients, and communities. But government and oil companies alike rarely sand fill water-logged areas to create new communities where they could relocate displaced people (OILG-01).

This statement is as contradictory as the lack of structured compensation itself. Although there is some form of compensation for deserving communities here, it is left for the oil company to decide how much and the qualification criteria. The lack of an effective regulatory framework appears to be the bane of oil and gas compensation problems in Nigeria (Okonofua, 2016; Okumagba, 2013). The regulatory gaps have been deliberate. Given the character of the Nigerian state where public and powerful private business leaders see every available opportunity as a potential avenue to dominate and control the people rather than to be used for the common good of all (Amundsen, 2019; Hoeffler, 2011; Ogbeidi, 2012). This precipitates tensions which sometimes lead to violent agitations and pipeline vandalism.

Further, a General Manager in charge of upstream exploration and production pointed out that,

> when an oil company sites a production facility in a community, a General Memorandum of Understanding (GMOU) is designed and signed between community representatives and the oil firms before the state Governor, industry, and community leaders. It details individual, collective compensation, and community development plans (OILG-06).

Although MOUs and GMOUs are not covered or enforceable by the oil and gas regulatory laws or courts, they are the closest means by which impacted communities' interface with oil firms to get direct compensation either in cash or construction of agreed infrastructure projects. MOU and GMOUs, in principle, are documents that stipulate what project the communities and oil firms agree on (see details in Chapters 1 and 2). Although these social contract documents are signed between a particular oil firm and a specific community, oftentimes, communities were not part of the drafting processes or agenda-setting, even if their kings were consulted. The community rarely sees the final document or project execution timeline (Okonofua, 2016). A security supervisor with an oil and gas firm said "anywhere crude oil is discovered, oil firms approach the community, sign Memorandum of Understanding which Bayelsa Governor is privy to and witnessed by the state executives and community leaders" (OILG-09). It is worthy of note that, signing MOUs is just one aspect of trying to compensate communities for the impact of oil and gas activities. Also, the problem is not the lack of social contract that signifies that communities will be compensated but how the projects are executed. The insights from some security respondents suggests that about nine out of every ten GMOUs signed are either neglected, abandoned, or haphazardly implemented, or the projects are swapped between communities due to some political interference or influence. There may have been some GMoUs schemes that worked, but this research could not verify such based on the documentary evidence examined. Therefore, GMoUs do not address the issue of compensating communities for displacement from their lands or hard suffering due to oil and gas activities. This is the gap that the ESG aims to close (see Chapter 4).

According to the chief operating officer of an oil and gas and pipeline operating company, some schools and health facilities constructed are often neglected by the communities, stating that:

> When oil companies construct schools, for instance, as benefits and part compensation for land, most locals refuse to attend them. They might prefer a town hall built or even money shared for them which may not be part of what the company had planned. This behavior is a common cause of tensions among the youths including the educated, uneducated, elders, and women groups alike (OILG-07).

This is, of course, problematic as oil and gas companies are there to make profits and not provide social services to the local communities which is the point Friedman makes in Chapter 2 (Friedman, 1993). He stressed that the greater social responsibility of businesses is to give dividends to their shareholders, but this theory continues to polarize scholars, businesses, and corporate capitalism advocates (Bruland, 1998; Schwab, 2021). CSR has further expanded from being limited to the generation of profit for shareholders alone to a broader sense of responsibility. Companies are now expected to be responsible for the generation of shared values (Agudelo et al., 2019). Shared values are organisational values developed by the leadership in consonance with the broader societal expectations such as ethical standards, and trust-based relationships with community partners, and academic, corporate, and government bodies. What Agudelo et al. are saying is that the social expectations of the communities are for the companies to take responsibility for the environment in which they operate (2019). The fact is that the contemporary business world has evolved into a complex reality where corporate executives need to refocus and balance internal and external priorities (Slocombe & Prno, 2012).

The societal expectation is that companies are obligated to undertake corporate social responsibilities beyond just payment of dividends to their shareholders to include the context of shared values such as ethical standards and community development. Alshbili et al. argue that governmental pressure through its regulatory frameworks and policies as well as external stakeholders have a considerable influence in promoting corporate-level CSR disclosure activities, especially as a legitimate mechanism in a fragile state like Nigeria (2020). Slocombe and Prno argued that oil companies should be encouraged to go beyond their "social licence to operate" (2012: 346). Also, a Nigerian Security and Civil Defence Deputy Superintendent of Corp observed that "family clashes arise when people believe the oil companies and government may have randomly compensated selected individuals or families whose lands were forcefully taken over or pollution suffered" (SEC-05). What this suggests is that corruption also influences compensation schemes and that corruption, poor governance, and nepotism determine who gets compensated (Amundsen, 2019). This indicates that there is a high level of corruption due to the involvement of influential political and business leaders who skew community compensation to friends and cronies (Amundsen, 2019; Ogbeidi, 2012). This provokes tensions and pipeline vandalism by communities who despite suffering the impact of oil spills and environmental degradation were neglected in the compensation scheme either because they did not agitate or have links to corrupt officials. A senior Intelligence Officer with DSS pointed out that

> Obodo community won compensation claims against environmental degradation in foreign courts against Shell petroleum setting judicial precedence. The Jurist mandated Shell to pay monies to some clustered communities of about 45,000 people who have suffered many years of environmental devastation (SEC-03).

According to Azubuike (2021), some communities have taken legal action against oil companies to get compensation for the damage caused by oil spills due to their operations. This suggests that there are legal hopes for communities that can fund challenges and therefore highlight their plight. Those unable to do so are left behind. For those left behind, vandalism becomes even more appealing. It appears the Nigeria Criminal Justice system may not be favourable to oil-bearing communities given that most of the compensatory cases are successfully decided in the home countries of operating firms (Azubuike, 2021).

Furthermore, three out of the 20 professionals, two security and one oil and gas respondent disagree that the payment for different categories of compensation such as land acquisition, compensation for pollution, and royalties was not enough. Given the regulatory hurdles, communities have to go through to get compensated (see Chapter 2). Whereas these few professional respondents did not specify which category of compensation is underpaid. They did not deny that some forms of compensation percolated the communities either through court rulings or private negotiations (Azubuike, 2021; Khalid, 2021). According to Igbinovia (2014), the compensation provided by the state and the oil companies does not reflect the damage done to the environment or the impact on displacement (physical, economic, and psychological) suffered. Also, it does not reflect the profits made by the government and the oil and gas companies. This inequality, along with the other reasons outlined in the above section, motivates some people to vandalise pipelines in the area. Given that these fall within the rubrics of CNADT. Excuses of difficult terrain and insecurity are often stated as reasons why no sustainable development is tied to community development schemes (Alamieyeseigha, 2008; Alagoa, 2005; Douglas & Okonta, 2003).

An Oil and Gas General Manager in charge of health and safety standards notes that:

> I don't believe we have done enough to assuage and compensate communities for the pains, suffering and economic deprivations oil activities have caused them. The oil and gas industry should compel a coordinated approach to community development to stop the age-long agitations (OILG-05)

Supporting the above claims, an environment commissioner states that:

> The majority of our people feel short-changed and attempt to force some of the oil and gas wealth back into those communities who feel they have not been fully compensated. Having seen how oil monies are been used in Lagos and Abuja. They use vandalism as a means to redirect monies into their pockets and resolve their predicament through illegal access to oil condensate lines. Agitations and Niger Delta militancy were a response to a dearth in infrastructural development in Bayelsa (OILG-04).

This shows that the people feel frustrated because of how oil and gas money is distributed and redistributed across states like Lagos and Abuja while leaving local oil-bearing communities behind to fend for themselves.

Furthermore, a Police Superintendent observed that there appears to be a correlation between increased vandalism and litigations in communities that have not received compensation either for lands forcefully taken by the government, oil pollution caused by vandalism, and/or structural blowouts. As well as the 13 per cent royalty payments and nonmandatory compensation through CSR and government investment in the areas (see Chapter 2 for discussion on CRS). He noted that:

> The people are not duly compensated for the many inconveniences oil activities have caused to their lives and environment. Neither do oil firms hardly concern themselves with the displacement and socio-economic well-being of the inhabitants. If it is established that the pipelines may have been tampered with, compensation payment becomes a tug of war. Sometimes individuals in communities conclude that either they steal what is inside the pipeline or let the oil spill into the environment even though it destroys their habitat (SEC-01).

A Deputy Superintendent of Corp with the Civil Defence agrees with this point. The objective is perhaps to mirror the litigation success in other communities (Igbinovia, 2014). A community may also institute litigation claiming negligence of the company when they are neglected and denied compensation for acquired lands, and damages (Amnesty International, 2018; James, 2018; Issa, 2015; see Chapter 3).

The analysis shows the compensation complexities and difficulties in its implementation in the Nigerian oil and gas sector were due to many factors. A flexible compensation scheme is beneficial especially when local communities are involved. At the same time powerful political, bureaucratic, and business leaders in Nigeria use the flexible compensation approach to exact undue influence either for their benefit or that of their family members. Mercer-Mapstone et al., (2017) argued that compensatory benefit-sharing and direct community investment create socio-economic development and build human capacity. 17 out of the 20 respondents believe that some communities and individuals have benefited from some form of compensation schemes. Even when compensation is paid, it often offers poor value for money and few tangible benefits for local communities. While the oil and gas firms and regulators employ professional and expert services of negotiators, the communities are often represented by either poorly educated or inexperienced traditional rulers and lawyers unskilled in the act of compensation negotiation.

Three out of the 20 respondents feel too little compensation has been disbursed, and when compensation is paid, the process is plagued by poor governance and corruption. Other times, Shell and many other oil and gas firms appear to reject compensatory recommendations like those made by Joint Investigation Visit (Oyadongha, 2020). The failure to meet the different compensation categories exacerbates frustration, resentment, and tensions. This is made worse by the absence of a community framework as reflected in the NOSDRA Act (2006) and the Oil Pipeline Act (2004).

The challenges of corruption and criminality, the impact of community projects on vandalism, environmental pollution, pipeline structural resilience, and community compensation scheme are not isolated to Nigeria's petroleum industry alone. These problems resonate with multidimensional problems observed in Colombia, Venezuela, Sudan, and many other countries in the Global South (see Chapters 2 and 4). Countries where these are entrenched make it easier for tensions and frustration that lead to overt and non-overt aggression to occur (see Chapters 2, 3, 4, and 5). It is also a clear demonstration that such a country is either lacking in policy or struggles to garner the political will to implement the UNSDGs or Agenda 20,230 (see Chapter 2). Multiple documentary evidence analysed and evaluated aligns with the fact that the themes discussed with the various professionals are directly tied to tensions, and insecurity problems in Bayelsa.

## CONCLUSION

The issues of pipeline vandalism and oil and gas infrastructure insecurity problems were explored in this chapter through the lens of oil and gas and security professionals in the public and private sectors. Their answers have shone a light on the causes of onshore oil and gas infrastructure pipeline insecurity in the historic Niger Delta region. The data demonstrate that the professional respondents overwhelmingly agree that the underlying issues mentioned above and throughout the thesis are causing frustration and triggering aggression across Bayelsa communities. It is these underlying issues that provoke anger within communities that can lead to the displacement of aggression against onshore pipelines resulting in vandalism. But the reforms suggested in the various NEITI reports (2015, 2021) and the new PIA Act (2021) that proposes a new and transparent regulatory regime for the petroleum industry would only be looking at the surface. NEITI and PIA both demonstrate that the government lacks adequate understanding of the underlying issues responsible for the insecurity and vandalism in Bayelsa. The agitations, tensions, militancy, vandalism, and oil theft are only responding to the issues which raise pertinent questions. It also suggests that Nigeria's security, political, economic, judicial, and traditional anti-social inhibitors are either weakened or broken and have become ineffective.

## REFERENCES

Addison, T. (2018). Climate Change and the Extractive Sector. In T. Addison & A. Roe (Eds.), *Extractive Industry: The Management of Resources as a Driver of Sustainable Development* (pp. 460–484). Oxford University.

Africa Oil and Gas Report. (2018). *In 24 Months Nembe Creek Trunk Line Will be Running Empty* (Vol. 19(8), pp. 1–10). Africa Oil and Gas Report.

Agudelo, M. A. L., Johannsdottir, L., & Davidsdottir, B. (2019). A Literature Review of the History and Evolution of Corporate Social Responsibility. *International Journal of Corporate Social Responsibility, 4*(1).

Akintunde, I. (2020). Nigeria's Recovery Means Rethinking Economic Diversification</Emphasis>. Chatham House. https://www.chathamhouse.org/2020/08/nigerias-recovery-means-rethinking-economic-diversification. Accessed 5 March 2022.

Akpomera, E. (2015). International Crude Oil Theft: Elite Predatory Tendencies in Nigeria. *Review of African Political Economy Journal, 42*(143), 156–165.

Alagoa, E. J. (2005). *A History of the Niger Delta*. Onyema Research Publications.

Alamieyeseigha, D. S. P. (2005). *Thoughts on Federalism*. Treasure Books.

Alamieyeseigha, D. S. P. (2008). The Environmental Challenge of Developing the Niger Delta. In S. S. Azaiki, D. S. P. Alamieyeseigha, & A. A. Ikein (Eds.), *Oil, Democracy and the Promise of True Federalism in Nigeria* (pp. 249–260). University Press of America.

Alshbili, I., Elamer, A. A., & Beddewela, E. (2020). Ownership Types Corporate Governance, and Corporate Social Responsibility Disclosures: Empirical Evidence from Developing Country. *Accounting Research Journal, 33*(1), 148–166.

Amnesty International Report. (2018). *Amnesty International Report 2017/18: The State of the World's Human Rights*. https://www.amnesty.org/en/documents/pol10/6700/2018/en/. Accessed 7 May 2024.

Amundsen, I. (2019). Extractive and Power-Preserving Political Corruption. In I. Amundsen (Ed.), *Political Corruption in Africa: An Extraction and Power Preservation* (pp. 1–28). Elgar.

Anand, V., & Ashforth, B. E. (2003). The Normalization of Corruption in Organisations. In *Research in Organisational Behaviour* (Vol. 25, pp. 1–52). Elsevier.

Anderson, C. A., & Dill, J. C. (1995). Effects of Frustration Justification on Hostile Aggression. *Aggressive Behaviour, 21*(5), 359–369.

Azubuike, V. (2021). International Court Orders Shell to Compensate Niger-Delta Communities over Oil Spillage. *Daily Post News.* https://dailypost.ng/2021/01/29/breaking-international-court-orders-shell-to-compensate-niger-delta-communities-over-oil-spillage/. Accessed 30 January 2021.

Bello, S. (1964). *Herzog*. Penguin Press.

Bergstresser, H. (2017). *A Decade of Nigeria: Politics, Economy and Society 2004–2016*. Brill.

Boro, I. (1982). *The Twelve-day Revolution*. Idodo Umeh.

Bruland, K. (1998). The Era of Corporate Capitalism. In K. Bruland & P. O'Brien (Eds.), *From Family Firms to Corporate Capitalism* (pp. 219–247). Claredon Press.

Collier, P. (2007). *The Bottom Billion* (pp. 39–52). Oxford University Press.

Collier, P., & Hoeffler, A. E. (2004). *Greed and Grievance in Civil War*. World Bank Development Research Group.

Devold, H. (2013). *Oil and Gas Production Handbook: An Introduction to Oil and Gas Production* (pp. 6–146). ABB. https://library.e.abb.com/public/34d5b70e18f7d6c8c1257be500438ac3/Oil%20and%20gas%20production%20handbook%20ed3x0_web.pdf. Accessed 12 December 2017.

Disu, K. (2021, July 24). How Bayelsa Lost Atala Field to Two-Year-Old Firm. *Vanguard News.* https://www.vanguardngr.com/2021/07/how-bayelsa-lost-atala-field-to-two-year-old-firm/. Accessed 24 July 2021.

Dodd, V. (2021, April 18). Tackling Poverty and Inequality to Reduce Crime, Says Police Chief. *The Guardian News.* https://www.theguardian.com/uk-news/2021/apr/18/tackle-poverty-and-inequality-to-reduce-says-police-chief. Accessed 18 April 2021.

Dokpesi, A. O., & Ibiezugbe, M. I. (2012). Assessment the Human Development Efforts of the Niger Delta Development Commission. In O. Ukaga, U. O. Ukiwo, & I. S. Ibaba (Eds.), *Natural Resources, Conflict, and Sustainable Development: Lessons from the Niger Delta* (pp. 60–78). Routledge.

Dollard, J., Miller, N. E., Doob, L. W., Mowrer, O. H., & Sears, R. R. (1939). *Frustration and Aggression*. Yale University Press.

Douglas, O., & Okonta, I. (2003). *Where Vultures Feast: Shell, Human Rights, and Oil in the Niger Delta*. Verso.

Ebiye, S. (2000). Community conflicts in the Niger Delta 1850 – 1980 and from 1981 to 1999. *Journal of Africana, 7*(ii), 102–108.

Eboh, M. (2021). DPR to Upgrade Downstream Petroleum Sector Operations. *Vanguard News*. https://www.vanguardngr.com/2021/02/dpr-to-upgrade-downstream-petroleum-sector-operations/. Accessed 9 February 2021.

Esiedesa, O. (2021). Nigeria Earned $418.5bn in 10 Years from Petroleum, NEITI Reveals. *Vanguard News*. https://www.vanguardngr.com/2021/06/nigeria-earned-418-5bn-in-10yrs-from-petroleum-neiti-reveals/. Accessed 19 June 2021.

Etemire, U. (2016). *Law and Practice on Public Participation in Environmental Matters: The Nigerian Example in Transnational Comparative Perspective.* Routledge.

Friedman, M. (1993). The Social Responsibility of Business is to Increase its Profits. In G. D. Chryssides & J. H. Kaler (Eds.), *An Introduction to Business Ethics* (pp. 249–265). Thomson.

Gbobo, I. P. (2020). Women and the Environment in Nigeria: The Experience of Women in the Niger Delta. In M. C. Green & M. Haron (Eds.), *Law, Religion and the Environment in Africa* (pp. 185–198). African Sun Media.

Gurr, R. T. (2015). *Political Rebellion: Causes.* Routledge.

Hairshine, K. (2021). Nigeria Faces a Tough Time Diversifying from Oil. *Deutsche Welle*. https://www.dw.com/en/nigeria-faces-a-tough-time-diversifying-from-oil/a-59494125. Accessed 5 March 2022.

Higgins, P. (2010). *Eradicating Ecocide: Laws and Governance to Stop the Destruction of the Planet.* Shepheard-Walwyn.

Hoeffler, A. (2011). Greed Versus Grievance: A Useful Conceptual Distinction in the Study of Civil War? *Studies in Ethnicity and Nationalism Journal, 11*(2), 274–284.

Idemudia, U. (2014). Oil Multinational Companies as Money Makers and Peace Makers: Lessons from Nigeria. In G. Eweje (Ed.), *Corporate Social Responsibility and Sustainability: Emerging Trends in Developing Economies* (pp. 191–214). Emerald.

Igbinovia, P. E. (2014). *Oil Thefts and Pipeline Vandalisation in Nigeria.* African Books.

Ioannides, E. (2017). *Fundamental Principles of EU Law Against Money Laundering.* Routledge.

Irvine, M. (2018). *A Practical Guide to Vicarious Liability.* Law Briefs Publication.

Issa, A. (2015). *Reflections on Industrial and Economy.* Maulthouse.

James, U. V. (2018). *Capacity Building for Sustainable Development.* Centre for Agriculture and Bioscience International-CABI Publication.

Janoski, T., Luke, D., & Oliver, C. (2014). *The Causes of Structural Unemployment: Four Factors that Keeps People from the Job they Deserve.* Polity Press.

Khalid, I. (2021). Shell in Nigeria: Polluted Communities Can Sue in English Supreme Courts. *BBC News.* https://www.bbc.co.uk/news/world-africa-560 41189. Accessed 13 February 2021.

Knutson, J. (2021). *Deepwater Horizon Oil Spill.* Cherry Lake Publishing.

Kuwornu, J. K. M. (2019). *Climate Change and Sub-Saharan Africa: The Vulnerability and Adaptation of Food Supply Chain Actors.* Vernon Art and Science Incorporated.

Land Use Act. (1978). *Vesting of All Land in the State; Control and Management of Land; Advisory Bodies; Designation of Urban Areas.* Applicable law for the interim management of land. https://faolex.fao.org/docs/pdf/nig67625. pdf. Accessed 7 May 2024.

Land Use Act. (2004). *The Complete Laws of Nigeria, a Searchable Compendium.* Land Use Act. https://lawsofnigeria.placng.org/view2.php?sn=228. Accessed 20 February 2022.

Linden, O., & Palsson, J. (2013). Oil Contamination in Ogoniland Niger Delta, Stockholm. *The Royal Swedish Academy of Sciences Journal, 42*(6), 685–701.

Loft, P., & Brien, P. (2023, September). Halfway to 2023: The Sustainable Development Goals. *UK House of Commons Library.* https://commonsli brary.parliament.uk/halfway-to-2030-the-sustainable-development-goals/. 31 October 2023.

Lynch, M. J., Stretesky, P. B., & Long, M. A. (2015). *Defining Crime: A Critique of the Concept and Its Implication.* Palgrave Macmillan.

Mahmood, Y., Yodo, N., Huang, Y., & Afrin, T. (2023). Sustainable Development for Oil and Gas infrastructure from Risk Reliability, and Resilience Perspectives. *Journal of Sustainability, 15*(3), 4953.

Makholm, J. D. (2012). *The Political Economy of Pipelines: A Century of Comparative Institutional Development.* University of Chicago Press.

Malici, A. (2007, Summer/Fall). Thinking about Rogue Leaders: Really Hostile or Just Frustrated? The *Whitehead Journal of Diplomacy and International Relations,* 1–9.

Mathias, Z. (2015). Providing All-Round Security against Oil and Gas Infrastructure Sabotage and Physical Attacks on the Staff of NNPC and Multinational Oil Companies in Nigeria as a Critical Article of Her National Security Efforts. *International Journal of Social Science and Humanities Research, 3*(2), 45–59.

Mba, H. C., Uchegbu, S. N., Udeh, C. A., & Moghalu, L. N. (2018). *Management of Environmental Problems and Hazards in Nigeria.* Routledge.

Mercer-Mapstone, L., Rafkin, W., Moffat, K., & Louis, W. (2017). Conceptualising the Role of Dialogue in Social License to Operate. *Journal of Resource Policy, 54,* 137–146.

Mickolus, E. (2018). *Terrorism Worldwide, 2016.* McFarland and Company.

National Bureau of Statistics. (2016). *Social Statistics Report December 2016.* National Bureau of Statistics.

National Bureau of Statistics. (2017). *Social Statistics Report December 2016*. National Bureau of Statistics.

National Bureau of Statistics. (2020). *Labour Force Statistics: Unemployment and Underemployment Report: Abridged Labour Force Survey Under COVID-19*. National Bureau of Statistics. https://www.nigerianstat.gov.ng/pdfuploads/Q2_2020_Unemployment_Report.pdf. Accessed 26 May 2021.

National Oil Spill Detection and Response Agency (Establishment) Act. (2006). As Amended. http://extwprlegs1.fao.org/docs/pdf/nig124170A.pdf. Accessed 5 August 2020.

Neumann, M., & Elsenbroich, C. (2017). Introduction: The Societal Dimensions of Organised Crime. *Trends in Organised Crime, 20*, 1–15.

Nigeria Extractive Industries Transparency Initiative. (2015). *Highlights of the 2015 Oil and Gas Audit Report*. NEITI.

Nigeria Extractive Industries Transparency Initiative. (2021). Oil and Gas Industry Audit Report 2019. NEITI. https://eiti.org/sites/default/files/attachments/neiti-oga-2019-report_compressed.pdf. Accessed 20 February 2022.

Nigeria Mineral and Mining Act. (2011). Administration of the Act. http://admin.theiguides.org/Media/Documents/Nigeruian%20Minerals%20and%20Mining%20Act,%202007.pdf. Accessed 5 October 2022.

Nigerian National Petroleum Corporation. (2016). *Monthly Financial and Operations Report September 2016* (pp. 2–9). Nigerian National Petroleum Corporation.

Nigerian National Petroleum Corporation. (2017). *Monthly Financial and Operations Report October 2017* (pp. 4–37). Nigerian National Petroleum Corporation.

Nigerian National Petroleum Corporation. (2018). Annual Statistical Bulletin 2018. https://www.nnpcgroup.com/NNPCDocuments/Annual%20Statistics%20Bulletin%E2%80%8B/ASB%202018%201st%20Edition.pdf. Accessed 24 September 2020.

Nigerian Oil and Gas Industry Content Development Act. (2010). An Act to Provide for the Development of Nigerian Content in the Nigerian Oil and Gas Industry, Nigerian Content Plan, Supervision, Coordination, Monitoring and Implementation of Nigerian Content. Available from https://www.ncdmb.gov.ng/images/GUIDELINES/NCACT.pdf. Accessed 13th December 2019.

Nye, S. J. (1967). Corruption and Political Development: A Cost-Benefit Analysis. *American Political Science Review, 61*(2), 417–427.

Ogbeidi, M. M. (2012). Political Leadership and Corruption in Nigeria since 1960: A Socio-economics Analysis. *Journal of Nigerian Studies, 1*(2), 1–24.

Ogundajo, G. O., Akintoye, I. R., & Olayinka, I. M. (2019). Taxing Informal Sector and Revenue Generation in Nigeria. *International Journal of Commerce and Management Research, 5*(4), 81–87.

Oil Pipeline Act. (2004). Chapter 338: Laws of the Federal Republic of Nigeria. https://www.chr.up.ac.za/images/researchunits/bhr/files/extractive_industries_database/nigeria/laws/Oil%20Pipelines%20Act.pdf. Accessed 28 March 2020.

Okafor, A., & Olaniyan, A. (2017). Legal and Institutional Framework for Promoting Oil Pipeline Security in Nigeria. *Journal of Sustainable Development Law and Policy, 8*(2).

Oki, R. A. (2017). *Barbarism to Decadence: Nigeria and Foreign Complicity.* Author Solutions.

Okonjo-Iweala, N. (2018). *Fighting Corruption is Dangerous: The Story Behind the Headlines.* MIT Press.

Okonkwo, E. C. (2020). *Environmental Justice and Oil Pollution Laws: Comparing Enforcement in the United States and Nigeria* (1st ed.). Routledge.

Okonofua, B. A. (2016). The Niger Delta Amnesty Program: The Challenges of Transitioning from Peace Settlements to Long-Term Peace. *Sage Open Journals, 6*(2), 1–16.

Okonta, I. (2016). Policy Incoherence and the Challenge of Energy Security. In A. Goldthau (Ed.), *The Handbook of Global Energy Policy* (pp. 501–520). Wiley.

Okumagba, P. (2012). Oil Exploration and Crisis in the Niger Delta: The Response of the Militia Groups. *Journal of Sustainable Society, 1*(3), 78–83.

Okumagba, P. (2013). Ethnic Militia and Criminality in the Niger Delta. *International Review of Social Sciences and Humanities, 5*(1), 239–246.

Olawuyi, D. S. (2012). Legal and Sustainable Development Impacts of Major Oil Spills. *The Journal of Sustainable Development, 9*(1), 1–15.

Onuoha, C. F. (2008). Oil Pipeline Sabotage in Nigeria: Dimensions, Actors and Implications for National Security. *African Security Review, 17*(3), 100–115.

Oriola, T. B. (2013). *Criminal Resistance?: The Politics of Kidnapping Oil Workers.* Ashgate publication.

Oriola, T. B. (2016). *Criminal Resistance: The Politics of Kidnapping Oil Workers.* Routledge.

Otokunefor, H. O. C. (2017). *Nigerian Petroleum Industry, Policies, and Conflicts Relations* (Vol. 2). Malthouse.

Oyadongha, S. (2020, October 28). NOSDRA Intervenes again in SPDC/Bayelsa Community Oil Spill Face-off. *Vanguard News Paper.* https://www.vanguardngr.com/2020/10/nosdra-intervenes-again-in-spdc-bayelsa-community-oil-spill-face-off/. Accessed 28 October 2020.

Oyadongha, S. (2021). We are Seeking International Help to Stop Nembe Oil Spill. *Vanguard News*. https://www.vanguardngr.com/2021/11/were-seeking-international-help-to-stop-nembe-oil-spill-aiteo/. Accessed 21 November 2021.

Paki, F. A. E., & Ebienfa, K. I. (2011). Militant Oil Agitations in Nigeria's Niger Delta and the Economy. *International Journal of Humanities and Social Sciences, 1*(5), 140–144.

Petroleum Industry Act. (2021). *PIA: Explanatory Memorandum*. https://eproofing.springer.com/ePb/books/pnXXkMoim97Z_a_rMD9rZeEbrTrR UQmOXjtKXvfLWedcljNJBuXmZZBNYj-SztuHljv8yt2gL-1Ccg7hvQhrTo jgqtjLQ2jAUWQdwYTjfbm05PWXyArOed10ZI9Y9nrGYFRl5Bl8liyVB1q XexaAfl7alFTrZ7252zWyo2Ivrw=. Accessed 4 May 2024.

Philp, M. (2015). The Definition of Political Corruption. In P. M. Heywood (Ed.), *Routledge Handbook of Political Corruption* (pp. 17–30). Routledge.

Prno, J., & Slocombe, D. S. (2012). Exploring the Origins of Social License to Operate in the Mining Sector: Perspectives from Governance and Sustainability Theories. *Journal of Resource Policy, 37*, 346–357.

Rieuwerts, J. (2017). *The Elements of Environmental Pollution*. Routledge.

Ross, M. L. (2012). *The Oil Curse: How Petroleum Wealth Shape the Development of Nations*. Princeton University Press.

Ross, M. L. (May, 2015). What Have We Learned about the Resource Curse? *Annual Review of Political Science Journal, 18*, 239–259.

Saro-Wiwa, K. (1992). *Genocide in Nigeria: The Ogoni Tragedy*. African Books.

Schwab, K. (2021). *Stakeholder Capitalism: A Global Economy that Works for Progress, People, and Planet*. Wiley.

Schwegler, V. (2017). The Disposable Nature: The Case of Ecocide and Corporate Accountability. *Amsterdam Law Reform Journal, 9*(3), 72–99.

Sinden, A. (2009). An Emerging Human Rights to Security from Climate Change: The Case Against Gas Flaring in Nigeria. In W. C. G. Burns & H. M. Osofsky (Eds.), *Adjudicating Climate Change: State, National, and International Approaches* (pp. 173–192). Cambridge University Press.

Theobald, R. (1990). *Corruption*. Palgrave Macmillan.

Timashev, S., & Bushinskaya, A. (2016). *Diagnostic and Reliability of Pipeline Systems*. Springer International Publishing.

Tomlinson, K. (2018). Oil and Gas Companies and the Management of Social and Environmental Impacts and Issues. In T. Addison & A. Roe (Eds.), *Extractive Industries: The Management of Resources as a Driver of Sustainable Development* (pp. 422–441). Oxford University Press.

Transparency International. (2019). Military Involvement in Oil Theft in the Niger Delta. https://ti-defence.org/publications/military-involvement-in-oil-theft-in-the-niger-delta/. Accessed 25 November 2020.

Transparency International. (2020). Corruption Perception Index 2020. https://www.transparency.org/en/cpi/2021. Accessed 24 November 2020.

Tysiachniouk, M. S. (2020). Disentangling Benefit-Sharing Complexities of Oil Extraction on the North Slope of Alaska. *Sustainability Journal, 12*(13), 1–31.

United Nations Environment Programme Report. (2012). Environmental Assessment of Ogoniland: Assessment of Vegetation, Aquatic and Public Health Issues. http://hdl.handle.net/20.500.11822/25286. Accessed 9 May 2018.

United Nations Sustainable Development Goals. (2016). The Sustainable Development Agenda. https://www.un.org/sustainabledevelopment/development-agenda-retired/#:~:text=%E2%97%8F,future%20for%20people%20and%20planet. Accessed 31 October 2023.

Vetter, S., Endrass, J., Schweizer, I., Teng, H. M., Rossler, W., & Gallo, W. T. (2006). The Effects of Economic Deprivation on Psychological Well-being Amongst the Working Population of Switzerland. *BMC Public Health, 6*(223), 1–10.

Zhao, Z. (2011). Non-Traditional Security and the New Concept of Security of China. In H. G. Brauch, J. Birkmann, U. O. Spring, J. Grin, C. Mesjasz, B. Chourou, P. Dunay, & P. K. Mbote (Eds.), *Coping with Global Environmental Change, Disasters and Security: Threats, Challenges, Vulnerabilities and Risks.* Springer.

# CHAPTER 7

# Pipeline Vandalism and the Impact of Oil and Gas Activities on Communities: Community Stakeholders' Perspectives

## IMPACT OF CORRUPTION AND CRIMINALITY

The 21 community stakeholders' perspectives on onshore oil and gas vandalism and infrastructure insecurity are the vital elements that this book contributes to the gap in literature and body of knowledge (see Chapter 6 into data presentation and analysis). This chapter will highlight the community stakeholders' perspectives on the continued negative impact the NCTL pipeline infrastructure and oil and gas activities have on local communities. It also evaluates the impact that ongoing corruption, poor governance, cyclical incompetent leadership that has become a curse, social inequalities, community neglect, poverty, and a lack of political engagement have on local communities and the wider security architecture in Bayelsa. Many peer-reviewed literature, books, and documentary evidence examined and analysed in previous chapters revealed that most of the above issues are also prevalent in most petrostates in the Global South (see Chapters 2 and 4). Insights and stories narrated by Bayelsa stakeholders could be used as bases to understanding what underpins the tensions and insecurity of oil and gas infrastructure in the petrostates in the Global South.

Corrupt practices have harmed the lives of many people especially the local communities in Nigeria (Ogbeidi, 2012). Powerful political and

A. L. A. Jatto, *Oil and Gas Pipeline Infrastructure Insecurity*, New Security Challenges, https://doi.org/10.1007/978-3-031-56932-6_7

239

bureaucratic classes in Nigeria sometimes divert public funds for pecuniary benefits which is partly responsible for either a dearth of investment in public infrastructures such as roads, schools, and hospitals or their poor maintenance (Amundsen, 2019; Nye, 1967; Ogbeidi, 2012). The criminality discussed here is a violation of the rule of law. But sometimes, corruption bears the element of criminality. Although pipeline vandalism and oil theft by some members of Bayelsa communities are morally reprehensible, their actions are mainly criminality, not corruption in the academic sense (see Chapters 1 and 5). Corruption is seen as a motivating factor for many young people to engage in pipeline vandalism. Some argue that the impact of oil and gas pipeline infrastructure and issues related to this are linked to corruption in Nigeria (Ogbeidi, 2012). The consistent failure of the state and private companies to tackle issues of environmental damage caused by oil and gas activities continues to agitate the local population (Alagoa, 2005; Alamieyeseigha, 2008a; Okumagba, 2013).

The 21 community interviewees are unanimous on the social, psychological, and economic impact of corruption and criminality on local communities. An in-depth analysis, reveals that 17 out of the 21 community respondents of five community leaders, four high-profile members, three professional NGOs, and all the five environmental activists agree. They argued that corruption and abuse of office had the greatest impact on communities. These participants insist that corruption and the consistent abuse of office reflected in poor governance and incompetent leadership do harm and violence to local communities. The link between the current situation and corruption is made by a community King, who stated that "community conflicts stem from a corrupt government and private influences" (Community Leader-01). Also supporting this claim, a senior professional NGO representative observed that,

> when you enter some communities in Kolo creek, you will see our women fish, drink, and soak their cassava in the same crude oil-polluted waters, you will see the raw oil on their faces, and efforts to get either the oil firm or government to clean up the river and address such neglect fall on deaf ears. This neglect provokes many community members to anger because they are frustrated. (Professional NGO-01)

The lack of data on oil spills and places that have been cleaned up makes it difficult to compare the stories of the community participants with those of oil and gas participants. Another professional NGO respondent noted that:

> The oil and gas industry and the political players are lobbying hard to reduce the proposed 10 per cent contribution of Operational Expenditure (OPEX) accruing to communities to 2.5 per cent which is supposed to be like royalties to local communities. This has led to a perception of corruption since their actions are meant to benefit the influential few. (Professional NGO-02)

This claim also aligns with the observation of four other professional NGO respondents. They pointed out that interested parties influence oil and gas regulations right from the national assembly which is to the detriment of the local communities. Douglas and Okonta explained that some local leaders collude with highly placed government officials to gain control over a large portion of the petroleum industry business chain (2003). A professional NGO leader stated:

> Some government representatives in connivance with the oil companies enrich themselves with our resources with the obnoxious land use Act of 2004 and 1978. It knowingly empowered the government to claim ownership of all the lands with petroleum and other mineral resources in Nigeria. They influence the allocation of oil blocks to people of their choice for a kickback and tacitly support the recklessness of oil companies. (Professional NGO-04)

Transparency International noted how the interference by government officials further promotes corruption and complicates transparency in the oil and gas industry (2019, 2020). An NGO representative supports this claim by stressing that, "some agents of Shell petroleum force contractors to pay 10 percent of the GMOU contract sum into proxy accounts before funds are released in turn affects the quality of the projects delivered to communities" (Professional NGO-04). 16 community members and three professional NGO representatives support this claim stressing that this type of corrupt practice was a major problem affecting quality project delivery to local communities.

An environmental activist who investigates environmental damage in Nembe and shares data on the economic, social, and traditional impact of oil spills on polluted fishing waters with NGOs observed that:

> Ministerial and bureaucratic leadership influence oil companies to award oil spill contracts to their competing proxies. The struggle for pecuniary gains by these powerful internal and external forces prevents and distracts the NOSDRA oil spill response agency from pollution. It also impedes community intervention projects and response to insecurity. (Environmental Activist-02)

Ong and Oriola have extensively discussed in Chapters 2 and 3 how political interference hinders effective response to oil spills and insecurity problems in the area (2016, 2017). Four high-profile members of Bayelsa-Nembe communities support the above claims. For example, they pointed out the NDDC is a classic case of a cesspool of corrupt and manipulated government agencies. A high-profile community member observed that:

> Exposure of the NDDC to political influences from the Presidency down to governors and Chiefs has made it a cesspool of corruption. Intervention projects and contracts are influenced and awarded in Abuja by those not statutorily empowered to do so often from other geopolitical regions to the detriment of the communities. It is now a yoke of burden and the cash cow that substitutes for political patronages by politicians. This is why it has failed to deliver on its mandate for the past 20 years. Our people want it scraped. (Community Member-02)

The corruption within the NDDC is also responsible for poor projects, tensions, mismanaged funds, and the abandonment of several community projects like the east–west coastal highway (see Chapters 2 and 3). Institutionalised corruption undermines trust between professional civil society NGO representatives, government, and oil and gas companies. A lack of trust impacts the relationship between NGOs, communities, the public, and the private sectors. According to a professional NGO representative,

> we stay away and don't take monies from any organisation we know is associated with the oil companies to avoid the corruption plague. We don't take their funding or attend programs sponsored by them. Our NGO boldly addresses issues of political influences and corruption by oil

regulators and operators by not meeting formerly with them. (Professional NGO-02)

This cannot be independently verified especially as many respondents had noted the complacency of some professional NGOs who collude with oil companies and even government agencies to publish unsubstantiated environmental reports. It suggests that oil companies manipulate NGOs to report findings in their favour.

This is why most local people challenge the findings of some NGOs that seem to blame communities for all the insecurity problems and oil spills. A senior professional NGO field officer in charge of the Bayelsa area claimed: "I immediately declined an invitation where I was supposed to be the resource person when I realised Chevron oil was sponsoring it. So, we can avoid enmeshing ourselves into the brown envelope thing" (Professional NGO-04). The behaviour of oil majors and their contractors exacts a negative influence on the traditional Nembe institutions supported by Akpomera (2015) and Okumagba (2012). Aligning with the above views, a community chief noted that corrupt monies from oil firms destroy community cohesion. "Management of oil companies use their vantage positions to influence and corrupt the traditional leadership structure of Nembe Youth Council funding them to turn against the collective interest of their people to keep the oil flowing" (Community Leader-02).

The analysed results reveal that corruption and its impact are made worse by the interference of oil companies anywhere they are deeply involved in local politics. A community King said, "corruption in Shell oil due to their influential positions directly caused the Nembe crisis in 2003 because of divide and conquer approach of Shell oil" (Community Leader-01). The crisis erupted because of heightened mutual distrust and suspicion between the Nembe Youth Council and the Nembe Council of Traditional Chiefs (Akpomera, 2015; Alagoa, 2005). All six high-profile community members, five environmental activists, three professional NGO representatives, and four other community leaders agreed with this statement. The two NGO respondents who disagreed pointed out that no concrete evidence linked Shell to the fracas that destroyed over 20 communities in 2003. Although their claim is against the popular account, what they did not deny was that the troubles were caused by the interference of oil and gas companies in Nembe local politics.

A professional NGO representative observed that:

> In one of our stakeholders' meetings with royal fathers and media houses, Shell was accused as the unseen hand influencing and distorting information coming out from the Niger Delta. For instance, they bribed some persons in Port Harcourt to give false testimonies in a documentary about purported houses built for displaced persons. Shell is covering up plenty of atrocities because they don't want to lose money. (Professional NGO-01)

The impact institutional and corporate corruption may be having on the younger generation in Nembe was also noted by a lawyer. "Our sense of culture and respect for traditional rulers, honour and good habit may all have been eroded, the younger people were only waiting for their turn and the community will be at their mercy" (Community Member-04). This aligns with the statement made by another high-profile Nembe community member.

> Senior security hierarchy influence the deployment of officers to the Niger Delta for their pecuniary gains. The security agencies are corrupt by influencing and protecting criminal vandals from being arrested in return for bribes and patronage of as much as 400,000 Nigerian Naira a week. These officers in the creeks send returns up to their commanding officers who influence their deployment. (Community Member-06)

However, only four out of the 21 respondents: two professional NGOs, and two high-profile community members argue that organised criminal gangs and the greed of some political and traditional leaders created the greatest environmental and economic impact on the communities. These participants were mainly concerned with organised criminal gangs, which is looking at the whole problem from a single lens (Neumann & Elsenbroich, 2017). The other 17 respondents disagreed with their claims. Pipeline vandalism, oil theft, bunkering, and operation of illegal refining facilities have contributed directly to the destruction of the natural environment in Nembe and the entire Bayelsa state. Often, perpetrators of vandalism go unpunished due to vested political interests, which protect them from law enforcement (Nye, 1967; Philp, 2015; see also Chapter 5). Such political and bureaucratic interferences heighten the impact of poor governance and poor and incompetent leadership. According to a professional NGO official:

> Vandalism and oil theft are criminalities. It appears to have contributed to the sudden riches of some people in the communities. There appears to

be some element of co-relation between drug abuse and disregard for hard work to the attractive rewards from criminality. This has violently disrupted the natural socio-economic equilibrium. (Professional NGO-05)

Often, these youths are supported by powerful forces with political and economic influences, with a vested interest, enabling them to evade justice. The extensive monopoly of politicians over the Nigerian criminal justice system, security, lack of accountability, and probity appears to favour the deviant behaviours of criminal youths (Philp, 2015). Supporting the above claims, a high-profile community member observed that:

Company staff sponsors willing hands within the communities as proxies to bid for contracts to clamp ruptured pipelines, spill recovery, and clean up. It is a vicious cycle of greed, and organised criminality I have witnessed since 2008 when I started visiting communities. (Community Member-04)

Further, the secretary of a senior citizens professional NGO stated that the act of oil theft and pipeline vandalisation directly impact the Niger Delta residents. In his words,

vandalism and oil theft are criminalities that have an extensive impact on the people and the environment of the entire Niger Delta area, especially Bayelsa. While it causes untold hardship, and underdevelopment due to displacement from agricultural activities, it has also worsened the poverty level and triggered tensions and insecurity problems. (Professional NGO-05)

This aligns with the views of Okonofua (2016) and Mathias (2015) discussed in Chapters 2 and 3 who stressed that organised criminality has the most direct impact on the social and economic lives of the people. The executive director of an NGO shared her worries that "some youths here in our community want to lead big life. They go from house-to-house extorting monies and properties to fund their drug use thereby committing a crime against their people" (Professional NGO-03). Therefore, the insecurity pervading communities in Bayelsa state is traced to youths and oil company personnel. Others believe that the communities were victims of organised criminal enterprise given that companies set aside huge budgetary allocations which incentivise crimes. Plenty Niger

Delta elders believe that the oil firms rather deploy money towards repairs of pipelines than engage youths in infrastructure development.

Others believe that communities are victims of organised criminal enterprise given that companies set aside huge budgetary allocations to dole out free oil money to any criminal group that causes problems to their operations thereby incentivising crimes (Mathias, 2015; Okonofua, 2016; Onuoha, 2008, 2016). Plenty Niger Delta elders argue that rather than develop infrastructure for the collective benefit of all communities and curtain youth restiveness most oil firms deploy a large per cent of their budget to pipeline repairs. The national secretary of a Niger Delta senior citizens professional NGO stated,

> We are victims of organised criminality by some oil workers who are aware of the huge budgetary allocation set aside for oil and gas pipeline infrastructure security. They lure a few boys to commit the criminal sabotage of pipelines. Some of the youths, who don't know better go and blast oil pipelines and similarly connive with these corrupt oil workers to arrange oil theft based on some pre-agreed bargain. However, when the pipeline is blasted, the community loses while the same white man working for Shell and Agip or other oil companies gets the million dollars contract to fix the broken pipeline. (Professional NGO-05)

Also, another high-profile community member supports most of the claims made by the professional NGOs stating that criminal activities of youths were more of a direct problem in communities.

> Oil thieves blew up an artery pipeline near Santabarbara claiming that their sons and daughters were excluded from the scholarship scheme and that the pipeline was obstructing their path destroying plantain and cocoyam farms in that area. (Community Member-03)

Bayelsa is motivated by the collective community neglect and bad public and private leadership that has failed to reciprocate the good gesture that many communities gave as most of their farmlands were acquired based on *national interest*, therefore, were not appropriately compensated (see Chapters 3 and 4 for various provisions of oil and gas regulations). Another high-profile community member pointed out that, this leads to anger, frustration, and different forms of aggressive reactions. According to a high-profile community member, areas, where more oil production activities take place, tend to experience heightened criminality like vandalism and bunkering given that most of the people would have been displaced from either their agricultural lands or fishing rivers or even both coupled with the outcome of oil activities that damage the natural habitat with direct consequences on the people. (Community Member-04)

He claimed further those Western nations are turning a blind eye to the problems of oil and gas infrastructure insecurity, oil bunkering, and pipeline vandalism given the silence of first-world democracies:

They are complicit and show that it is an international enterprise with severe consequences for communities. The oil companies at that level are owned by first-world businesses. It takes weeks to siphon oil into drums-barges-canoe-tug boats to load unto a 500,000 to one-million-barrel ocean liner in the Gulf of Guinea. These vessels are major monuments transporting criminal crude oil into first-world nations such as England, America, and the Netherlands, to sell stolen oil. They are visible to satellites and the maritime sector. So, the government is aware that the oil on board such Ocean liners is gotten illegally. The western government just chooses to close its eyes. (Community Member-04)

The lack of geopolitical cooperation between Nigeria and other countries in the Gulf of Guinea heightens the trade in stolen crude oil and insecurity in the historic Niger Delta (Mickolus, 2018). Also, the security deployed to the Niger Delta is believed to support the criminal enterprise due to the greed of some of the officials (Transparency International, 2019). As an NGO representative puts it,

we believe some security officers arm the boys to perpetrate the crime of disrupting oil supplies. When you send the Navy to the shore and waterways to protect facilities, we hear they collaborate with international criminals who infiltrate the Niger Delta to steal oil and pocket the money. (Professional NGO-05)

Sometimes, the line between corruption and criminality is blurred. Corrupt government and private officials collude in several ways like facilitating vandalism and oil bunkering, award intervention contracts to cronies, and taking kickbacks for infrastructure that end up not executed. Many of the respondents recognised that corruption is not the only factor that leads to vandalism and oil and gas pipeline insecurity as noted by Madubuko (2017) and Onuoha (2016). Some also identified manipulations by oil companies, extensive government, and bureaucratic influences. Furthermore, compromised security and the deliberate uncooperative geopolitical and international systems worsen the matter. Although most of the respondents believe corruption impacts the lives of people, serious organised criminal gangs are perceived as being much more problematic. As shown in this and previous chapters, corrupt public and private officials collude with local criminal gangs. This increased insecurity in the historic Niger Delta region and makes solutions to the problems more difficult.

## LACK OF SOCIO-ECONOMIC AND POLITICAL RESOURCES

Access to socio-economic and political resources, for example, social inclusion, are vital developmental indices that contribute to human and economic security (Giugni & Passy, 2014; Hercog, 2019). The limitations or lack of political resources like inclusion from political participation, access to skills and knowledge, and money to mention a few have negatively influenced the behaviour of the people. The government ought to use these resources to douse tensions while productively engaging with the people. Whereas improvement in the legal status grows access to political resources. Political exclusion reinforces a dearth of social and economic opportunities. Therefore, the inaccessibility to various socio-economic and political resources in Bayelsa feeds tensions and encourages criminality. Gates and Akyeampong pointed out that preventing access to socio-economic and political resources was a way of dominating and controlling local communities (2012; see Chapters 2 and 3). This has contributed to tensions within and between communities.

16 out of the 21 community respondents argued that exclusion from national political participation and lack of socio-economic resources contributes to loss of household incomes and heightens the level of poverty which triggers tensions and anger. Further analysis showed that all six high-profile community members, five community leaders, two professional NGO representatives, and three environmental activists agreed that lack of access to socio-economic and political resources harms household incomes. Oil and gas activities prevent Bayelsa communities from freely accessing their natural resources. This is made worse by a dearth of infrastructure projects to recreate socio-economic equilibrium. According

to an environmental activist, "our existence revolves around our fishing waters and scarce farmlands which are facing extreme human and hydro-carbon pollution and damages" (Environmental Activist-01). Inadequate economic empowerment programs, and reduction in revenue also significantly impact the economy of the state and the income of individuals. According to Alamieyeseigha (2008a) and Alagoa (2005) socio-economic stagnation and political isolation are frustrating and drive some people to engage in aggression and vandalism in Bayelsa.

An environmental activist argues that their lack of income is linked to a lack of access to farmlands, harvest, and sale of farm produce. He pointed out that:

> We are losing financial and economic resources because our farmlands no longer yield as much as they used to do in past years due to oil spillage, and destruction of our farm produce. Most residents go to their farms and return with little or nothing. It is difficult to eke out a living these days. And even the fish in the water are not increasing so there is nothing to survive on or sell to generate income. (Environmental Activist-01)

Sixteen other respondents say similar things. The leader of another professional NGO whose activities are spread across Bayelsa gave an instance of the economic impact caused by the Fantoum oil spill.

> The people complained about their inability to catch fish, crabs, end even periwinkles which they depended upon for protein and trade. Other sources of income were all wiped out by an extensive oil spill in the Fantoum facility owned and operated by Shell. It destroyed all the tall mangrove economic trees because the oil had percolated their roots and the trees succumbed to extensive asphyxiation. (Professional NGO-02)

The soil composition is weak and unable to sustain mangrove forests because of oil pollution which worsens the problems noted by Teme (2018). The impact of environmental issues will be discussed in more detail in the subsequent section. The above claim is consistent with the views expressed by a community environmental data gathering specialist who works closely with a professional NGO situated in Nembe. He observed the damaging impact a pipeline explosion and oil spillages have on the Nembe environment. This affects the communities' ability to maintain subsistence agriculture. He pointed out that

Plenty of fishermen and women are unable to provide for their families when a pipeline blowout. There is this particular fish we love in Nembe which fetches a lot of money called *Afaro* (sardine), this has completely disappeared because oil spills have destroyed and contaminated its natural breeding habitat. An uncleaned oil spill has directly and indirectly removed food and economic power and income from our people who now struggle to feed their families. (Environmental Activist-03)

All the 20 other respondents agree with this point. As natural sources become polluted income derived from agriculture and fishing dries up which is a precursor to community neglect aggression displacement tendencies. This means those affected need to seek out other, often rare, and violent sources of income (see Chapter 2). A Nembe environmental activist stated that "most people are unable to find decent options for economic empowerment hence some have taken to a different aspect of illegalities especially vandalism to augment for economic losses due to environmental damage" (Environmental Activist-02).

The wider literature suggests that the impact of insecurity problems in Bayelsa cannot be decoupled from the broader national economic problems (Mathias, 2015; NBS, 2017; see Chapters 2 and 3). Income deprivation has a ripple effect on political participation and limits people's access to many resources (Bejakovic & Mrnjavac, 2018; Janoski, et al., 2014; see Chapter 2). According to an executive director of a professional NGO

Our people are an easy target for politicians due to the high prevalence of poverty. Both the youths especially women and girls may not be able to engage in certain illegal acts for survival. Our people need support to get directly involved in state and national political processes which is the only way they can legitimately influence governance and regulatory framework for public policies that yield collective benefit for all. (Professional NGO-03)

Further, a high-profile community member who is a Magistrate that has been involved in litigation cases between oil and gas operators and local communities noted that:

In Bayelsa, the inclusion of women in politics is very low which impacts their ability to support and contribute to their families and debate on governance in terms of their social and economic wellbeing. Violence is partly responsible. Right now, we are creating awareness and campaigning on "stop violence against women in politics" sponsored by different civil society groups in Bayelsa. (Community Member-04)

The inclusion of women is not only a problem for women in Bayelsa and Nigeria but also across local communities in the Global South. Women are less than a quarter of employees working in Venezuela's oil and gas industry (Colgan, 2013). There is an impression that the percentage of women actively engaged in the oil and gas industry varies in Libya, Iraq, Iran, Saudi Arabia, Sudan, and many other countries in the Global South heightening tensions and widening the socio-economic disequilibrium. The popular consensus is that women are disproportionately represented in the traditional global oil and gas workforce, women accounted for less than a quarter between 15 and 22 percent up until 2021 post global COVID-19 pandemic (Energy World, 2021; Wells, 2019). The equitable participation of women is essential for sustaining a vibrant democracy and economic development (Agbalajobi, 2021). Orisadare (2019) points out that women make up just over half the population in Nigeria, yet women's issues remain secondary, which is why women are disproportionately represented in the oil and gas sector. Both economic and political participation is negatively impacted by this. Understanding this may explain some of the frustrations and tensions that lead to vandalism (Okumagba, 2013). This partly explains why some scholars and NGOs are advocating for inclusive economic empowerment and training programs for women and men in faith-based organisations and Bayelsa Women Forum (BWF) (Tonunarigha & Oghenekohwo, 2019). The focus of BWF is the training and empowerment of Bayelsa women and girls from ages 16 to 65 years.

According to Akpomera, Bayelsa women are deprived of many socio-economic opportunities (2015). They are often excluded from politics, and therefore their interest is least represented. Supporting this view, a professional NGO executive noted that:

We are working with USAID on strengthening public awareness about violence against women in politics. We are working with stakeholders like Women Groups, the National Orientation Agency, the Independent National Electoral Commission-INEC, Political Parties, CSOs, and the Federation of Female Lawyers (FEDAL). Encouraging women to get involved and exercise their franchise in all electoral processes. (Professional NGO-03)

Only seven respondents share this same view. The remaining 14 respondents argue that women do not always support the interest of women. Although it is good for more women to occupy public positions and take up seats in national and state houses of assemblies. This does little to alleviate the struggles of the rural women and the grassroots population. For instance, a classic case is Rwanda's over 50 percent of women parliamentarians who have had less impact on rural, and working-class women (Burnet, 2012a, b: 193; 2018: 573). They should engage more and look beyond numbers to achieve the expected result.

A professional NGO respondent also argued that Sea piracy has a significant negative impact on the economic initiatives of residents, particularly women and girls. In his words,

> Sea piracy from the Gulf of Guinea has truncated a major economic preoccupation of our people in the Nembe area. We can't farm because of indiscriminate pipeline networks and oil spills. The women go to Yenagoa or Onitsha to buy things to sell in Nembe but are sometimes robbed of their monies, belongings, and even phones by Sea pirates at the end of the day they are economically crumbled. (Professional NGO-03)

Over the last decade or so, Bayelsa State has not created an enabling environment in terms of infrastructure where the private sector can create opportunities and thrive (Dickson, 2018; Toakodi & Assi, 2016). There are few opportunities for the 5000 or so graduate students churned out annually in the state, nor are there opportunities for those with lower levels of education and the unskilled (Toakodi & Assi, 2016). The absence of opportunities created significant frustrations amongst those affected, which in turn can lead to tensions and a worsening of the insecurity situation in Bayelsa (Alamieyeseigha, 2008a). A King of seven communities, who also works with youths and liaises with the oil and gas companies observed that,

> We used to be very rich in forest flora and fauna which ordinarily sustained our livelihood before the discovery of crude oil which has changed this beautiful natural socio-economic equilibrium-a balanced ecosystem. Now we have lost all these to hydrocarbon pollution. Our sources of livelihood are gone while we remain unemployed and on top of that deprived of

education. How else do you stay alive or have any economic value? This is what we describe as *economic genocide*. This type of genocide agenda has been done against the Ijaws, Bayelsa-Nembe, and the entire Niger Delta people. (Community Leader-01)

While 16 of the 21 respondents agree with this claim as well as a paramount ruler and head of two communities. Others feel it may have been over-amplified regarding focusing on the Ijaws. The neglect does not affect the Ijaw alone but all the people who live within the Niger Delta area. The paramount ruler stated that the government and oil and gas operators should take the blame for the worsening socio-economic and environmental situation in the state, he said;

They milk my people and destroy the sources of their economic power evidenced by the degradation of land, fishing waters, seas, and oceans that we see around us. If this is not psychologically degrading enough to cause tensions and aggression, then tell me what is. (Community Leader-04)

The failure of government and oil and gas firms to address these issues raised by the Paramount ruler is a classic case of collective community neglect that triggers Community Neglect-Aggression Displacement-CNADT. There is a perception of extreme ingratitude on the part of the oil beneficiaries to their benefactors-the local communities. Over the years, pipeline operations and oil spillages have contributed significantly to the displacement of around 120,000 people within Bayelsa State alone (Daniel & Edet, 2018). The people were dispossessed of their lands and natural fishing and agricultural settlements. They were never constructively resettled which is another reason for CNADT.

In another instance, the paramount ruler explained how his family was displaced and disposed of their ancestral lands.

My family gave about 4.97 hectares of farm and fishing pond business lands to Shell to construct a pipeline route. We wrongly thought that royalties and other compensations will be paid by Shell to enable us take care of our families. We did not know they will pay royalties only once in five years. The last time, they paid only 4 million Naira to be shared amongst 110 members of the family. People received only a few thousand. It is frustrating and a major economic loss to wait for another five years for this kind of peanut. (Community Leader-04)

Major stakeholders like pipeline regulators, oil companies, the NOSDRA response agency, and the Ministry of Petroleum are less concerned about how the communities survive (Daniel & Edet, 2018). This sort of collective neglect is what the proposed community neglect-aggression displacement theory-CNADT says provokes aggressive reactions that lead to vandalism and attacks on oil and gas infrastructure. What the inhabitants see is the destruction of lives and their heritage. According to the view of a king,

> Your mother is dying, your father and your children are dying and even you are also dying of hunger and diseases, which then pushes you into some criminality of a sort. In Nembe, Ekpetiama, and Okodia Kingdoms, and such places, you find that the oil blocks that would have been seceded to communities as economic advantage have been given to some private concerns owned by persons from outside our communities. They do not suffer the impact of oil activities but reap the benefits. Giving my ancestorial economic inheritance to someone from the north or west as an oil block is mentally disturbing and a classic case of economic injustice. (Community Leader-01)

The apathy by the government and the oil and gas companies towards affected communities is staggering and fits into the proposition made by CNADT. This combined with the political and economic disempowerment has continued to fuel frustrations and tensions within local communities (Okumagba, 2012, 2013). A high-profile community member observed that:

> The economic power or potential of an average Bayelsan has been eroded. They live in abject poverty. You will see it written on their faces. Some of them may not afford two square meals a day, especially those fishermen, women, and farmers experiencing decreasing harvest. (Community Member-06)

Further, five out of the 21 community respondents, including three professional NGO representatives, and two environmental activists hold the view that, though lack of access to socio-economic and political resources harms household incomes and the political empowerment of people. They pointed out that vandalism and oil and gas infrastructure insecurity are down to an individual's laziness and innate violent behaviour. According to an NGO representative, "there are instances where access to education and upskilling training were provided but the potential beneficiaries rejected them, rather they preferred free money to be handed out to them" (Professional NGO-01). 16 out of the 21 community respondents disagreed with this point stressing that most of the training institutes were either located in the middle of nowhere or lacked good structures and teachers. But another executive of a collection of NGO representatives operating in the communities supports the earlier claim, stating that, "many of our people are lazy and uneducated, and seem to have a knack for violence" (Professional NGO-04).

These arguments are backed up by Umar and Othman's assertions that it is not the deprivation nor disengagement from politics that leads to such deviant behaviours, though they do not deny that this exists, rather, it is self-inflicted due to laziness and people's innate tendencies to be violent (2017). An environmental activist in Nembe observed that,

> At times the oil regulators, acting on behalf of the government, collaborate with some oil firms and may want to site or construct intervention projects in a particular community, suddenly you see the youths trooping out and insisting that the projects cannot start until and unless they are first paid, thus stagnating development, and stalling collective benefits. (Environmental Activist-05)

Nevertheless, such views neglect underlying structural factors and the impact of long-term unemployment and deprivation on individuals' mental health, and how they view themselves within the larger society (Bejakovic & Mrnjavac, 2018). The environmental damage has destroyed subsistent farming leading to income deficiency and restricted living standards (Vetter et al., 2006; see Chapter 2). Therefore, many youths are moving to urban centres. An executive chairman of some NGOs operating in the communities observed that,

> The sudden movement to urban centres has seen few schools built in communities where these people settle fully. Youths are leaving for the cities with the hope of getting easy oil money. Many such youths have been wrongly oriented by Shell, Agip, and others to assume and think in such a way leading to laziness, and this has become a social problem. (Professional NGO-04)

Closely related to the above point, an environmental activist pointed out that money motivates some involvement in criminality, insisting that:

Some youths agitate with the view that oil companies will pay them some money. Laziness and greed play a better part in it. Even when empowerment programs are created, they refuse to participate, they disappear after a few days looking for easier means to make money which is vandalism and oil bunkering. (Environmental Activist-02)

There is a dearth in accessing economic and political opportunities. These structural issues further increase the likelihood of rural–urban migration and/or engagement in criminal activities, rather than seeking out the few opportunities that arise. The data demonstrate that the perception of laziness amongst many young people and some older generation of Bayelsans as well as innate violence explain insecurity in the area. This is despite the overwhelming evidence that such behaviour is driven by the negative impact of corruption, political disengagement, the environmental impact of long-term unemployment/underemployment, and other forms of deprivations (Egbe, 2010; Etekpe, 2018; Etete, 2017; Okumagba, 2012). The wider literature links the violent behaviour of Bayelsa and Nembe youths to a learned culture from decades of militarisation of the area (Okumagba, 2013; Omeje, 2017c). Paying selected youths, leaders, and high-profile community members without working intensified tensions and created violent competition which further deprives communities of economic incomes and political participation (Alamieyeseigha, 2008b; Sagay, 2008). Data also shows that the benefits from oil and gas may not always be evenly spread across communities.

While the respondents' experiences and perceptions about the people and youths being lazy, maybe accurate, their experiences may or may not be completely reflective of everyone's reality in the region. If even these experiences reflect reality, they must be seen in the wider context of persistent poverty, rampant inequality, hunger, lack of household incomes, a lack of opportunities for even skilled people, and the negative impact that long-term unemployment has on an individual's mental state (Bejakovic & Mrnjavac, 2018; Ingo et al., 2014; Vetter et al., 2006). Plenty of studies show that the unemployed have no significantly different personality traits or that they are more prone to violence (Madson, 2018; More et al., 2017; Walker & Mendolia, 2015). According to a study in Sweden, the long-term unemployed develops one of the three discourses: conformity, distancing, or resistance (Hobbins, 2016). The examples provided by both the professional respondents in the previous chapter and the examples provided here by the community respondents suggest that many of those affected are also *buying into similar* discourse with distancing and resistance. These discourses are of course shaped by the local context which created the very conditions in which pipeline vandalism becomes part of the discourse of resistance. To accept that the people are lazy and prone to violence is hugely problematic and makes findings solutions to the underlying issues of onshore pipeline vandalism and oil and gas infrastructure insecurity in the area difficult.

## Environmental Pollution

A sustainable extractive industry is central to the UNSDG 2030 agenda (see Chapter 2). Responses to oil spillages and environmental damages are influenced by political, and bureaucratic interference, outright denial by operators, and regulatory frameworks in Nigeria (Ekpenyong, 2010; Etowah, 2012; OPA Act, 2004; Oyadongha, 2021; PIA Act, 2021; see Chapter 2). This conflicts with the UNSGD framework on climate action. Such tendencies increase the environmental degradation and damage to the general ecosystem as well as worsen frustration due to loss of livelihood and the neglect that comes with it. Environmental pollution and degradation are central to the tensions causing CNAD tendencies against onshore pipelines and infrastructure insecurity in the historic Niger Delta. Some scholars stated that these tensions and insecurity in Bayelsa and Nembe are self-inflicted problems by the oil and gas companies (Alamieyeseigha, 2008a; Okumagba, 2012). The impact of environmental damage is discussed in detail by Higgins in Chapter 2 (2010).

All 21 respondents, six high-profile community members, five community leaders, five professional NGO representatives, and five environmental activists agree that oil and gas companies and government agencies neglect the pollution of the local environment and its impact on communities. This neglect contributes significantly to the environmental damage which impacts the lives of people leading to tensions, loss of lives, and incomes exacerbating poverty which triggers the proposed CNAD tendencies. A high-profile community member who is a Barrister at law pointed out that:

> When you are traveling out of this place drive through the LNG road, after the army checkpoint, you will see an oil-bearing village where gas is

flared, you will feel the stench of condensed air. You can hardly breathe fresh air in that community because hydrocarbon trappings are dispersed in the atmosphere. (Community Member-04)

This is a classic example of poor governance and/or corruption manifested in the design and implementation of various environmental regulatory frameworks (Awosika, 2014). The environmental problems faced in Bayelsa reflect the extent of poor implementation of regulations that are not wholly reflective of environmental reality across the communities. Another influential community member who is a professor of surgery noted that the natural marine ecosystem around some communities has been devasted by pipelines,

Oil pipelines laid inside the river in the Ogboloma community, for instance, have altered and destroyed the natural water temperature because the water is extremely hot due to the movement of crude oil inside the pipeline. A classic case of the social impact of environmental pollution is seen in the rise in poor health of children who bathe in such waters used as pipeline transit routes. (Community Member-02)

This suggests that the fishing rivers are not spared by the activities of oil and gas and the communities bear the attendant consequences (Omeje, 2017c). He further noted that "people exposed to hydrocarbon and those who live close to pipeline routes stand to inhale dangerous particles from gas flaring which could manifest as lung cancer and congenital malformations" (Community Member-02).

Supporting the above claims, a community King made a critical observation stating that, "our people are dying of asthma due to oil pollution, asphyxiation due to hydrocarbon in the air, cancer due to poisoned fish and contaminated vegetable plants, and defective houses caused by acid rain which are all as a result of long-term neglect" (Community Leader-01). Oil and gas chemicals have percolated into the soil contaminating the underground water table. A professional NGO representative stated that, "a woman almost lost her life to gas leakage in her farm at Ibamah community when she tried to burn something but unknowingly ignited an inferno because of the gas leak" (Professional NGO-01). This is another case of how gas pollution in the atmosphere directly impacts the lives of individuals who may not return to such farms to eke out a living thereby worsening their state of hunger and frustration. It also validates some other views that extractive activities create accidental blowouts in communities (Oyadongha, 2020, 2021). According to an environmental activist, a teacher of chemistry,

> When I visited the Sonkre area where Agip operates the Ibiama flow station, a woman who had newly given birth said to me that oil pollution was not the only problem, but that they cannot drink the river water or natural rainwater that falls from the sky. If they put their basins outside to fetch rainwater [this is] filled with water mixed with hydrocarbon soot trapped in the air. (Community Activist-02)

Scholars have argued in the previous chapter that environmental destruction of such magnitude suggests one thing, the government is not meeting its social obligations to the citizens in local communities (LUA Act, 2004, 1978; Onakpohor et al., 2020). The government and oil companies take the largest blame for the state of the Bayelsa and Nembe environment, as claimed by a respondent who states that, the "government arrogated everything about the oil and gas industry to itself and Shell and other oil companies who are their business partners" (Professional NGO-02). Therefore, they should be taking responsibility for the environmental damages in the state. Also, a marine engineer environmental activist supports this view arguing that "oil activity is causing erosions and washing away topsoil because the oil companies and government have neglected the environmental protection of communities by failing to pile our coastal communities to prevent floods" (Community Activist-03). The people become increasingly vulnerable to loss of farmland, damage to their ecosystem, and a polluted environment which translates into a loss of income and mental health, and confidence leading to reactive aggression (Hobbins, 2016).

Further, the chair of a professional NGO represented in the Nembe area claims that providing environmental safety and protection is another way of securing lives and properties.

> Nothing links oil companies to environmental safety in their operational guidelines-OPG. This was one outcome of the research I conducted with a colleague to evaluate the impact of the GMOUs in Bayelsa. Environmental safety concerns issues of the people. Pollution from exploration and processing companies with their local collaborators has exacerbated the environmental damages suffered by the local people. (Professional NGO-04)

This claim agrees with the suggestion by Owen (2004) and Haq (1995) noted that environmental safety and protection of human lives are aspects of human security which is the fulcrum of political security. According to an environmental activist, a senior lecturer at one of the institutes, the amount of environmental degradation done to communities means that:

> The aquaculture has been permanently destroyed and the indigenous residents depend on aquaculture and agriculture for survival. Therefore, no number of resources deployed to these communities would ever be enough or said to be too much given that the entire Nigeria depends on the Niger Delta for survival. (Community Member-03)

The impact of pollution on all strata of life in the area is significant, it has triggered tensions. Describing his experience, a high-profile community member who is an accountant in a federal ministry noted that,

> a busted pipeline sometimes spills up to five to six inches thick of oil which prevents you from seeing the water. People paddle their canoes on top of the crude oil spills. This destroys fishing nets, and if you are using a flying boat, it often destroys the engine propeller and sometimes causes fire. (Community Member-06)

A similar event occurred recently in the Santa Barbara axis of the NCTL in Nembe where a structural wellhead blowout led to an oil spill of magnitude proposition into the rivers for up to a month because NOSDRA and Aiteo, the operating oil firm, could not clamp the leak (Oyadongha, 2021). A community King while supporting this claim expressed the view that their lives revolved around the community and by destroying the environment meant the destruction of their livelihood. He noted that

> When you go to Beseni, you will find out that there are some old rusty oil pipelines still lying on the roads which constitute environmental hazards. I believe when you ask people there how old some of those pipelines are, they will tell you 20 to 40 years old. The community is our life, destroying the environment you finish us which is why we are like this because the environment is already destroyed. (Community Leader-01)

This is supported by the claims of a former National Assembly member who noted the negative impact that old pipelines have caused on the lives of people. He argued that;

> In the Okoroma community in Nembe pipelines are laid in shallow waters, not deep down the riverbed, which destroys fishing nets, and most have not been changed. Since they started exploiting oil in Nembe territory to date-2019, not one single pipeline has been changed in the Nembe area despite several protests and National Assembly resolutions. (Community Member-02)

This clearly shows political corruption and that the system is compromised given that the National Assembly were acutely aware that their resolutions were not implemented and yet do nothing about it. International best practice requires that oil pipelines are replaced every 10 years (Devold, 2013; Mickolus, 2018; Timashev & Bushinskaya, 2016a). Another interviewee noted that the "polluted Gbaran-toro coast eventually impacts the daily lives of people in the Brass area, this is worse during the flood season because the oil permeates ground soil. Instead of taking responsibility, oil companies accuse communities" (Professional NGO-05). According to Sinden (2009), oil spills spread downstream or along with the coast and have affected local communities severely, in particular those reliant on fishing.

Furthermore, hydrocarbon pollution has environmental and health implications on a local level. The pollution affects the air and, destroys plants and animals. More damage is done by the emissions of toxic gasses and chemicals which are carcinogenic and causes other chronic diseases, hair loss, and neurological damage to name a few (Adams, 2019; Olawuyi, 2012). Due to the interconnectedness of the environment, the impact of the pollution can be felt beyond the Bayelsa and Niger Delta region (Okonofua, 2016; UNEP, 2012). A Nembe youth leader and high-profile community facilitator noted:

> We have seen migratory birds from Spain several times here in Nembe, Fishes that spawn in our waters here tend to swim as far back as Maimi-US. Some Americans kill and eat them in Maimi, without knowing the fish comes from polluted waters of the Niger Delta, not knowing the health implications. Nobody is shielded from the after-effect of oil pollution. (Community Member-05)

This is an important observation that stresses the fact that the global ecosystem is linked and the destruction of the ecosystem in one part of the world directly affects people in other parts. Therefore, highlights the need for the western countries to rein in their erring oil and gas companies operating in Nigeria given that marine water pollution in the Niger Delta may have a negative impact on their marine life and the food chain of their citizens. The toxic waste dumped by Shell and Agip around some Nembe communities worsens the chances of reclamation of the land and fishing waters. A professional NGO representative noted that:

> Toxic waste materials were dumped at Twon-Brass. The Chiefs took Nigerian Agip Oil Company-NAOC to the courts requesting that they remove their toxic dumps. We later discovered that the oil companies dug up trenches like wells they call slumps and dumped this toxic waste inside them against international laws. Wherever these toxic wastes are dumped aquatic life is extinguished which eventually affects the life of the inhabitants. (Professional NGO-03)

Another respondent who is a barrister and high-profile community member also put some of the blame for pollution on the oil and gas companies. Drawing on many years of experience in the oil and gas sector, he stated that

> Some contractors working for Agip and Shell burn spilled oil into the environment by setting fire to the oil to speedily conclude their clean-up exercise which further damages the environment. When it rains trapped hydrocarbon falls back down as soot defacing houses across the area. The health implications are strange respiratory diseases that are alien to the Nembe people making it impossible to eat natural foods. Some of these diseases affected the thorax causing bronchitis in some people. Some reports claim one in 10 Nembe residents might have cancer due to environmental pollution. (Community Member-04)

An environmental activist pointed out that the impact of air pollution was significant. He stated that:

> The entire atmosphere in Nembe is covered in thick black smoke once gas turbines that run on crude oil are switched on. At such times we are unable to see any bright skylight for weeks. It takes about two to three weeks for the smoke to clear for us to be able to see the sky again. Our

people either evacuate the environment for their safety or hide inside their houses with their children. (Environmental Activist-05)

The problem, however, goes beyond oil spills, gas flaring, and illegal dumping of waste materials by oil and gas companies. Illegal oil refineries shut down by the security forces also contribute to wider environmental pollution. A Paramount ruler pointed out that,

> Asking the security to bomb and burn artisanal refining facilities sometimes causes widespread inferno that burnt people and this was a big polluter of the environment since the oil is spilled into the ecosystem deliberately. When traveling through Nembe creek to the Brass-Okpoma area, you will discover that the mangrove which formed very good vegetation for the environment is vanquished with the trees dried up and some whitish materials appearing there. Aquatic life that was previously a source of income for the fisher folks is almost obliterated and those still fishing around there are constantly doing so in pain. (Community Leader-04)

Listening to members of the local communities and indeed the professionals (see Chapter 6) and triangulating their stories and account of oil and gas activities with the wider literature, it is difficult to neglect the impact that oil and gas extraction has on the local environment (see Chapters 2, 3, and 4). As noted, the damage comes from poor practices within the oil and gas sector, vandalism, and the destruction of illegal refineries by security services. All these culminate into general socio-economic loss that triggers frustration which further angers the people leading to CNADT theoretical proposition. Mckenzie et al. (2018) and Holdway (2002) noted there was a significant correlation between living near oil facilities and poor health, with neurological, haematological, and impairment of the hepatic system in the blood. The community argued that the oil and gas pipeline regulators, over many decades, have been unable to design effective monitoring measures (Ikelegbe, 2014; NESREA Act, 2007; OPA Act, 2004; UNEP, 2012). This has made it harder to effectively supervise the oil operators or hold them accountable for the widespread environmental damages in Bayelsa. Therefore, the increasing rate of mechanical blowout and vandalism is put at the doorstep of poor governance and unethical operation practices of oil firms. The data evaluated contextualises the nature and extent of environmental degradation across Bayelsa communities. It appears tensions over environmental degradation and ecological destruction of Bayelsa and

Nembe will remain a criminal part of the security dynamics of the region for a long time.

## COMPENSATION AND SOCIAL INJUSTICE

There are three distinct forms of oil and gas compensation identified in this book. Compensation for acquired lands, compensation for environmental damages due to vandalism or operational blowouts as well as payment of royalties as compensation. These are generally found within the rubrics of ESG criteria (see Chapter 4). CSR and local investments in communities have negatively impacted communities and have been extremely narrow which is what ESG is designed to correct (Ibagere, 2012; O'Connor, 2022; Shastry, 2023; see Chapters 3 and 4). Whereas the injustice begins from the lack of compensation for acquired lands blessed with natural resources and/or needed for pipeline routes (see various oil and gas regulations discussed in chapter two; LUA Act, 2004; OPA Act, 2004). The tensions that feed vandalism and CNAD tendencies focus on the impact that the inadequate or neglect of compensation for environmental damages, CRS, and investment have on the local communities. Agudelo and Davidsdottir et al. pointed out that CSR should extend beyond profit sharing but must include or/and extend to the generation of shared values such as ethics (2019). The community participants believe that virtually all the oil and gas regulations operational in Nigeria are designed with the oil and gas companies in mind and neglect the impact oil activities may or/ may not have on communities. This is evidence of poor implementation due to poor governance and political corruption. Thereby enabling oil and gas companies to shape policies that allow them to get away with systematic murder (Olawuyi, 2012; Sinden, 2009; UNEP, 2012). The discrimination against economic and environmental rights constitutes the hallmark of social injustice that impacts the life of the people (Okumagba, 2012).

All the 21 community interviewees agree that there is a heightened sense of poor compensation and social injustice in Bayelsa communities and the historic Niger Delta which is what is triggering CNAD disposition amongst the communities. This sense of injustice has led to collective frustration which leads to further deterioration of the security situation in the region (Okumagba, 2012; Onuoha, 2008). Many people in Bayelsa face displacement from their farmlands, natural habitat, and cultural fishing festivals like the Seigbien fishing festival (Alagoa, 2005;

Okumagba, 2012). Such injustices are aspects of what Ruffin referred to as constituting *environmental racism* (2012). This involves dislocating indigenous people from their natural sources of livelihood. The participants pointed out that Bayelsa communities deserve to be adequately compensated given that the oil and gas resources are found under their soil (Alamieyeseigha, 2008b).

Referring to published public statistics, a senior representative of a professional NGO stated that:

> When you deny fisher folks their means of livelihood like fishing and farming, you infringe on their rights to survive which increases hunger and access to income that boost self-confidence and this triggers frustration and crime, prostitution, and attacks on oil pipelines. (Professional NGO-02)

The other 20 respondents agree with this claim. The importance of creating economic opportunities for every person in Bayelsa through entrepreneurship, business start-ups, skills acquisition, business grants, and mentorship cannot be over-emphasised. This motivated the creation of the "Social Performance Interface" compensation scheme by Green Energy International Limited (GEIL). They designed this in their MOU with communities they are located as their CSR and local investments. This compensation scheme pushes for the effective delivery of development outcomes in target communities to mitigate many decades of environmental and economic neglect and address youth restiveness as well as boost government taxation.

Human rights abuses and destruction of communities reinforce social injustices when, "you take away education, and social enlightenment since the people are forced to accept whatever you stretch to them", stated a high-profile community participant (Community Member-02). Pointing out that

> Nembe people do not realise that oil from their backyard is what the government connived with operators to name "Bonny light". There is no oil drilled in the Bonny area. It ought to be called "Nembe light". There are massive socio and infrastructure development ongoing right now in the Bonny axis due to the Liquified Natural Gas (LNG) processed from our Nembe oil while we are deprived. It is injustice and frustrating that the NCTL trunk line pumps crude from here to the export terminal in Bonny Island. (Community Member-02)

The Niger Delta region has been historically been perceived as an economic satellite or annex of successive colonial rules to the current Nigerian government and oil companies (see Chapter 2). This seemingly explains the disproportionality with which the government treats the people and their environment (Douglas & Okonta, 2003). Residents have suffered abuses, discrimination, and deprivations from oil and gas companies, and the government (Okumagba, 2012; Olawuyi, 2012). A community king stated that

> our underaged girls, as young as 12 years, are lured and abused, and before you know it the man who caused this had disappeared. This was how the staff of oil companies destroyed the social and cultural fabric of our local communities. This damage is a perpetual signature on every oil-producing community across Nembe, Bayelsa, and the entire Niger Delta. It is expensive and difficult to get justice in this country. (Community Leader-01)

Further, a paramount ruler pointed out that the oil and gas sector is undermining the quest for environmental justice for the people of Bayelsa state and the wider Niger Delta region (Olawuyi, 2012). He noted that

> Critical issues like lack of transparency in the oil and gas sector, unemployment, militarisation of oil production, lack of/or inadequate skills acquisition opportunities, and marginalisation of oil-producing states are some of the injustices provoking the frustration that triggers displaced aggression against pipelines. Bayelsa crude oil earns multi-billion dollars in revenue to the Nigerian government daily, yet they deny the people justice. (Community Leader-04)

As has been noted above, and in previous chapters, the suffering of the Niger Delta people comes down to a lack of leadership, corruption, and lack of investment in the socio-economic infrastructure (Ogbeidi, 2012; Okumagba, 2012). A community chief and former National Assembly representative argued that:

> I am passionate to ensure the world knew how atrocious oil businesses have been in Bayelsa. How much it has retrogressed, demonised, and destroyed our social existence turning us into a ghost of ourselves. We had over 3,000 men, young active randy men, most of whom were not married, while others left their wives in Britain and America but came to Bayelsa

and became sexual predators wreaking social havoc on our girls, women, and the larger society. Shell and Agip turned their faces and denied us justice thus failing in their vicarious liability. (Community Leader-02)

His anger has been echoed by many of the other participants. It explains some of the despair and extreme frustrations that are felt amongst local communities (Bushman et al., 2018; Dollard et al., 1939; see Chapter 3).

The literature suggests that oil companies have displaced well over 200 small fishing communities from the NCTL routes in Nembe alone (Akpomera, 2015; Onuoha, 2008). In the early 2000s, Shell took some extreme measures to ensure it was able to build the pipeline. In the process, thousands of locals were displaced. An environmental activist and Biologist pointed out that:

The NCTL Joint Venture operators and Shell displaced and forcefully removed many small fishing settlements and communities from their natural ancestorial lands to gain unhindered access to the creeks and upland in the Nembe-Ewelesuo community. We mobilised and vigorously resisted the government and the oil firm from forcefully removing about 3000 to 5000 Ewelesuo indigenes from their ancestral lands. (Environmental Activist-02)

Whereas 18 out of the 21 respondents seem to back these claims, the others argued that there is no evidence. Some argue that the compensation provided to local communities is not enough (Alamieyeseigha, 2008b; Douglas & Okonta, 2003; Saro-Wiwa, 1992). When compensation is paid it has created more tensions because of political interference which is a reflection of corruption and poor governance. Oriola (2018) argued that compensation should include participatory ownership in the oil business value chain like allocation of marginal oil blocks (see Chapter 5). Prno and Slocombe (2012) and Tysiachniouk (2020) suggest that some of the income generated by oil and gas companies should be distributed to local communities. Although the 13 percent establishment Act and PIA (2021) suggest this poor governance and corruption are making their implementation ineffective. There are problems in how different categories of compensation are implemented. Relevant clauses in the Land Use Act (2004) and Oil Pipeline Act (2004) leave the issue of compensation for acquired lands with mineral resources and the amount to be paid in compensation to local communities to the courts. A high-profile community member who is an accountant noted that "authorities and oil and gas operators are aware communities hardly know the difference between proposed 10 percent or 3 percent undeclared profit, and 10 percent operating cost" (Community Member-06). A lack of understanding of corporate jargon around operating costs and profits is partly responsible for the endless local and international litigation cases that are instituted against oil operators (Azubuike, 2021; Khalid, 2021).

Further, a professional NGO representative and national secretary of the Niger Delta senior citizens civil society group noted that:

> some communities sued Mobil for the 1998 Idoho oil spillage that affected the whole Niger Delta through late Chief J.L.D. Dagogo for 92 billion Naira in damages. Honourable Justice Okeke Federal high court Lagos gave judgment in favour of the communities for 15 billion Naira, but it was frustrating that Mobil's appeal was upheld against our claims. (Professional NGO-05)

19 out of the 21 respondents agreed with this claim, stating that this way some communities are getting compensated for environmental damages and loss of sources of livelihood. Adopting different approaches to compensation could help, but plenty of communities are missing out due to the way it is implemented (see Chapter 2 for LUA Act and OPA Act on compensation). "Despite over 100 operating oil wells across Nembe-Ewelesuo, the community has remained the most polluted creek in Nembe, I can't say that anybody or the community has been duly compensated in the last 30 years", stated a high-profile community youth leader (Community Member-05).

The failure of the Nigerian government to acknowledge the importance of the environment to local communities has led to a lack of proportionate compensation (Douglas & Okonta, 2003; UNEP, 2012). According to an environmental activist who is also an agriculturist in Nembe;

> The government can't give an accurate value to our forests, creeks, and the mangrove. Neither do oil firms account for the exact financial and production losses. They used these skewed statistical resources to calculate their GDP, leading to miscalculation of compensation claims due to impacted communities and providing infrastructure intervention. (Environmental Activist-05)

Azubuike (2021) and Tonunarigha and Oghenekohwo (2019) noted that trees, mangroves, and other natural endowments in Bayelsa were usually ignored when discussing environmental impacts. According to a Paramount ruler of two communities;

> The slow nature of land registration, documentation, and issuance of a Certificate of Occupancy to communities slows validation of ownership of polluted ancestral lands which is tied to poor governance structures. Some leaders use this excuse to confiscate monies meant for impacted families. (Community Leader-04)

Closely aligned with the claims above, a community environmental activist observed that;

> Communities have experienced a varying degree of damage and environmental impact from extractive activities. It makes perfect sense for regulators and oil companies to adopt a loose compensation structure otherwise just as it is today the main sufferers will not get anything which is why we have women and girls accessing our programs. (Environmental Activist-01)

According to a high-profile community businesswoman, the problem with implementing compensation schemes is the difficulty in calculating what is due to the different categories of compensation above which is reflected in many MOU and GMOUs. She pointed out that,

> We get little or nothing from oil money compared to what we suffer. How do we suffer degradation, abuse, and nothing to show? Claims that communities are compensated with employment only destroy existing trust and values. GMOU may suggest employment but hardly is there any evidence to support this claim. (Community Member-01)

The poorly negotiated nature and amount of what should be the compensation are reflected in the unproductive social contracts in GMOUs and MOUs. Different compensation strategies or schemes are hardly the problem. Given that various compensation schemes come with plenty of complexities and often escalated tensions, a senior executive of a cluster of professional NGO representatives noted that;

compensation should entail human capital and sustainable development. Transform damaged environment across communities, land reclamation, and clean-up of fishing waters. Bridges should be constructed to link all small creek communities thereby opening Bayelsa up for sustainable economic development and poverty eradication. Transparent conflict resolution mechanism, and structure for rapid response to oil spills and cleanup. (Professional NGO-05)

The only way around the tensions and insecurity, a high-profile community youth leader claimed is that "government and oil companies should accurately enumerate impacted local communities and individuals for a more direct compensation" (Community Member-05). In the words of a professional NGO representative, "oil and gas firms should develop the will to implement a standardised CSR policy program, and avoid divide and rule tactics" (Professional NGO-03). The opinion of this book is that the reclamation of farmlands, replanting the mangrove forests, and trees, re-breeding fish species, and cleaning up polluted waters should be a precursor to whatever form of a compensation scheme that is adopted by relevant stakeholders.

The scale of the injustices which the communities have suffered says a lot about how the various oil and gas and pipeline regulations have been framed. Although this section focused mostly on compensation, the fact remains that it constitutes an aspect of social injustices (see Chapter 2). Rewarding a few private investors such as facilitating the purchase of OML 17 by Total Nigeria Oil and Gas and allocating oil fields to political supporters is not community compensation because it only widens the socio-economic inequality gaps (Oki, 2017; see Chapters 2, 3, and 5). The widening socio-economic inequality is a factor that motivates the proposed CNADT theoretical framework. The fact that it could take quite some time to serve justice and compensate people whose lives have been forever impacted and changed due to oil and gas activities heightens the general distrust and tensions between the communities, government, and oil firms. Thus, tensions over social and environmental injustice will remain an integral part responsible for the security dynamics in the Niger Delta region.

## CONCLUSION

There is broad agreement, that tensions and frustrations have been triggered by poorly regulated oil and gas extraction laws, and by the inability of the state to rein the damage caused by these companies. As a result, the environment and local communities continue to suffer. Many community respondents believe that criminality and the lack of compensation or the way it is distributed are bigger issues. Amongst participants is the perception that youths and criminals are lazy and innately violent. Environmental degradation, poor infrastructure, poverty, inequality, and a lack of opportunities remain huge barriers and triggers of frustration that can and has turned violent. Only an accelerated socio-economic and infrastructure development of the state will mitigate the scale of insecurity problems, revert the factors that cause CNADT, and even this will take years to be effective. There are consequences when government celebrates oil and gas innovations and expansion based on investment inflow, and increased royalties alone. Given the evidence, it is difficult to agree with the idea, that what is best for private oil and gas companies is also good for the local communities. The starkest reminder of this is the devastating damage to the local environment. The wider implication of this can be seen in the people's health with a significant dearth of evidence showing that local community residents were linked to the activities of oil and gas companies.

Across the public and private sectors, there seems to be a total disregard and neglect for the health and safety of residents of local communities, the environment, and those working in the oil and gas sector. Oil and gas infrastructure insecurity literature seems to suggest that pipeline vandalism and oil theft can only be mitigated by the deployment of physical security and/or preventative technologies. Given the evidence presented so far, it is evident that increases in security will only provide temporary respite. Any security measures will provide only Ghost Security as outlined by Skoczylis and Andrews (2021) and cannot and will not resolve the problem of onshore oil and gas pipeline infrastructure insecurity in the historic Niger Delta. It is only by addressing underlying economic issues such as poverty and inequalities as well as poor governance, and human security by providing political security like defense against human rights abuses that true security can be achieved. Shifting the focus towards the protection of human and environmental rights of communities would positively change the insecurity dynamics and revert

CNADT. Failure to do so will continue to heighten and provoke political, socio-economic, and physical insecurity in the historic Niger Delta region.

# REFERENCES

Adams, P. (2019). Salt Marsh Restoration. In G. M. E. Parilla, E. Wolanski, D. R. Cahoon, & C. S. Hopkinson (Eds.), *Coastal Wetlands: An Integrated Ecosystem Approach* (2nd ed., pp. 817–861). Elsevier.

Agbalajobi, D. (2021, May 3). Nigeria has Few Women in Politics: Here's Why, and What to do About It. *The Conversation*. https://theconversation.com/nigeria-has-few-women-in-politics-heres-why-and-what-to-do-about-it-159578. Accessed 15 March 2022.

Agudelo, M. A. L., Johannsdottir, L., & Davidsdottir, B. (2019). A Literature Review of the History and Evolution of Corporate Social Responsibility. *International Journal of Corporate Social Responsibility, 4*(1).

Akpomera, E. (2015). International Crude Oil Theft: Elite Predatory Tendencies in Nigeria. *Review of African Political Economy Journal, 42*(143), 156–165.

Alagoa, E. J. (2005). *A History of the Niger Delta*. Onyema Research Publications.

Alamieyeseigha, D. S. P. (2008a). The Environmental Challenge of Developing the Niger Delta. In S. S. Azaiki, D. S. P. Alamieyeseigha, & A. A. Ikein (Eds.), *Oil, Democracy and the Promise of True Federalism in Nigeria* (pp. 249–260). University Press of America.

Alamieyeseigha, D. S. P. (2008b). The Niger Delta: Treasure Base of Energies. In S. Azaika, A. A. Ikein, & D. S. P. Alamieyeseigha (Eds.), *Oil Democracy and the Promise of True Federalism in Nigeria* (pp. 290–310). University Press of America.

Amundsen, I. (2019). Extractive and Power-Preserving Political Corruption. In I. Amundsen (Ed.), *Political Corruption in Africa: An Extraction and Power Preservation* (pp. 1–28). Elgar.

Azubuike, V. (2021). International Court Orders Shell to Compensate Niger-Delta Communities Over Oil Spillage. *Daily Post News*. https://dailypost.ng/2021/01/29/breaking-international-court-orders-shell-to-compensate-niger-delta-communities-over-oil-spillage/. Accessed 30 January 2021.

Bejakovic, P., & Mrnjavac, Z. (2018). The Dangers of Long-Term Unemployment and Measures for Its Reduction: The Case of Croatia. *Economic Research Journal, 31*(1), 1837–1850.

Burnet, J. E. (2012a). Rwanda: Women's Political Representation and Its Consequences. In S. Franceschet, M. L. Krook, & N. Tan (Eds.), *The Palgrave Handbook of Women Political Rights* (pp. 563–576). Palgrave Macmillan.

Burnet, J. E. (2012b). Women's Empowerment and Cultural Change in Rwanda. In S. Franceschet, M. L. Krook, & J. M. Piscopo (Eds.), *The Impact of Gender Quotas* (pp. 190–207). Oxford University Press.

Bushman, B. J., Anderson, C. A., & Allen, J. J. (2018). The General Aggression Model. *Current Opinions in Psychology Journal, 9*, 75–80.

Colgan, J. (2013). *Petro-Aggression: When Oil and Causes War*. Cambridge.

Daniel, E., & Edet, A. (2018). Displacement and the Development of Highway Communities in Nigeria's Niger Delta Region. *Journal of Developing Country Studies, 8*(8), 102–110.

Devold, H. (2013). *Oil and Gas Production Handbook: An Introduction to Oil and Gas Production* (pp. 6–146). ABB. https://library.e.abb.com/public/34d5b70e18f7d6c8c1257be500438ac3/Oil%20and%20gas%20production%20handbook%20ed3x0_web.pdf. Accessed 12 December 2017.

Dickson, S. H. (2018). Bayelsa Removes 28,000 Ghost Workers from Payroll. *Punch News*. https://punchng.com/Bayelsa-removes-28000-ghost-workers-from-payroll/. Accessed 23 May 2021.

Dollard, J., Miller, N. E., Doob, L. W., Mowrer, O. H., & Sears, R. R. (1939). *Frustration and Aggression*. Yale University Press.

Douglas, O., & Okonta, I. (2003). *Where Vultures Feast: Shell, Human Rights, and Oil in the Niger Delta*. Verso.

Egbe, R. E., & Thompson, D. (2010). Environmental Challenges of Oil Spillage for Families in Oil Producing Communities of the Niger Delta Region. *Journal of Home Economics Research, (13)*, December.

Ekpenyong, A. S. (2010). The Oil Economy, Environmental Laws, and Human Rights Violations in Niger Delta Region: Implications and Suggested Solutions. *International Journal of Social Policy Research and Development, 1*(2).

Energy World. (2021). *Women Make Up 22 Percent of the Workforce in Oil and Gas Industry: Survey*. https://energy.economictimes.indiatimes.com/news/oil-and-gas/women-make-up-22-per-cent-of-the-workforce-in-oil-gas-industry-survey/88197709. Accessed 14 November 2023.

Etekpe, A. (2018). The Challenges of Climate Change on the Livelihood and Sustainable Development of Selected Coastal Communities in Nigeria's Niger Delta (1990–2015). In V. U. James (Ed.), *Capacity Building for Sustainable Development* (pp. 254–264). CAB International.

Etete, E. (2017, July 7). Ovom in Yenagoa City: A Cradle of Development but Shadow of itself. *Headline News Nigeria*. http://headlinenewsnigeria.com/ovom-yenagoa-city-cradle-development-shadow/. Accessed 2 March 2018.

Etowah, U. E. & Effiong, S. A. (2012), Oil Spillage Cost, Gas Flaring Cost, and Life Expectancy Rate of the Niger Delta People of Nigeria. *Advances in Management and Applied Economics Journal, 2*(2), pp. 211–228.

Gates, H. L., & Akyeampong, E. K. (2012). *Dictionary of African Biography*. Oxford University Press.

Giugni, M., & Passy, F. (2014). Migrant Mobilization Between Political Institutions and Citizens Regimes: A Comparison of France and Switzerland. *European Journal of Political Research*, *43*, 51–82.

Haq, U. M. (1995). *Reflections on Human Development*. Oxford University Press.

Hercog, M. (2019). Skill Levels, as a Political Resource: Political Practices of Recent Migrants in Switzerland. In I. Steiner & P. Wanner (Eds.), *Migrants and Expats: The Swiss Migration and Mobility Nexus* (pp. 243–263). Springer.

Higgins, P. (2010). *Eradicating Ecocide: Laws and Governance to Stop the Destruction of the Planet*. Shepheard-Walwyn.

Hobbins, J. (2016). Young Long-Term Unemployed and the Individualisation of Responsibility. *Nordic Journal of Working Life Studies*, *6*(2), 43–59.

Holdway, D. A. (2002). The Acute and Chronic Effects of Wastes Associated with Offshore Oil and Gas Production on Temperate and Tropical Marine Ecological Processes. *Marin Pollution Bulletin*, *44*(3), 185–203.

Ikelegbe, O. A. (2014). The Resource Curse: Oil, Communal Agitation and State Repression in the Niger Delta. In O. A. Ikelegbe (Ed.), *Oil, Environmental and Resource Conflicts in Nigeria* (pp. 109–142). Lit Verlag.

Ingo, V., Pelzer, B., & Schaffrath, S. (2014). Coping with Unemployment: The Impact of Unemployment on Mental Health Personality, and Social Interaction Skills. *Work: A Journal of Prevention, Assessment and Rehabilitation*, *48*(2), 289–295.

Janoski, T., Luke, D., & Oliver, C. (2014). *The Causes of Structural Unemployment: Four Factors That Keeps People from the Job They Deserve*. Polity Press.

Khalid, I. (2021). Shell in Nigeria: Polluted Communities Can Sue in English Supreme Courts. *BBC News*. https://www.bbc.co.uk/news/world-africa-560 41189. Accessed 13 February 2021.

Land Use Act, (1978). Vesting of all land in the State; Control and management of land; advisory bodies; Designation of urban areas; Applicable law for the interim management of land, Available from https://faolex.fao.org/docs/pdf/nig67625.pdf. [Accessed 7 May 2024].

Land Use Act. (2004). *The Complete Laws of Nigeria, a Searchable Compendium*. Land Use Act. https://lawsofnigeria.placng.org/view2.php?sn=228. Accessed 20 February 2022.

Madson, T. (2018). The Conception of Laziness and the Characterisation of Others as Lazy. *Journal of Human Arenas*, *1*, 288–304.

Madubuko, C. C. (2017). Oiling the Guns and Gunning for Oil: The Youths and Niger Delta Oil Conflicts in Nigeria. In E. M. Mbah & T. Falola (Eds.), *Dissent, Protest and Dispute in Africa* (pp. 260–289). Routledge.

Mathias, Z. (2015). Providing All-Round Security Against Oil and Gas Infrastructure Sabotage and Physical Attacks on the Staff of NNPC and Multinational Oil Companies in Nigeria as a Critical Article of Her National Security Efforts. *International Journal of Social Science and Humanities Research, 3*(2), 45–59.

McKenzie, L. M., Blair, B., Hughes, J., Allshouse, W. B., Blake, N. J., Helmig, D., Milmoe, P., Halliday, H., Blake, D. R., & Adgate, J. L. (2018). Ambient Nonmethane Hydrocarbon Levels Along Colorado's Northern Front Range: Acute and Chronic Health Risk. *Journal of Environmental Science and Technology, 52*(8), 4514–4525.

Mickolus, E. (2018). *Terrorism Worldwide, 2016.* McFarland and Company.

More, P., Dougherty, D. S., & Rick, J. M. (2017). Unemployment and Social Class Stigmas. *Journal of Applied Communication Research, 45*(5).

National Bureau of Statistics. (2017). *Social Statistics Report December 2016.* National Bureau of Statistics.

National Environmental Standards and Regulation Enforcement Agency Act. (2007). *Discharge of Hazardous Substance and Related Offences.* http://lawsofnigeria.placng.org/laws/nesrea.pdf. Accessed 22 February 2022.

Neumann, M., & Elsenbroich, C. (2017). Introduction: The Societal Dimensions of Organised Crime. *Trends in Organised Crime, 20,* 1–15.

Nye, S. J. (1967). Corruption and Political Development: A Cost-Benefit Analysis. *American Political Science Review, 61*(2), 417–427.

O'Connor, B. (2022). *The ESG Investment Handbook: Insights and Developments in Environmental, Social and Governance Investment.* Harriman House.

Ogbeidi, M. M. (2012). Political Leadership and Corruption in Nigeria Since 1960: A Socio-Economics Analysis. *Journal of Nigerian Studies, 1*(2), 1–24.

Oil Pipeline Act. (2004). *Chapter 338: Laws of the Federal Republic of Nigeria.* https://www.chr.up.ac.za/images/researchunits/bhr/files/extractive_industries_database/nigeria/laws/Oil%20Pipelines%20Act.pdf. Accessed 28 March 2020.

Oki, R. A. (2017). *Barbarism to Decadence: Nigeria and Foreign Complicity.* Author Solutions.

Okonofua, B. A. (2016). The Niger Delta Amnesty Program: The Challenges of Transitioning from Peace Settlements to Long-Term Peace. *Sage Open Journals, 6*(2), 1–16.

Okumagba, P. (2012). Oil Exploration and Crisis in the Niger Delta: The Response of the Militia Groups. *Journal of Sustainable Society, 1*(3), 78–83.

Okumagba, P. (2013). Ethnic Militia and Criminality in the Niger Delta. *International Review of Social Sciences and Humanities, 5*(1), 239–246.

Olawuyi, D. S. (2012). Legal and Sustainable Development Impacts of Major Oil Spills. *The Journal of Sustainable Development, 9*(1), 1–15.

Omeje, K. (2017a). *Extractive Economies and Conflicts in the Global South: Multiregional Perspectives on Rentier Politics*. Taylor and Francis.

Omeje, K. (2017b). *High Stakes and Stakeholders: Oil Conflict and Security in Nigeria*. Routledge.

Omeje, K. (2017c). The Egbesu and Bakassi Boys: African Spiritism and Mystical Re-rationalisation of Security. In D. J. Francis (Ed.), *Civil Militia: Africa's Intractable Security Menace* (pp. 71–86). Routledge.

Onakpohor, A., Fakinle, B. S., Sonibare, J. A., Oke, A. M., & Akeredolu, A. F. (2020). Investigation of Air Emissions from Artisanal Petroleum Refineries in the Niger Delta, Nigeria. *Heliyon Journal, 6*(11), 1–9.

Ong, D. (2017). Litigation against Multinational Oil Companies in their Home State Jurisdictions: An Alternative Legal Response to Pollution Damage in Foreign 362 Jurisdictions? In C. Tan & J. Faundez (Eds.), *Natural Resources and Sustainable Development: International Economic Law Perspectives*, Gloucestershire, Edward Elgar, pp. 278–297.

Onuoha, C. F. (2008). Oil Pipeline Sabotage in Nigeria: Dimensions, Actors and Implications for National Security. *African Security Review, 17*(3), 100–115.

Onuoha, C. F. (2016). *The Resurgence of Militancy in Nigeria's Oil-Rich Niger Delta and the Dangers of Militarisation*. Al Jazeera Centre for Studies.

Oriola, B. T. (2016). *Criminal Resistance: The Politics of Kidnapping Oil Workers*. London, Routledge.

Orisadare, M. A. (2019). An Assessment of the Role of Women Group in Women Political Participation, and Economic Development in Nigeria. *Frontiers in Sociology Journal, 4*(52), 1–7.

Owen, T. (2004). Challenges and Opportunities for Defining and Measuring Human Security. *Disarmament Forum Journal, 3*, 15–23.

Oyadongha, S. (2020, October 28). NOSDRA Intervenes again in SPDC/ Bayelsa Community Oil Spill Face-off. *Vanguard News Paper*. https://www. vanguardngr.com/2020/10/nosdra-intervenes-again-in-spdc-bayelsa-com munity-oil-spill-face-off/. Accessed 28 October 2020.

Oyadongha, S. (2021). We are Seeking International Help to Stop Nembe Oil Spill. *Vanguard News*. https://www.vanguardngr.com/2021/ 11/were-seeking-international-help-to-stop-nembe-oil-spill-aiteo/. Accessed 21 November 2021.

Petroleum Industry Act, (2021). PIA: Explanatory Memorandum. Available from https://eproofing.springer.com/ePb/books/pnXXkMoim97Z_a_r MD9rZeEbrTrRUQmOXjtKXvfLWedcljNJBuXmZZBNYj-SztuHljv8yt2gL-1Cc-g7hvQhrTojgqtjLQ2jAUWQdwYTjfbm05PWXyArOed10ZI9Y9nrG YFRl5Bl8liyVB1qXexaAf17alFTrZ7252zWyo2Ivrw=. [Accessed 04/05/2024].

Philp, M. (2015). The Definition of Political Corruption. In P. M. Heywood (Ed.), *Routledge Handbook of Political Corruption* (pp. 17–30). Routledge.

Prno, J., & Slocombe, D. S. (2012). Exploring the Origins of Social License to Operate in the Mining Sector: Perspectives from Governance and Sustainability Theories. *Journal of Resource Policy, 37*, 346–357.

Ruffin, S. (2012). Royal Dutch Shell Environmentally Degrades Nigeria's Niger Delta Region: A Land of Blacks. *Environmental Justice, 5*(3), 140–152.

Sagay, I. (2008). Nigeria: Federalism, the Constitution and Resource Control. In S. S. Azaiki, D. S. P. Alamieyeseigha, & A. A. Ikein (Eds.), *Oil, Democracy and the Promise of True Federalism in Nigeria* (pp. 370–379). University Press of America.

Saro-Wiwa, K. (1992). *Genocide in Nigeria: The Ogoni Tragedy*. African Books.

Shastry, V. (2023). *The Notorious ESG: Business, Climate, and the Race to Save the Planet*. Emerald.

Sinden, A. (2009). An Emerging Human Rights to Security from Climate Change: The Case Against Gas Flaring in Nigeria. In W. C. G. Burns & H. M. Osofsky (Eds.), *Adjudicating Climate Change: State, National, and International Approaches* (pp. 173–192). Cambridge University Press.

Skoczylis, J., & Andrews, S. (2021). The Spectacle of Ghost Security: Security Politics and British Civil Society. In: E. T. Njoku and S. N. Romaniuk (eds.), *Counter-Terrorism and Civil Society: Post 9/11 Progress and Challenges*, Manchester, Manchester University Press, pp. 109–126.

Teme, S. C. (2018). Pre-Design Site Investigation for an Oil and Gas Facility in the Marginal Lands of the Nigerian Niger Delta Sub-region. In J. Wasowski, D. Giordan, & P. Lillino (Eds.), *Engineering Geology and Geological Engineering for Sustainable Use of the Earth's Resources* (pp. 20–40). Springer.

Timashev, S., & Bushinskaya, A. (2016a). *Diagnostic and Reliability of Pipeline Systems*. Springer International Publishing.

Timashev, S., & Bushinskaya, A. (2016b). Methods of Assessing Integrity of Pipeline Systems with Different Types of Defects. In S. Timashev & A. Bushinskaya (Eds.), *Diagnostics and Reliability of Pipeline Systems* (Vol. 30, pp. 9–43). Springer.

Toakodi, A., & Assi, E. (2016). Corruption in the Civil Service: A Study of Payroll Fraud in Selected Ministries, Departments and Agencies (MDAS) in Bayelsa State, Nigeria. *Research on Humanities and Social Sciences Journal, 6*(3), 53–69.

Tonunarigha, Y. D., & Oghenekohwo, J. E. (2019). Empowerment Programmes of Faith-Based Organisations (FBOs) and Socio-economic Well-being of Members in Yenagoa Community Bayelsa State, Nigeria. *International Journal of Education and Literacy Studies, 7*(4), 192–198.

Transparency International. (2019). Military Involvement in Oil Theft in the Niger Delta. https://ti-defence.org/publications/military-involvement-in-oil-theft-in-the-niger-delta/. Accessed 25 November 2020.

Transparency International. (2020). Corruption Perception Index 2020. https://www.transparency.org/en/cpi/2021. Accessed 24 November 2020.

Tysiachniouk, M. S. (2020). Disentangling Benefit-Sharing Complexities of Oil Extraction on the North Slope of Alaska. *Sustainability Journal, 12*(13), 1–31.

Umar, A. T., & Othman, M. S. H. (2017). Causes and Consequences of Crude Oil Pipeline Vandalism in the Niger Delta of Nigeria: A Confirmatory Factor Analysis Approach. *Cogent Economics and Finance Journal, 5*(1), 1–15.

United Nations Environment Programme Report. (2012). *Environmental Assessment of Ogoniland: Assessment of Vegetation, Aquatic and Public Health Issues.* http://hdl.handle.net/20.500.11822/25286. Accessed 9 May 2018.

Vetter, S., Endrass, J., Schweizer, I., Teng, H. M., Rossler, W., & Gallo, W. T. (2006). The Effects of Economic Deprivation on Psychological Well-being Amongst the Working Population of Switzerland. *BMC Public Health, 6*(223), 1–10.

Walker, I., & Mendolia, S. (2015). Youth Unemployment and Personality Traits. *IZA Journal of Labour Economics, 4*(19).

Wells, J. (2019). Just 15% of the Oil and Gas Workforce is Female-these Women Want to Change that. *CNBC News.* https://www.cnbc.com/2019/01/04/15percent-of-oil-and-gas-workers-are-female-these-women-want-to-change-that.html. Accessed 14 November 2023.

# CHAPTER 8

# Discussion and Conclusion

## COMPARING FINDINGS: OIL AND GAS PROFESSIONALS AND COMMUNITY STAKEHOLDERS

This book uses the case study of the vandalism of the NCTL onshore oil and gas pipeline infrastructure insecurity in Nembe Bayelsa State, Nigeria as a lens to understand the recurrent threats, tensions, and conflicts in oil and gas producing local communities in the Global South. By addressing the following objectives, which are to:

1. Identifying the causes of onshore oil and gas pipeline infrastructure insecurity in Bayelsa state (Chapters 3, 4, 6, and 8);
2. Evaluating how the government and oil and gas companies respond to oil spillage, in particular, vandalism of the NCTL pipeline infrastructure (Chapters 2, 3, 4, 6, and 8);
3. Identifying the strategies deployed in protecting oil and gas pipeline infrastructure from vandalism and the impact on local communities in Bayelsa (Chapters 2, 6, and 8);
4. Exploring the impact of the construction of the NCTL onshore pipeline on local communities (Chapters 2, 3, 4, and 7).

This chapter does two things: synthesis the findings of the book bring together, the views of the community stakeholders and those of the

© The Author(s), under exclusive license to Springer Nature Switzerland AG 2024
A. L. A. Jatto, *Oil and Gas Pipeline Infrastructure Insecurity*, New Security Challenges,
https://doi.org/10.1007/978-3-031-56932-6_8

professionals. It is mainly organised around and sums up the four objectives: causes of vandalism, the response of government and corporations, strategies for protecting onshore oil and gas pipelines and the impact the NCTL on local communities. Each section is underpinned by the three literature review chapters. Evidence in this book has shown that some of the violence and criminality that are experienced are directed toward the oil and gas infrastructure, which includes pipeline vandalism. Continued pipeline vandalism increases and worsens the environmental damage and heightens the deterioration of security in the region. Ironically, as suggested in Chapter 6, this leads to further tensions and violent behaviours. As outlined in the previous chapters, this vicious cycle continues and little is done to break it. Previous chapters provided a detailed analysis of the underlying social, economic, environmental, and political reasons that continue to plague the region and how and why they led to the vandalism of the NCTL pipeline. This concluding chapter synthesis the findings from previous chapters and looks at the implications of onshore oil and gas infrastructure insecurity in Bayelsa State, Nigeria.

The analysis of the interview data with professionals and community representatives in Chapters 6 and 7 has provided a much deeper insight into the four research questions outlined above. Whereas the insights from the community respondents only provide a partial story and/or perspective as to what caused the vandalism of pipelines and onshore oil and gas infrastructure insecurity in Bayelsa state, particularly Nembe communities. Combining the professional and community data gave a fuller picture of why some of this anger and frustration exists within Bayelsa State and why this may lead to pipeline vandalism. The findings reveal that the majority of the professional and community respondents believe that corruption and criminality are huge problems that not only challenge the government but also the oil and gas sector. This corruption and mismanagement of public funds have a lasting effect on the socio-economic and political environment in the Niger Delta. The data clearly shows the extent to which corruption shapes the behaviours of public officials, oil and gas executives, regulatory agencies, and the way the petroleum sector is "regulated". Corruption and public sector mismanagement, have exacerbated the already unstable economic and environmental damage. Although most participants agreed that corruption was a problem across the board, almost a quarter of the participants believed that charges of corruption leveled at the oil and gas sector were overblown.

This same group of participants also believe that criminality by the local communities, community leaders, state officials, politicians, and criminal gangs—driven by greed—was a much more significant issue than corruption. According to Transparency International, those who say criminality was more problematic either benefit from corruption, are compromised officials, or were economical with the truth (2019; addressed in Chapter 3). The findings imply that corruption and criminality cannot be decoupled from understanding the issues underlying the vandalism of pipelines. The little increase in investment flow into the oil and gas sector does not necessarily suggest good ethical conduct, professionalism, and effective regulations. Much of the funding has gone to protecting and supporting the oil and gas companies. Local communities continue to be neglected and have not benefited from the increase in spending or the presence of the oil and gas sector in their area. According to Tysiachniouk extractive industry benefit-sharing complexities must be disentangled (2020). This sort of community neglect is what Okumagba (2013) and Dollard et al. (1939) say provokes collective frustration that leads to aggression.

As outlined in Chapters 6 and 7, the wealth that accompanies oil and gas production has not trickled down to local communities. There is a dearth of community projects and the few tangible infrastructures remain in a perpetual state of disrepair. This, coupled with inadequate access to socio-economic and political resources heightens tensions. Whereas professional respondents focused on oil and gas revenue, most of the community participants focused on how a lack of access to resources contributes to loss of household incomes as well as heightens poverty levels, which in turn increases tensions. Surprisingly, a small number of professional and community representatives still believe that vandalism was down to an individual's laziness and innate violent behavioural disposition of some Bayelsa people rather than a lack of access to resources and/or a dearth of community projects that cause vandalism. The pioneers of the *community neglect hypothesis* are saying that ignoring the communities creates perfect conditions for aggression (Coleman, 2015; Ekpenyong, 2010; Etowah & Effiong, 2012; Okonta, 2016; Okumagba, 2012, 2013; Saro-Wiwa, 1992; see Chapters 3, 4 and 5).

This book drew on the argument raised by the pioneers of the community neglect hypothesis to propose the Community Neglect Aggression Displacement theoretical framework (see Chapters 3, 4 and 5). CNADT explains that the neglect of socio-economic and environmental issues decreases household incomes, increases health problems, worsens poverty levels, and increased unemployment. This in turn creates the perfect conditions for anger and frustration that triggers the displacement of aggression against onshore pipelines. It also ties in with what Dollard et al. argued that when individuals are prevented from achieving their goals and set objectives, it triggers aggression displacement to resist the source of the obstruction (1939). Collective community neglect triggers tensions and frustrations that result in aggression and displacement against pipelines (see Chapters 6 and 7).

The majority of the respondents agreed that oil and gas exploration and the continued vandalism of pipelines have caused serious damage to the environment and ecosystem. Surprisingly, many oil and gas professionals agreed that the unethical and unprofessional behaviour of oil and gas operators was at least partly to blame for some of the environmental damage. Community representatives were unanimous that much of the damage to the environment, traditional and customary festivals like the boat regatta and fishing contests, and the local economy was down to the oil and gas companies and the poor response by state authorities. It is not surprising, that some of the professionals, however, attempted to shift the blame for worsened environmental degradation and violence, vandalism, oil bunkering, and theft as well as illegal artisanal refineries onto the community and criminals. The data is clear, while some blame must be attached to individuals engaging in criminality and vandalism, the wider socio-economic, political, and environmental context and decades of corruption and mismanagement of public funds play a huge part in creating and perpetuating the disappointment, anger, and frustration of the local communities. This has created the perfect conditions in which criminality and vandalism flourish.

Another implication of these findings is that resolving the underlying issues of socio-economic and environmental damage will continue to be contested especially by the few who directly or indirectly benefit which partly explains the UNSDG rhetoric (see Chapter 2). It also means that communities will continue to focus on, blame, and displace aggression on the oil and gas industry for environmental degradation, *ecocide,* and disorder to the natural habitat of Nembe and the larger Bayelsa. The most significant revelation of this finding is that all the stakeholders including the vandals in local communities take some portion of the blame for the destruction of the ecosystem of Bayelsa and the historic Niger Delta (see Chapters 6 and 7). To this day, there are no publicly available documents that demonstrate that the government and/or oil and gas companies have calculated the impact of oil and gas extraction on the environment and human health in Bayelsa or the wider Niger Delta (Ubong et al., 2010).

The problem is that Part III S.13(1) of the Flare Gas, Prevention of Waste and Pollution Regulations (2018) suggests US$2 accrues to the Nigerian government per every 28.317 standard cubic meters of gas flared. But advertently or inadvertently, no oil and gas regulatory document examined, including the Flare Gas Act, published any matrix for calculating and disentangling the benefit of oil and gas extraction and production to local communities for the destruction of the ecosystem and economic forest. The continued neglect significantly heightens the environmental damage leading to tensions, loss of lives, and household incomes which are the precursor to community neglect-aggression displacement (see Okumagba, 2012; see Chapters 2, 3, and 4). As outlined in earlier chapters and echoed by Bushman, Anderson, and Allen's work, the socio-economic and environmental context increases aggression amongst locals who at times turn to criminality and vandalism in an act of resistance, defiance, and rebellion, or to generate "wealth" through illicit means (2018).

Most professional participants agreed that poor oil and gas infrastructure increased operational and mechanical blowouts and amplified the damage caused by vandalism. What is not in dispute is that significant investment into the oil and gas infrastructure is required to minimise the damage from blowouts and vandalism. While this may somewhat lower tensions unless there is a significant investment into the local economy and local infrastructure and major efforts are made to repair the decade-old environmental damage, then insecurity will remain a way of life in the historic Niger Delta region. The majority of the professional and community respondents agreed that although it is hard to decouple the benefit-sharing and compensation complexities from environmental damages demanded by the local communities and other forms of social injustices. The broader compensatory framework largely responds to the needs of the communities (see Chapters 1, 2, 6, and 7). The interesting thing about this finding is that all the community respondents believe that ineffective implementation of regulatory laws and lack of clarity and timeline for the enforcement of different categories intensifies social injustices, Human rights abuses, and destruction of communities (see Chapters 2, 6, and 7).

The above position of all the community participants is further re-echoed by a few professionals who believe the community has not got a fair deal and/or share from the oil and gas benefits accruing to Nigeria and the oil firms. They pointed out that the payment for different categories of compensation such as land acquisition, compensation for pollution, royalties, CSR, and community projects was not enough which heightens the importance of ESG (O'Connor, 2022; Shastry, 2023). The implication of this is that different forms of compensation were not the problem or source of tension. The problem lies in the implementation of existing regulatory policy frameworks. Also, most of the professional and community respondents inadvertently agreed that the neglect of adequate compensation is a form of social injustice and causes frustration that leads to vandalism and insecurity of onshore oil and gas pipeline infrastructure (Okumagba, 2012). Different forms of tensions and insecurity issues would be mitigated where people are adequately compensated and the devasted farmlands reclaimed (Azubuike, 2021; see Chapter 7). While the professional and community participants did not disagree with most of the issues raised by the interviewer, they paid less attention to some, and others were interpreted from different perspectives. Both sample groups did not inherently differ in the combination of underlining factors that provoke the vandalism of pipelines. The different impacts and benefits that the professional and community sectors derive or suffer from petroleum activities influenced the pattern and way they narrated their stories.

## Causes of Vandalism, Threats, Conflicts, and Insecurity in the Niger Delta

This book highlights multidimensional factors causing onshore oil and gas pipeline vandalism and infrastructure insecurity, particularly the NCTL, are anger and frustration. This came about based on collective community neglect reinforced by corruption and organised criminality, poor governance, socio-economic deprivation, lack of infrastructure, and the continued environmental damage caused by oil and gas exploration (see Chapters 6 and 7). These findings are supported by the wider literature on the topic (Alamieyeseigha, 2008a; Anand & Ashforth, 2003; Ioannides, 2017; Lynch et al., 2015; Nye, 1967; Ogbeidi, 2012). Underlying socio-economic issues are a lack of social housing, hospitals, transport infrastructure, an increase in household poverty, unemployment, and inequality which persists because of neglect leading to frustration (see Chapter 2, 3, and 4; Bergstresser, 2017; Ibaba, 2009: 555; Okonofua, 2016; Okumagba, 2012). These issues are also prevalent in many petrostates in the Global South.

The environmental issues are pollution caused by oil exploration, deforestation of the mangrove trees from oil spills, waste disposal, acidification of fishing waters, and the ocean (Chapters 2 and 4; Douglas & Okonta, 2003; Etemire, 2016; Linden & Palsson, 2013; Olawuyi, 2012; Sinden, 2009; UNEP, 2012). Neglecting to address these issues conversely intensified what this book coined as the "Contemporary Poor Governance Cycle" (CPGC), socio-economic, and environmental and political issues highlighted. Implying that there is a forward and backward nexus between the factors causing vandalism and the underlying micro-foundational variables and triggers of the factors causing vandalism. My findings complement and re-echo the findings of others (Anderson & Dill, 1995; Berkowitz, 2011; Bushman et al., 2018; Dollard et al., 1939; Krueger, 1996; Lazarus, 1994; Okumamagba, 2012; Sanderson, 2010). All of these factors are present at varying degrees in a majority of local communities in petrostates in the Global South. Figure 8.1 demonstrates the correlation between the factors that cause oil and gas pipeline vandalism and micro-foundational triggers that reinforce those factors.

The symptomatic factors that cause vandalism and oil and gas pipeline infrastructure insecurity are directly linked to the micro-foundational variables and triggers that reinforce the causes of insecurity. The figure indicates that anytime the underlying micro-foundational variables and triggers remain unchanged, unaddressed, or unresolved, there is bound to be consistency of the factors causing the oil and gas pipeline vandalism in the area. The neglect that the Niger Delta region has suffered, over many decades, is reflected in the micro-foundational triggers that are responsible for their frustration and aggression displacement against pipelines leading to vandalism.

One of the core findings is the critical role that the issue of corruption plays in causing pipeline vandalism and infrastructure insecurity in Nigeria and most petrostates in the Global South. The government's attempt at improving the local economy and infrastructure has woefully been inadequate in Bayelsa and Nigeria. There is a downward drop in public-sector perception levels of corruption within 10 years (2012–2021) in Nigeria (Transparency International, 2021). Corruption in the Global South, as

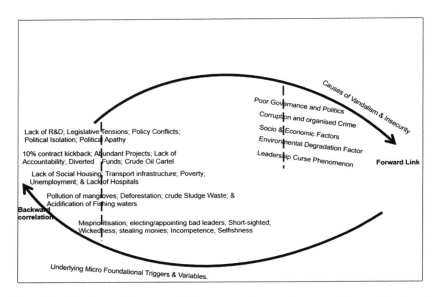

**Fig. 8.1**    Onshore oil and gas infrastructure insecurity nexus (*Source* Designed by Author (2023))

in Nigeria's context goes beyond bribery. The UNODC (2019) corruption report concludes that the Nigerian government's anti-corruption agenda has only a marginal effect on corrupt practices. As outlined in Chapters 6 and 7, the high level of corruption and lack of transparency contributes to tensions and intensifies insecurity problems in the historic Niger Delta region. The Nigerian government has made some efforts to tackle the systemic and growing culture of corruption and crimes amongst the youths, but this has been woefully inadequate (Transparency International, 2020). A United Nations report notes that "public officials continue to meet with little resistance when requesting bribes…and mechanisms for reporting bribery remain the Achilles' heel of the anti-corruption system" (UNODC, 2019: 9). This corruption is of course not confined to the public sector alone.

Poor governance factor continues to disrupt the effective regulation of the oil and gas industry in Nigeria, particularly the implementation of extractive industry regulatory policy frameworks in the Niger Delta which goes against the UNSDG goals. The broader concept of Poor Governance which also interconnects with the factor of corruption, plays a central role in this book due to its evolving nature. Poor governance, analysed here within the context of conflicting policies, legislative tensions, and lack of investment in R and D is a factor that causes vandalism. Other factors are environment, corruption, and socio-economic. Although these are connected with poor governance but they are analysed separately as issues that trigger the tensions that lead to pipeline vandalism. There is a distinction between the conventional component of poor governance and the contemporary components coined as the Contemporary Poor Governance Cycle (CPGC), discussed in the final part of poor governance.

FADT argues that conflicting instrumental policies prevents the legitimate participation of local communities in the oil and gas business chain which trigger resistance, resentment, and anger that leads to aggression (Dollard et al., 1939; Okumagba, 2012; Sanderson, 2010). This is supported by the proposed Community Neglect Aggression Displacement theory which argues that the collective neglect by the government and oil operators worsens poverty, and decreases household incomes. This in turn triggers tensions and displacement of aggression against pipelines. A classic example is the defective design and implementation of most oil and gas regulatory guidelines such as the Land Use Act, Oil Pipeline Act, NDDC Act, and even the Presidential Amnesty Establishment Act. They are designed with the oil and gas companies in mind with no significant input from the host communities (see Chapters 3 and 4). The regulatory frameworks continue to be beset by poor governance and hence are unable to resolve the very issue they were designed to resolve. It is this situation that continues to inflame and frustrate local populations making vandalism continue to occur. The data from the study shows that regulations and the operational policies of oil firms seldom reflect the realities across communities (see Chapters 6 and 7). Nigerian politicians and bureaucratic bottlenecks, just like elsewhere in the Global South, do not always accept the rational outcomes of evidence-based research to support government regulatory frameworks due to a lack of a standardised process.

Sequel to this, the Community Stakeholders' Policy Development Model (CSPDM) in Fig. 8.2 is proposed as a standardised data-gathering model. CSPDM is an interconnected, inclusive, and participatory model for gathering empirical resource-based data.

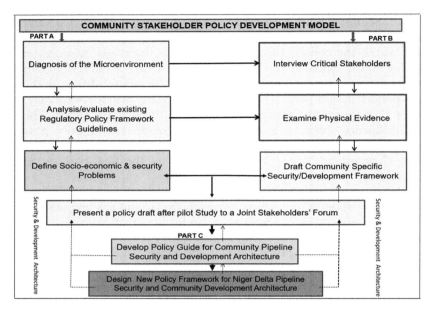

**Fig. 8.2** Community stakeholders' policy development model (CSPDM) (*Source* Author (2023))

This CSPDM does three things (1); Part A and B are interlinked and work together to enable the design of part C. Whilst A uses existing policies and evidence from the community to redefine the problem, (2) it relies on B to validate or invalidate the evidence through interviews and physical examination of materials before designing a security and development policy draft which is then presented to the stakeholders. (3) Part C triangulates and integrates the evidence-based socio-economic problems with the outcome of the pilot study from stakeholders and designs a new framework policy guide for community pipeline security and development architecture. This CSPDM model can be leveraged to redesign a new policy framework for the Niger Delta pipeline security. The researchers and policy drafters must, as a necessity, examine physical evidence in the communities, using the government empirical data resources to design a draft policy targeted at the specific problem, combined with the clearly defined problems presented to community stakeholders, after the pilot study leads to the design of a community-specific security and development policy that can be mirrored in the entire Niger Delta area. The final, but extremely crucial in the process, is the upward pointing arrows which indicate that the entire policy processes are interconnected, and must reflect the data of the preceding stages in the final composite policy framework. This model will resolve the issues of policy conflicts, duplication, and collective resentment.

Another outcome of poor governance discussed in this book is the lack of investment in R and D. This shows the inadequacy of the government because communities are further deprived of gainful employment in the oil and gas sector by the lack of industries. The lack of investment in R and D, statutory environmental and oil spill agencies like NOSDRA, and specialised equipment is a function of corruption and political processes which are the hallmark of poor governance. The failure of the Nigerian government, as in many other petrostates in the Global South contradicts the UNSGD 2030 which aligns with the argument of Loft and Brien (2023; see Chapter 2). The lack of equipment on its own does not cause vandalism. But the inability of NOSDRA and oil firms to locally galvanise resources with which to respond to oil spillage conversely impacts the environment which hinders communities' livelihood. As outlined in earlier chapters, this can provoke frustration and collective community aggression displacement (Gurr, 2015; see Chapters 2 and 3). Uncleaned oil spills worsen the economic life of the people, reinforce unemployment, and intensify youth restiveness leading to frustration and anger that triggers more vandalism. The findings reveal that delay and sometimes refusal of oil companies, the oil service industry, and regulatory authorities to invest in Research and Development not only hinder clamping of accidental blowouts and gas leaks it also worsens pollution. The lack of these initiatives hinders the development of industry expertise, competitiveness, reduction in revenue, and effective recovery of onshore petroleum resources, and more difficult to meet the UNSDGs Global Goals 2030. A classic example of what lack of investment in infrastructure does is the inability of Aiteo to contain the Santa Barbara oil well spillage on the OML 29 oilfield in November 2021 (Oyadongha, 2021). A situation where the oil continues to pollute the fishing waters, and farmlands and destroy the ecosystem demonstrate a perfect precursor that triggers collective anger that leads to community aggression displacement, and vandalism of other oil and gas infrastructure.

The third element in the poor governance factor that causes vandalism is the intense federal legislative tensions which heighten insecurity against infrastructures. Tensions, vandalism, conflicts, and pollution are some of the underlying social issues that trigger humans to vandalise pipelines. These federal legislative tensions are created by intensified oppositions from other geopolitical zones in Nigeria create another source of concern, worsen pipeline vulnerability, and heighten infrastructure insecurity. Some of the tensions are because federal lawmakers from the Niger Delta capitulate to external pressure and the interest of other geopolitical zones when it comes to oil and gas legislation. Other times, deliberate closure in communication channels between the government, and oil operators, and preventing communities from effective participation in legislative inputs create tensions. Most community inhabitants are their leaders are unaware of the terms of engagement with the oil firms working in their back-yards depriving direct benefits to oil-bearing communities. The generality of Bayelsans believes that the best part of their ancestral inheritance in terms of oil blocks has been appropriated by vested regional interests that do not share the same anthropology with Nembe and the historic Niger Delta people. The agitation by many federal legislative members to protect the interest of non-oil-producing regions is disproportionate, undermines, and delays the legislation on improving the oil and gas host communities. For instance, the latest Petroleum Industry Act, 2021, took about 20 years to pass, due to the need for individual pecuniary gains.

These regional federal legislative geopolitical interplays are hijacked by oil firms to further deepen the divisions in communities. For instance, the division of Nembe into Ogbolomabiri and Basambiri Ruling Houses favours the operator because the section that is not in power is isolated enabling the oil firms to execute fewer intervention projects. Another instance is that federal legislative tensions and maneuvering influenced the naming of the NCTL infrastructure rather than the "Ewelesuo Creek Trunk Line" given that the oil field and wellhead are located in their community, it was named the NCTL. Many indigenes believe this type of stagnated socio-economic growth of Ewelesuo because the opportunity that the NCTL attracts goes to Nembe central rather than come to their community. This way socio-economic activities would have been stimulated. The resentment that follows eventually explodes into tensions and vandalism of the NCTL. Wherever immediate underlying social issues causing the vandalism of pipelines, there are less obvious geopolitical legislative contentions. Leading to confrontations between the States in the Niger Delta and those from other zones. This sort of behavior defines the contemporary character of Nigeria's politics.

The problematic nature of poor governance makes it extremely harder to deliver public goods. This book has further established that the concept of CPGC goes beyond the above three issues of conflicting policies, legislative tensions, and lack of investment in Research and Development. It expands it by dividing CPGC into four sub-themes to cover some complexities of postmodernity. These sub-themes are security architecture; infrastructure underdevelopment; Human Development Index and Politics. This thematic categorisation enabled an in-depth discussion of 30 components of social issues, as shown in Fig. 8.2, that have redefined tensions and insecurity problems. These CPGC components further illuminate emerging socio-economic and cultural issues responsible for varying tensions in modern society especially in the Global South (see Chapters 2 and 4). This extends beyond the conventional discussion around the concept of poor governance limited to issues bothering on corruption, insecurity, conflicts, organised crime, disrespect for the rule of law/human rights, and others (Anand & Ashforth, 2003; Neumann & Elsenbroich, 2017; Nye, 1967; Ogbeidi, 2012). Multiple issues within the CPGC typically require a combination of reform in ethics, leadership, integrity, transparency, accountability, and conscious citizen engagement. Evidence in Chapters 6 and 7 of this book shows that poor governance and corruption play crucial roles in reinforcing the socio-economic and environmental problems in Nigeria's Niger Delta region, as replicated in many oil and gas producing countries in the Global South (see Chapter 2).

Figure 8.3 shows that CPGC continues to expand reflecting emerging cyclical micro-foundation issues global issues. An in-depth interrogation reveals each of the four sub-set components, though interconnected, stands alone with each defined by its own peculiar underpinning elements. They are tightly linked, though distinct, however, problems easily diffuse across them, making it harder to deliver public goods, both in Nigeria and other countries in the Global South (see Chapters 2, 3, 4, and 5). Politics and HDI are the biggest issues catalysts confronting CPGC in Niger and many countries in the Global South. If nations get the politics right, other issues that reinforce poor governance could be significantly mitigated. After critically scrutinising over 30 pieces of documentary evidence on about 20 countries in the Global South suggests that in countries where HDI and political components are challenging such as Nigeria, Brazil, and Venezuela. There is bound to be poor security architecture which heightens infrastructure underdevelopment. However, in countries where aspects of Politics and HDI were less challenging, does not always necessarily translate to the achievement of infrastructure development or secure governance.

Another factor is the socio-economic in nature together with its underlying issues. The socio-economic factor is made worse by some underlying issues leading to the vandalism of pipelines in Bayelsa. Some of these issues are a lack of social housing, lack of hospitals, lack of transport

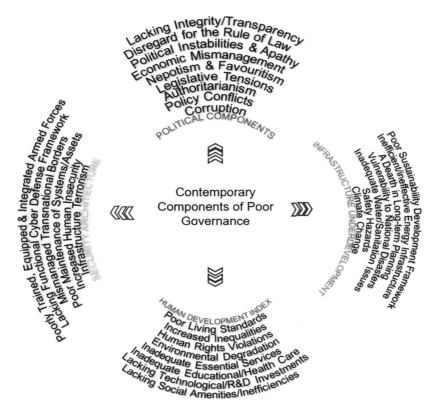

**Fig. 8.3** Contemporary poor governance cycle (CPGC) (*Source* Designed by Author (2023))

infrastructure, an increase in household poverty, massive youth unemployment, and a wide gap of social inequality. The lack of social security for displaced persons, lack of household incomes, and industries to add value to the crude oil, poor standard of living, and increased social inequalities are some of the underlying socio-economic problems that provoke vandalism (Bergstresser, 2017; Ibaba, 2009: 555). These social issues are woven into the issue of poor governance and therefore the failure to provide and improve on these social and economic issues is what Okonta (2016) and Etowah and Effiong (2012) described as collective community neglect (see Chapter 3). Such economic issues that link to vandalism are the lack of political resources, household poverty, unemployment, and preventing communities from participating in the oil and gas sector (Alagoa, 2005; Alamieyeseigha, 2008a). The economic indices in terms of industries, household incomes, and social inequalities in Bayelsa and the wider historic Niger Delta area demonstrate that the benefits from oil and gas have not percolated to the grassroots. Hence some of the youths try to normalise and justify their illegal acts arguing that they were indeed getting their share of the "national cake" by engaging in criminal acts.

In addition, little has been done to fix the ever-worsening environmental factor which puts pressure against the UNSDG agenda (2016; see Chapters 2 and 4). Over decades, the worsening situation has increased the tensions, anger, and discontent of the local population leading to frustration like vandalism, despite its negative impact on the environment while criminality has become part of life in the region. This has brought further instability to the region (see Chapters 6 and 7). The underlying environmental issues such as pollution caused by oil exploration, deforestation of the mangrove trees by oil spills, waste disposal, acidification of fishing waters, and the ocean also reflect on poor governance and lead to anger and vandalism including CNADT. Although environmental pollution might be a by-product of vandalism the fact that mechanical blowouts also result in oil spillages frustrates the livelihood of people which provokes anger against pipelines. The data reveal that the oil and gas activities of corporations are the single largest contributors to environmental degradation which Higgins (2010) described as ecocide. Historical facts suggest that oil and gas companies have been polluting the Niger Delta environment and oil-bearing communities for many decades. Many years of uncleaned oil spillages resulting from mechanical and operational blowouts are the provocateur for further attacks on the pipelines.

According to Berkowitz (1993) and Balham (1985) aggression is a relationship imposed by an actor to devastate the physical and psychological well-being of others (see Chapter 3).

By vandalising the pipelines, the perpetrators demonstrate their resolve to inflict psychological and mental pain as well as economic losses on both the Nigerian government and the oil and gas operators who are seen as provocateurs. Krueger pointed out that aggression will occur when and only when there is frustration (1996). Kee states that aggressive policies trigger frustration, hostilities, and insecurity (2012). This research argues that since the state has statutory control over the instrument of political, security, and judicial power, and distributes scarce resources while determining who gets "what" and "when" the overwhelming fault should be blamed on the government. The government should take full responsibility for the abuse of the natural environment and abuse of sustainability as well as a lack of community development (Esiedesa, 2021).

## Responding to Oil Spillages and Vandalism

The policy framework of environmental sustainability adopted by the Nigerian Federal Government and the implementation strategies followed by the federal Ministry of Petroleum do not reflect the UNSDG framework (2016). If anything, they are in contradiction support the environmental devastation of oil and gas producing communities especially Nembe and other Bayelsa communities. Operational blowout and pipeline vandalism that leads to oil spillages elicit different responses from both the government statutory response agencies like NOSDRA, Nigeria Federal Environmental Protection Agency, and the oil and gas operators. Evidence from this research shows that the government responds to oil spillages through NOSDRA and NFEPA in close collaboration with the oil firms concerned (see Chapter 2). In principle, the 2006 NOSDRA Act stipulates that affected oil firms must report cases of oil spills immediately to both NOSDRA and NFEPA. But in practice, political, security, and technical reasons prevent this from happening. This is made worse by the lack of equipment available to NOSDRA. According to the evidence from this study, oil firms respond by deciding whether the oil spill is a result of human vandalism or structural failure which dictates how they will respond, even where a report from the Joint Investigation Visit team which involves environmentalists, NGOs, DPR, NOSRDA, Security, and oil firms says otherwise (see Chapters 2, 6, and 7).

For instance, Shell Petroleum Development Company (SPDC) rejected the Joint Investigation findings of a recent blowout of the Joint Venture pipeline at the Nun River in Bayelsa. Utebor claims that Shell ignored the obvious fact that the pipeline was overtly corroded and demonstrated plenty of signs of loss of structural integrity due to age (2021). Given that blame is placed on vandalism, Shell can withhold any compensation and delay the activation of cleanup operations. Thereby pushing the responsibility to NOSDRA. This sort of thing is what Okumagba says leads to anger and frustration because the exposure to methane gases worsens the environmental issues, reduces farm yields, and increases hunger (2012). Oil firms randomly blame communities for vandalism to escape condemnations from civil society and government sanctions. In their analysis of FADT, Dollard et al. describe this as a classic case of corporate instrumental aggression that triggers anger (1939; see Chapters 2, 3, and 4). The significance of the findings is that the oil and gas extractive industry remain the focal point or central point of attention as it concerns the environmental degradation of Nembe and Bayelsa's natural habitat.

An effective federal legislative assembly that works with the executive and judiciary to determine who gets what, when, and how is one core characteristic element of good governance (Lasswell, 1936, 2018). The constant tension in Nigeria's National Assembly reinforces and intensifies poor governance and response to oil and gas spillages and gas leaks and worsens the inability to address the problem of vandalism. Federal legislative tensions have a wider implication on government functions and effectiveness. Such as conflict of policies, and a dearth of state and corporate investment in oil and gas research and development. The culture of looking for pecuniary gains influences legislation in the petroleum sector (Amundsen, 2019). Political and legislative leaders who consider their interests first rather than those of communities are the sets of people Bellow described as "a class of people profoundly dangerous to the rest... I mean the leaders. Invariably, the most dangerous people seek the power" (Bello, 1964: 51). Often, the federal lawmakers from the Niger Delta capitulate to external pressure and the interest of other geopolitical zones when it comes to oil and gas legislation that will benefit local communities, for instance, the Niger Delta rejection of the new PIA Act (see Chapter 3).

## Impact of Security Strategies on Local Communities

The data discovered that the Nigerian government applies two-prong strategies, hard military kinetic force, and soft socio-economic and infrastructural development strategies like the Presidential amnesty program (see Chapters 2 and 3). Evidence from this research suggests that soft options such as socio-economic development are a secondary measure. Much of the state's focus is on traditional security which includes the use of the military (Okonofua, 2016; Mathias, 2015; see Chapter 2). Leaving the communities behind in setting mid and long-term economic and infrastructure development is partly what scholars described as community neglect that leads to aggression displacement (Chapters 2 and 3). Although current security measures may have prevented a full-scale oil war in the historic Niger Delta, they have not eliminated constant internal conflicts and communal wars. The findings show that the activities of OPDS have been counterproductive in many ways. Alamieyeseigha (2008a; Isaac Boro, 1982; Saro-Wiwa, 1992) argues that the military approach has its roots and historic foundation in the British Nembe-Brass 1895 massacre. The British used force of arms to seize lands and oil palm trading routes and plantations that originally belonged to the local indigenous merchants, landowners, and Kings (see Chapters 2 and 3).

The findings revealed that the security approach is contributing to the escalation of vandalism as Okonofua (2016) stated, the security design and its implementation frameworks violate human rights. Poor governance and corruption hamper security operations, with some security personnel actively engaging in illegal oil bunkering and artisanal refining activities (Transparency International, 2019, 2020; see Chapters 5 and 6). Furthermore, the soft approach is the Presidential Amnesty Program introduced over a decade ago as human security approach. This has been hampered by political meddling. Its implementation and ineffectiveness have precipitated clashes between different groups which has worsened insecurity across communities (Abidde, 2017; Okonofua, 2016; Onuoha, 2016). Whereas some people are benefiting from the amnesty program, the government has deliberately refused to activate the infrastructural development phase of the program. This would have involved land reclamation and infrastructure development. The wait is frustrating and leads to more resistance and aggression (Dollard et al.,

1939; Sanderson, 2010). This is in tandem with the community neglect hypothesis (Okonta, 2016; Okumagba, 2012; Saro-Wiwa, 1992). Many have argued that the Presidential Amnesty Program is a glorified settlement scheme. Given that it tends to favour politicians and a few selected former militants.

## IMPACT OF THE NCTL CONSTRUCTION ON LOCAL COMMUNITIES

The socio-economic and environmental impact of the construction of the NCTL on communities is addressed here. The research findings show evidence of the devastating economic, cultural, traditional, and environmental impact that the NCTL has on communities leading to loss of economic incomes, farm produce increased household unemployment, and displacement. The wider literature argued that the NCTL traverses over 80 communities in Nembe-Ewelesuo in Bayelsa alone and over 100 communities by the time it reaches the Bonny export terminal axis in Rivers state (Mickolus, 2018; Onuoha, 2016). The construction of the NCTL has led to the destruction of many natural habitats including asphyxiation of the mangrove forests that destroys and hinders their natural ability to de-carbonise hydrocarbon pollution from the atmosphere. It is hard to gauge the environmental and economic losses Nembe communities have suffered since the operationalisation of the NCTL pipeline. The data supports the narrative of the participants that, the ineffectiveness of the pipeline regulators reinforced the unprofessional practices in the construction, operation, and management of pipelines and particularly the NCTL (see Chapters 6 and 7).

There is a persistent disagreement between the professional and community participants about how the operation of the NCTL heightens the level of insecurity problems in the area. Whereas the construction of the NCTL benefits the government and Aiteo, at the same time it has impoverished local communities. Even though the government is aware that the majority of the Fishing Creek communities along the NCTL pipeline route were displaced yet the government programs broadly leave such communities behind which is a precursor to the overwhelming neglect they face (see Chapters 2 and 3). According to Dollard et al. when people are prevented from achieving their set objectives and goals, they get frustrated, angry, and aggress against their obstructor or in their frustration displace their aggression against softer targets linked to the provocateur (1939). On the other hand, when socio-economic issues are left unresolved, it worsens poverty, youth unemployment, and widens inequality. This leads to CNADT proposed in Chapter 3. The refusal to address the impact of the NCTL on the communities is what this thesis describes as community neglect that results in aggression displacement against pipelines (see Chapters 3, 4 and 5).

## Solving the Problems. Is this Possible?

This book makes it clear that solving the problem of onshore pipeline vandalism, threats, tensions, and conflicts with its attendant socio-economic and infrastructural deficits lies in adoption and clear understanding of the UNSDGs. It has also been established elsewhere in this book that setting practical policy mechanisms that draw on the UNSDG framework for the implementation of the Global Agenda 2030 is the irreducible minimum to achieve sustainable progress. This will enable the design of a lasting solution for resolving vandalism, threats, and infrastructure insecurity problems in Nigeria and most petrostates in the Global South (Loft & Brien, 2023; UNSDG, 2016). This section is about understanding what the 41 professional and community stakeholders' respondents think needs to happen for the onshore oil and gas pipeline and infrastructure to be secured in the Bayelsa case study area. Most of the professional and community respondents suggested that reforms to the socio-economic and infrastructure development of communities, and reforms to regulations and policy frameworks are required. Working with, rather than on behalf of, communities in Nigeria and the other extractive states in the Global South is essential to policy success. The participation of communities is what Akpan stated is the best way oil companies can improve the lives and situation of local communities as well as optimize the performance of their assets (2021). The Community Stakeholders' Policy Development Model (CSPDM—Fig. 8.2) above has been designed to help stakeholders effectively achieve collective ownership of the policy processes. Stakeholders from different sectors including the communities should create an "*Oil and Gas Stakeholders' Forum*" to facilitate the synergy between local communities and oil production companies. The fiduciary benefits to communities are achieved only when an inclusive framework is created for them to thrive (Leipziger, 2017).

The widespread and deep-rooted socio-economic inequalities which percolate the entire fabric in the area, make it harder to find a solution (see Chapter 2, 3, 4, and 5). The community respondents suggest the upscaling of local illegal refining facilities into *cleaner and legal mainstream modular refining infrastructure* to employ youths (Onakpohor et al., 2020; see Chapters 2 and 6). Modular refineries are oil production infrastructure that contributes to the stimulation of the petroleum value chain while expanding sources of petroleum product supplies (Ochayi & Eromosele, 2021). By integrating all artisanal refineries into the modular model, the government closes the employment gaps and works with restive youths to ensure that further establishment of illegal artisanal refining facilities is checked. The upscaling of artisanal refineries to modular refineries will benefit the state in terms of taxes and jump-start the industrial base in the oil and gas states. While expanding the mid and downstream components of the oil industry. Provisions and improved infrastructure in Bayelsa State are, certainly, part of a more lasting solution. While these may be a welcome idea, the underlying issues that arise due to political corruption, poor governance, incompetent leadership, and vested interests of the oil and gas companies have to be addressed. Until these issues are addressed in tandem with the socio-economic issues insecurity of oil and gas infrastructure especially vandalism and the oil spills that come with it will remain a problem.

All the community and professional respondents agree that there should be complete reform of the oil and gas regulations that deliver public good to the communities and meets the interest of oil firms. Whereas the professionals want effective oil and gas regulatory laws, they argued that there should be a demonstration of transparent implementation and monitoring regimes. The community respondents suggested that the *oil and gas operating headquarters* should be relocated to the Niger Delta. Also, the laws should stipulate the establishment of community-to-community *truth and reconciliation commission* that will bring together affected communities, oil-bearing communities, oil and gas operators, civil society representatives, and industry regulators. This should facilitate the phased payment of reparation in terms of coordinated development and comprehensive cleanup of fishing waters and farmlands, reclamation, and replanting of the destroyed mangrove forests to trigger an agricultural revolution. "A combination of oil and gas and socio-economic policy changes would be a game-changer", the head of civil society and NGO representatives stated (Professional NGO-04). Although this cannot happen in isolation except through the effective collaboration of all oil and gas companies, the government, regulators, local authorities, and communities.

Further, a few professional oil and gas and security respondents advocated for the deployment of preventative technologies and military power to mitigate vandalism. These respondents were two oil and gas and three security professionals. Evidence from this research suggests that the continued sustenance of military presence in the Niger Delta cannot be decoupled from the need to sustain their pecuniary benefits (Transparency International, 2019, 2020; see Chapters 2, 3, 5, and 6). What these respondents do not explain is how to overcome the widespread poverty or provide legitimate opportunities for the many unemployed youths to keep them off the streets and become productive for themselves and the larger society. It is worthy of note that, the scares of many decades of socio-economic delays will be visible for many years to come. There are also no quick fixes or silver bullets that will automatically erase the long history of community neglect and poverty which has been worsened by environmental degradation and violence suffered.

The views of the professional and community respondents have shone some light on why local communities support and engage in pipeline vandalism. They give sufficient and in-depth views about what is going on and why. What is less acknowledged is who is to blame as both sample groups often try to shift the blame. As outlined above most professionals and communities agree that poverty, poor infrastructure, lack of socio-economic opportunities, poor governance, incompetent leadership, neglect, and corruption are some of the leading underlying causes of frustration. It is such frustration that leads individuals to engage in pipeline vandalism. Although the problems are mostly acknowledged, many professionals attempted to minimise and shift the blame from themselves and their organisations. As noted above, some professional respondents openly acknowledged the role of their organisation in creating the conditions of insecurity in the region. While some community respondents somewhat suggested that some of their youths engaged in outright criminality. At the same time, they all believed that it is a collaboration with this very same sector that can provide the solutions to the problems.

In addition, this thesis supports the idea of oil and gas regulatory framework reforms but this should be done along with the reforms of the Oil Pipeline Act to include three distinctive phases of the *oil and gas pipeline life cycle*. This thesis divides the pipeline life cycle into three distinctive phases which are planning, implementation, and operationalisation. The whole purpose is to ensure that the community and civil society can relate, and gauge tangible and physical benefits accruing to the local communities right from the start to the end of each of the three phases of the pipeline life cycle. In addition to supporting FADT with the community neglect hypothesis (see Chapters 2 and 3), this thesis also suggests a review of the different phases in the pipeline life cycle. The thesis proposes the inclusion of tangible socio-economic infrastructure and environmental benefits in the planning, implementation, and operationalisation of pipelines. The neglect of these direct benefits in oil pipeline operation and management in the Oil Pipeline Act (2004) is one gap that creates tensions because it intensifies hunger and poverty. It intensifies every other issue discussed so far which causes anger, frustration, and aggression. Hunger is increased along with lack of income and worsening household poverty (Okumagba, 2013). Given that pipeline networking and operation of onshore pipelines displaces communities from their legitimate sources of income.

Each phase of the pipeline operation should be transparently verifiable to ensure the completion of all stated measurable community benefits. These are:

- *In the planning phase*; community development experts should be included to represent community interest in pipeline project conceptualisation, route selection, and the selection of impactful community infrastructure. Undertake a demographic diagnosis and threat characteristics.
- *In the implementation phase;* reclaim lands, re-plant trees destroyed, clean polluted waterways, and rebreed marine life. Recreate new socio-economic opportunities for displaced communities impacted by the pipelines.

*In the operationalisation phase;* intensification of public safety awareness campaigns and reinforcement of physical barriers around pipeline routes. There should be a continuation of land reclamation, replanting of mangrove trees, and green vegetation destroyed, and rebreeding of different fish species and marine life. As well as compensation to impacted communities, whenever an oilfield stops production and a pipeline route, is decommissioned.

# Pipeline Operations and Community Development Life Cycle (POCDLC)

The adoption of each of the phases of this proposed pipeline life cycle will be novel to the manufacturing, deployment, operationalisation, and management of oil and gas pipelines in Nigeria. Given the inclusion of targeted community development and re-integration deliverables at environmental, economic, and social levels before the completion of each phase. Communities will engage with the step-by-step processes of the pipeline operation and management chain. Particularly aspects that directly impact their socio-economic lives. Thus, mitigating tensions since they can measure the trickle-down benefits at every stage of the pipeline development process, see the three-phased Pipeline Operation and Strategic Community Development Life Cycle in Figs. 8.4, 8.5, and 8.6. These three phases should be adopted by petrostates in the Global South as part of best practices in onshore oil and gas pipeline operation and management. The three-phase pipeline life cycle does two things differently; (1) it includes the UNSDGs at every level putting the community as the central referent point; and (2) it focuses on the physical structurality and resilience of the pipeline.

The planning phase of the proposed three-phased oil and gas pipeline cycle includes community development, infrastructure security, and environmental reclamation that will contribute to the socio-economic, environmental, and human security of host communities. It draws on the communities' perspectives in the selection of pipeline route, social infrastructural, and human capital development index in the communities. This thesis argued that seeking the views of the communities advances socio-economic cohesion, well-being, and psychological and mental health. Phase two outlines the implementation of different elements needed to make the pipeline secure and functional.

After the seven stages in the planning cycle are verified triggers the implementation phase. This will curtail tensions that cascade into conflicts and infrastructure insecurity problems. The implementation phase shows that the reinforcement and reclamation of destroyed farmlands, fishing waters, and waterways ensures that communities can return to their natural economic, and traditional activities while managing pipelines. Where these are left unresolved constitute, the underlying micro-functional triggers reinforcing the factors of vandalism. Also, the intensification of very mechanical aspects and testing of a manufactured

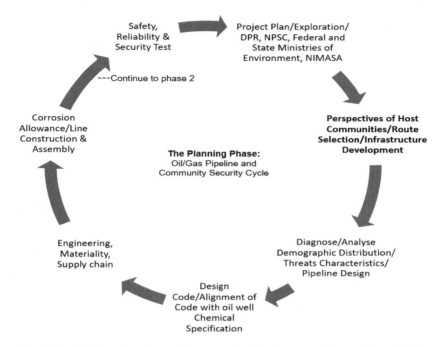

**Fig. 8.4** Pipeline planning and community development (*Source* Compiled by Author (2023))

pipeline prevents mechanical blowouts and protects the best interest of the community (see infrastructure insecurity nexus above).

The operational phase shows the extent to which the third phase of the model can contribute to the socio-economic, human development, sustainable environment, and security of the local community and the oil and gas infrastructure. This third phase of the proposed pipeline life cycle emphasizes the importance of adopting a structural safety mechanism in pipeline operations. It also involves an increase in public safety awareness campaigns as well as structured maintenance, decommissioning, and retirement culture of pipelines to prevent hazards to communities. Whilst the planning phase may not have an immediate impact on the socio-economic life of the communities, the implementation and operational phases have direct impacts human capital development.

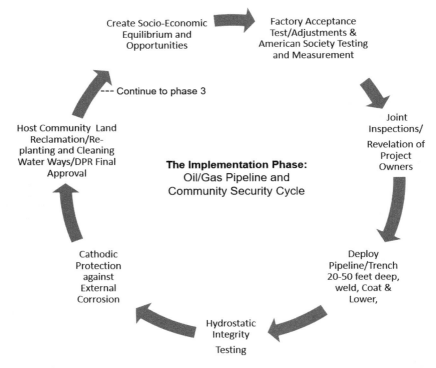

**Fig. 8.5** Pipeline implementation and community development (*Source* Compiled by Author (2023))

Canada Energy Pipeline Association-CEPA (2016) identified planning; application; construction; and operations for pipelines. CEPA included the post-construction phase which suggest the testing, cathodic protection, cleanup, land restoration; monitoring-control centers, emergency preparedness, and innovative technologies. What global oil and gas pipeline industry professionals are pointing out is that developing a structured pipeline life cycle framework was an important element in framing a strategic pipeline operational chain. CEPA clearly omitted community development as a critical element of the pipeline life cycle. Failure to recognise the critical role community development plays in ensuring the security of the pipeline infrastructure creates a gap and a problem. Therefore, leaves many things to the discretion, imagination, and manipulations

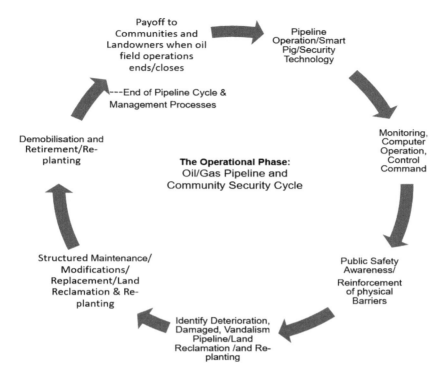

**Fig. 8.6** Pipeline operation and community development (*Source* Compiled by Author (2023))

of industry operators. This gap is closed in the new designs shown above. Although the stages TC Energy and Canada Energy Pipeline Association adopt might work in some climes like in Canada, empirical evidence suggests their designs may not completely apply or work in Nigeria. Given the peculiarity of the national political economy, social behaviors, security, and infrastructure as well as the character of the Nigerian state (Devold, 2013; Jega, 2000; Joseph, 2014). The differentiation and simplification of pipeline operation processes in a detailed manner would enlighten Bayelsa stakeholders especially the communities on pipeline operational processes and management.

Some of the professionals and communities say it would be harder to mobilise stakeholders' to support ideas that would chart a new course towards resolving vandalism and the oil and gas infrastructure insecurity problems. While corruption prevents the implementation of new oil and gas reforms leading to more hunger, poverty, and tensions. Environmental Pollution and damages provoke anger and vandalism. Operational blowouts weaken the pipelines and worsen the spate of vandalism. There is a strong case for increasing the role of communities to tackle the insecurity problems in the area. This will, however, require concerted efforts by the state and private sector to tackle rampant corruption and poor governance so that issues such as inequalities and poverty can be addressed. But communities must be at the heart of the way forward (Dodd, 2021). Durable infrastructure like bridges that link different isolated Islands and lagoons traversing Bayelsa communities, just like the pipelines do, would be a good starting point. This would trigger a new socio-economic equilibrium for the communities.

The data suggest that the problem is not a lack of oil and gas CSR initiatives, but the implementation process is compromised by the same incompetent political class that has corrupted the processes of implementing various petroleum industry regulatory guidelines. This has led to the failure of many CSR initiatives including corrupted compensation processes. Either compensation for lands with farms and private properties, polluted fishing waters, gas leaks, and/or the transparent use of the 13 percent royalty/derivatives designed to improve the lives of oil-producing states. Inadequate implementation of CSR principles in some communities or the complete lack of CSR initiative in most local communities heightens frustration and aggression and justifies the outcomes of the Community Neglect Aggression Displacement theory. This has significantly contributed to the hardship, tensions, and backwardness of displaced and/or neglected local communities (see Chapters 3 and 4). At the same time, the CSR intervention program has failed to achieve the desired outcomes and objectives in local communities. Due in part to a lack of commitment by oil and gas corporations, institutional influences, political manipulations and/or distractions, and a dearth of interface with civil society and NGO professional representatives. The corruption of the few privileged private oil and gas workers and contractors, as well as the government, some NGO activists, and community leaders, hinder the delivery of public good (Collier, 2007; Hoeffler, 2011; Ross, 2012). This further widens the socio-economic divide responsible for the inequalities that aggravate tensions. This leads to more frustration, aggression, and pipeline vandalism in Bayelsa and Nembe communities (Okumagba, 2012, 2022).

Why do criminal elements in local communities vandalise onshore oil and gas pipelines, particularly the NCTL resulting in oil spills and causing other insecurity problems? This study used two theories, FADT and CNADT, to explain why the NCTL pipeline is been vandalised exposing Bayelsa to insecurity problem. The first theory represents the frustration-aggression displacement theory proposed by Dollard et al. (1939) the author of this thesis proposes the CNADT. FADT argue that when the set objectives and self-esteem of an individual or collective are disrupted, they will instinctively react against the disruptor. When a collective is prevented from achieving their goals it harms its self-esteem which triggers an instinctive reaction against the original provocateur (Dollard et al., 1939; Okumagba, 2012; Sanderson, 2010). The instrumental laws and oil and gas regulatory guidelines designed for the operation of the oil and gas industry disrupt the way of life of all local communities. These instruments have caused socio-economic, and environmental disequilibrium as well as prevented the local communities from achieving their set objectives. This frustrates communities triggering aggression.

Preventing the local communities from participating in the oil and gas business and supply chain, obstructing access to farmlands and fishing waters due to pollution and acidification including the destruction of the mangrove forest hinders the socio-economic objective trajectory of the communities (see Chapters 3, 5, and 6). This means men and women in the local communities are unable to fend for themselves, their children, and their families which leads to frustration-aggression displacement. This is what is manifested in vandalism against pipelines and oil theft in Bayelsa (Dollard et al., 1939; Okumagba, 2012). As Lazarus argued, when an individual or collective community's self-esteem and ego are directly impacted by an external aggressor it will result in an instinctive aggressive reaction against the source of the original disruption (1994; Okumagba, 2012; Sanderson, 2010). This frustration is directly responsible for the vandalism and aggression reactions of the local communities against oil and gas infrastructure.

The Community Neglect-Aggression Displacement theory is the second theory that explains why the NCTL pipeline has been vandalised and caused other insecurity problems to occur in Bayelsa (Amnesty International, 2018; Hoeffler, 2011; Samuelson, 1954; see Chapter 3). It identified and explained the factors responsible for the vandalism of the NCTL pipeline causing insecurity problems in Bayelsa. CNADT's theoretical framework argues that failure to resolve many underlying socio-economic issues worsens the environmental devastation, impoverishment, and unemployment situations across local communities. Unresolved socio-economic and environmental issues lead to tensions that degenerate into insecurity problems (Langford, 1986). CNADT theory is used to explain the causes of onshore oil and gas pipeline vandalism; collective frustration-aggression; and infrastructure insecurity problems in the Niger Delta and Nigeria. The factors that cause onshore oil and gas pipeline vandalism and infrastructure insecurity problems, highlighted throughout this thesis, and the micro-foundational variables and triggers of those factors are found in the micro-foundational and operational variables that underpins CNADT.

The CNADT has some varied and wider implications on the evolving tensions and insecurity problems fast spreading across the six geopolitical zones of contemporary Nigeria. CNADT explains the Boko Haram terrorists in the northeast, militancy, pipeline vandalism and oil theft in the South-South Niger Delta, unknown gunmen in the Southeast, Banditry and largescale kidnappings in the northwest, Fulani herders' terrorism in the Middle belt, and kidnapping in the southwest region. The socio-economic, environmental, and political factors that lead to CNADT tendencies are similar to issues of poor governance, environmental degradation, and other factors that cause onshore pipeline vandalism. What this thesis is saying is that though some of the causes of onshore NCTL pipeline vandalism in Bayelsa share similar characteristics with those factors that trigger the CNADT, they result in a common outcome of reactive aggression. Despite having differing underlying root causes.

The deliberate neglect of the people and failure of the government, state, and federal institutions including private corporations in addressing the issues of poverty, unemployment, climate change, out-of-school children vise-a vise lack of access to education, and decreased households are sources of frustration. These trigger instinctive aggressive reactions. The collective neglect has triggered collective anger due to shared collective frustration leading to diverse forms of aggression and insecurity problems in the historic Niger Delta and the entire Nigeria. Particularly the insecurity and vandalism of the NCTL pipeline in the area of study. The wider implication of some aspects of the CNADT is that the factors could be logically generalised. Given that corruption, environmental disaster, and socio-political and economic inequalities are diffused across all the Niger

Delta states. Bell et al., (2018: 18) called this 'case-to-case transfer', which is generalising common similarities from one case to another case (state to state). The social and economic situations of the sample population interviewed in Bayelsa are broadly present across Nigeria and many other parts of the world.

Some of these neglects are a reflection of the colonial legacies demonstrated in the arbitrary and reactive policies of the Nigerian government, and the exclusion of the indigenous people from the political processes. The local communities in Nigeria, Myanmar, Venezuela, Colombia to name a few, in the Global South, are still prevented from participating in the oil and gas business chain. Thereby socio-economically emasculating the local communities. The various oil and gas multinational corporations demonstrate contemporary neocolonial and imperialist dominance of the oil and gas industry. First, the major multinational oil and gas operators like Shell, Chevron, BP, Addax, Total, and Mobil oil and gas corporations represent the interest of the colonial powers, and these are largely the new faces of contemporary imperialistic forces. Secondly, these private businesses have succeeded in ensuring that Nigeria does not refine oil and gas within its shores. The data suggest that they are complacent in aiding the export of stolen crude oil from Nigerian shores. Given that the large foreign Ocean Liners that export the stolen crude oil off the coast of Nigeria belong to the big western business conglomerates in the world. The stolen oil is sold at the western international oil market to the same western powers who are acutely aware of the footprint and origin of the crude oil. The western buyers of this illegal crude oil know it was stolen from Nigeria, but ignore that fact because it is sold to them and their proxies at a cheaper price. Most evidence shows that the majority of the illegally exported crude oil from Nigeria is bought and consumed by other countries, especially the Western nations.

## CONCLUSION

Many writers highlight various devastations caused by oil and gas exploration and production in Nigeria's Niger Delta, Myanmar, Sudan, Libya, South Africa, Niger, and Most GCC countries such as socio-economic exploitation and poverty (Alamieyeseigha, 2008a; Ibaba, 2012; Isidiho & Sabran, 2015; Okumagba, 2013). Environmental destruction, and pollution (Alagoa, 2005; Ite et al., 2018; Olawuyi, 2012; Sinden, 2009; UNSDG, 2016). Oil and gas ghost workers (Douglas & Okonta, 2003;

Ikelegbe, 2014; Okonjo-Iweala, 2018). Youth unemployment, violence, increase in household poverty, and destruction of natural and traditional sources of economic income and livelihood (Boro, 1982; Igbinovia, 2014; Madubuko, 2017; Nicholas et al., 2013; Saro-Wiwa, 1992). Interference with political institutions, and cultural and traditional disequilibrium (Alagoa, 1999, 2005; Ikein, 2008; Makholm, 2012). All these and many more are some of the fundamental ingredients that trigger the underlying causes of vandalism and onshore oil and gas pipeline infrastructure insecurity in Bayelsa State. The refusal to resolve these problems conversely intensifies anger and aggression toward pipelines. Although Nigeria is the largest producer of oil and gas resources in Africa and a force in the global hydrocarbon landscape. This feat has been marred by complex environmental and climatic impacts (Transparency International, 2020; UNEP, 2012).

Hardly has Nigeria's crude oil production capacity and those of many other countries in the Global South translated into physical and accelerated development for many of the population, particularly the local communities. After over 63 years of exploration, production, exportation, and earning huge revenue from crude oil and natural gas resources supported by intellectual capital and a workforce of national and international reckoning, Nigeria like many Global South countries faces worsening socio-economic realities. It is unintelligible to understand why Nigeria blames its colonial or the relics of imperialism and complex global technological and economic dynamics for its poor regulatory policy framework coupled with its abysmal structural-developmental backwardness. At the same time, the imperialists share part of the blame going by the cause-and-effect principle. Although my thesis has not focused on how the Western economies encourage the stealing of public monies from Nigeria.

But stealing public funds is inherently connected to corruption which has been discussed extensively in this thesis and thus ties in with this aspect of my conclusion. Given that the Western economies have consistently looked away, Nigerian political and business oligarchs, advertently or inadvertently see such a posture as encouraging them to steal and launder public funds and finances into Western banks, which they have indeed done (Enweremadu, 2013; Jatto et al., 2023). Some of these banks are in London, Switzerland, and other Western financial capitals (Enweremadu, 2013; Mimiko & Olawadayisi, 2016). The sophisticated Western banking systems and intelligence infrastructure hardly question, apply transparency and due diligence or reject laundered funds from Nigeria's public officials and politicians and those from elsewhere. If the Western banks had prevented laundered monies from Nigeria from entering their private banks, Nigeria's public officers and politically exposed persons would have probably been disinterested in the mindless and reckless stealing of public funds from Nigeria (Jatto et al., 2023).

The idea of many Western financial regulatory frameworks allowing laundered public funds into banks in capital cities before later seizing the money has not discouraged but rather has encouraged the mindless plundering of public coffers and treasury in Nigeria (Enweremadu, 2013). Drawing on this aspect of corruption, every stratum of Nigerian social class should share in the blame and be held accountable for the contemporary shambolic state of socio-economic, political, and insecurity problems that Nigeria has found itself. Rather than blame it all on natural resources and/or energy dynamics. The question is, to what extent is the historical background and failure of past political regimes relevant to the current oil and gas infrastructure insecurity problems in Bayelsa (Alamieyeseigha, 2008a; Willink Commission Report, 1958)? Should references not also be made to the divergent roles played by local communities and their leaders? There should also be a sincere national discussion on ethnicity paradox, nepotism, military incursions, religious interference and manipulations, and the influence of socio-cultural leaning. All of this camouflage themselves within the implementation of regulatory policy frameworks. Including the implementation of the federal character principle in the name of national cohesion that results in the emergence and sometimes appointment of mediocre, incompetent, wicked, and unpatriotic public officials (see Demarest al., 2020).

Many researchers on Niger Delta oil and gas conflicts and insecurity problems such as Mathias, Onuoha, Alamieyeseigha, Douglas, and Okonta as well as Oriola have not explored a range of underlying socio-economic, poor governance, environmental conditions, and politics as responsible for the vandalism of the NCTL pipeline. Development economists like Collier (2003, 2007); Collier & Hoeffler (2004); have elaborated extensively on some of these issues like socio-economic and poor governance. The Adelphi Papers (original policy-related monograph series that publishes the academic research of the International Institute for Strategic Studies), also, examined links between economic development and social tensions. Most scholars prefer to concentrate on the political economy perspective (Igwe, 2020) while others on socio-economic dimensions (Okumagba, 2013; Onuoha, 2008). However, this research explored the borderline areas. It drew on inferences from both political and socio-economic, and environmental factors and linked them to structural issues to analyse the causes of onshore pipeline vandalism, and oil and gas infrastructure insecurity. Based on the research findings, it has become obsolete and rhetorical to lay the entire blame for socio-economic stagnation, pipeline vandalism, and oil and gas infrastructure insecurity in the historic Niger Delta at the doorstep of a few disgruntled community members. Including the neglected local communities, or some youths (Igbinovia, 2014; Mathias, 2015; Onuoha, 2008; Saro-Wiwa, 1992).

The entire stakeholders of Nigeria's petroleum industry such as the government, regulatory authorities, multinational and indigenous oil and gas corporations, some professional civil society groups, some community leaders, some youth groups, the security architecture, contractors, and regulators all play a contributory role. They have all provoked the underlying issues that influence the CNADT factors that cause insecurity and pipeline vandalism, but some are much more prominent than others (see Chapter 3). This is against the popular perception that insecurity and pipeline vandalism problems in Bayelsa and the oil and gas industry were squarely caused by the government and/or oil and gas companies alone (Alagoa, 2005; Alamieyeseigha, 2008b; Douglas & Okonta, 2003; see Chapter 2). *The onshore oil and gas infrastructure insecurity nexus* is coined by this researcher to define the forward and backward correlation between the factors that cause vandalism and the underlying micro foundational variables and triggers of the factors causing vandalism. The failure to address decreased household income, poverty, and social inequality issues conversely intensify and worsens poor governance—recycling of wicked and incompetent leaders—which this thesis referred to as *cursed leadership*, economic, and environmental factors. These underlying issues that cause tensions and violence have forward and backward correlation with the outcomes of insecurity and vandalism. This is not only in Bayelsa State but also across the entire historic Niger Delta, and the Global South. The factors that cause vandalism and oil and infrastructure insecurity are reinforced.

To that extent, this thesis partly disagrees with Michael Ross's "oil curse hypothesis" that says petro-rich countries were less democratic with frequent civil wars than those without crude oil (2012). And Collier's "resource curse hypothesis," notes that many low-income commodities export countries will experience slower economic growth than those with fewer resources (2008). As well as those who argued that the reason for tensions, underdevelopment, and insecurity in the Niger Delta region of Nigeria is due to poor governance and corruption. This thesis argues throughout that crude oil and gas and/or other resources left under-ground are not a curse by themselves nor cause underdevelopment and tensions. But the combination of poor governance and wicked and incom-petent leadership—this thesis coined as the *leadership curse hypothesis* is the problem causing and intensifying insecurity in Nigeria.

The leadership curse is coined to describe the cyclical emergence of successive Nigerian leaders who invoke a perpetual supernatural power that makes them inflict harm to Nigerian citizens and on Nigeria. It is beyond normal to persistently witness or experience the emergence of many political and corporate leaders who continually steal and cart away public funds year-in-year-out throughout different regimes without ever getting tired (Jatto et al., 2023). Even though they are acutely aware that their wicked intentions and actions against Nigeria and Nige-rians truncate socio-economic growth and infrastructure development in terms of spreading the common good (see Chapters 2, 3, and 4). It is the frequency of the emergence of such wicked leaders into the socio-economic and political space of Nigeria and other countries in the Global South that makes it a *leadership curse*. This continues to harm the collec-tive progress the Global South and thereby heightening tensions and insecurity problems of both humans and infrastructures (see Chapters 2, 3, and 4).

The different impacts and benefits that the professional and community sector derive or suffer from petroleum activities influenced the pattern and way they narrated their stories. They all narrated their experiences from different perspectives. The findings suggest that the professional and community respondents did not inherently differ on the combination of underlying issues that trigger those factors mentioned above which leads to vandalism. The theme represents the local provocateurs that trigger frustration leading to the vandalism of the NCTL and onshore oil and gas infrastructure insecurity. While it is difficult to say whether the different narrative of the professional respondents was due to a lack of a unifying framework. It is uncertain whether the views from different sectors of the community would advertently force the government, oil pipeline, and environmental regulators as well as oil and gas corporations to be more professional and ethical in their interaction with the local communities and the environment. Also, it is hard to say whether the professional and community narrations would trigger systematic and institutional change and reforms to occur.

As exhaustively discussed throughout this thesis, political corruption, and its underpinnings is responsible for Nigeria's socio-economic, human, and infrastructure insecurity problems. This laid, feeds, and maintains the foundation that has sustained a "vicious circle of accursed leadership" in Nigeria (see Chapter 3 on Nembe-Ewelesuo). This is reflected in decades of environmental pollution, secrecy in oil and gas theft and accrued revenue data, community neglect, ignoring of the structural integrity of pipeline structures, a dearth of socio-economic and political resources, and engineered social injustice and compensation problems. Every factor that causes vandalism of the NCTL and oil and gas infrastructure insecurity in the case study area is either directly or indirectly linked to the corrosive political corruption that is bedeviling Nigeria. The character of the state, ethnicity and religious paradoxes, and the political economy reflect and mirror the intricate essence of political corruption. The tensions, militancy, kidnapping, onshore oil and gas pipeline infrastructure insecurity, oil theft, communal crisis, socio-economic stagnation of Nembe, Bayelsa, the historic Niger Delta region, and indeed the entire Nigerian state is put on the doorstep of political corruption.

## RECOMMENDATIONS

This book has achieved its initial objectives and questions overarching the central question of oil and gas pipeline infrastructure insecurity-focusing on vandalism, threats, and conflicts in the case study area of Bayelsa Nembe in the Niger Delta and the Global South. All the participants approached took part, except the operations director and production manager in Nigeria Agip oil company-Eni. The data gathered and analysed were comprehensive and robust enough to analyse each of the four objectives set out in Chapter 1 and re-emphasised in the earlier part of this chapter. The effective participation of senior executive professionals in oil and gas, security officials, and professional civil society representatives on one hand and critical community stakeholders kings, paramount rulers, chiefs, youth leaders, and local NGOs on the other enabled this book to bring together professional and community perspectives of oil and gas pipeline infrastructure insecurity in the Niger Delta and informed conclusion of tensions and insecurity happening in the wider petrostates in the Global South.

It makes recommendations in two key areas of pipeline operations and management, and regulatory policy frameworks. Aspects of critical security theories propose a different route to approach security issues (Browning & McDonald, 2011). The relationships between societies and their various population groups are inseparable from their developmental processes and agendas. It is important to think of the meaning of security within the context of politics and ethics, and develop new approaches to understanding and achieving security in Bayelsa and the historic Niger Delta region. This book makes the following recommendations: It recommends that the Nigerian government grants Special Status Recognition (SSR) to all oil and gas communities in the Niger Delta. This will mandate the authorities and oil companies to accelerate infrastructure development like roads, public housing units, among others in the region. SSR should mandate the afforestation of deforested lands, with mangrove trees, flora, fauna, and green vegetation to aid the de-carbonisation of the region (a Marshal Plan). As well as re-breeding aquatic life, fish, and other marine species to restore nature and boost socio-economic and cultural activities.

Further, evidence-based research data should be used to create oil and gas legislation, law, and policy regulations to demonstrate relevance to the broader realities across communities which will encourage support during implementation. Also, the government should create the Niger Delta Environmental Restoration Development Commission (NDERDC). The NDERDC will focus mainly on the restoration of every inch of the devastated environment and ecosystem within a 20 years' time frame to forestall the impact of climate change. NDERDC should focus specifically on the coastal Niger Delta states to reverse and restore the 60 years of environmental damage that has put it six decades behind other regions in Nigeria. And ensure an accelerated reconstruction. This will justify the appreciation of the huge revenue that the crude oil extracted from the area has earned for Nigeria. The infrastructure development should be enhanced with 15 percent derivation to oil-producing states.

Finally, the Niger Delta Development Commission-NDDC Act should be repealed. The NDDC should be disentangled from all forms of political influences while undertaking a comprehensive reform of infrastructure Development Agencies. The proposed new Niger Delta development agencies like NDERDC should be administered by professional independent civil society representatives and high-profile community members.

Their positions should be rotated every two years. The board of the above body should report directly to houses of assembly in the historic Niger Delta states, and the federal judiciary for oversight functions. This will significantly reduce the political influence of the Presidency, state government, national assembly as well as oil companies. This will help focus and deliver a people-oriented infrastructure development program, at record spread, to local communities that have been left behind.

## REFERENCES

Abidde, S. O. (2017). *Nigeria's Niger Delta: Militancy, Amnesty, and the Post Amnesty Environment*. Lexington.

Akpan, U. (2021). 1.1bn OML 17 Development, Operations will Boost Local Content. *Vanguard News*. https://www.vanguardngr.com/2021/01/1-1bn-oml-17-development-operations-will-boost-local-content-rewane/. Accessed 22 January 2021.

Alagoa, E. J. (1999). *The Land and People of Bayelsa State: Central Niger Delta*. Onyema Research Publications.

Alagoa, E. J. (2005). *A History of the Niger Delta*. Onyema Research Publications.

Alamieyeseigha, D. S. P. (2008a). The Environmental Challenge of Developing the Niger Delta. In S. S. Azaiki, D. S. P. Alamieyeseigha, & A. A. Ikein (Eds.), *Oil, Democracy and the Promise of True Federalism in Nigeria* (pp. 249–260). University Press of America.

Alamieyeseigha, D. S. P. (2008b). The Niger Delta: Treasure Base of Energies. In S. Azaika, A. A. Ikein, & D. S. P. Alamieyeseigha (Eds.), *Oil Democracy and the Promise of True Federalism in Nigeria* (pp. 290–310). University Press of America.

Amundsen, I. (2019). Extractive and Power-Preserving Political Corruption. In I. Amundsen (Ed.), *Political Corruption in Africa: An Extraction and Power Preservation* (pp. 1–28). Elgar.

Amnesty International Report, (2018). *Amnesty International Report 2017/18: The State of the World's Human Rights*, Available from https://www.amnesty.org/en/documents/pol10/6700/2018/en/ Accessed 7 May 2024

Anand, V., & Ashforth, B. E. (2003). The Normalization of Corruption in Organisations. In *Research in Organisational Behaviour* (Vol. 25, pp. 1–52). Elsevier.

Anderson, C. A., & Dill, J. C. (1995). Effects of Frustration Justification on Hostile Aggression. *Aggressive Behaviour, 21*(5), 359–369.

Azubuike, V. (2021). International Court Orders Shell to Compensate Niger-Delta Communities over Oil Spillage. *Daily Post News*. https://dailypost.ng/2021/01/29/breaking-international-court-orders-shell-to-compensate-niger-delta-communities-over-oil-spillage/. Accessed 30 January 2021.

Bell, E., Bryman, A., & Harley, B. (2018). *Business Research Methods* (5th ed.). Oxford University Press.

Bello, S. (1964). *Herzog*. Penguin Press.

Bergstresser, H. (2017). *A Decade of Nigeria: Politics, Economy and Society 2004–2016*. Brill.

Berkowitz, L. (2011). A Cognitive-No Association Theory of Aggression. In A. W. Kruglanski, P. A. M. Van Lange, & E. T. Higgins (Eds.), *The Handbook of Theories of Social Psychology* (pp. 90–120). Sage.

Berkowitz, L. (1993). *Aggression: Its Causes, Consequences, and Control*. McGraw-Hill.

Boro, I. (1982). *The Twelve-day Revolution*. Idodo Umeh.

Browning, S. C., & McDonald, M. (2011). The Future of Critical Security Studies: Ethics and the Politics of Security. *European Journal of International Relations, 19*(2), 220–230.

Bushman, B. J., Anderson, C. A., & Allen, J. J. (2018). The General Aggression Model. *Current Opinions in Psychology Journal, 9*, 75–80.

Canada Energy Pipeline Association. (2016). Five Phases of the Pipeline Life Circle. https://www.aboutpipelines.com/en/blog/five-phases-of-the-pipeline-life-cycle/. Accessed 9 August 2020.

Coleman, J. S. (2015). The Politics of Sub-Saharan Africa. In A. G. Almond & J. S. Coleman (Eds.), *The Politics of the Developing Areas* (pp. 247–354). Princeton University Press.

Collier, P. (2003). *Breaking the Conflict Trap: Civil Wars and Development Policy*. Oxford University Press.

Collier, P. (2007). *The Bottom Billion* (pp. 39–52). Oxford University Press.

Collier, P., & Hoeffler, A. E. (2004). *Greed and Grievance in Civil War*. World Bank Development Research Group.

Demarest, L., Langer, A., & Ukiwo, U. (2020). Nigeria's Federal Character Commission (FCC): A Critical Appraisal. *Oxford Development Studies, 48*(4), 315–328.

Devold, H. (2013). *Oil and Gas Production Handbook: An Introduction to Oil and Gas Production* (pp. 6–146). ABB. https://library.e.abb.com/public/34d5b70e18f7d6c8c1257be500438ac3/Oil%20and%20gas%20production%20handbook%20ed3x0_web.pdf. Accessed 12 December 2017.

Dodd, V. (2021, April 18). Tackling Poverty and Inequality to Reduce Crime, Says Police Chief. *The Guardian News*. https://www.theguardian.com/uk-news/2021/apr/18/tackle-poverty-and-inequality-to-reduce-says-police-chief. Accessed 18 April 2021.

Dollard, J., Miller, N. E., Doob, L. W., Mowrer, O. H., & Sears, R. R. (1939). *Frustration and Aggression.* Yale University Press.

Douglas, O., & Okonta, I. (2003). *Where Vultures Feast: Shell, Human Rights, and Oil in the Niger Delta.* Verso.

Ekpenyong, A. S. (2010). The Oil Economy, Environmental Laws, and Human Rights Violations in Niger Delta Region: Implications and Suggested Solutions. *International Journal of Social Policy Research and Development, 1*(2).

Enweremadu, D. (2013). Nigeria's Quest to Recover Looted Assets: The Abacha Affair. *African Spectrum Journal, 48*(2), 51–70.

Esiedesa, O. (2021). Nigeria Earned $418.5bn in 10 Years from Petroleum, NEITI Reveals. *Vanguard News.* https://www.vanguardngr.com/2021/06/nigeria-earned-418-5bn-in-10yrs-from-petroleum-neiti-reveals/. Accessed 19 June 2021.

Etemire, U. (2016). *Law and Practice on Public Participation in Environmental Matters: The Nigerian Example in Transnational Comparative Perspective.* Routledge.

Etowah, U. E., & Effiong, S. A. (2012). Oil Spillage Cost Gas Flaring Cost, and Life Expectancy Rate of the Niger Delta People of Nigeria. *Advances in Management and Applied Economics Journal, 2*(2), 211–228.

Gurr, R. T. (2015). *Political Rebellion: Causes, Outcomes and Alternatives.* Routledge.

Higgins, P. (2010). *Eradicating Ecocide: Laws and Governance to Stop the Destruction of the Planet.* Shepheard-Walwyn.

Hoeffler, A. (2011). Greed Versus Grievance: A Useful Conceptual Distinction in the Study of Civil War? *Studies in Ethnicity and Nationalism Journal, 11*(2), 274–284.

Ibaba, I. S. (2009). Violent Conflicts and Sustainable Development in Bayelsa State. *Review of African Political Economy,* (122), 555–573.

Ibaba, I. S. (2012). Introduction: Interrogating Development Deficits in the Niger Delta. In S. I. Ibaba (Ed.), *Niger Delta: Constraints and Pathways to Development* (pp. 1–9). Newcastle upon Tyne.

Igbinovia, P. E. (2014). *Oil Thefts and Pipeline Vandalisation in Nigeria.* African Books.

Igwe, U. (2020). *A Political Economy Perspective on Oil and Conflict in Nigeria's Niger Delta.* The London School of Economics and Political Science. https://www.blogs.lse.ac.uk/africaatlse/2020/09/16/political-economy-perspective-oil-conflict-security-nigeria-niger-delta/. Accessed 2 November 2021.

Ikein, A. (2008). Introduction to Nigeria and the Politics of Niger Delta. In D. S. P. Alamieyeseigha, S. Azaika, & A. A. Ikein (Eds.), *Oil Democracy and the Promise of True Federalism in Nigeria* (pp. 2–20). University Press of America.

Ikelegbe, O. A. (2014). The Resource Curse: Oil, Communal Agitation and State Repression in the Niger Delta. In O. A. Ikelegbe (Ed.), *Oil, Environmental and Resource Conflicts in Nigeria* (pp. 109–142). Lit Verlag.

Ioannides, E. (2017). *Fundamental Principles of EU Law Against Money Laundering*. Routledge.

Isidiho, A. O., & Sabran, M. S. B. (2015). Socio-Economic Impact of Niger Delta Development Commission (NDDC) Infrastructural Projects in Selected Communities in Imo State Nigeria. *Asian Journal of Humanities and Social Sciences, 3*(2), 109–115.

Ite, A. E., Harry, T. A., Obadimu, C. O., & Inim, I. J. (2018). Petroleum Hydrocarbons Contaminations of Surface Water and Ground Water in the Niger Delta Region of Nigeria. *Journal of Environment Pollution and Human Health, 6*(2), 51–61.

Jatto, A. A., Skoczylis, J., & Horner, G. (2023). UK Anti-Money Laundering and Counter-Terrorist Financing Measures. In S. N. Romaniuk, C. Kaunert, & A. P. H. Fabe (Eds.), *Countering Terrorist and Criminal Financing* (1st ed.), Routledge & CRC Press. https://doi.org/10.4324/9781003092216. Accessed 18 November 2023.

Jega, A. (2000). The State and Identity Transformation under Structural Adjustment in Nigeria. In A. Jega (Eds.), *Identity Transformation and Identity Politics Under Structural Adjustment in Nigeria* (pp. 24–40). Nordic African Institute.

Joseph, R. A. (2014). *Democracy and Prebendal Politics in Nigeria*. Cambridge University Press.

Kee, C. (2012). *Global Sales and Contract Law*. Oxford University Press.

Krueger, I. J. (1996). Probabilistic National Stereotypes. *European Journal of Social Psychology, 26*, 960–985.

Langford, P. (1986). *Modern Philosophies of Human Nature: Their Emergence from Christian Thoughts*. Lancaster.

Lasswell, H. D. (1936). *Politics: Who Gets What, When, How*. McGraw-Hill.

Lasswell, H. D. (2018). *Politics: Who Gets What, When, How*. Papamoa Press.

Lazarus, R. S. (1994). *Emotion and Adaptation*. Oxford University Press.

Leipziger, D. (2017). *The Corporate Responsibility Code Book*. Routledge.

Linden, O., & Palsson, J. (2013). Oil Contamination in Ogoniland Niger Delta, Stockholm. *The Royal Swedish Academy of Sciences Journal, 42*(6), 685–701.

Loft, P., & Brien, P. (2023, September). Halfway to 2023: The Sustainable Development Goals. *UK House of Commons Library*. https://commonslibrary.parliament.uk/halfway-to-2030-the-sustainable-development-goals/. 31 October 2023.

Lynch, M. J., Stretesky, P. B., & Long, M. A. (2015). *Defining Crime: A Critique of the Concept and Its Implication.* Palgrave Macmillan.

Madubuko, C. C. (2017). Oiling the Guns and Gunning for Oil: The Youths and Niger Delta Oil Conflicts in Nigeria. In E. M. Mbah & T. Falola (Eds.), *Dissent, Protest and Dispute in Africa* (pp. 260–289). Routledge.

Makholm, J. D. (2012). *The Political Economy of Pipelines: A Century of Comparative Institutional Development.* University of Chicago Press.

Mathias, Z. (2015). Providing All-Round Security against Oil and Gas Infrastructure Sabotage and Physical Attacks on the Staff of NNPC and Multinational Oil Companies in Nigeria as a Critical Article of Her National Security Efforts. *International Journal of Social Science and Humanities Research, 3*(2), 45–59.

Mickolus, E. (2018). *Terrorism Worldwide, 2016.* McFarland and Company.

Mimiko, M. O., & Olawadayisi, A. O. (2016). Effects of Money Laundering on the Economy of Nigeria. *Beijing Law Review, 7*(2).

Neumann, M., & Elsenbroich, C. (2017). Introduction: The Societal Dimensions of Organised Crime. *Trends in Organised Crime, 20,* 1–15.

Nicholas, A., Mitchell, J., & Lindner, S. (2013). *Consequences of Long-Term Unemployment.* The Urban Institute.

Nye, S. J. (1967). Corruption and Political Development: A Cost-Benefit Analysis. *American Political Science Review, 61*(2), 417–427.

O'Connor, B. (2022). *The ESG Investment Handbook: Insights and Developments in Environmental, Social and Governance Investment.* Harriman House.

Ochayi, C., & Eromosele, F. (2021). PIB: FG Holds Summit on Artisanal, Modular Refineries Operations. *Vanguard News.* https://www.vanguardngr.com/2021/03/pib-fg-holds-summit-on-artisanal-modular-refineries-operat ions/. Accessed 2 June 2021.

Ogbeidi, M. M. (2012). Political Leadership and Corruption in Nigeria since 1960: A Socio-economics Analysis. *Journal of Nigerian Studies, 1*(2), 1–24.

Oil Pipeline Act. (2004). Chapter 338: Laws of the Federal Republic of Nigeria. https://www.chr.up.ac.za/images/researchunits/bhr/files/extrac tive_industries_database/nigeria/laws/Oil%20Pipelines%20Act.pdf. Accessed 28 March 2020.

Okonjo-Iweala, N. (2018). *Fighting Corruption is Dangerous: The Story Behind the Headlines.* MIT Press.

Okonofua, B. A. (2016). The Niger Delta Amnesty Program: The Challenges of Transitioning from Peace Settlements to Long-Term Peace. *Sage Open Journals, 6*(2), 1–16.

Okonta, I. (2016). Policy Incoherence and the Challenge of Energy Security. In A. Goldthau (Ed.), *The Handbook of Global Energy Policy* (pp. 501–520). Wiley.

Okumagba, P. (2012). Oil Exploration and Crisis in the Niger Delta: The Response of the Militia Groups. *Journal of Sustainable Society, 1*(3), 78–83.

Okumagba, P. (2013). Ethnic Militia and Criminality in the Niger Delta. *International Review of Social Sciences and Humanities, 5*(1), 239–246.

Okumagba, E. O. (2022), Examine Global Court Practices in Reducing Climate Change Impacts through Litigation: Lessons for Nigeria, E. O. Ekhator, S. Miller and E. Igbinovia (eds.), *Implementing the Sustainable Development Goals in Nigeria: Barriers, Prospects, and Strategies*, London, Routledge, pp.98–118

Olawuyi, D. S. (2012). Legal and Sustainable Development Impacts of Major Oil Spills. *The Journal of Sustainable Development, 9*(1), 1–15.

Onakpohor, A., Fakinle, B. S., Sonibare, J. A., Oke, A. M., & Akeredolu, A. F. (2020). Investigation of Air Emissions from Artisanal Petroleum Refineries in the Niger Delta Nigeria. *Heliyon Journal, 6*(11), 1–9.

Onuoha, C. F. (2008). Oil Pipeline Sabotage in Nigeria: Dimensions, Actors and Implications for National Security. *African Security Review, 17*(3), 100–115.

Onuoha, C. F. (2016). *The Resurgence of Militancy in Nigeria's Oil-Rich Niger Delta and the Dangers of Militarisation*. Al Jazeera Centre for Studies.

Oyadongha, S. (2021). We are Seeking International Help to Stop Nembe Oil Spill. *Vanguard News*. https://www.vanguardngr.com/2021/11/were-seeking-international-help-to-stop-nembe-oil-spill-aiteo/. Accessed 21 November 2021.

Ross, M. L. (2012). *The Oil Curse: How Petroleum Wealth Shape the Development of Nations*. Princeton University Press.

Samuelson, P. A. (1954). The Pure Theory of Public Expenditure. *Review of Economics and Statistics Journal, 36*(4), 387–389.

Sanderson, C. A. (2010). *Social Psychology*. Wiley.

Saro-Wiwa, K. (1992). *Genocide in Nigeria: The Ogoni Tragedy*. African Books.

Shastry, V. (2023). *The Notorious ESG: Business, Climate, and the Race to Save the Planet*. Emerald.

Sinden, A. (2009). An Emerging Human Rights to Security from Climate Change: The Case Against Gas Flaring in Nigeria. In W. C. G. Burns & H. M. Osofsky (Eds.), *Adjudicating Climate Change: State, National, and International Approaches* (pp. 173–192). Cambridge University Press.

Transparency International. (2019). Military Involvement in Oil Theft in the Niger Delta. https://ti-defence.org/publications/military-involvement-in-oil-theft-in-the-niger-delta/. Accessed 25 November 2020.

Transparency International. (2020). Corruption Perception Index 2020. https://www.transparency.org/en/cpi/2021. Accessed 24 November 2020.

Transparency International. (2021). Corruption Perception Index 2021: Sub-Saharan Africa: How does your Country Measure Up?. https://images.transparencycdn.org/images/CPI2021_Report_EN-web.pdf. Accessed 19 April 2022.

Tysiachniouk, M. S. (2020). Disentangling Benefit-Sharing Complexities of Oil Extraction on the North Slope of Alaska. *Sustainability Journal, 12*(13), 1–31.

Ubong, U. I., Chibuogwu, E., Aroh, K. N., Umo-Otong, J. C., Harry, I. M., & Gobo, A. E. (2010). Oil Spill Incidents and Pipeline Vandalisation in Nigeria: Impact on Public Health and Negation to Attainment of Millennium Development Goals: The Ishiagu Example. *Disaster Prevention, and Management International Journal, 19*(1), 70–87.

United Nations Environment Programme Report. (2012). Environmental Assessment of Ogoniland: Assessment of Vegetation, Aquatic and Public Health Issues. http://hdl.handle.net/20.500.11822/25286. Accessed 9 May 2018.

United Nations Office on Drugs and Crime. (2019). *Corruption in Nigeria: Pattern and Trends: Second Survey on Corruption as Experienced by the Population.* https://www.unodc.org/documents/data-and-analysis/statis tics/corruption/nigeria/Corruption_in_Nigeria_2019_standard_res_11MB. pdf. Accessed 16 October 2021.

United Nations Sustainable Development Goals. (2016). The Sustainable Development Agenda. https://www.un.org/sustainabledevelopment/dev elopment-agenda-retired/#:~:text=%E2%97%8F,future%20for%20people% 20and%20planet. Accessed 31 October 2023.

Utebor, S. (2021). Shell, Bayelsa Communities at Loggerheads Over Oil Spillages. *The Nations.* https://thenationonlineng.net/. Accessed 2 November 2021.

Willink Commission Report. (1958). *Nigeria: Report of the Commission Appointed to Inquire into the Fears of Minorities and the Means of Allaying them.* Her Majesty's Stationary Office.

# Appendix A

© The Editor(s) (if applicable) and The Author(s), under exclusive
license to Springer Nature Switzerland AG 2024
A. L. A. Jatto, *Oil and Gas Pipeline Infrastructure Insecurity*,
New Security Challenges,
https://doi.org/10.1007/978-3-031-56932-6

UNIVERSITY OF
LINCOLN

# RISK ASSESSMENT SUMMARY SHEET

## 1. Location

| Campus: Brayford Pool | Assessment Date: February 2018 |
|---|---|
| Department/Faculty: School of Social and Political Sciences | Re-assessment Date: |
| Building/Area: BH2105 | Risk assessment team members: |
| | Dr. Joshua Skoczylis and Dr. Andrew Defty |

**Accountable Manager:** Prof. Jacqui Briggs

## 2. Details of further action necessary to control risk (with dates)

| Task | Action | Who is Responsible | Date |
|---|---|---|---|
| To conduct field interviews in Bayelsa state | Undertake risk assessment before traveling to Bayelsa state | J. Skoczylis | 28/02/2018 |

## 3. Summary of risks (with controls in place)

| Assessment of risk | Low | X | Medium | | High | | Very High | |
|---|---|---|---|---|---|---|---|---|

| Risk to Pregnant Workers? | Yes | No | X |
|---|---|---|---|
| Or to Disabled Workers? | Yes | No | X |

## 4. Evaluation

This assessment is an accurate statement of the known hazards, risks, and precautions. I certify that the control measures will prevent or, if this is not possible, control the risk subject to the level shown in section 3 (above) and that staff will be adequately trained and supervised, and the identified control measures implemented. The contents of this assessment will be communicated to staff and all relevant persons.

| Signature of Assessor: | Date: |
|---|---|
| Signature of Accountable Manager (if not Assessor): | Date: |

Severity of Injury/Loss/Harm (S)

| 1 | Minor | Mild bruising, minor cuts, mild chemical irritation to eyes or skin. No absence from work or absence of less than 3 days. | Minor property damage |
|---|---|---|---|
| 2 | Serious | Loss of consciousness, burns, breaks or injury resulting in absence from work for more than 3 days. Other non-permanent chemical effects. | Serious property damage confined to the workroom or area |
| 3 | Major | Permanent disability or other reportable injury or disease. | Major property damage affecting the |

Probability of Injury/Loss/Harm (P)

| 1 | Very Unlikely |
|---|---|
| 2 | Possible |
| 3 | Probable |

## Risk Assessment Detail Sheet

**General hazards**

| Task | Hazard | Who might be harmed | Before Controls (Initial risk) | | | Control Measures (Existing) | Control Measures (Proposed) | After Controls (Revised risk) | | Overall Risk |
|---|---|---|---|---|---|---|---|---|---|---|
| | | | P[1] | S[1] | 3+ | | | P | S | P X S |
| Interviews in Bayelsa | Familiar with the state and region | Investigator and participants | 1 | 1 | 2 | The visible presence of a joint security task force (military, police, Navy, and Civil defence) in the state. Oil and gas firms have their security apparatus. | Subsisting security arrangements are good enough including adding the on-site risk assessment by the security and petroleum sectors | 1 | 1 | 2 |
| | | Investigator and participants | 1 | 1 | 1 | The investigator and participants will adhere to the latest security tips given by the gatekeepers and their lead contacts within the sample groups about the environment | Subsisting security arrangements are good enough including adding the on-site risk assessment by the security and petroleum sectors | 1 | 1 | 2 |
| Travel to Bayelsa | Failure to adhere to security plans | Investigator and participants | 1 | 1 | 1 | Investigator and participants MUST follow security advice from lead contacts within each sample group | Subsisting security arrangements are good enough including adding the on-site risk assessment by the security and petroleum sectors | 1 | 1 | 2 |
| Open discussions with gatekeepers and prepare for Bayelsa's visit | Cutting communication links with gatekeepers/lead contacts within the sample groups | Investigator and participants | 1 | 1 | 1 | Follow local and national news updates and information from gatekeepers and their contacts within the sample groups about security in the region | Subsisting security arrangements are good enough including adding the on-site risk assessment by the security and petroleum sectors | 1 | 1 | 2 |

| Flight to Nigeria and hire a vehicle to Bayelsa | Private drive to Bayelsa State | Investigator | 2 | 2 | 4 | Follow local and national news updates and information from gatekeepers about the region | Subsisting security arrangements are good enough including, adding the on-site risk assessment by the security and petroleum sectors | 1 | 1 | 2 |
|---|---|---|---|---|---|---|---|---|---|---|
| Safety whilst in Bayelsa | Accidents, and other Unforeseen emergencies | Investigator and participants | 2 | 2 | 3 | There is professional medical personnel on the ground working with the security and oil and gas sectors. Call contacts introduced by the gatekeepers including national emergency on 112 or 199 in case of fire, police assistance, and ambulance services. | Subsisting security arrangements are good enough including, adding the on-site risk assessment by the security and petroleum sectors | 2 | 2 | 3 |

**Risk Assessment:**    Low [X]  Medium [ ]  High [ ]

Highest Score on any line [4]

| Score | Overall Risk | Acceptability |
|---|---|---|
| 1 – 5 | Low risk | Reasonably acceptable risk. Modify wherever possible. Implement control measures. Monitor. |
| 6 – 12 | Medium risk | Tolerable risk. Review and modify wherever possible. Enforce control measures. Review regularly. Monitor. |
| 13 – 16 | Very High risk | Unacceptable risk. Stop work and modify urgently. Enforce control measures. |

# Appendix B

**Participants Information Sheet**
(The data used for this book is derived from my Ph.D. research at the University of Lincoln, UK).
**The Research Title:** The Causes of Onshore Oil and Gas Pipeline Infrastructure Insecurity Problems in Historic Niger Delta Region.

**Introducing the Study:**

My name is Abraham Abdul Jatto a doctoral research candidate in Politics at the School of Social and Political Sciences at the University of Lincoln United Kingdom. The purpose of this research is to explore the scale and causes of onshore oil and gas pipeline infrastructure insecurity in the historic Niger Delta particularly the Nembe Creek Trunk Line (NCTL). Since the NCTL became operational, the pipeline has been destroyed over 220 times, causing ecological and socio-economic damage to the local communities.

**Participation:**

This research would involve a tape-recorded face-to-face interview. Participants for the interview exercises will be selected from three groups of the oil and gas sector, the security, and local communities to give the researcher different perspectives on the Bayelsa security question focusing on the insecurity of pipeline infrastructure. You have been invited to take part in this face-to-face tape-recorded interview because you belong to one of these groups and hence might have some understanding and

A. L. A. Jatto, *Oil and Gas Pipeline Infrastructure Insecurity*,
New Security Challenges,
https://doi.org/10.1007/978-3-031-56932-6

knowledge of the scale of onshore pipeline insecurity across communities in the state. The United Niger Delta Energy Development Security Strategy (UNDEDSS) NGO was the primary gatekeeper for the study. Please note that participation is completely voluntary and you can refuse to participate or answer any question. The interview will take about 30–40 minutes and will comprise questions about the scale and causes of oil and gas pipeline insecurity in Bayelsa state and its impact on local communities. You can stop the interview at any time. After the interview, a verbatim written record will be created, and you will receive a copy of the transcript to review. After receiving the transcript, you will have 21 days to withdraw from the research. After this time frame, it will be at the discretion of the researcher to decide whether the verbatim written record created from the interview will be withdrawn or not.

**Data Handling/Confidentiality and Anonymity**

The data and any personal information gathered from you will be kept confidential and stored securely and I will be the only person that can access it. Your personal information and data will not be used for anything different in line with the confidentiality principles of the National Committee on Human Research Ethics (NCHRE) in Nigeria and the European Union's General Data Protection Regulation (GDPR) legislation. A review of the data will occur regularly and any data that is no longer needed will be deleted permanently. Your details will be kept confidential while quotes including interview data used in the project outputs will be anonymised by using participants' identification numbers which means quotes and data cannot be traced back to the participants. Also, be aware that your details will be held separately from the interview transcript. Please note that the outcome of this research will be published in this Ph.D. thesis, academic journal articles, books, seminars, and public policy recommendations. You will receive an executive summary with details of where to access any publications.

**Risks:**

The participants who disclose past or ongoing criminal activity might face the risk of being reported and their identities disclosed to appropriate authorities; they might be arrested to face trial and as such may lose their privacy including dismissal from employment. There is also the risk of collective community unrest resulting from the arrest of participants who might have confessed to any form of criminality.

**Benefits:**

Although no direct financial benefits are accruing from this study to participants, they will receive an executive summary of the main findings of the study or an email address to follow up on any publications. The direct benefit to communities will by way of creating the opportunity for different segments of OGHCs to articulate their inputs into government and the oil OGMNCs' relevant community policies which will be a structured process of addressing resentment and frustrations amongst the residents. Other benefits include; fast track cleanup of oil spills across OGHCs communities including government partnership with OGMNCs to regenerate devastated farmlands in the historic Niger Delta region. Finally, the benefits of this study outweigh the potential risks identified above because the outcomes create an enabling environment that could bring about sustainable peace and prosperity in the larger Niger Delta region.

**Research Approval:**

The Ph.D. study was approved by the School of Social and Political Sciences Ethics Committee at the University of Lincoln, in 2018 in accordance with the University of Lincoln's ethical standards and regulations. The project-specific phone number will be revealed to potential participants when the information sheet and consent form are been administered.

# Appendix C

**Informed Consent Form**

### Participant's Copy

**Research Title:** The causes of onshore oil and gas pipeline infrastructure insecurity problem in historic Niger Delta region.

**Name of Researcher:** Abraham Abdul Jatto

**Pseudonym assigned to Participant:** _____

If you decide to take part in the research, kindly read and sign this consent form.

**Please initial box**

---

I have read and understood the information sheet about the purpose of this research

My questions and concerns about my role have been adequately addressed

I understand I do not have to answer any questions I do not wish to respond to and can stop the interview at any point

I can withdraw my consent to the use of the interview data within 21 days of receiving a copy of the interview transcript

I am aware the anonymised data from the interview will be used in the Ph.D. thesis, academic journal articles, books, seminars, and public policy recommendations

I understand that my private details will be kept strictly confidential and the interview transcript data will be anonymised and stored securely to avoid unauthorised access

---

(continued)

© The Editor(s) (if applicable) and The Author(s), under exclusive license to Springer Nature Switzerland AG 2024
A. L. A. Jatto, *Oil and Gas Pipeline Infrastructure Insecurity*,
New Security Challenges,
https://doi.org/10.1007/978-3-031-56932-6

(continued)

| I voluntarily accept to participate in this study | | |
|---|---|---|
| Please send me an executive summary with details of where to access any publications resulting from this research or an email address for follow-up | | **YES/ NO** |

.................................................................................

**Name of participant**          **Date**          **Signature**

.................................................................................

**Name of researcher**          **Date**          **Signature**

Researcher's Copy

**Research Title:** The scale and causes of onshore oil and gas pipeline infrastructure security problem in historic Niger Delta.

**Name of Research:** Abraham Abdul Jatto

**Pseudonym assigned to Participant:** _____

**If you decide to take part in the research, kindly read and sign this consent form.**

**Please initial box**

| I have read and understood the information sheet about the purpose of this research |
|---|
| My questions and concerns about my role have been adequately addressed |
| I understand I do not have to answer any questions I do not wish to respond to and can stop the interview at any point |
| I can withdraw my consent to the use of the interview data within 21 days of receiving a copy of the interview transcript |
| I am aware the anonymised data from the interview will be used in the Ph.D. thesis, academic journal articles, books, seminars, and public policy recommendations |
| I understand that my private details will be kept strictly confidential and the interview transcript data will be anonymised and stored securely to avoid unauthorised access |
| I voluntarily accept to participate in this study |

| Please send me an executive summary with details of where to access any publications resulting from this research or an email address for follow-up | **YES/ NO** |
|---|---|

.................................................................................

**Name of participant**          **Date**          **Signature**

.................................................................................

**Name of researcher**          **Date**          **Signature**

# Appendix D

**Interview Questions**
**Section A: Questions for the Professional Participants**
**(Security and Oil and Gas)**
**Section A: Introduction**

1. Tell me about yourself and your current job role
2. What do you think are the main advantages of oil and gas production for local communities?
3. What do you think are the downsides of oil and gas production for local communities?
4. In your opinion, what are the main socio-economic and political issues in Bayelsa state?
5. From your observations, do you think the environmental issues are related to the activities of oil and gas companies?
6. What impact will climate change have on continued oil and gas production in these areas for both companies and local communities?
7. In what ways are the issues you have just raised affect the security of onshore oil and gas infrastructure?
8. Have you come across your organisational policy on the pipeline life cycle?

© The Editor(s) (if applicable) and The Author(s), under exclusive license to Springer Nature Switzerland AG 2024
A. L. A. Jatto, *Oil and Gas Pipeline Infrastructure Insecurity*,
New Security Challenges,
https://doi.org/10.1007/978-3-031-56932-6

## Section B: Oil and Gas Pipelines

1. Let's talk about security issues in more detail. What are the main security challenges facing onshore oil and gas pipelines in Bayelsa state?
2. You mentioned vandalism and disruption. In your opinion, what are the reasons that locals engage in vandalism and/or disruption of the oil and gas pipelines?
3. How many incidents of pipeline vandalism and/or disruption has your organisation recorded across communities in Bayelsa in the last 12 months?
4. How many of such disruptions have been on NCTL?
5. How are these incidences of damage recorded?
6. What impact does this vandalism have on your company/ organisation?
7. How does your company/ organisation deal with these disruptions?
8. What sort of protective security measures are put in place to prevent future damage to the onshore oil and gas pipeline infrastructure?
9. How effective has this protective security been? Why/ Why not?
10. What is the economic cost of the disruption to your company/ organisation?
11. In your opinion, what impact has the vandalisation of NCTL pipelines had on local communities?

## Section C: Suggestions

1. Do you think the problems leading to vandalism and disruption currently, can be solved?
2. In your opinion, what roles should regulators/ operators play in solving the underlying problems that disrupt the oil and gas pipelines?
3. Why do you think communities should /shouldn't be involved in finding solutions to these issues?

4. Given that the trust between communities, companies, and authorities has been eroded, how can this trust be rebuilt to ensure effective engagement?
5. What socio-economic issues do you think need to be addressed to provide a more effective solution for the future?
6. How do you think the misunderstanding between communities, operators, and government can be resolved?

### Section D: Closing Questions

1. Do you have any questions for me?
2. Finally, is there anything you would like to add?

## Section B:

### The Local Community Stakeholders' Participants (Non-governmental Organisation Professionals, Community Activists, Community Leaders-Kings/Chiefs, and High-Profile Community Members)

### Part A: Introduction

1. Could you tell me a few things about yourself, and some of the problems you have experienced living in the Nembe community for the past few years?
2. What are some of the socio-economic issues that you and your community face?
3. How do you feel about oil and gas extraction in Nembe, Bayelsa, and the Niger Delta region?
4. What benefits have you and your communities seen as a result of this?
5. What are some of the negative impacts that oil and gas production had on you and your communities?

### Part B: Oil and Gas Pipelines

1. How has the construction and operation of oil and gas pipelines affected you, your family, and your community?

2. Before the construction and development of the NCTL pipeline infrastructure, have you and the wider community ever been consulted?

    i. (if yes) What issues did you and others in your community raise during the consultation?

    ii. (if no) How do you feel about not being consulted?

    iii. (if displacement is mentioned) How has displacement because of the pipelines affected you, your family, and your community?

3. How has constant vandalism and disruption of the oil and gas pipeline infrastructure affected your life?

4. How do you feel about this vandalism and disruption?

5. From your observations, what causes members of your community to engage in vandalism and disruption?

6. What do you think oil firms and government could do for your communities and or groups that might positively affect the operation of NCTL in the future?

## Part C: Suggestions

1. What do you think oil companies and the government should do to improve the socio-economic well-being of affected communities?

2. How do you think the trust between oil companies, the government, and your community can be rebuilt?

3. What role do you think the oil companies/government should play in addressing the issues that lead members of your communities to engage in vandalism and disruption?

4. What role do you think you and your community can play in improving the conditions that might lead individuals to vandalism?

5. What impact have protective security measures, introduced by the oil and gas firms and/or government, had on your community?

6. How do you think this situation can be resolved?

## Part D: Closing Questions

1. Do you have any questions for me?

2. Finally, is there anything you would like to add?

# Bibliography

Abadom, D. C., & Nwankwoala, H. O. (2018). Investigations of Physio-Chemical Composition of Groundwater in Otuoke and Environs, Bayelsa State, Nigeria. *International Journal of Environmental Sciences and Natural Resources, 9*(1), 1–9.

Abah, B. (2011, January–March). Agonies of Niger Delta Women. In *Environmental Rights Action/Friends of the Earth.* https://womin.africa/wp-content/uploads/2020/09/Environmental-Rights-Action-Agonies-of-Niger-Delta-Women.pdf. Accessed 10 June 2019.

Abidde, S. O. (2017). *Nigeria's Niger Delta: Militancy, Amnesty, and the Post Amnesty Environment.* Lexington.

Ablo, D. A. (2020). Enterprise Development? Local Content, Corporate Social Responsibility, and Disjunctive Linkages in Ghana's Oil and Gas Industry. *Extractive Industry and Society Journal, 7*(2), 321–327.

Abrahams, R., & Abraham, R. G. (1998). *Vigilant Citizens: Vigilantism and the State.* Polity Press.

Achebe, C. (1984). *The Trouble with Nigeria.* Heinemann Educational Publishers.

Achebe, C. H., Nneke, U. C., & Anisiji, O. E. (2012). Analysis of Oil Pipeline Failures in the Oil and Gas Industries in the Niger Delta Area of Nigeria. *International Association of Engineers: International MultiConference of Engineers and Computer Scientists, II*, 1–5.

Ackerman, B. (2004). The Emergency Constitution. *Yale Law Journal, 113*(5), 1029–1091.

Adam, C., Knill, C., & Steinebach, Y. (2018). Neglected Challenges to Evidence-Based Policy-Making: The Problem of Policy Accumulation. *Policy Science Journal, 51,* 269–290.

Adams, P. (2019). Salt Marsh Restoration. In G. M. E. Parilla, E. Wolanski, D. R. Cahoon, & C. S. Hopkinson (Eds.), *Coastal Wetlands: An Integrated Ecosystem Approach* (2nd ed., pp. 817–861). Elsevier.

Addink, H. (2019). *Good Governance: Concept and Context.* Oxford University Press.

Addison, T. (2018). Climate Change and the Extractive Sector. In T. Addison & A. Roe (Eds.), *Extractive Industry: The Management of Resources as a Driver of Sustainable Development* (pp. 460–484). Oxford University.

Adedeji, H. O., & Elegbede, I. O. (2018). Mapping and Modeling Ecosystem Services in Petroleum Producing Areas in Nigeria. In P. E. Ndimele (Ed.), *The Political Economy of Oil and Gas Activities in the Nigerian Aquatic Ecosystem* (pp. 159–170). Academic Press.

Adedeji, A. (1999). *Comprehending and Mastering African Conflicts: The Search for Sustainable Peace and Good Governance.* Zed Books.

Adedeji, T. (2021, September 22). Weeds, Reptiles take over Abandoned NNPC and SEPLAT 200-Bed Infectious Diseases Centre in Imo. *Daily Post News.* https://dailypost.ng/2021/09/22/weeds-reptiles-take-over-abandoned-nnpc-seplat-200-bed-infectious-diseases-centre-in-imo/. Accessed 22 September 2021.

Adejoh, O. F. (2014). Petroleum Pipelines Spillages and the Environment of the Niger Delta Region of Nigeria. *World Environment Journal, 4*(3), 93–100.

Adekoya, R. (2019, February 4). Nigeria's President Isn't a Democrat. He is a liar: Twenty Years after its return to Democratic Rule, Nigeria is on the Verge of Re-electing a Dictator. *Foreign Policy.* https://foreignpolicy.com/2019/02/04/nigerias-president-isnt-a-democrat-hes-a-liar/. Accessed 5 June 2019.

Aderogba, A. (2016). Government Amnesty Programme and Peace Efforts in the Niger Delta Region: An Analysis of Newspaper Coverage. *European Scientific Journal, 12*(20), 1–12.

Adeyemi, A. E. (2015). *Terrorism and Transnational Security Threats in West Africa: A Global Perspective.* Author Solutions.

Adeyeri, J. O. (2018). Oil, Conflict and Sustainable Development in Nigeria. In V. U. James (Ed.), *Capacity Building for Sustainable Development* (pp. 231–240). CABI.

Adler, P. A., & Adler, P. (No Date). *How Many Qualitative Interviews is Enough?.* National Centre for Research Method. https://eprints.ncrm.ac.uk/id/eprint/2273/4/how_many_interviews.pdf. Accessed 2 March 2022.

Adogame, A. (2005). Politicisation of Religion and Religionalisation of Politics in Nigeria. In C. J. Korieh & G. U. Nwokeji (Eds.), *Religion, History, and Politics in Nigeria: Essays in Honor of Ogbu U. Kalu* (pp. 125–139). University Press of America.

Adunbi, O. (2015). *Oil Wealth and Insurgency in Nigeria*. Indiana University Press.

Africa Oil and Gas Report. (2018). *In 24 Months Nembe Creek Trunk Line Will be Running Empty* (Vol. 19(8), pp. 1–10). Africa Oil and Gas Report.

Agagu, A. A. (2013). Public Policy and the Niger Delta Question: The Case of Interventionist Development Agencies. In A. Ikelegbe (Ed.), *Oil, Environment and Resource conflicts in Nigeria* (pp. 93–108). Lit Verglag.

Agbalajobi, D. (2021, May 3). Nigeria has Few Women in Politics: Here's Why, and What to do About It. *The Conversation*. https://theconversation.com/nigeria-has-few-women-in-politics-heres-why-and-what-to-do-about-it-159578. Accessed 15 March 2022.

Agbonifo, J. (2004). Beyond Greed and Grievance: Negotiating Political Settlement and Peace in Africa. *Journal of Peace, Conflict, and Development*, (4), 1–14.

Agbonifo, J. (2019). *Environment and Conflict, the Place and Logic of Collective Action in the Niger Delta*, New York. Routledge.

Aghedo, I., & Thomas, A. N. (2015). Security Architecture and Insecurity Management: Context, Content, and Challenges in Nigeria. *Sokoto Journal of the Social Sciences, 1*(4), 22–36.

Agudelo, M. A. L., Johannsdottir, L., & Davidsdottir, B. (2019). A Literature Review of the History and Evolution of Corporate Social Responsibility. *International Journal of Corporate Social Responsibility, 4*(1).

Ahmed, H. H. (2005). Palestinian Resistance and Suicide Bombing: Causes and Consequences. In T. Biorgo (Ed.), *Root Causes of Terrorism: Myths, Reality, and Ways Forward* (pp. 87–102). Routledge.

Ahram, A. I. (2021). Hybrid Security Governance and the Search for the State in the Middle East, War the Rocks. *Texas National Security Review*. https://warontherocks.com/2021/01/hybrid-security-governance-and-the-search-for-the-state-in-the-middle-east/. Accessed 12 February 2022.

Ajala, F. (2019). Nigeria: Trapped in a Militarised Democracy. *The Republic, 3*(2). https://republic.com.ng/vol3-no2/nigeria-trapped-in-a-militarized-democracy/. Accessed 5 June 2019.

Ajibola, I. O. (2015). Nigeria's Amnesty Program: The Role of Empowerment in Achieving Peace and Development in Post-Conflict Niger Delta. *Sage Open*, 1–11. https://doi.org/10.1177/2158244015589996

Akemu, O., Comiteau, L., & Mes, A. (2018). Shell Nigeria: Changing the Community Engagement Model. In N. C. Smith & G. G. Lenssen (Eds.),

*Managing Sustainable Business: An Executive Education Case and Textbook* (pp. 273–297). Springer.

Akentyeva, E. M. (2010). Requirements of Oil and Gas Operations for Climate Data, Information, Products, and Services in the High Latitudes. In A. Troccoli (Ed.), *Management of Weather and Climate Risk in the Energy Industry* (pp. 165–171). Springer.

Akinsola, B. (2017). *Nigeria: Study Predicts "Epidemic" of Cancer in Nigeria's Oil Producing Region by 2025* (Business and Human Rights Resource Centre Report). https://www.business-humanrights.org/en/latest-news/nigeria-study-predicts-epidemic-of-cancer-in-nigerias-oil-producing-region-by-2025/. Accessed 8 May 2018.

Akintunde, I. (2020). *Nigeria's Recovery Means Rethinking Economic Diversification.* Chatham House. https://www.chathamhouse.org/2020/08/nigerias-recovery-means-rethinking-economic-diversification. Accessed 5 March 2022.

Ako, R. (2011). Resource Exploitation and Environmental Justice: The Nigerian Experience. In F. N. Botchway (Ed.), *Natural Resource Investment, and Africa's Development* (pp. 50–72). Edward Elgar.

Ako, R. (2014). Environmental Justice in Nigeria's Oil Industry: Recognising and Embracing Contemporary Legal Developments. In R. V. Percival, J. Lin, & W. Piermattei (Eds.), *Global Environmental Law at a Crossroads* (pp. 160–176). Edward Edger Publication.

Akonye, A. E. (2013). Kidnapping: The Terror of the 21st Century? Lessons from Southeastern Nigeria. In T. Falola & C. Thomas (Eds.), *Security Africa: Local Crises and Foreign Interventions* (pp. 139–147). Routledge.

Akpan, U. (2021). 1.1bn OML 17 Development, Operations will Boost Local Content. *Vanguard News.* https://www.vanguardngr.com/2021/01/1-1bn-oml-17-development-operations-will-boost-local-content-rewane/. Accessed 22 January 2021.

Akpeninor, J. O. (2012). *Modern Concepts of Security.* Author House.

Akpeninor, J. O. (2013). *Merger Politics of Nigeria and the Surge of Sectarian Violence.* Author House.

Akpomera, E. (2015). International Crude Oil Theft: Elite Predatory Tendencies in Nigeria. *Review of African Political Economy Journal, 42*(143), 156–165.

Akuaibit, S. P. U. (2017). Sea Level Rise and Coastal Submergence Along the South East Coast of Nigeria. *Journal of Oceanography and Marine Research, 5*(4), 2–8.

Akujieze, C. (2019). *Nigeria: An Experiment in Nation Building.* Author House.

Akujobi, A. T. (2009). Corporate Social Responsibility in Nigeria: An Evaluation. In E. Emiri & G. Deinduomo (Eds.), *Law and Petroleum Industry in Nigeria: Current Challenges* (pp. 211–221). Malthouse.

Alabi, J. O. (2013). Resource Conflicts: Energy Worth Fighting for? In M. J. Trombetta & H. Dyer (Eds.), *International Handbook on Energy Security* (pp. 70–92). Edward Elgar.

Alagoa, E. J. (1999). *The Land and People of Bayelsa State: Central Niger Delta*. Onyema Research Publications.

Alagoa, E. J. (2005). *A History of the Niger Delta*. Onyema Research Publications.

Alamieyeseigha, D. S. P. (2005). *Thoughts on Federalism, South–South and Resource Control*. Treasure Books.

Alamieyeseigha, D. S. P. (2008a). The Environmental Challenge of Developing the Niger Delta. In S. S. Azaiki, D. S. P. Alamieyeseigha, & A. A. Ikein (Eds.), *Oil, Democracy and the Promise of True Federalism in Nigeria* (pp. 249–260). University Press of America.

Alamieyeseigha, D. S. P. (2008b). The Niger Delta: Treasure Base of Energies. In S. Azaika, A. A. Ikein, & D. S. P. Alamieyeseigha (Eds.), *Oil Democracy and the Promise of True Federalism in Nigeria* (pp. 290–310). University Press of America.

Albrecht, J. F., Heyer, D. G., & Stanislas. (2019). *Policing and Minority Communities: Contemporary Issues and Global Perspectives*. Springer.

Al-Hashemi, H. (2016). The Role of Institutions in Economic Diversification: The Case of the UAE. In Y. Al-Saleh & S. Mahroum (Eds.), *Economic Diversification Policies in Natural Resource Rich Economies* (pp. 236–266). Routledge.

Ali, D. A. (2019). The Dilemma of Colonial Transportation on the Lower Niger and Benue Rivers 1879–1960. *Jebat: Malaysian Journal of History Politics & Strategy, 46*(1), 155–171.

Alkire, S. (2003). *A Conceptual Framework for Human Security* (CRISE Working Paper 2). University of Oxford. https://assets.publishing.service. gov.uk/media/57a08cf740f0b652dd001694/wp2.pdf. Accessed 24 January 2022.

Allen, F. (2011). *Implementation of Oil Related Environmental Policies in Nigeria: Government Inertia and Conflict in the Niger Delta*. Cambridge Scholar.

Allen, J., & Catron, C. E. (2007). *Early Child Curriculum: A Creative Play Model*. Prentice-Hall.

Almond, A. G. (2015). Introduction: A Fundamental Approach to Comparative Politics. In G. A. Almond & J. S. Coleman (Eds.), *The Politics of the Developing Ages* (pp. 3–57). Princeton University Press.

Alshbili, I., Elamer, A. A., & Beddewela, E. (2020). Ownership Types Corporate Governance, and Corporate Social Responsibility Disclosures: Empirical Evidence from Developing Country. *Accounting Research Journal, 33*(1), 148–166.

Al-Tamimi, A. K. (2016). High-Performance Materials and Corrosion. In R. Javaherdashti, C. Nwaoha, & H. Tan (Eds.), *Corrosion and Materials in the Oil and Gas Industries* (pp. 13–24). CRC Press.

Aluko, M. A. O. (2015). Social Dimensions and Consequences of Environmental Degradation in the Niger Delta of Nigeria: Suggestions for the Next Millennium. In N. P. Nchoji & P. N. Nkwi (Eds.), *The Anthropology of Africa: Challenges for the 21st Century* (pp. 199–208). Langaa Research and Publishing.

Amadi, L. A., & Alapiki, H. (2018). Environmental Security Threats and Policy Response in the Niger Delta, Nigeria 1990–2016. In A. N. Eneanya (Ed.), *Handbook of Research on Environmental Policies for Emergency Management and Public Safety* (pp. 189–208). IGI Global.

Amaiwo, S., & Samuel, C. Z. (2015, May 20). Niger Delta Indigenes Petitions UNO, Demands the Niger Delta Republic. *Urhobo Today.* http://urh obotoday.com/niger-delta-indigenes-petition-uno-demands-niger-delta-rep ublic/. Accessed 2 March 2018.

Ambituuni, A., Hopkins, P., Amezaga, J. M., Werner, D., & Wood, J. M. (2015). Risk Assessment of a Petroleum Product Pipeline in Nigeria: The Realities of Managing Problems of theft/Sabotage. In C. A. Brebbia, F. Garzia, & D. Poljak (Eds.), *Safety and Security Engineering* (pp. 49–60). WIT Press.

Amsel, A. (1992). *Frustration Theory: An Analysis of Dispositional Learning and Memory.* Cambridge University Press.

Amundsen, I. (2019). Extractive and Power-Preserving Political Corruption. In I. Amundsen (Ed.), *Political Corruption in Africa: An Extraction and Power Preservation* (pp. 1–28). Elgar.

Amnesty International Report, (2018). *Amnesty International Report 2017/18: The State of the World's Human Rights,* Available from https://www.amnesty. org/en/documents/pol10/6700/2018/en/ Accessed 7 May 2024

Anand, V., & Ashforth, B. E. (2003). The Normalization of Corruption in Organisations. In *Research in Organisational Behaviour* (Vol. 25, pp. 1–52). Elsevier.

Anderson, C. (2010). Presenting and Evaluating Qualitative Research. *American Journal of Pharmaceutical Research, 74*(8), 141.

Anderson, C. A., & Dill, J. C. (1995). Effects of Frustration Justification on Hostile Aggression. *Aggressive Behaviour, 21*(5), 359–369.

Anderson, J. A. (2011). *Media Research Methods: Understanding Metrics and Interpretive Approaches.* Sage.

Andoh-Arthur, J. (2019). *Gatekeepers in Qualitative Research.* Sage.

Aneek, C. (2010). *International Relations Today: Concepts and Applications.* Pearson.

Anheier, H. K., & Toepler, S. (2010). *International Encyclopedia of Civil Society.* Springer.

Aniche, E. T. (2019). Youth Militancy in the Niger Delta Region. In O. O. Shita, I. M. Alumna, & F. C. Onuoha (Eds.), *Internal Security Management in Nigeria: Perspectives, Challenges and Lessons* (pp. 139–164). Palgrave.

Aniello, A., Luna, D. G., Lodi, G., & Baldoni, R. (2011). A Collaborative Event Processing System for Protection of Critical Infrastructures from Cyber Attacks. In F. Flammini, S. Bologna, & V. Vittorini (Eds.), *Computer Safety, Reliability, and Security* (pp. 310–323). Springer.

Aning, S. (2016). Oil and Gas Security Issues. In K. Appiah-Adu (Ed.), *Governance of the Petroleum Sector* (pp. 233–250). Routledge.

Aremu, A. O. (2012). The Impact of Emotional Intelligence on Community Policing in Democratic Nigeria: Agenda Setting for National Development. In A. Verma, D. K. Das, & M. Abraham (Eds.), *Global Community Policing: Problems and Challenges* (pp. 25–40). CRC Press.

Aris, B. (2023). Niger Coupe Threatens Nigeria-Morocco 30bcm Gas Pipeline Project. *Intelli News*. https://intellinews.com/niger-coup-threatens-nigeria-morocco-30bcm-gas-pipeline-project-286426/. Accessed 27 October 2023.

Arner, R. (2010). *Consistently Pro-Life: The Ethics of Bloodshed in Ancient Christianity*. Pickwick.

Aronu, O. K. (2017). *Integrity Management in The Energy Sector: An Investigation of Oil and Gas Assets*. Norwegian University of Science and Technology.

Arteaga, F. (2010). *International Security: Energy Security in Central Asia: Infrastructure and Risks*. Elcano Royal Institute.

Asika, N. (2004). *Research Methodology in the Behavioural Sciences*. Longman.

Asselin, M. E. (2003). Insider Research: Issues to Consider when Doing Qualitative Research in your Setting. *Journal for Nursing in Staff Development, 19*(2), 99–103.

Astalin, P. K. (2013). Qualitative Research Designs: A Conceptual Framework. *International Journal of Social Science and Interdisciplinary Research, 2*(1), 118–124.

Asuni, B. J. (2009). *Special Report: Blood Oil in the Niger Delta* (pp. 2–19). United States Institute of Peace. https://www.usip.org/sites/default/files/blood_oil_nigerdelta_0.pdf. Accessed 3 March 2019.

Asuo, O. O., Metuonu, I. C., & Ochulor, C. L. (2011). Corruption in Contemporary Nigeria: The Way Out. *American Journal of Social and Management Sciences, 2*(1), 90–99.

Auzer, K. A. (2017). *Institutional Design and Capacity to Enhance Effective Governance of Oil and Gas Wealth: The Case of Kurdistan Region*. Springer.

Avwunudiogba, A. (2023). Environmental Degradation and Community Poverty: Lessons from the Niger Delta of Nigeria. In B. I. Gill & G. K. Danns (Eds.), *Comparative Assessment of Social Issues in Africa, Latin America, and the Caribbean* (pp. 97–114). Rowman and Littlefield.

Azubuike, V. (2021). International Court Orders Shell to Compensate Niger-Delta Communities over Oil Spillage. *Daily Post News*. https://dailypost.ng/2021/01/29/breaking-international-court-orders-shell-to-compensate-niger-delta-communities-over-oil-spillage/. Accessed 30 January 2021.

Babatunde, B., Zabbey, N., Mekuleyi, G. O., & Akpu, V. (2017). Bunkering Activities in Nigerian Waters and Their Eco-Economic Consequences. In P. E. Ndimele (Ed.), *The Political Economy of Oil and Gas Activities in the Nigerian Aquatic Ecosystem* (pp. 439–446). Academic Press.

Babbie, E. (2015). *The Practice of Social Research* (14th ed.). Cengage Learning.

Baecher, G. B. (2013). Risk Evaluation of Threats to Critical Infrastructure. In N. A. Makhutove & G. B. Baecher (Eds.), *Comparative Analysis of Technological and Intelligent Terrorism Impacts on Complex Technical Systems* (pp. 12–21). IOP Press.

Bagayoko, N., Hutchful, E., & Luckham, R. (2016). Hybrid Security Governance in Africa: Rethinking the Foundations of Security, Justice and Legitimate Public Authority. *Journal of Conflict, Security and Development, 16*(1), 1–32.

Bahadori, A. (2017). *Oil and Gas Pipelines and Piping Systems: Design, Construction, Management, and Inspection*. Elsevier.

Bahgat, G. (2012). Sovereign Wealth Funds in the Gulf: Opportunities and Challenges. In R. E. Looney (Ed.), *Handbook of Oil Politics*. Routledge.

Bailey, K. D. (2006). Systems Theory. In J. H. Turner (Ed.), *Handbook on Sociological Theory* (pp. 379–404). Springer.

Baiyewu, L., & Akinkuotu, E. (2021, July 5). PIB: North, Ogun's Quest for Oil get Boost, Exploration Receives 30%. *The Punch News Paper*. https://punchng.com/pib-north-oguns-quests-for-oil-get-boost-exploration-receives-30/. Accessed 8 July 2021.

Baker, S. E., & Edwards, R. (2012). *How Many Qualitative Interviews is Enough?*. ESRC National Centre for Research Methods.

Baku-Tbilisi-Ceyhan Corporation. (2014). *Protecting Pipelines-BTC as a Case Study*. In M. Edwards (Ed.), *Critical Infrastructure Protection* (pp. 55–58). IOS.

Baldwin, D. A. (1998). The Concept of Security. *Review of International Studies, 23*(1), 5–26.

Balogun, A. O. (2018). Muhammed Chris Ali and the Politics in the Nigerian Army: A Philosophical Approach. In M. Dukor (Ed.), *Muhammed Chris Ali's The Federal Republic of Nigerian Army Symposium on Sage Philosophy* (pp. 24–57). Malthouse.

Bandura, A. (1973). *Aggression: A Social Learning Analysis*. Prentice-Hall.

Bassey, C. O., & Dokubo, C. Q. (2011). *Defence Policy of Nigeria: Capability and Context: A Reader*. Author House.

Bauman, C. E. (2012). *The Diplomatic Kidnappings: A Revolutionary Tactics of Urban Terrorism*. Springer.

Bayelsa Ministry of Health Report. (2013). *State Wide Rapid Health Facility Assessment: In Preparation of for the Elimination of Mother-to-Child Transmission of HIV* (pp. 2–27). Bayelsa State Ministry of Health and FHI 360.

BBC News. (2021, November 23). EndSars Protests: Nigeria's Lekki Massacre Report Fake. *Says Minister*. https://www.bbc.co.uk/news/topics/cezwd6k5k6vt/endsars-protests. Accessed 20 January 2022.

Bejakovic, P., & Mrnjavac, Z. (2018). The Dangers of Long-Term Unemployment and Measures for its Reduction: The Case of Croatia. *Economic Research Journal, 31*(1), 1837–1850.

Bell, E., Bryman, A., & Harley, B. (2018). *Business Research Methods* (5th ed.). Oxford University Press.

Bello, B., & Abdullahi, M. M. (2021, October–December). Farmers-Herdsmen Conflict, Cattle Rustling, and Banditry: The Dialectics of Insecurity in Anka and Maradun Local Government Area of Zamfara State, Nigeria. *Sage Open Journal*, 1–12.

Bello, S. (1964). *Herzog*. Penguin Press.

Bensted, R. (2011). A Critique to Paul Collier's 'Greed' and 'Grievance' Thesis of Civil Wars. *Africa Security Review, 20*(3), 84–90.

Bento, F., Mercado, M. P., & Garotti, M. (2021). Organisational Resilience in Oil and Gas Industry: A Scoping Review. *Safety Science Journal, 133*, 1–11.

Berg, L. B. (2007). *Qualitative Research Methods for the Social Sciences* (6th ed.). Pearson Education.

Bergkamp, L. (2021). *Liability and Environment: Private and Public Law Aspects of Civil Liability for environmental Harm in an International Context*. Brill.

Bergstresser, H. (2017). *A Decade of Nigeria: Politics, Economy and Society 2004–2016*. Brill.

Berkowitz, L. (1989). Frustration-Aggression Hypothesis: Examination and Reformulation. *American Psychological Association Journal, 106*(1), 59–73.

Berkowitz, L. (1993). *Aggression: Its Causes, Consequences, and Control*. McGraw-Hill.

Berkowitz, L. (2011). A Cognitive-No Association Theory of Aggression. In A. W. Kruglanski, P. A. M. Van Lange, & E. T. Higgins (Eds.), *The Handbook of Theories of Social Psychology* (pp. 90–120). Sage.

Berman, J. J. (2013). *Principles of Big Data: Preparing, Sharing, and Analysing Complex Information*. Newnes.

Berton, P. (2012). *The Great 1929–1939 Depression*. Doubleday.

Best, B., Idemudia, U., & Cragg, W. (2016). Confronting Corruption Using Integrity Pacts: The Case of Nigeria. In R. J. Burke, E. C. Tomlinson, & C.

L. Cooper (Eds.), *Crime and Corruption in Organisations: Why It Occurs and What to do About It* (pp. 297–322). Routledge.

Bianchi, R. (2014). *Interest Groups and Political Development in Turkey.* Princeton University Press.

Bielecki, J. (2010). Energy Security; Past Accomplishments, Emerging Challenges. In P. Bilgin, P. D. Williams, M. Sekiguchi, J. K. Galbraith, S. T. Inayatullah, J. Wiener, R. A. Schrire, & I. L. Murphy (Eds.), *Global Security, and International Political Economy* (Vol. 5, pp. 329–346). EOLSS.

Bigo, D. (2014). Globalised Insecurity: The Field and the Ban-opticon. In A. Tsoukala & D. Bigo (Eds.), *Terror, Insecurity and Liberty: Illiberal Practices of Liberal Regimes after 9/11* (pp. 15–41). Routledge.

Billion, P. L., & Bridge, G. (2013). *Oil.* Polity.

Binuomoyo, Y. K., Ogbewo, J. B., Okoro, E. A., & Ukaga, O. (2012). Land Reforms, Land Rights, and Development Challenges. In U. U. Ibaba & O. Ukaga (Eds.), *Natural Resources, Conflicts, and Sustainable Development: Lessons from the Niger Delta* (pp. 115–131). Routledge.

Biringer, B. E., Warren, D. E., & Vugrin, E. D. (2016). *Critical Infrastructure System Security and Resiliency.* CRC Press.

Blaikie, N. (2007). *Approaches to Social Enquiry: Advancing Knowledge* (2nd ed.). Polity.

Blatz, W. E. (1966). *Human Security some Reflections.* University of Toronto Press.

Boix, C. (2008). Economic Roots of Revolution Civil Wars in the Contemporary World. *Journal of World Politics, 60*(3), 390–437.

Bolaji, S. D., Gray, J. R., & Evans, G. C. (2015). Why do Policies Fail in Nigeria. *Journal of Education and Social Policy, 2*(5), 57–64.

Bollier, S. (2013). All is Not Well in Northern Iraq's Oilfields. *Global Policy Forum.* https://archive.globalpolicy.org/the-dark-side-of-natural-resources-st/oil-and-natural-gas-in-conflict/middle-east/52194-all-is-not-well-in-nor thern-iraqs-oilfields.html%3Fitemid=id.html#40291. Accessed 27 October 2023.

Booth, K. (1991). Security and Emancipation. *Reviews of International Studies Journal, 17*(4), 313–326.

Booth, K. (2007). *Theory of World Security.* Cambridge University Press.

Booth, K., & Wheeler, J. N. (2008). *The Security Dilemma: Fear, Cooperation, and Trust in World Politics.* Palgrave Macmillan.

Bordoff, J., & O'Sullivan, M. L. (2023, May/June). The Age of Energy Insecurity: How the Fight for Resources Is Upending Geopolitics, *Foreign Affairs Journal.* https://www.foreignaffairs.com/world/energy-insecurity-cli mate-change-geopolitics-resources. Accessed 27 October 2023.

Boris, O. H. (2015). The Upsurge of Oil Theft and Illegal Bunkering in the Niger Delta Region of Nigeria: Is there a Way Out? *Mediterranean Journal of Social Sciences, 6*(3), 563–571.

Boro, I. (1982). *The Twelve-day Revolution.* Idodo Umeh.

Bosold, D. (2010). Development of the Human Security Field: A Critical Examination. In D. Chandler & N. Hynek (Eds.), *Critical Perspectives on Human Security: Rethinking Emancipation and Power in International Relations* (pp. 25–31). Routledge.

Bouchat, C. J. (2019). *The Causes of Instability in Nigeria and Implications for the United States.* Strategic Studies Institute.

Bowen, G. A. (2009). Document Analysis as a Qualitative Research Method. *Qualitative Research Journal, 9*(2), 27–40.

Bradshaw, C., Doody, O., & Atkinson, S. (2017). Employing a Qualitative Description Approach in Health Care Research. *Global Qualitative Nursing Research Journal, 4,* 1–8.

Brauch, H. G. (2015). Environmental and Energy Security: Conceptual Evolution and Potential Applications to European Cross-Border Energy Supply Infrastructure. In S. J. Booth, A. S. Victorov, M. G. Culshaw, & V. I. Osipov (Eds.), *Environmental Security of the European Cross-Border Energy Supply Infrastructure* (pp. 155–186). Springer.

Brennan, J. (2016). *Against Democracy: New Preface.* Princeton.

Bretthauer, J. M. (2016). *Climate Change and Resource Conflicts: The Role of Scarcity.* Routledge.

Briggs, D. A. (2007). *Critical Reflections on the Niger Delta Question.* Larigraphics.

Brinkhoff, T. (2017). City Population: Nembe Population. https://www.citypopulation.de/php/nigeria-admin.php?adm2id=NGA006004. Accessed 3 January 2019.

Brisibe, W. G., & Tepple, D. T. (2018). Lessons Learnt from the 2012 Flood Disaster: Implications for Post-Flood Building Design and Construction in Yenagoa Nigeria. *Journal of Civil Engineering and Architecture, 6*(3), 171–180.

Broderick, C. B. (1993). *Understanding Family Process: Basics of Family Systems Theory.* Sage.

Brown, W. (2023). Why France's Exit from Niger Could Spark a Uranium Rush. *Sensemaker Daily.* https://www.tortoisemedia.com/2023/09/26/why-frances-exit-from-niger-could-spark-a-uranium-rush/. Accessed 27 October 2023.

Brown, M. E. (2003). *Grave New World: Security Challenges in the 21st Century.* George Town University Press.

Brown, S., & Sessions, J. G. (2000). Employee Militancy in Britain: 1985–1990. *Applied Economics Journal, 32,* 1767–1774.

Browning, S. C., & McDonald, M. (2011). The Future of Critical Security Studies: Ethics and the Politics of Security. *European Journal of International Relations, 19*(2), 220–230.

Bruland, K. (1998). The Era of Corporate Capitalism. In K. Bruland & P. O'Brien (Eds.), *From Family Firms to Corporate Capitalism* (pp. 219–247). Claredon Press.

Bryman, A. (2016). *Social Research Methods* (5th ed.). Oxford University Press.

Bryman, A., & Buchanan, D. (2009). 'The Organisational Research Context: Properties and Implications. In A. Bryman & D. Buchanan (Eds.), *The Sage Handbook of Organisational Research Methods* (pp. 1–18). Sage publication.

Brynjar, L., & Ashild, K. (2001). *Terrorism and Oil- An Explosive Mixture? A Survey of Terrorist and rebel Attacks on Petroleum Infrastructure 1968–1999* (pp. 3–49). Norwegian Defense Research Establishment. https://public ations.ffi.no/nb/item/asset/dspace:2244/01-04031.pdf. Accessed 31 March 2018.

Bukarti, A. B. (2017). *Hate Speech Threatens Co-Existence in Nigeria*. Tony Blair Institute for Global Change. https://institute.global/policy/hate-speech-thr eatens-co-existence-nigeria. Accessed 28 November 2018.

Bulhan, H. A. (1985). *Frantz Fanon and the Psychology of Oppression*. Plenum.

Burlton, A. H. A. (2007). *Pleasure and Instinct: A Study in the Psychology of Human Action*. Routledge.

Burnard, P. (1991). *A Method of Analysing Interview Transcripts in Qualitative Research*. University of Wales.

Burnet, J. E. (2012a). Rwanda: Women's Political Representation and Its Consequences. In S. Franceschet, M. L. Krook, & N. Tan (Eds.), *The Palgrave Handbook of Women Political Rights* (pp. 563–576). Palgrave Macmillan.

Burnet, J. E. (2012b). Women's Empowerment and Cultural Change in Rwanda. In S. Franceschet, M. L. Krook, & J. M. Piscopo (Eds.), *The Impact of Gender Quotas* (pp. 190–207). Oxford University Press.

Burnham, P., Lutz, K. G., Layton-Henry, Z., & Grant, W. (2008). *Research Methods in Politics* (2nd ed.). Palgrave Macmillan.

Burns, B. R. (2000). *Introduction to Research Methods*. Sage.

Bush, W. (2003). *The National Strategy for the Physical Protection of Critical Infrastructures and Key Asset*. Diane.

Bushman, B. J., & Anderson, C. A. (2002). Human Aggression. *Annual Review Psychology Journal, 53*, 27–51.

Bushman, B. J., Anderson, C. A., & Allen, J. J. (2018). The General Aggression Model. *Current Opinions in Psychology Journal, 9*, 75–80.

Buzan, B. (1991). *People, States, and Fear: An Agenda for International Security Studies in the Post-Cold War Era*. Lynn Rienner.

Buzan, B. (1984a). Peace, Power, and Security: Contending Concepts in the Study of International Relations. *Journal of Peace Research, 21*(2), 109–125.

Buzan, B. (1984b). *People, States, and Fear: The National Security Problems in International Relations.* University of North Carolina.

Buzan, B., & Hansen, L. (2009). *The Evolution of the International Security Studies.* Cambridge University Press.

Bybee, R. W. (2013). *The Case for STEM Education: Challenges and Opportunities.* NSTA Press.

Cabot, C. (2016). *Climate Change, Security Risks and Conflict Reduction in Africa: A Case of Farmer-Header Conflicts over Natural Resources in Cote d'Ivoire, Ghana and Burkina Faso 1960–2000.* Springer.

Cameron, R. (2014). A More 'Human' Human Security: The Importance of Existential Security in Resilient Communities. In C. Hobson, P. Bacon, & R. Cameron (Eds.), *Human Security, and Natural Disasters* (pp. 159–172). Routledge.

Campbell, D. (1998). *Writing Security* (Revised). University of Minnesota Press.

Campbell, J. (2013). *Nigeria: Dancing in the Brink.* Rowman, and Littlefield.

Canada Energy Pipeline Association. (2016). Five Phases of the Pipeline Life Circle. https://www.aboutpipelines.com/en/blog/five-phases-of-the-pip eline-life-cycle/. Accessed 9 August 2020.

Carvalho, H. (2017). *The Preventive Turn in Criminal Law.* Oxford University Press.

Cashman, G. (2014). *What Causes War? An Introduction to Theories of International Conflicts* (2nd ed.). Rowman, and Littlefield.

Cassino, Y. B., & Cassino, D. (2018). *Social Research Methods by Example: Application in the Modern World.* Routledge.

Centre for the Protection of National Infrastructure. (2018). *Critical National Infrastructure.* Centre for the Protection of National Infrastructure. https://www.cpni.gov.uk/critical-national-infrastructure-0. Accessed 29 September 2018.

Centre for Strategic and International Studies. (2021). *A New Revolution in the Middle East.* CSIS. https://www.csis.org/analysis/new-revolution-mid dle-east. Accessed 27 October 2023.

Cha, V. D. (2011). Globalisation and Security. In M. Y. Lai & C. W. Hughes (Eds.), *Security Studies.* Routledge.

Charles, V., Crow, G., Wiles, R., & Heath, S. (2006). Research Ethics and Data Quality: The Implication of Informed Consent. *International Journal of Social Research Methodology, 9,* 83–95.

Chemerinsky, E., & Gillman, H. (2017). *Free Speech on Campus.* Yale University Press.

Cheney, G., Gill, R., & Kendall, B. E. (2007). Consumer Activism and Corporate Social Responsibility: How Strong a Connection? In S. May, G. Cheney, & J. Roper (Eds.), *The Debate Over Corporate Social Responsibility* (pp. 241–266). Oxford University Press.

Cherp, A., Adenikinju, A., & Vakulenko, S. (2012). Energy and Security. In T. B. Johansson, N. Nakicenovic, A. Patwardhan, & L. G. Echeverri (Eds.), *Global Energy Assessment: Towards a Sustainable Future* (pp. 325–380). Cambridge University Press.

Chomsky, N. (2016). *Who Rules the World? Reframing.* Penguin.

Chomsky, N. (2003). *Hegemony or Survival: America's Quest for Global Dominance.* Henry Holt.

Christopher, O., & Stanley, A. (2016). Analysis Towards Effective Policing in Nigeria. *African Research Review-Journal, 10*(1), Serial (40), 61–72.

Chukwurah, D. (2014). *Last Train to Biafra.* Grosvenor House.

Clark, A. (2006). *Anonymising Research Data* (ESRC National Centre for Research Methods Working Paper Series). https://eprints.ncrm.ac.uk/id/eprint/480/1/0706_anonymising_research_data.pdf. Accessed 3 January 2018.

Clarke, V., & Braun, V. (2006). Using Thematic Analysis in Psychology. *Qualitative Research in Psychology Journal, 3*, 77–101.

Cole, D. (2016). *Engine of Liberty: The Power of Citizen Activists to Make Constitutional Law.* Hachette.

Coleman, J. S. (2015). The Politics of Sub-Saharan Africa. In A. G. Almond & J. S. Coleman (Eds.), *The Politics of the Developing Areas* (pp. 247–354). Princeton University Press.

Colgan, J. (2013). *Petro-Aggression: When Oil and Causes War.* Cambridge.

Collier, P. (2003). *Breaking the Conflict Trap: Civil Wars and Development Policy.* Oxford University Press.

Collier, P. (2007). *The Bottom Billion* (pp. 39–52). Oxford University Press.

Collier, P., & Hoeffler, A. E. (2004). *Greed and Grievance in Civil War.* World Bank Development Research Group.

Constitution of the Federal Republic of Nigeria. (1999). Third Amendment, Section 43(3). https://publicofficialsfinancialdisclosure.worldbank.org/sites/fdl/files/assets/law-library-files/Nigeria_Constitution_1999_en.pdf. Accessed 5 August 2020.

Cook, N. A. (1943). *British Enterprise in Nigeria.* Cass.

Coon, D., & Mitterer, J. O. (2010). *Introduction to Psychology: Gateways to Mind and Behaviour* (12th ed.). Wadsworth-Cengage Learning.

Cordesman, A. H. (2016). *The Underlying Causes of Stability and Instability in the Middle East and North Africa (MENA) Region.* Center for Strategic and International Studies.

Courson, E. (2006). *Odi Revisited: Oil and State Violence in Odioma, Brass Local Government Area* (Bayelsa State, Working Paper Number 7). http://geog.berkeley.edu/ProjectsResources/ND%20Website/NigerDelta/WP/7-Courson.pdf. Accessed 10 June 2019.

Cox, D. G. (2005). Political terrorism and Democratic and Economic Development in Indonesia. In W. J. Crotty (Ed.), *Democratic Development and*

*Political Terrorism: The Global Perspective* (pp. 255–267). Northeastern University Press.

Cramer, C. (2003). Does Inequality Cause Conflict? *Journal of International Development, 14*(4), 397–412.

Creswell, J. W. (2007). *Qualitative Inquiry and Research Design: Choosing Among Five Approaches* (2nd ed.). Sage.

Creswell, J. W. (2013). *Research Design: Qualitative, Quantitative, and Mixed Methods Approaches* (2nd ed.). Sage.

Creswell, J. W. (2015). *A Concise Introduction to Mixed Methods Research.* Sage.

Cronin, A., Alexander, V. D., Fielding, J., Moran-Ellis, J., & Thomas, H. (2008). The Analytic Integration of Qualitative Data Sources. In P. Alasuutari, L. Bickman, & J. Brannen (Eds.), *The Sage Handbook of Social Research Methods* (pp. 572–584). Sage.

Croucher, S. M., & Mills, C. D. (2015). *Understanding Communication Research Methods: A Theoretical and Practical Approach.* Routledge.

Curley, M., & Pettiford, L. (1999). *Changing Security Agendas and the Third World.* Pinter.

D' Arcy, S. (2013). *Languages of the Unheard: Why Militant Protests is Good for Democracy.* Zed Books.

Daka, T., Abuh, A., & Jeremiah, K. (2021, March 18). After $25b on Maintenance, FEC Approves New $1.5b for PH Refinery. *The Guardian News.* https://guardian.ng/news/after-25b-on-maintenance-fec-approves-new-1-5b-for-ph-refinery/. Accessed 18 July 2022.

Daly, D. L., & Sterba, M. N. (2011). *Working with Aggressive Youth: Positive Strategies to Teach Self-Control and Prevent Violence.* Boy Town Press.

Dambo, L. B. (2006). *Nembe: The Divided Kingdom.* Paragraphs.

Daniel, E., & Edet, A. (2018). Displacement and the Development of Highway Communities in Nigeria's Niger Delta Region. *Journal of Developing Country Studies, 8*(8), 102–110.

Dattalo, P. (2008). *Sample-Size Determination in Quantitative Social Work Research.* Oxford University Press.

Daum, P. (2013). *International Synergy Management: A Strategic Approach for Raising Efficiencies in the Cross-border Interaction Process.* Anchor Academic.

Dawson, T. (2021, November 25). Pipelines Will Be Blown Up, Says David Suzuki, If Leaders Don't Act on Climate Change. *National Post.* https://nationalpost.com/news/canada/pipelines-will-be-blown-up-says-david-suzuki-if-leaders-dont-act-on-climate-change. Accessed 25 November 2021.

De Leon, A. (2018). Beyond the Wall: Race and Immigration Discourse. In M. G. Urbina & S. E. Alvarez (Eds.), *Immigration and the Law: Race, Citizenship, and Social Control* (pp. 30–46). The University of Arizona Press.

Demarest, L., Langer, A., & Ukiwo, U. (2020). Nigeria's Federal Character Commission (FCC): A Critical Appraisal. *Oxford Development Studies, 48*(4), 315–328.

Denscombe, M. (2007). *The Good Research Guide for Small-Scale Social Research Projects* (3rd ed.). Open University Press.

Denzin, N. (2009). *The Elephant in the Living Room*. Sage.

Department of Petroleum Resources Flare-Gas-Prevention-of-Waste-and-Pollution-Regulations-Gazette. (2018, July 9). *Federal Republic of Nigeria Official* Gazette (Vol. 105(88)). https://ngfcp.dpr.gov.ng/media/1120/flare-gas-prevention-of-waste-and-pollution-regulations-2018-gazette-cleaner-copy-1.pdf. Accessed 10 August 2020.

Devold, H. (2013). *Oil and Gas Production Handbook: An Introduction to Oil and Gas Production* (pp. 6–146). ABB. https://library.e.abb.com/public/34d5b70e18f7d6c8c1257be500438ac3/Oil%20and%20gas%20production%20handbook%20ed3x0_web.pdf. Accessed 12 December 2017.

Dewalt, K. M., & Dewalt, B. R. (2011). *Participant Observation: A Guide for Fieldworkers* (2nd ed.). Rowman, and Littlefield.

Diamond, S. (2007). Who Killed Biafra? *Journal of Dialectical Anthropology, 31*, 339–362.

Dickson, S. H. (2018). Bayelsa Removes 28,000 Ghost Workers from Payroll. *Punch News*. https://punchng.com/Bayelsa-removes-28000-ghost-workers-from-payroll/. Accessed 23 May 2021.

Dinstein, Y. (2011). *War, Aggression and Self-Defense*. Cambridge University Press.

Disu, K. (2021, July 24). How Bayelsa Lost Atala Field to Two-Year-Old Firm. *Vanguard News*. https://www.vanguardngr.com/2021/07/how-bayelsa-lost-atala-field-to-two-year-old-firm/. Accessed 24 July 2021.

Dixon, J. C., Singleton, R. A., & Straits, B. C. (2016). *The Process of Social Research*. Oxford University.

Dodd, V. (2021, April 18). Tackling Poverty and Inequality to Reduce Crime, Says Police Chief. *The Guardian News*. https://www.theguardian.com/uk-news/2021/apr/18/tackle-poverty-and-inequality-to-reduce-says-police-chief. Accessed 18 April 2021.

Dodd, N., & Merwe, J. V. D. (2019). *The Political Economy of Underdevelopment in the Global South: The Government-Business-Media Complex*. Palgrave Macmillan.

Doerffer, J. W. (2013). *Oil Spill Response in the Marine Environment*. Elsevier.

Dokpesi, A. O., & Ibiezugbe, M. I. (2012). Assessment the Human Development Efforts of the Niger Delta Development Commission. In O. Ukaga, U. O. Ukiwo, & I. S. Ibaba (Eds.), *Natural Resources, Conflict, and Sustainable Development: Lessons from the Niger Delta* (pp. 60–78). Routledge.

Dollard, J., Miller, N. E., Doob, L. W., Mowrer, O. H., & Sears, R. R. (1939). *Frustration and Aggression*. Yale University Press.

Don Pedro, I. (2006). *Oil in the Water, Crude Power and Militancy in the Niger Delta*. Forward Communications Limited.

Donaldson, L. (1985). *In Defense of Organisation Theory: A Reply to Critics*. Cambridge University Press.

Donovan, C., & Ahmed, R. (1992). *Issues of Infrastructural Development: A Synthesis of the Literature*. International Food Policy Research Institute.

Doro-on, A. (2012). *Risk Assessment for Water Infrastructure Safety and Security*. CRC.

Doro-on, A. M. (2014). *Risk Assessment and Security for Pipelines, Tunnels, and Underground Rails and Transit Operations*. CRC Press.

Douglas, O. (2008). A Community Guide to Understanding Resource Control. In A. Ikein, D. S. P. Alamieyeseigha, & S. Azaiki (Eds.), *Oil, Democracy, and the Promise of True Federalism* (pp. 331–340). University Press of America.

Douglas, O., & Okonta, I. (2003). *Where Vultures Feast: Shell, Human Rights, and Oil in the Niger Delta*. Verso.

Dragos Incorporated Report. (2021). Oil and Natural Gas Cyber Threat Perspective for the GCC 2021. https://www.dragos.com/resource/gcc-ong-cyber-threat-perspective/. Accessed 26 October 2023.

Duda, D., & Wardin, K. (2013). Characteristics of Piracy in the Gulf of Guinea and its Influence on International Maritime Transport in the Region. In A. Weintrit & T. Neumann (Eds.), *Marine Navigation and Safety Transportation* (pp. 177–185). CRC Publication.

Duquet, N. (2011). Swamped with Weapons: The Proliferation of illicit Small Arms and Light Weapons in the Niger Delta. In C. Obi & S. A. Rustad (Eds.), *Oil and Insurgency in the Niger Delta: Managing the Complex Politics of Petrol-Violence*. Zed Books.

Duquette, G. (1997). *Classroom Methods and Strategies for Teaching at the Secondary School Level*. E. Mellen Press.

Durkheim, E. (1956). *Education and Sociology*. Free Press.

Durojaye, O. (2012). *Peace Research Methods*. National Open University of Nigeria.

Dwyer, S., & Buckle, J. (2009). The Space Between on Being an Insider-Outsider in Qualitative Research. *International Journal of Qualitative Methods, 8*(1), 54–63.

Eagleton, T. (2013). *The Illusions of Postmodernism*. Blackwell.

Ebiye, S. (2000). Community conflicts in the Niger Delta 1850 – 1980 and from 1981 to 1999. *Journal of Africana, 7*(ii), 102–108.

Eboh, M. (2021). DPR to Upgrade Downstream Petroleum Sector Operations. *Vanguard News*. https://www.vanguardngr.com/2021/02/dpr-to-upgrade-downstream-petroleum-sector-operations/. Accessed 9 February 2021.

Eboreime, M. I., & Omotor, D. G. (2010). Development Interventions of Oil Multinationals in Nigeria's Niger Delta: For the Rich or the Poor? In V. Ojakorotu (Ed.), *Anatomy of the Niger Delta Crisis: Causes, Consequences, and Opportunities for Peace* (pp. 63–78). Lit Verlag.

Ecumenical Council for Corporate Responsibility (ECCR). (2010). *Shell in the Niger Delta: A Framework for Change.* Cordaid.

Eden, C., & Ackermann, F. (2011). *Making Strategy: Mapping Out Strategic Success.* Sage.

Edigin, L., & Okonmah, I. E. (2010). Mystifying Development Policy Strategies in the Niger Delta: The Unending Mistake. *Journal of Research in National Development, 8*(2).

Edoni, E. R., McFubara, K. G., & Akwagbe, R. E. E. (2012, November). Health Manpower Development in Bayelsa State, Nigeria. *Risk Management and Healthcare Policy Journal, 5,* 127–135.

Edwards, R., & Holland, J. (2013). *What is Qualitative Interviewing?* Bloomsbury.

Effiong, J. (2010). Oil and Gas Industry in Nigeria: The Paradox of the Black Gold. In D. E. Taylor (Eds.), *Environmental and Social Justice: An International Perspective* (Vol. 18, pp. 323–352). Emerald.

Egbe, R. E., & Thompson, D. (2010, December). Environmental Challenges of Oil Spillage for Families in Oil Producing Communities of the Niger Delta Region. *Journal of Home Economics Research,* (13).

Eisenmenger, N., Pichler, M., Krenmayer, N., Noll, D., Plank, B., Schalmann, K., Wandl, M. T., & Gingrich, S. (2020). The Sustainable Development Goals Prioritized Economic Growth Over Sustainable Resource Use: A Critical Reflection on the SDGs from Socio-ecological Perspective. *Journal of Sustainable Science, 15,* 1101–1110.

Ejeh, E. U., Bappah, A. I., & Dankofa, Y. (2019). Nature of Terrorism and Anti-terrorism Laws in Nigeria. *Nnamdi Azikiwe University Journal of International Law and Jurisprudence, 10*(2), 186–192.

Ejiofor, C. (2012). *Biafra's Struggle for Survival.* Catholic Institution for Development Justice and Peace.

Ekpenyong, A. S. (2010). The Oil Economy, Environmental Laws, and Human Rights Violations in Niger Delta Region: Implications and Suggested Solutions. *International Journal of Social Policy Research and Development, 1*(2).

Emmel, N. (2013). *Sampling and Choosing Cases in Qualitative Research: A Realist Approach.* Sage.

Emmer, R. (2016). Securitisation. In A. Collins (Ed.), *Contemporary Security Studies* (4th ed., pp. 168–182). Oxford University Press.

Enders, W., & Sandler, T. (2012). *The Political Economy of Terrorism* (2nd ed.). Cambridge University Press.

Eneh, S., & Enuoh, R. (2015). Corporate Social Responsibility in the Niger Delta Region of Nigeria: In Who's Interest? *Journal of Management and Sustainability, 5*(3), 74–82.

Energy World. (2021). Women Make Up 22 Percent of the Workforce in Oil and Gas Industry: Survey. https://energy.economictimes.indiatimes.com/news/oil-and-gas/women-make-up-22-per-cent-of-the-workforce-in-oil-gas-industry-survey/88197709. Accessed 14 November 2023.

Environmental Rights Action. (2002). *A Blanket of Silence: Images of the Odi Genocide, Special Reports.* Environmental Rights Action/Friends of the Earth.

Environmental Performance Index. (2020). 2020 EPI Results. https://epi.yale.edu/epi-results/2020/component/epi. Accessed 23 October 2021.

Enweremadu, D. (2013). Nigeria's Quest to Recover Looted Assets: The Abacha Affair. *African Spectrum Journal, 48*(2), 51–70.

Erford, B. T. (2015). *Research and Evaluation in Counseling* (2nd ed.). Cengage Learning.

Esiedesa, O. (2021). Nigeria Earned $418.5bn in 10 Years from Petroleum, NEITI Reveals. *Vanguard News.* https://www.vanguardngr.com/2021/06/nigeria-earned-418-5bn-in-10yrs-from-petroleum-neiti-reveals/. Accessed 19 June 2021.

Etekpe, A. (2018). The Challenges of Climate Change on the Livelihood and Sustainable Development of Selected Coastal Communities in Nigeria's Niger Delta (1990–2015). In V. U. James (Ed.), *Capacity Building for Sustainable Development* (pp. 254–264). CAB International.

Etemire, U. (2016). *Law and Practice on Public Participation in Environmental Matters: The Nigerian Example in Transnational Comparative Perspective.* Routledge.

Etete, E. (2017, July 7). Ovom in Yenagoa City: A Cradle of Development but Shadow of itself. *Headline News Nigeria.* http://headlinenewsnigeria.com/ovom-yenagoa-city-cradle-development-shadow/. Accessed 2 March 2018.

Etikerentse, G. (1985). *Nigerian Petroleum Law.* Macmillan.

Etowah, U. E., & Effiong, S. A. (2012). Oil Spillage Cost Gas Flaring Cost, and Life Expectancy Rate of the Niger Delta People of Nigeria. *Advances in Management and Applied Economics Journal, 2*(2), 211–228.

Evers, J. C., & Staa, A. (2010). Qualitative Analysis in Case Study. In A. J. Mills, G. Eurepos, & E. Wiebe (Eds.), *Encyclopedia of Case Study Research* (Vol. 1, pp. 749–755). Sage.

Ewalefoh, J. O. (2020). The Political Economy of Insecurity in Africa: Focus on North East, Nigeria. In S. O. Oloruntoba & T. Falola (Eds.), *The Palgrave Handbook of African Political Economy* (pp. 927–946). Palgrave Macmillan.

Fagel, M. J. (2012). Agroterrorism. In M. J. Fagel (Ed.), *Principles of Emergency Management: Hazard Specific Issues and Mitigation Strategies* (pp. 375–402). CRC Press.

Fahim, M. A., Abdel-Aal, H. K., & Aggour, M. A. (2015). *Petroleum and Gas Field Processing* (2nd ed.). CRC Press.

Fairclough, N. (2013). *Critical Discourse Analysis: The Critical Study of Language* (2nd ed.). Routledge.

Fairclough, N., & Wodak, R. (1997). Critical Discourse Analysis. In T. van Dijk (Ed.), *Discourse as Social Interaction* (pp. 258–284). Sage.

Faleti, A. S. (2006). *Theories of Social Conflicts*. Spectrum.

Falola, T. (2009). *Colonialism and Violence in Nigeria*. Indiana University Press.

Falola, T., & Genova, A. (2005). *The Politics of the Global Oil Industry: An Introduction*. Praeger.

Fang, H., & Duan, M. (2014). *Offshore Operation Facilities: Equipment and Procedures*. Elsevier.

Farah, D. (2001, May 18). Nigeria's Oil Exploitation Leaves Delta Poisoned, Poor. https://www.washingtonpost.com/archive/politics/2001/03/18/nigerias-oil-exploitation-leaves-delta-poisoned-poor/1353516c-6c79-4df0-879377fc7dbd4880/?utm_term=.f07d9d93647c. Accessed 5 May 2018.

Faust, D., & Aktan, A. E. (2003). A Holistic Integrated Systems Approach to Assure the Mobility, Efficiency, Safety, and Integrity of Highways Transportation. In Z. Wu & M. Abe (Eds.), *Structural Health Monitoring and Intelligent Infrastructure: Structures and Infrastructure Sustainability* (Vol. 1, pp. 7–18). Balkema.

Federal Ministry of Environment. (2015). Shell Petroleum Development Company Environmental Impact Assessment Report of Agbada Non-Associated Gas (NAG) Project in Obio Akpor LGA, Rivers State. https://www.shell.com.ng/sustainability/environment/environment-impact-assessments/_jcr_content/par/textimage.stream/1481187344977/1e0d17d75a2015f74ec44eee92a4a225db6a7775a99d5e15d708c1c987705376/report-agbada-non-associated-gas-nag-project-eia.pdf. Accessed 22 August 2018.

Federal Republic of Nigeria Official Gazette. (2018). Flare Gas, Prevention of Waste and Pollution Regulation (Vol. 105(88)). Retrieved from PR https://ngfcp.dpr.gov.ng/media/1120/flare-gas-prevention-of-waste-and-pollution-regulations-2018-gazette-cleaner-copy-1.pdf. Accessed 14 December 2020.

Fentiman, A. (2014). The Anthropology of Oil: The Impact of the Oil Industry on a Fishing Community in the Niger Delta. In C. Williams (Ed.), *Environmental Victims* (pp. 75–87). Routledge.

Ferabolli, S. (2021). Space Making in the Global South: Lessons from the GCC-Mercosur Agreement. *Contexto International, 43*(1).

Fierke, K. M. (2015). *Critical Approaches to International Security* (2nd ed.). Polity.

Finkel, M. L. (2018). *Pipeline Politics: Assessing the Benefits and Harms of Energy Policy*. Abe-Clio.

Fisher, J. J. (2018). Decolonizing Nigeria, 1945–1960: Politics, Power, and Personalities by Toyin Falola and Bola Dauda (review). *Journal of Global South Studies, 35*(1), 174–174.

Floyd, R. (2010). *Security and the Environment: Securitisation Theory and US Environmental Security Policy.* Cambridge University Press.

Folorunsho, R., & Awosika, L. (2014). Estuaries and Ocean Circulation Dynamics in the Niger Delta, Nigeria: Implication for Oil Spill and Pollution Management. In S. Diop & J. P. Barusseau (Eds.), *The Land/Ocean Interactions in the Coastal Zone of West and Central Africa* (pp. 77–86). Springer.

Forest, J. J. F., & Sousa, M. V. (2006). *Oil and Terrorism in the New Gulf: Framing U. S. Energy and Security Policies for the Gulf of Guinea* (p. 54). Rowman, and Littlefield.

Fox, M. A., & Whitesell, J. K. (2004). *Organic Chemistry* (3rd ed.). Jones, and Bartlett.

Franks, S., & Nunnally, S. (2011). *Barbarians of Oil: How the World's Oil Addiction Threatens Global Prosperity and Four Investments to protect Your Wealth.* Wiley.

Freud, S. (2015). *Beyond Pleasure Principle.* Dover.

Friedman, M. (1993). The Social Responsibility of Business is to Increase its Profits. In G. D. Chryssides & J. H. Kaler (Eds.), *An Introduction to Business Ethics* (pp. 249–265). Thomson.

Frynas, G. J. (2000). *Oil in Nigeria: Conflicts and Litigation Between Oil Companies and Village Communities* (pp. 8–50). LIT Verlag.

Fukuyama, F. (2018). *Identity: The Demand for Dignity and the Politics of Resentment.* Profile Books.

Gall, M. D., Gall, J. P., & Borg, W. R. (1996). *Educational Research: An Introduction* (6th ed.). Longman.

Galletta, A. (2013). *Mastering the Semi-Structured Interview and Beyond: From Research Design to Analysis and Publication.* New York University Press.

Ganor, B. (2010). Defining Terrorism: Is One Man's Terrorist Another Man's Freedom Fighter? *Journal of Police Practice and Research, 3*(4), 287–304.

Gary, D. E. (2018). Secondary Data and Research. In J. Skoczylis (Ed.), *Applying Research* (pp. 634–660). Sage.

Gates, H. L., & Akyeampong. (2012). *Dictionary of African Biography.* Oxford University Press.

Gaughran, A. (2015). *Hundreds of Oil Spills Continue to Blight Niger Delta* (Amnesty International Report). https://www.amnesty.org/en/latest/news/2015/03/hundreds-of-oil-spills-continue-to-blight-niger-delta/. Accessed 9 October 2018.

Gbobo, I. P. (2020). Women and the Environment in Nigeria: The Experience of Women in the Niger Delta. In M. C. Green & M. Haron (Eds.), *Law, Religion and the Environment in Africa* (pp. 185–198). African Sun Media.

Geary, W. M. N. (2013). *Nigeria Under British Rule (1927)*. Routledge.

General Data Protection Regulation. (2018). *Guide to the General Data Protection Regulation (GDPR)*. Information Commissioner's Office. https://assets.publishing.service.gov.uk/government/uploads/system/uploads/attachment_data/file/711097/guide-to-the-general-data-protection-regulation-gdpr-1-0.pdf. Accessed 10 January 2019.

George, L. N. (2009). American Insecurities and the on politics of the US Pharmacotic Wars. In F. Debrix & M. J. Lacy (Eds.), *The Geopolitics of American Insecurity: Terror* (pp. 34–53). Routledge.

Gheorghe, A. V., Pulfer, R., Vamanu, D. V., & Katina, P. F. (2017). *Critical Infrastructures, Key Resources, Key Assets: Risk, Vulnerability, Resilience, Fragility and Perception Governance*. Springer.

Ghosh, T. K., & Prelas, M. A. (2009). *Energy Resources and Systems: Fundamentals and Non-Renewable Resources* (Vol. 1). Springer.

Gibbs, G. (2018). *Analysing Qualitative Data: The Sage Qualitative Research Kit* (2nd ed.). Sage.

Gillie, M., Schoenung, S., Klebanoff, L., & Keller, J. (2016). The Need for Hydrogen-Based Energy Technologies in the 21st Century. In L. Klebanoff (Ed.), *Hydrogen Storage Technology: Materials and Applications* (pp. 3–30). CRC.

Gillion, J. T. (2012). *Phonological Awareness: From Research to Practice*. Guilford Press.

Gilmore, J. (2015). *The Cosmopolitan Military: Armed Forces and Human Security in the 21st Century*. Springer.

Gimbel, K., & Newsome, J. (2018). Using Qualitative Methods in Quantitative Survey Research Agenda. In L. R. Atkeson & R. M. Alvarez (Eds.), *The Oxford Handbook of Polling and Survey Methods* (pp. 505–532). Oxford University Press.

Ginsberg, B. (2013). *The Value of Violence*. Prometheus Books.

Giugni, M., & Passy, F. (2014). Migrant Mobilization between Political Institutions and Citizens Regimes: A Comparison of France and Switzerland. *European Journal of Political Research, 43*, 51–82.

Gjorv, G. H. (2018). Chapter 15: Human Security. In P. D. Williams & M. McDonald (Eds.), *Security Studies: An Introduction* (3rd ed.). Routledge.

Global Terrorism Index. (2015). *Measuring and Understanding the Impact of Terrorism*. Institute for Economics and Peace Publication. http://economicsandpeace.org/wp-content/uploads/2015/11/2015-Global-Terrorism-Index-Report.pdf. Accessed 15 April 2020.

Global Partnership for the Prevention of Armed Conflict. (2017). Conflict Analysis Framework: Filed Guidelines and Procedures. https://www.gppac. net/files/2018-11/GPPAC%20CAFGuide_Interactive%20version_febr2018_. pdf. Accessed 1 October 2020.

Global Patriot. (2019, May 24). Aiteo Pledges N500 M Support to Bayelsa Education Fund: Laments Frequent Vandalism on NCTL. *Global Patriot Newspaper*. https://globalpatriotnews.com/aiteo-pledges-n500-m-support-to-bayelsa-education-fund-laments-frequent-vandalism-on-nctl/. Accessed 20 September 2020.

Gold, R. L. (1958). Roles in Sociological Field Observations. *Journal of Social Forces, 36*(3), 217–223.

Goodall, J. (2010). *In the Shadow of Man*. Orion.

Goodman, A., Moynihan, D., & Goodman, D. (2016). *Democracy Now!: Twenty Years Covering the Movements Changing America*. Simon and Schuster.

Gopakumar, G. (2012). *Transforming Urban Water Supply in India: The Role of Reform and Partnerships in Globalisation*. Routledge.

Gormley, T. P., & Kristensen, M. (2019). Regulating Offshore Petroleum Resources: The British and Norwegian Models. In E. O. Pereira & H. Bjornebye (Eds.), *Hydrocarbon Policy and Legislation: Norway* (pp. 39–94). Edward Elgar.

Goumandakoye, H. (2016). Oil in Niger: A Foundation for Promise or a New Resource Curse? *The Extractive Industries and Society Journal, 3*(2), 361–366.

Griffiths, R. J. (2016). *U.S. Security Cooperation with Africa: Political and Policy Challenges*. Routledge.

Grigg, N. S. (2010). *Infrastructure Finance: The Business of Infrastructure for a Sustainable Future*. Wiley.

Grix, J. (2010). *Demystifying Postgraduate Research from MA to Ph.D*. University of Birmingham Press.

Grossman, H. I. (1999). Kleptocracy and Revolutions. *Oxford Economic Papers Journal, 51*, 267–283.

Grove, S. K., Burns, N., & Grey, J. (2010). *Understanding Nursing Research: Building an Evidence-Based Practice* (5th ed.). Elsevier.

Guest, G., Macqueen, K. M., & Namey. (2012). *Applied Thematic Analysis*. Sage.

Gultekin, K. (2007). Women Engagement in Terrorism: What Motivates Females to Join in Terrorist Organisations? In D. M. Al-Badayneh, S. Ozeren, & I. D. Gunes (Eds.), *Understanding Terrorism: Analysis of Sociological and Psychological Aspects, the NATO Science for Peace and Security Programme* (Vol. 22, pp. 169–174). IOS.

Gundlach, E. R. (2018). Oil-Related Mangrove Loss East of Bonny River, Nigeria. In C. Makowski & C. W. Finkl (Eds.), *Threats to Mangrove Forests: Hazards, Vulnerability, and Management* (pp. 267–322). Springer.

Gupta, D. K. (2008). *Understanding Terrorism and Physical Violence: The Life Cycle of Birth, Growth, Transformation and Demise.* Routledge.

Gurr, R. T. (2015). *Political Rebellion: Causes, Outcomes and Alternatives.* Routledge.

Haas, T. (2014). Qualitative Case Study Methods in Newsroom Research and Reporting: The Case of the Akron Beacon Journal. In S. H. Lorio (Ed.), *Qualitative Research in Journalism: Taking it to the Streets* (pp. 59–74). Routledge.

Hai-Jew, S. (2016). Conducting Sentiment Analysis and Post-Sentiment Data Exploration through Automated Means. In S. Hai-Jew (Ed.), *Social Media Data Extraction, and Content Analysis* (pp. 202–241). IGI Global.

Hain, D., & Pisoiu, S. (2017). *Theories of Terrorism: An Introduction.* Routledge.

Hairshine, K. (2021). Nigeria Faces a Tough Time Diversifying from Oil. *Deutsche Welle.* https://www.dw.com/en/nigeria-faces-a-tough-time-diversifying-from-oil/a-59494125. Accessed 5 March 2022.

Haken, N., & Taft, P. (2015). *Violence in Nigeria: Patterns and Trends.* Springer.

Halibozek, E., & Kovacich, G. L. (2017). *The Manager's Handbook for Corporate Security: Establishing and Managing a Successful Assets Program* (2nd ed.). Butterworth-Heinemann.

Hall, H. L., & Manfull, A. (2016). *Getting the Story Straight: Principles of Effective News and Caption Writing.* Rosen.

Hamalai, L., Egwu, S., & Omotola, S. J. (2017). *Nigeria's 2015 General Election: Continuity and Change in Electoral Democracy.* Palgrave Macmillan.

Hammond, J. L. (2011). The Resource Curse and Oil Revenues in Angola and Venezuela. *Science and Society Journal, 75*(3), 348–378.

Haq, U. M. (1995). *Reflections on Human Development.* Oxford University Press.

Harding, J. (2013). *Qualitative Data Analysis from Start to Finish.* Sage.

Harrington, N., Jones, S. G., Bermudez, J. S., & Newlee, D. (2019). *Iran's Threat to Saudi's Critical Infrastructure: The Implications of U.S.–Iranian Escalation.* Centre for Strategic and International Studies.

Hashim, A. S., Gramescu, B., & Nitu, C. (2018). Pipe Leakage Detection Using Humidity and Microphones Sensors—A Review. In G. I. Gheorghe (Eds.), *Proceedings of the International Conference of Mechatronics and Cyber-Mix Mechatronics—2018* (pp. 129–137). Springer.

Heck, R. H. (2004). *Studying Educational and Social Policy: Theoretical Concepts and Research Methods.* Lawrence Erlbaum Associates.

Heleta, S. (2009). *The Darfur Conflict from the Perspective of the Rebel Justice and Equality Movement.* Nelson Movement University.

Hendriksz, M., Chetty, M., & Teljeur, E. (2017). Africa's Prospect for Infrastructure Development and Regional Integration: Energy Sector. In N. Ncube &

C. L. Lufumpa (Eds.), *Infrastructure in Africa: Lessons for Development* (pp. 185–256). Policy Press.

Henry, A. D. (2016). A Concise View of Niger Delta Region of Nigeria: An Interpretation of a Nigerian Historian. *International Research Journal of Interdisciplinary and Multidisciplinary Studies, 2*(10), 56–63.

Herbst, D., & Ndlangisa, M. (2010). CII Protection- Lessons for Developing Countries: South Africa as a Case Study. In R. Bloomfield & E. Rome (Eds.), *Critical Information Infrastructures Security*. Springer.

Hercog, M. (2019). Skill Levels, as a Political Resource: Political Practices of Recent Migrants in Switzerland. In I. Steiner & P. Wanner (Eds.), *Migrants and Expats: The Swiss Migration and Mobility Nexus* (pp. 243–263). Springer.

Herington, J. (2015). Philosophy: The Concepts of Security, Fear, Liberty, and the State. In P. Bourbeau (Ed.), *Security Dialogue Across Disciplines* (pp. 22–44). Cambridge University Press.

Hermans, H. J. M. (2018). *Society in the Self: A Theory of Identity for Democracy*. Oxford University Press.

Heurlin, B., & Kristensen, K. (2010). International Security. In P. D. Williams, P. Bilgin, Sekiguchi, J. K. Galbraith, S. T. Inayatullah, J. Wiener, R. A. Schrire, & I. L. Murphy (Eds.), *Global Security, and International Political Economy* (Vol. III, pp. 65–109). EOLSS Publication.

Higgins, P. (2010). *Eradicating Ecocide: Laws and Governance to Stop the Destruction of the Planet*. Shepheard-Walwyn.

Hill, J. (2020). *Environmental, Social, and Governance (ESG) Investing: A Balanced Analysis of the Theory and Practice of a Sustainable Portfolio*. Academic Press.

Hirshleifer, J. (2001). *The Dark Side of the Force: Economic Foundations of Conflict Theory*. Cambridge University Press.

Hobbins, J. (2016). Young Long-term Unemployed and the Individualisation of Responsibility. *Nordic Journal of Working Life Studies, 6*(2), 43–59.

Hoeffler, A. (2011). Greed Versus Grievance: A Useful Conceptual Distinction in the Study of Civil War? *Studies in Ethnicity and Nationalism Journal, 11*(2), 274–284.

Holborn, M., & Haralambos, M. (2021). *Sociology: Themes and Perspectives* (8th ed.). Collins.

Holcomb, J. (2016). *Definitive Guide to Cybersecurity for the Oil and Gas Industry* (pp. 3–27). Leidos. https://www.ciosummits.com/Online_Assets_Leidos_Definitive_Guide_to_Cyber_for_Oil_and_Gas_eBook.pdf. Accessed 27 March 2018.

Holden, E., Linnerud, K., & Banister, D. (2014). Sustainable Development: Our Common Future Revisited. *Journal of Global Environmental Change, 26*, 130–139.

Holdway, D. A. (2002). The Acute and Chronic Effects of Wastes Associated with Offshore Oil and Gas Production on Temperate and Tropical Marine Ecological Processes. *Marin Pollution Bulletin, 44*(3), 185–203.

Hosen, A. (2011). Religion and Security: What's Your Motive? In N. Hosen & R. Mohr (Eds.), *Law and Religion in Public Life: The Contemporary Debate* (pp. 137–151). Routledge.

Hough, P. (2004). *Understanding Global Security.* Routledge.

House of Commons. (2013). *Serious and Organised Crime Strategy.* Stationery Office.

Howell, J. (2011). Civil Society in China. In M. Edwards (Ed.), *The Oxford Handbook of Civil Society* (pp. 159–170). Oxford University Press.

Huberman, M. A., & Miles, M. B. (1994). *Data Management and Analysis Methods.* Sage.

Hudson, N. F. (2010). *Gender, Human Security and the United Nations: Security Language as a Political Platform for Women.* Routledge.

Huesmann, L. R. (2013). *Aggressive Behaviour: Current Perspectives.* Springer Science.

Hughes, S., & Sengupta, K. (2020). Priti Patel Repeatedly Backed Company Accused of Obtaining Nigerian Gas Contract through Corruption. *Independent News.* https://www.independent.co.uk/news/uk/politics/priti-patel-gas-contract-corruption-nigeria-process-industrial-development-b1759441.html. Accessed 21 November 2020.

Human Rights Watch. (1999). *Nigeria: Crackdown in the Niger Delta* (Vol. 11(2)). Human Rights Watch.

Human Rights Watch. (1999). *Nigeria the Price of Oil: Corporate Responsibility and Human Rights Violations in Nigeria's Oil Producing Communities, January 1999.* Human Rights Watch.

Human Rights Watch. (2002). *The Niger Delta: No Democratic Dividend* (Vol. 14(7), pp. 30–41). Human Rights Watch.

Human Security Report Project. (2013). *The Decline of Global Violence: Evidence, Explanation, and Contestation.* Human Security Press. https://reliefweb.int/sites/reliefweb.int/files/resources/HSRP_Report_2013_140226_Web.pdf. Accessed 3 July 2020.

Hunt, L. W. (2018). *The Retrieval of Liberalism in Policing.* Oxford University Press.

Hussain, F., & Al-Marri, M. A. (2017, November). *The Impact of the Oil Crisis on Security and Foreign Policy in GCC Countries: Case Studies of Qatar, KSA and UAE.* Arab Centre for Research and Policy Studies.

Hustedde, R. J. (2014). Seven Theories for Seven Community Developers. In R. Phillips & R. H. Pittman (Eds.), *An Introduction to Community Development* (2nd ed., pp. 22–44). Routledge.

Ibaba, I. S. (2009). Violent Conflicts and Sustainable Development in Bayelsa State. *Review of African Political Economy*, (122), 555–573.

Ibaba, I. S. (2012). Introduction: Interrogating Development Deficits in the Niger Delta. In S. I. Ibaba (Ed.), *Niger Delta: Constraints and Pathways to Development* (pp. 1–9). Newcastle upon Tyne.

Idemudia, U. (2014). Oil Multinational Companies as Money Makers and Peace Makers: Lessons from Nigeria. In G. Eweje (Ed.), *Corporate Social Responsibility and Sustainability: Emerging Trends in Developing Economies* (pp. 191–214). Emerald.

Igbinovia, P. E. (2014). *Oil Thefts and Pipeline Vandalisation in Nigeria*. African Books.

Igwe, U. (2020). *A Political Economy Perspective on Oil and Conflict in Nigeria's Niger Delta*. The London School of Economics and Political Science. https://www.blogs.lse.ac.uk/africaatlse/2020/09/16/pol itical-economy-perspective-oil-conflict-security-nigeria-niger-delta/. Accessed 2 November 2021.

Ikein, A. (2008). Introduction to Nigeria and the Politics of Niger Delta. In D. S. P. Alamieyeseigha, S. Azaika, & A. A. Ikein (Eds.), *Oil Democracy and the Promise of True Federalism in Nigeria* (pp. 2–20). University Press of America.

Ikelegbe, A. (2013). The Crisis in Relations: Multinational Oil Companies and Host Communities in the Niger Delta. In A. Ikelegbe (Ed.), *Oil, Environment and Resource Conflicts in Nigeria*. Lit Verglag.

Ikelegbe, A., & Oshita, O. O. (2019). An Overview of Theoretical and Practical Issues in Internal Security Management in Nigeria. In O. O. Oshita, I. M. Alumona, & F. C. Onuoha (Eds.), *Internal Security Management in Nigeria: Perspectives, Challenges, and Lessons* (pp. 29–48). Palgrave.

Ikelegbe, A. (2005). The Economy of Conflict in the Oil Rich Niger Delta Region of Nigeria. *Nordic Journal of African Studies, 14*(2), 207–235.

Ikelegbe, O. A. (2014). The Resource Curse: Oil, Communal Agitation and State Repression in the Niger Delta. In O. A. Ikelegbe (Ed.), *Oil, Environmental and Resource Conflicts in Nigeria* (pp. 109–142). Lit Verlag.

Imokhai, C. (2015). *The People's Choice*. Author House.

Inengite, P. (2018). The 1914 Amalgamation of North and South: A Historic Misadventure: A History of the Niger Delta Question...- Part 2. https://patnengii.blogspot.com/20/16/06/amalgamation-of-norths outh-historical14.html. Accessed 16 December 2021.

Ingo, V., Pelzer, B., & Schaffrath, S. (2014). Coping with Unemployment: The Impact of Unemployment on Mental Health Personality, and Social Interaction Skills. *Work: A Journal of Prevention, Assessment and Rehabilitation, 48*(2), 289–295.

Information Resources Management Association. (2015). Research Methods: Concepts, Methodologies, tools, and Applications, USA, IGI.

Intergovernmental Panel on Climate Change. (2007). *Summary for Policymakers, in Climate Change 2007: Impacts, Adaptation, and Vulnerability, Contribution of Working Group II to the Fourth Assessment Report of the Intergovernmental Penal on Climate Change* (pp. 15–17). Cambridge University.

Intergovernmental Panel on Climate Change. (2022). *The Ocean and Cryosphere in a Changing Climate: Special Report of the Intergovernmental Panel on Climate Change*. Cambridge University Press.

International Monetary Fund. (2019). Nigeria: Mobilizing Resources to Invest in People. https://www.imf.org/en/News/Articles/2019/04/01/na040219-nigeria-mobilizing-resources-to-invest-in-people. Accessed 19 June 2021.

Ioannides, E. (2017). *Fundamental Principles of EU Law Against Money Laundering*. Routledge.

Irvine, M. (2018). *A Practical Guide to Vicarious Liability*. Law Briefs Publication.

Isidiho, A. O., & Sabran, M. S. B. (2015). Socio-Economic Impact of Niger Delta Development Commission (NDDC) Infrastructural Projects in Selected Communities in Imo State Nigeria. *Asian Journal of Humanities and Social Sciences, 3*(2), 109–115.

Issa, A. (2015). *Reflections on Industrial and Economy*. Maulthouse.

Ite, A. E., Harry, T. A., Obadimu, C. O., & Inim, I. J. (2018). Petroleum Hydrocarbons Contaminations of Surface Water and Ground Water in the Niger Delta Region of Nigeria. *Journal of Environment Pollution and Human Health, 6*(2), 51–61.

Iwuoha, V. C. (2021). Strategic Security Planning and Protection of Multinational Oil Pipeline Assets in the Niger Delta International. *Journal of Intelligence, Security, and Public Affairs, 23*(3), 343–366. https://doi.org/10.1080/2300992.2021.2005933

Izuaka, M. (2021, March 29). Nigeria Will Continue to Rely on Natural Gas as a Transitional Fuel. *Premium Times*. https://www.premiumtimesng.com/business/business-news/451981-nigeria-will-continue-to-rely-on-natural-gas-as-a-transition-fuel-sylva.html. Accessed 8 July 2021.

Jackson, P., Kassaye, D., & Shearon, E. (2019). I Fought the Law and the Law Won: Evidence on Policing Communities in Dire Dawa, Ethiopia. *British Journal of Criminology, 59*(1), 126–143.

Jackson, K., & Bazeley, P. (2013). *Qualitative Data Analysis with Nvivo* (2nd ed.). Sage.

Jaffee, D. (1998). *Levels of Socio-economic Development Theory* (2nd ed.). Praeger.

Jaison, J. (2018). *Qualitative Research and Transformative Results: A Primer for Students and Mentors in Theological Education*. South Asian Institute of Advanced Christian Studies Publication.

James, A. (2012). SPDC Alleges Sabotage after Discovery of 51 Operational Leaks in Niger Delta. *Daily Post News Nigeria.* https://dailypost.ng/2021/06/15/spdc-alleges-sabotage-after-discovery-of-51-operational-leaks-in-n-delta/. Accessed 15 June 2021.

James, D. D. (1995). The Value of Security: Hobbs, Marx, Nietzche, and Baudrillard. In R. D. Lipchitz (Ed.), *On Security* (p. 24). Colombia University Press.

James, R. K., & Gilliland, B. E. (2013). *Crisis Intervention Strategies* (7th ed.). Cengage.

James, U. V. (2018). *Capacity Building for Sustainable Development.* Centre for Agriculture and Bioscience International-CABI Publication.

Janoski, T., Luke, D., & Oliver, C. (2014). *The Causes of Structural Unemployment: Four Factors that Keeps People from the Job they Deserve.* Polity Press.

Jarmuth, M. R. (2009). *The Psychology of American Fascism: The Triumph of the Authoritarian Id in Post-Christian USA.* CreateSpace.

Jatto, A. A., Skoczylis, J., & Horner, G. (2023). UK Anti-Money Laundering and Counter-Terrorist Financing Measures. In S. N. Romaniuk, C. Kaunert, & A. P. H. Fabe (Eds.), *Countering Terrorist and Criminal Financing* (1st ed.). Routledge & CRC Press. https://doi.org/10.4324/9781003092216. Accessed 18 November 2023.

Jatto, A. A., & Stanislas, P. (2017). Contemporary Security Challenges Facing Edo State Nigeria. *Journal of Geopolitics, History, and International Relations, 9*(2), 118–140.

Jega, A. (2000). The State and Identity Transformation under Structural Adjustment in Nigeria. In A. Jega (Eds.), *Identity Transformation and Identity Politics Under Structural Adjustment in Nigeria* (pp. 24–40). Nordic African Institute.

Jenkins, L. (2022). *Sisters and Sisterhood: The Kenney Family, Class, and Suffrage 1890–1965.* Oxford University Press.

Johl, S. K., & Renganathan, S. (2010). Strategies for Gaining Access in Doing Fieldwork: Reflection of Two Researchers. *The Electronic Journal of Business Research Methods, 8*(1), 42–50.

John, M. (2017). *Al-Shabaab and Boko Haram: Guerrilla Insurgency or Strategic Terrorism.* World Scientific.

Johnsen, S. (2016). Mitigating Vulnerabilities in Oil and Gas Assets via Resilience. In M. Rice & S. Shenoi (Eds.), *Critical Infrastructure Protection X* (pp. 43–62). Springer.

Johnson, B., & Christensen, L. (2008). *Educational Research: Qualitative, Quantitative and Mixed Approaches.* Sage.

Johnson, B., & Christenson, L. B. (2017). *Educational Research: Quantitative, Qualitative and Mixed Approaches* (6th ed.). Sage.

Johnson, P. (2010). *Making the Market: Victorian Origins of Corporate Capitalism*. Cambridge University Press.

Jones, S. R., Torres, V., & Arminio, J. (2014). *Negotiating the Complexities of Qualitative Research in Higher Education: Fundamental Elements and Issues* (2nd ed.). Routledge.

Joseph, S. (1988). *Political Theory and Power*. E. J. Brill.

Joseph, R. A. (2014). *Democracy and Prebendal Politics in Nigeria*. Cambridge University Press.

Juke, P., & Kenny, S. (2015). Pipeline/Soil Interaction Modelling in Support of Pipeline Engineering Design and Integrity. In R. W. Revie (Ed.), *Oil and Gas Pipelines Integrity and Safety Handbook* (pp. 101–130). Wiley.

Justice, J. B. (2008). Purpose and Significance of Research Design. In K. Yang & G. J. Miller (Eds.), *Handbook of Research Methods in Public Administration* (pp. 75–92). CRC.

Kabir, S. M. Z., & Momtaz, S. (2013). *Evaluating Environmental and Social Impact Assessment in Developing Countries*. Elsevier.

Kaldor, M. (2020). *Cities at War: Global Insecurity and Urban Resistance*. Colombia University Press.

Kalu, K. N. (2009). *State Power, Autarchy, and Political Conquest in Nigeria's Federalism*. Lexington.

Kalu, K. N. (2018). *Political Culture, Change, and Security Policy in Nigeria*. Routledge.

Kant, I. (2018). *Project for Perpetual Peace: A Philosophical Essay*. Creative Media.

Kaplan, O. (2017). *Resisting War: How Communities Protect Themselves*. Cambridge University Press.

Karasz, M., & Pustisek, A. (2017). *Natural Gas: A Commercial Perspective*. Springer.

Kashubsky, M. (2016). *Offshore Oil and Gas Installations Security: An International Perspective*. Routledge.

Katsouris, C., & Sayne, A. (2015). *Nigeria's Criminal Crude: International Options to Combat the Export of Stolen Oil*. Chatham House.

Kay, S. (2012). *Global Security in the Twenty-First Century: The Quest for Power and the Search for Peace* (2nd ed.). Rowman, and Littlefield.

Keck, M. E., & Sikkink, K. (2014). *Activists beyond Borders: Advocacy Networks in International Politics*. Cornell University Press.

Kee, C. (2012). *Global Sales and Contract Law*. Oxford University Press.

Keiding, H. (2015). *The Game Theory: A Comprehensive Introduction*. World Scientific.

Kelly, S. (2017). *Governing Literate Populations: The Political Uses of Literacy in Securing Civil Society*. Routledge.

Kennedy, J. L. (1993). *Oil and Gas Pipelines Fundamentals*. Penn Well.

Kennedy, S. (2021, July 7). Revealed: Fossil Fuel Companies Lobby UK Government for Gas 'Compromise' Ahead of COP26. *Channel 4 News*. https://www.channel4.com/news/revealed-fossil-fuel-companies-lobby-uk-government-for-gas-compromise-ahead-of-cop26. Accessed 8 July 2021.

Keynes, J. M. (2019). *The General Theory of Employment, Interest and Money*. General Press.

Khalid, I. (2021). Shell in Nigeria: Polluted Communities Can Sue in English Supreme Courts. *BBC News*. https://www.bbc.co.uk/news/world-africa-560 41189. Accessed 13 February 2021.

Khan, K., Faura, J. C., & Khurshid, A. (2023, June). Energy Security Analysis in a Geopolitically Volatile World: A Causal Study. *Resources Policy Journal, 83*.

King, S. O. (2016). Engineering Students' Approaches to Learning Mathematics. In L. Ling & P. Ling (Eds.), *Methods and Paradigms in Education Research* (pp. 167–190). IGI.

King, M. L., Jr. (1967). *The Other America and Black Power*. Beacon Press.

King, N. (2004). Using Templates in the Thematic Analysis of Text. In C. Cassell & G. Symon (Eds.), *Essential Guide to Qualitative Methods in Organisational Research* (pp. 257–270). Sage.

Klare, M. T. (2014). Twenty-first Century Energy Wars: How Oil and Gas are Fuelling Global Conflicts. *Energy Post.EU*. https://energypost.eu/twenty-first-century-energy-wars-oil-gas-fuelling-global-conflicts/. Accessed 23 April 2019.

Knutson, J. (2021). *Deepwater Horizon Oil Spill*. Cherry Lake Publishing.

Kofigah, F. E. (2015). *The Security Challenges in Africa. Bridging the Gap between Human Security and State Security through Institutional Reforms: A Case Study of Nigeria*. Grin.

Koknar, A. M. (2009). The Epidemic of Energy Terrorism. In G. Luft & A. Korin (Eds.), *Energy Security Challenges for the 21st Century* (pp. 18–30). ABC-CLIO.

Kollewe, J. (2018, November 11). Alarm Over Talks to Implant UK Employees with Microchips. *The Guardian*. https://www.theguardian.com/technology/2018/nov/11/alarm-over-talks-to-implant-uk-employees-with-microchips. Accessed 24 November 2018.

Krahmann, E. (2008). Security: Collective Good or Commodity? *European Journal of International Relations, 14*(3), 382–383.

Krishnaswamy, K. N., Sivakumar, A. I., & Mathirajan, M. (2009). *Management Research Methodology: Integration of Principles, Methods and Techniques* (3rd ed.). Pearson Education.

Krueger, I. J. (1996). Probabilistic National Stereotypes. *European Journal of Social Psychology, 26*, 960–985.

Kulungu, M. (2021). Movement for the "Emancipation of the Niger Delta" (MEND) Constitutes a Threat to the U.S National Security. *Open Access Library Journal, 8*, 1–17.

Kundnani, H. (2017). What is the Liberal International Order? *The German Marshal Fund of the United States.* https://www.gmfus.org/news/what-lib eral-international-order. Accessed 8 December 2018.

Kurtulus, E. N. (2018). Chapter 3: Is There a 'New Terrorism' in Existence Today? The Relevance of the New Terrorism Concept. In R. Jackson & D. Pisoiu (Eds.), *Contemporary Debates on Terrorism.* Routledge.

Kuwornu, J. K. M. (2019). *Climate Change and Sub-Saharan Africa: The Vulnerability and Adaptation of Food Supply Chain Actors.* Vernon Art and Science Incorporated.

Kyuka, U. A. (2017). *Nigerian Oil and Gas Industry Law: Policies and Institutions.* Malthouse.

Lagoke, O., Adesola, S., & Vita, D. G. (2015). Nigerian Oil and Gas Industry Local Content Development: A Stakeholder Analysis. *Journal of Public Policy Administration, 3*(1), 1–38.

Lamnisos, D., Lambrianidou, G., & Middleton, N. (2019). Small-Area Socioeconomic Deprivation Indices in Cyprus: Development and Association with Premature Mortality. *BMC Public Health, 19*(627), 1–11.

Lamont, C. (2015). *Research Methods in International Relations.* Sage.

Land Use Act. (2004). *The Complete Laws of Nigeria, a Searchable Compendium.* Land Use Act. https://lawsofnigeria.placng.org/view2.php?sn=228. Accessed 20 February 2022.

Langford, P. (1986). *Modern Philosophies of Human Nature: Their Emergence from Christian Thoughts.* Lancaster.

Land Use Act, (1978). Vesting of all land in the State; Control and management of land; advisory bodies; Designation of urban areas; Applicable law for the interim management of land, Available from https://faolex.fao.org/docs/pdf/nig67625.pdf. [accessed 7 May 2024].

Lanoszka, A. (2018). *International Development: Socio-Economic Theories, Legacies, and Strategies.* Routledge.

Larus, E. F. (2005). China's New Security Concept and Peaceful Rise: Trustful Cooperation or Deceptive Diplomacy? *American Journal of Chinese Studies, 12*(2), 218–241.

Lasswell, H. D. (1936). *Politics: Who Gets What, When, How.* McGraw-Hill.

Lasswell, H. D. (2018). *Politics: Who Gets What, When, How.* Papamoa Press.

Lawrence, M. (2013). *Three Approaches to Security: Prevention. Protection, and Resilience.* Centre for Security Governance. https://www.secgovcentre.org.2013/02/three-approaches-to-security-prevention-protection-and-resile ince/. Accessed 12 April 2020.

Lazarus, R. S. (1994). *Emotion and Adaptation.* Oxford University Press.

Leeuw, E. D. D. (2008). Choosing the Method of Data Collection. In E. D. D. Leeuw, J. J. Hox, & D. A. Dillman (Eds.), *International Handbook of Survey Methodology* (pp. 113–135). Lawrence Erlbaum Associates.

Leffler, W. L. (2014). *Natural Liquids: A Nontechnical Guide.* Pennwell.

Leipziger, D. (2017). *The Corporate Responsibility Code Book.* Routledge.

Lencucha, R., Thow, A. M., & Kulenova, A. (2023). Framing Policy Objectives in the Sustainable Development Goals: Hierarchy, Balance, or Transformation? *Journal of Globalisation and Health, 19*(5).

Leonardo, D. A. (2012). Pirates and Militants in the Niger Delta: An Overview. In S. C. Giotti (Ed.), *Piracy and Maritime Terrorism: Logistics, Strategies, Scenarios* (pp. 170–190). IOS Press.

Leong, F. T. L., & Austin, J. T. (2006). *The Psychology Researcher Handbook: A Guide for Graduate Students and Research Assistance* (2nd ed.). Sage.

Lesar, D. J. (2001). *Securing Oil and Natural Gas Infrastructures in the New Economy.* Diane.

Lester, A. D. (2003). *The Angry Christian: A Theology for Care and Counselling.* Westminster John Knox Press.

Leuven, L. J. V. (2011). Chapter 2: Water/Wastewater Infrastructure Security: Threats and Vulnerabilities. In R. M. Clark, S. Hakim, & A. Ostfeld (Eds.), *Handbook of Water and Wastewater Systems Protection* (pp. 27–46). Springer.

Levan, A. C. (2019). *Contemporary Nigerian Politics: Competition in a Time of Transition and Terror.* Cambridge University Press.

Levang, P., & Rival, A. (2014). *Palms of Controversies: Oil Palm and Development Challenges.* Centre for International Forestry Research.

Levitsky, S., & Ziblatt, D. (2018). *How Democracies Die: What History Reveals About our Future.* Penguin.

Lewis, A. (2008). *Freedom for the thoughts that we Hate: A Biography of the First Amendment.* Hachette.

Lewis, T. G. (2015). *Critical Infrastructure Protection in Homeland Security: Defending a Networked Nation* (2nd ed.). Wiley.

Lilly, C. C. (2013). Case Studies. In A. A. Trainor & E. Graue (Eds.), *Reviewing Qualitative Research in the Social Sciences* (pp. 54–65). Routledge.

Lincoln, S. Y., & Denzin, K. N. (2011). *The Sage Handbook of Qualitative Research* (4th ed.). Sage.

Lincoln, Y., & Guba, E. G. (1985). *Naturalistic Inquiry.* Sage.

Linden, O., & Palsson, J. (2013). Oil Contamination in Ogoniland Niger Delta, Stockholm. *The Royal Swedish Academy of Sciences Journal, 42*(6), 685–701.

Liu, H. (2017). *Pipeline Engineering.* CRC Press.

Lodico, M. G., Voegtle, K. H., & Spaulding, D. T. (2010). *Methods in Educational Research from Theory to Practice* (2nd ed.). John-Wiley.

Loft, P., & Brien, P. (2023, September). Halfway to 2023: The Sustainable Development Goals. *UK House of Commons Library.* https://commonsli brary.parliament.uk/halfway-to-2030-the-sustainable-development-goals/. 31 October 2023.

Looy, A. V. (2014). *Business Process Maturity: A Comparative Study on a Sample Business Process Maturity.* Springer.

Loucks, D. P. (2021). Impacts of Climate Change on Economies, Ecosystems, Energy, Environments, and Human Equity: A Systems Perspective. In T. M. Letcher (Ed.), *The Impacts of Climate Change: A Comprehensive Study of Physical, Biophysical, Social, and Political Issues* (pp. 20–39). Elsevier.

Lowi, T. J. (2015). *Arena of Power.* Routledge.

Lugard, F. D. (1965). *The Dual Mandate in British Tropical Africa with a New Introduction by Margery Perham* (5th ed.). Frank Cass.

Luong, P. J., & Weinthal, E. (2010). *Oil is Not a Curse.* Cambridge University Press.

Luthra, G. (2015). Conceptualising Energy Security for the Indian Ocean Region. In S. Chaturvedt & D. Rumley (Eds.), *Energy Security and the Indian Ocean Region* (pp. 18–33). Routledge.

Lynch, M. J., Stretesky, P. B., & Long, M. A. (2015). *Defining Crime: A Critique of the Concept and Its Implication.* Palgrave Macmillan.

Macaulay, T. (2016). *Critical Infrastructure: Understanding Its Component Parts, Vulnerabilities, Operating Risks, and Interdependence.* CRC Press.

Madson, T. (2018). The Conception of Laziness and the Characterisation of Others as Lazy. *Journal of Human Arenas, 1,* 288–304.

Madubuko, C. C. (2017). Oiling the Guns and Gunning for Oil: The Youths and Niger Delta Oil Conflicts in Nigeria. In E. M. Mbah & T. Falola (Eds.), *Dissent, Protest and Dispute in Africa* (pp. 260–289). Routledge.

Mahmood, Y., Yodo, N., Huang, Y., & Afrin, T. (2023). Sustainable Development for Oil and Gas infrastructure from Risk Reliability, and Resilience Perspectives. *Journal of Sustainability, 15*(3), 4953.

Maizland, L. (2023, September). Global Climate Agreements: Successes and Failures. *Council on Foreign Relations.* https://www.cfr.org/backgrounder/paris-global-climate-change-agreements. Accessed 2 November 2023.

Makholm, J. D. (2012). *The Political Economy of Pipelines: A Century of Comparative Institutional Development.* University of Chicago Press.

Malici, A. (2007, Summer/Fall). Thinking about Rogue Leaders: Really Hostile or Just Frustrated? The *Whitehead Journal of Diplomacy and International Relations,* 1–9.

Mallin, C. (2016). *Corporate Governance* (5th ed.). Oxford University Press.

Manby, B., & Watch, H. R. (1999). *The Price of Oil: Corporate Social Responsibility and Human Rights Violations in Nigeria's Oil Producing Communities.* Human Rights Watch.

Manning, F. S., & Thompson, R. E. (1995). *Oilfield Processing of Petroleum: Volume Two Crude Oil.* Pennwell Books.

Marmot, M. G. (2004). Evidence-Based Policy or Policy-Based Evidence. *BMJ Journal, 328,* 906. https://www.bmj.com/content/328/7445/906. Accessed 20 September 2021.

Masson, J. (2004). The Legal Context. In S. Fraser, V. Lewis, S. Ding, M. Kellett, & C. Robinson. *Doing Research with Children and Young People* (pp. 95–118). Sage.

Masys, A. J. (2016). Manufactured Risk, Complexity and Non-traditional Security: From World Risk Society to a Networked Risk Model. In A. J. Masys (Ed.), *Exploring the Security Landscape: Non-Traditional Security Challenges* (pp. 313–320). Springer.

Mathias, B. A. (2011). The Social Effects of Oil Production in Gbaran Ubie Bayelsa State, Nigeria. *International Journal of Development and Management Review, 6,* 151–159.

Mathias, Z. (2015). Providing All-Round Security against Oil and Gas Infrastructure Sabotage and Physical Attacks on the Staff of NNPC and Multinational Oil Companies in Nigeria as a Critical Article of Her National Security Efforts. *International Journal of Social Science and Humanities Research, 3*(2), 45–59.

May, T. (1997). *Social Research: Issues, Methods, and Process.* Open University Press.

Maya, A. (1994). *Wouldn't Take Nothing for My Journey Now.* Hachette Digital.

Mba, H. C., Uchegbu, S. N., Udeh, C. A., & Moghalu, L. N. (2018). *Management of Environmental Problems and Hazards in Nigeria.* Routledge.

Mbu, M. T. (2018). *Dignity in Service.* Safari Books.

McAreavey, R., & Das, C. (2013). A Delicate Balancing Act: Negotiating with Gatekeepers for Ethical Research when Researching Minority Communities. *International Journal of Qualitative Methods, 12*(1), 113–131.

McDougall, A., & Radvanovsky, R. (2016). *Critical National Infrastructure: Homeland Security and Emergency Preparedness* (3rd ed.). CRC Press.

McGill University. (2020). *Climate and Sustainability Strategy 2020–2025.* https://www.mcgill.ca/sustainability/files/sustainability/mcgillclimatesustainability2025_-_reduced.pdf. Accessed 30 October 2023.

McGuire, J. (2020). Niger Delta Still Waiting for the Big Oil to Clean Up Devastating Pollution. *EcoWatch.* https://www.ecowatch.com/niger-delta-pollution-2646218738.html. Accessed 16 April 2022.

McKenzie, L. M., Blair, B., Hughes, J., Allshouse, W. B., Blake, N. J., Helmig, D., Milmoe, P., Halliday, H., Blake, D. R., & Adgate, J. L. (2018). Ambient Nonmethane Hydrocarbon Levels Along Colorado's Northern Front Range: Acute and Chronic Health Risk. *Journal of Environmental Science and Technology, 52*(8), 4514–4525.

McNabb, D. E. (2015). *Research Methods for Political Science: Qualitative and Quantitative Methods*. Routledge Publication.

Meissner, H. (2016). Corruption, Favouritism, and Institutional Ambiguity as Political Risks: Insights from the Concept of Neopatrimonialism. In J. Leiner & H. Meissner (Eds.), *State Capture, Political Risks, and International Business: Cases from Black Sea Region Countries* (pp. 11–25). Routledge.

Menon, E. S. (2015). *Transmission Pipeline Calculations and Simulations Manual*. Gulf professional.

Mensah, J., & Casadevall, S. R. (Reviewing Editor). (2019). Sustainable Development: Meaning, History, Principles, Pillars, and Implications for Human Action: Literature Review. *Journal of Cogent Social Sciences, 51*(1).

Mercer-Mapstone, L., Rafkin, W., Moffat, K., & Louis, W. (2017). Conceptualising the Role of Dialogue in Social License to Operate. *Journal of Resource Policy, 54*, 137–146.

Meredith, M. (2014). *Fortunes of Africa: A 5,000 Year History of Wealth, Greed and Endeavour*. Simon and Schuster.

Merriam, S. B., & Grenier, R. S. (2019). *Qualitative Research in Practice: Examples for Discussion and Analysis* (2nd ed.). Jossey-Bass.

Mewett, F. H. (2018). *The New Security: Individual, Community and Cultural Experiences*. Palgrave Macmillan.

Mhlanga, G., & Chirisa, I. (2023). Building more Sustainable and Resilient Urban Energy Infrastructures in Southern Africa. In R. Brinkmann (Ed.), *The Palgrave Handbook of Global Sustainability* (pp. 985–1005). Palgrave Macmillan.

Mickolus, E. (2018). *Terrorism Worldwide, 2016*. McFarland and Company.

Mignolo, W. D. (2011). The Global South and World Dis/Order. *Journal of Anthropological Research, 67*(2), 165–188.

Mill, S. J. (1863). *Utilitarianism, On Liberty and Considerations on Representative Government*. Parker, Son, and Bourn.

Miller, T., & Bell, L. (2012). Consenting to What? Issues of Access, Gatekeeping and 'Informed Consent.' In T. Miller, M. Birch, M. Mauthner, & J. Jessop (Eds.), *Ethics in Qualitative Research* (2nd ed., pp. 61–75). Sage.

Mimiko, M. O., & Olawadayisi, A. O. (2016). Effects of Money Laundering on the Economy of Nigeria. *Beijing Law Review, 7*(2).

Ministry of Budget and National Planning. (2016). *Strategic Implementation Plan for the 2016 Budget of Change*. Ministry of Budget and National Planning.

Mitchell, C. (2023). Niger Coup, Financing Woes Rock Nigeria's Plan to Supply Gas to Europe, S and P Global Commodity Insight. https://www.spglobal.com/commodityinsights/en/market-insights/latest-news/natural-gas/090823-niger-coup-financing-woes-rock-nigerias-plan-to-supply-gas-to-europe. Accessed 27 October 2023.

Mojid, A. (2019). How the South Was Born: Reflections in the Geography and Culture of Inequality. In J. Dargin (Ed.), *The Rise of the Global South: Philosophical, Geopolitical and Economic Trends of the 21st Century* (pp. 3–28). World Scientific.

Momah, S. (2013). *Nigeria: Beyond Divorce: Amalgamation in Perspective*. Safari.

Moody, J. (2016). The Niger Delta Avengers: A New Threat to Oil Producers in Nigeria. *James Foundation Journal of Terrorism Monitor, 14*(12). https://jamestown.org/program/the-niger-delta-avengers-a-new-thr eat-to-oil-producers-in-nigeria/. 13 November 2021.

More, P., Dougherty, D. S., & Rick, J. M. (2017). Unemployment and Social Class Stigmas. *Journal of Applied Communication Research, 45*(5).

More, T. (2020). *Utopia*. Open Road Media.

Morrow, S. L. (2011). Honor and Respect: Feminist Collaborative Research with Sexually Abused Women. In C. T. Fisher (Ed.), *Qualitative Research Methods for Psychologists: Introduction through Empirical Studies* (pp. 143–172). Academic Press.

Mou, D. (2017). *National Security, Democracy and Good Governance in Post-Military Rule Nigeria*. Author House.

Mounk, Y. (2018). *The People vs. Democracy: Why Our Freedom is in Danger and How to Save it*. Harvard University Press.

Mowrer, O., Dollard, J., Miller, N., Doob, L., & Sears, R. (1939). *Frustration and Aggression*. Oxford University Press.

Moyo, D. (2011). *Dead Aid: Why Aid is Not Working and How There is Another Way for Africa*. Penguin.

Mpofu, S. (2021). *The Politics of Laughter in the Social Media Age: Perspectives from the Global South*. Springer International.

Murphy, M. N. (2013). Petrol-Piracy: Predation and Counter-Production in Nigerian Waters. In G. Guilfoyle (Ed.), *Modern Piracy: Legal Challenges and Responses* (pp. 61–90). Edward Elgar.

Murshed, S. M., & Cuesta, J. (2013). Greed, Grievance, and Globalisation. In P. Justino, T. Bruck, & P. Verwimp (Eds.), *A Micro-Level Perspective on the Dynamics of Conflict, Violence, and Development* (pp. 50–68). Oxford University Press.

Naanen, B. (2012). The Nigerian State, Multinational Oil Corporations, and the Indigenous Communities of the Niger Delta. In S. Sawyer & E. T. Gomez (Eds.), *The Politics of Resource Extraction: Indigenous Peoples, Multinational Corporations, and the State*. Palgrave Macmillan.

Nacos, B. L. (2016). *Terrorism and Counterterrorism* (5th ed.). Routledge.

National Academies of Sciences, Engineering, and Medicine, National Academy of Engineering, Division on Engineering and Physical Sciences National Materials and Manufacturing Board and Committee on Connector Reliability for

Onshore Oil and Natural Gas Operations. (2018). *High-Performance Bolting Technology for Offshore Oil and Natural Gas Operations.* National Academies.

National Bureau of Statistics. (2017). *Social Statistics Report December 2016.* National Bureau of Statistics.

National Bureau of Statistics. (2020). *Labour Force Statistics: Unemployment and Underemployment Report: Abridged Labour Force Survey Under COVID-19.* National Bureau of Statistics. https://www.nigerianstat.gov.ng/pdfuploads/Q2_2020_Unemployment_Report.pdf. Accessed 26 May 2021.

National Bureau of Statistics. (2022). *Nigeria Multidimensional Poverty Index (2022).* National Bureau of Statistics.

National Climate Change Policy. (2021). Federal Ministry of Environment, Department of Climate Change: Climate Change Policy for Nigeria 2021–2030. https://climatechange.gov.ng/wp-content/uploads/2021/08/NCCP_NIGERIA_REVISED_2-JUNE-2021.pdf. Accessed 22 February 2022.

National Environmental Standards and Regulation Enforcement Agency Act. (2007). Discharge of Hazardous Substance and Related Offences. http://lawsofnigeria.placng.org/laws/nesrea.pdf. Accessed 22 February 2022.

National Oil Spill Detection and Response Agency (Establishment) Act. (2006). As Amended. http://extwprlegs1.fao.org/docs/pdf/nig124170A.pdf. Accessed 5 August 2020.

Neack, L. (2007). *Elusive Security: States First, People Last.* Rowman, and Littlefield.

Nef, J. (2003). *Human Security and Mutual Vulnerability: The Global Political Economy of Development and Underdevelopment* (2nd ed., Chapter 1). International Development Research Centre.

Neocleous, M. (2000a). *The Fabrication of Social Order: A Critical Theory of State Power.* Pluto.

Neocleous, M. (2000b). Against Security. *Radical Philosophy Journal,* (100), 7–14.

Neocleous, M. (2007). Security Liberty and the Myth of Balance: Towards a Critique of Security Politics. *Contemporary Political Theory Journal, 6,* 131–149.

Neocleous, M. (2008). *Critique of Security.* Edinburgh University Press.

Neuman, W. L. (2011). *Social Research Methods: Qualitative and Quantitative Approaches.* Pearson.

Neumann, M., & Elsenbroich, C. (2017). Introduction: The Societal Dimensions of Organised Crime. *Trends in Organised Crime, 20,* 1–15.

Newman, E. (2004). A Normatively Attractive but Analytically Weak Concept. *Journal of Security Dialogue, 35*(3), 355–360.

Newsom, D., Kruckeberg, D., & Turk, J. V. (2013). *Cengage Advantage Book: This is PR: The Realities of Public Relations* (11th ed.). Cengage.

Nfam, O. T. (2017). Poverty in the Midst of Plenty: A Study of Poverty and Underdevelopment in the Niger Delta Region of Nigeria. In M. Mawere (Ed.), *Underdevelopment, Development and the Future of Africa* (pp. 191–212). Langaa Research.

Nicholas, A., Mitchell, J., & Lindner, S. (2013). *Consequences of Long-Term Unemployment*. The Urban Institute.

Niger Delta Development Commission Act. (2000). Functions and Powers of the Commission. https://www.chr.up.ac.za/images/researchunits/bhr/files/extractive_industries_database/nigeria/laws/Niger-Delta%20Development%20Commission.pdf. 22 February 2022.

Nigeria Federal Environmental Protection Agency. (1991). Guidelines and Standards for Environmental Pollution Control in Nigeria. https://lawsofnigeria.placng.org/laws/F10.pdf. Accessed 6 May 2021.

Nigeria Mineral and Mining Act. (2011). Administration of the Act. http://admin.theiguides.org/Media/Documents/Nigeruian%20Minerals%20and%20Mining%20Act,%202007.pdf. Accessed 5 October 2022.

Nigeria Extractive Industries Transparency Initiative. (2015). *Highlights of the 2015 Oil and Gas Audit Report*. NEITI.

Nigeria Extractive Industries Transparency Initiative. (2021). Oil and Gas Industry Audit Report 2019. NEITI. https://eiti.org/sites/default/files/attachments/neiti-oga-2019-report_compressed.pdf. Accessed 20 February 2022.

Nigeria's Flare-Gas-(Prevention of Waste and Pollution) Regulations. (2018). Flare Gas (Prevention of Waste Pollution) Regulations. https://ngfcp.dpr.gov.ng/media/1120/flare-gas-prevention-of-waste-and-pollution-regulations-2018-gazette-cleaner-copy-1.pdf. Accessed 19 September 2021.

Nigerian Oil and Gas Industry Content Development Act. (2010). An Act to Provide for the Development of Nigerian Content in the Nigerian Oil and Gas Industry, Nigerian Content Plan, Supervision, Coordination, Monitoring and Implementation of Nigerian Content. https://www.ncdmb.gov.ng/images/GUIDELINES/NCACT.pdf. Accessed 13 December 2019.

Nigerian National Petroleum Corporation. (2013). *NNPC Annual Statistical Bulletin* (1st ed.), *Corporate Planning and Strategy*. https://www.nnpcgroup.com/NNPCDocuments/Annual%20Statistics%20Bulletin%E2%80%8B/2013%20ASB%201st%20edition.pdf. Accessed 24 September 2020.

Nigerian National Petroleum Corporation. (2016). *Monthly Financial and Operations Report September 2016* (pp. 2–9). Nigerian National Petroleum Corporation.

Nigerian National Petroleum Corporation. (2017). *Monthly Financial and Operations Report October 2017* (pp. 4–37). Nigerian National Petroleum Corporation.

Nigerian National Petroleum Corporation. (2018). *Annual Statistical Bulletin 2018*. https://www.nnpcgroup.com/NNPCDocuments/Annual%20Statist ics%20Bulletin%E2%80%8B/ASB%202018%201st%20Edition.pdf.    Accessed 24 September 2020.

Nigerian Investment Promotion Commission. (2018). *Shell Begins Gas Production in Second Phase of Bayelsa Project*. Nigerian Investment Promotion Commission. https://www.nipc.gov.ng/2017/08/24/shell-begins-gas-production-second-phase-bayelsa-project/. Accessed 31 December 2018.

Niskanem, J. (2018). *Mainstreaming Passive Houses: A study of Energy Efficient Residential Buildings in Sweden*. Linkoping University Press.

Njoku, A. O. (2016). Oil Pipelines Vandalism and its Effects on the Socio-Economic Development in Nigerian Society. *International Journal of Multidisciplinary Academic Research, 4*(7), 45–57.

Norman, J. (2009). Got Trust? The Challenge of gaining Access in Conflict Zones. In C. L. Sriram, J. C. King, J. A. Mertus, O. M. Ortega, & J. Herman (Eds.), *Surviving Field Research: Working in Violent and Difficult Situations* (p. 75). Routledge.

Novotny, D. D. (2007). What is Terrorism. In E. V. Linden (Ed.), *Focus on Terrorism* (pp. 23–31). Nova.

Nowell, L. S., Moules, N. J., White, D. E., & Norris, J. M. (2017). Thematic Analysis: Striving to Meet the Trustworthiness Criteria. *International Journal of Qualitative Methods, 16*, 1–13.

Numbere, A. O. (2018). The Impact of Oil and Gas Exploration: Invasive Nypa Palm Species and Urbanisation on Mangroves in the Niger River Delta, Nigeria. In C. Makowski & C. W. Finkl (Eds.), *Threats to Mangrove Forests: Hazards, Vulnerability, and Management* (pp. 247–266). Springer.

Numbere, A. O., & Camilo, G. R. (2017). Mangrove Leaf Litter Decomposition under Mangrove Forest Stands with Different Levels of Pollution in the Niger Delta. *African Journal of Ecology, 55*(2), 162–167.

Nuttall, M. (2023). *The Shaping of Greenland's Resource Spaces: Environment, Territory, and Geo-Security*. Routledge.

Nwagboso, C. I. (2018). Nigeria and the Challenge of Internal Security in the 21st Century. *European Journal of Interdisciplinary Studies, 4*(2), 15–30.

Nwagwu, F. (2019). Bayelsa Guber Race: Only the Fittest Will Win. *Premium Times*. https://opinion.premiumtimesng.com/2019/08/29/bayelsa-guber-race-only-the-fittest-will-win-by-fidelis-nwagwu/. Accessed 30 March 2022.

Nwankwoala, H. O., Obafemi, A. A., & Berezi, O. K. (2019). Flood Vulnerability Assessment of Communities in the Flood Prone Areas of Bayelsa State Nigeria. *International Journal of Geology and Earth Science, 5*(3), 19–36.

Nwobueze, C. C., & Osemene, O. J. (2018). The Resurgence of Militant Groups in the Niger Delta: A Study of Security Threats and the Prospects for Peace in Nigeria. In C. Obi & T. B. Oriola (Eds.), *The Unfinished Revolution in*

*Nigeria's Niger Delta: Prospects for Environmental Justice and Peace* (pp. 120–135). Routledge.

Nwuke, K. (2021). *Nigeria's Petroleum Industry Act: Addressing Old Problems, Creating New Ones.* Africa in Focus. https://www.brookings.edu/blog/afr ica-in-focus/2021/11/24/nigerias-petroleum-industry-act-addressing-old-problems-creating-new-ones/. Accessed 19 February 2022.

Nye, S. J. (1967). Corruption and Political Development: A Cost-Benefit Analysis. *American Political Science Review, 61*(2), 417–427.

Nyiayaana, K. (2016). Arming Community Vigilantes in the Niger Delta: Implications for Peace Building. In J. I. Lahai & T. Lyons (Eds.), *African Frontiers: Insurgency, Governance, and Peace Building in Post-Colonial States* (pp. 131–142). Routledge.

O'Connor, B. (2022). *The ESG Investment Handbook: Insights and Developments in Environmental, Social and Governance Investment.* Harriman House.

O'Grady, S. (2016). Boris Johnson Called Africa a Country, But Are We Surprised? *Foreign Policy.* https://foreignpolicy.com/2016/10/03/boris-joh nson-called-africa-a-country-but-are-we-really-surprised/. Accessed 11 March 2019.

O'Grady, R. (2018). *The Passionate Imperialists: The True Story of Sir Frederick Lugard, Anti-slavery, Adventurer and the Founder of Nigeria, and Flora Shaw.* Conrad Press.

Obi, C. I. (1997). *Oil, Environmental Conflict and National Security in Nigeria: Ramifications of the Ecology-Security Nexus for Sub-Regional Peace.* Arms Control and Disarmament and International Security.

Obi, C. I. (2013). The Petroleum Industry: A Paradox or (Sp)oiler of Development, In O. Obadare & W. Adewanbi (Eds.), *Nigeria at Fifty: The Nation in Narration* (pp. 65–80).

Obi, C. I. (2016). From Homeland to Hopeland? Economic Globalisation and Ogoni Migration in the 1990s. In S. Gupta & T. Omoniyi (Eds.), *The Culture of Economic Migration: International Perspectives* (pp. 116–127). Routledge.

Obi, C., & Oriola, T. B. (2018). Introduction: The Unfinished Revolution, the Niger Delta Struggle since 1995. In C. Obi & T. B. Oriola (Eds.), *The Unfinished Revolution in Nigeria's Niger Delta: Prospects for Environmental Justice and Peace.* Routledge.

Obozuwa, O. G., Nagy, H., Kaposzta, J., & Neszmelyi, G. I. (2017). Effects of International Trade Agreements on the Economy and the Society of Africa: Special Focus on Nigeria. In V. Erokhin (Ed.), *Establishing Food Security and Alternatives to International Trade in Emerging Economies* (p. 196219). IGI Global.

Ochayi, C., & Eromosele, F. (2021). PIB: FG Holds Summit on Artisanal, Modular Refineries Operations. *Vanguard News*. https://www.vanguardngr.com/2021/03/pib-fg-holds-summit-on-artisanal-modular-refineries-operations/. Accessed 2 June 2021.

Odudu, C. O. (2017). Compensation Issues in the Niger Delta-A Case Study of Boboroku Jesse, Delta State, Nigeria. *International Journal of Civil Engineering, Construction and Estate Management, 5*(4), 21–43.

Oduntan, O. B. (2017). Decolonisation and Ethnic Minority Question in Nigeria: The Willink Commission Revisited. In U. Usuanlele & B. Ibhawoh (Eds.), *Minority Rights and the National Question in Nigeria* (pp. 17–40). Palgrave Macmillan.

OECD. (2020). OECD Employment Outlook 2020: Worker Security and the COVID-19 Crisis. https://www.oecd-ilibrary.org/employment/oecd-employment-outlook_19991266. Accessed 26 May 2021.

Offu, K. A. (2013). *The Nigerian Dependent Management and Leadership Development in the Postwar II Colonial Nigeria*. Author House.

Ogbeidi, M. M. (2012). Political Leadership and Corruption in Nigeria since 1960: A Socio-economics Analysis. *Journal of Nigerian Studies, 1*(2), 1–24.

Ogundajo, G. O., Akintoye, I. R., & Olayinka, I. M. (2019). Taxing Informal Sector and Revenue Generation in Nigeria. *International Journal of Commerce and Management Research, 5*(4), 81–87.

Ogunleye, E. K. (2017). Political Economy of Nigerian Power Sector Reform. In D. Arent, C, Arndt, M. Miller, F. Tarp, & O. Zinaman (Eds.), *The Political Economy of Clean Energy Transitions* (pp. 391–409). Oxford University Press.

Ohwo, O. (2015). Public Perception on Climate Change in Yenagoa. *Geography Journal, 2015*, 1–10.

Oil Pipeline Act. (2004). Chapter 338: Laws of the Federal Republic of Nigeria. https://www.chr.up.ac.za/images/researchunits/bhr/files/extractive_industries_database/nigeria/laws/Oil%20Pipelines%20Act.pdf. Accessed 28 March 2020.

Oil and Gas Climate Initiative Report. (2018, September). At Work: Committed to Climate Action: A Report from the Oil and Gas Climate Change Initiative. https://www.ogci.com/wp-content/uploads/2018/09/OGCI_Report_2018.pdf. Accessed 9 December 2018.

Ojeleye, O. (2016). *The Politics of Post-War Demobilisation and Reintegration in Nigeria*. Routledge.

Okafor, A., & Olaniyan, A. (2017). Legal and Institutional Framework for Promoting Oil Pipeline Security in Nigeria. *Journal of Sustainable Development Law and Policy, 8*(2), pp.210-224

Okafor, C., Madu, C., Ajaero, C., Ibekwe, J., Bebenimibo, H., & Nzekwe, C. (2021). Moving Beyond Fossil Fuel in an Oil-Exporting and Emerging Economy: Paradigm Shift. *AIMS Energy Journal, 9*(2), 379–413.

Okafor, N. (2016). *Reconstructing Law and Justice in a Postcolony*. Routledge.

Oki, R. A. (2017). *Barbarism to Decadence: Nigeria and Foreign Complicity*. Author Solutions.

Okolie, A. M., & Ugwueze, M. I. (2015). Securitisation of Politics and Insecurity in Nigeria: The Boko Haram Experience. *International Affairs, and Global Strategy Journal, 36*, 28–40.

Okomus, F., Altinary, L., & Roper, A. (2007). Gaining Access to Research: Reflections from Experience. *Annals of Tourism Research Journal, 34*(1), 7–26.

Okonjo-Iweala, N. (2018). *Fighting Corruption is Dangerous: The Story Behind the Headlines*. MIT Press.

Okonkwo, E. C. (2020). *Environmental Justice and Oil Pollution Laws: Comparing Enforcement in the United States and Nigeria* (1st ed.). Routledge.

Okonofua, B. A. (2016). The Niger Delta Amnesty Program: The Challenges of Transitioning from Peace Settlements to Long-Term Peace. *Sage Open Journals, 6*(2), 1–16.

Okonta, I. (2016). Policy Incoherence and the Challenge of Energy Security. In A. Goldthau (Ed.), *The Handbook of Global Energy Policy* (pp. 501–520). Wiley.

Okumagba, E. O. (2022). Examine Global Court Practices in Reducing Climate Change Impacts through Litigation: Lessons for Nigeria. In E. O. Ekhator, S. Miller, & E. Igbinovia (Eds.), *Implementing the Sustainable Development Goals in Nigeria: Barriers, Prospects, and Strategies* (pp. 98–118). Routledge.

Okumagba, P. (2012). Oil Exploration and Crisis in the Niger Delta: The Response of the Militia Groups. *Journal of Sustainable Society, 1*(3), 78–83.

Okumagba, P. (2013). Ethnic Militia and Criminality in the Niger Delta. *International Review of Social Sciences and Humanities, 5*(1), 239–246.

Oladipo, S. B. (2013). *Vision 2020 and the Menace of Vandalism*. African World Press.

Olaiya, A., Adetunji, A., & Olorunfemi, M. (2014). *Nigerian Oil and Gas A Mixed Blessing?: A Chronicle of NNPC's Unfinished Mission*. Kachifo.

Olaiya, T. A., & Folami, T. M. (2017). Environmental Conflict, Collective Anger, and Resolution: Strategies in the Niger Delta Conflict. In S. C. Cloninger & S. A. Leibor (Eds.), *Understanding Angry Groups: Multidisciplinary Perspectives on their Motivations and Effects on Society* (pp. 309–332). Praeger.

Olalere, O. P. (2021, August 19 Monday). Nigeria: Behold the Brand-New Nigerian Petroleum Industry Act, 2021. https://www.mondaq.com/nigeria/oil-gas-electricity/1103114/behold-the-brand-new-nigerian-petroleum-industry-act-2021. Accessed 19 February 2022.

Olaniyan, A. (2017). The Multi-Agency Response Approach to the Management of Oil Spill Incidents: Legal Framework for Effective Implementation in Nigeria. *Journal of Sustainable Development Law and Policy, 6*(1), 2–15.

Olawuyi, D. S. (2012). Legal and Sustainable Development Impacts of Major Oil Spills. *The Journal of Sustainable Development, 9*(1), 1–15.

Oliveira, A. D. (2010). *Energy Security in South America: The Role of Brazil*. International Institute for Sustainable Development.

Olowu, D. (2010). *International Law: A Textbook for the South Pacific*. CD Publishing.

Olsen, M. (1965). *The Logic of Collective Action: Public Goods and the Theory of Groups*. Harvard University Press.

Oluduro, O. (2014). *Oil Exploitation and Human Rights Violations in Nigeria's Oil Producing Communities*. Intersentia.

Olusanya, O. (2014). Using the Macro-Micro Integrated Theoretical Model to Understand the Dynamics of Collective Violence. In I. Bantekas & E. Mylonaki (Eds.), *Criminological Approaches to International Criminal Law* (pp. 222–239). Cambridge University Press.

Oluyemi, A. O. (2020). The Military Dimension of Niger Delta Crisis and Its Implications on Nigeria National Security. *Sage Open Journal*. https://doi.org/10.1177/2158244020922895

Omagu, D. O. (2012). Oil Multinationals: 'Environmental Genocide' and Socioeconomic Development in Nigeria's Niger Delta. In T. Falola & A. Paddock (Eds.), *Environment and Economics in Nigeria* (pp. 107–124). Routledge.

Omand, D. (2011). *Securing the State*. C. Hurst, and Co.

Omeje, K. (2017). *Extractive Economies and Conflicts in the Global South: Multiregional Perspectives on Rentier Politics*. Taylor and Francis.

Omeje, K. (2017). *High Stakes and Stakeholders: Oil Conflict and Security in Nigeria*. Routledge.

Omeje, K. (2017). The Egbesu and Bakassi Boys: African Spiritism and Mystical Re-rationalisation of Security. In D. J. Francis (Ed.), *Civil Militia: Africa's Intractable Security Menace* (pp. 71–86). Routledge.

Omeje, K. C. (2017). *High Stakes and Stakeholders: Oil Conflict and Security in Nigeria*. Ashgate.

Omeni, A. (2018). *Counterinsurgency in Nigeria: The Military and Operations against Boko Haram, 2011–2017*. Routledge.

Omoweh, D. (2008). Governance, Democratization and Development of the Niger Delta. In S. S. Azaiki, D. S. P. Alamieyeseigha, & A. A. Ikein (Eds.), *Oil, Democracy and the Promise of True Federalism in Nigeria* (pp. 167–186). University Press of America.

Onakpohor, A., Fakinle, B. S., Sonibare, J. A., Oke, A. M., & Akeredolu, A. F. (2020). Investigation of Air Emissions from Artisanal Petroleum Refineries in the Niger Delta Nigeria. *Heliyon Journal, 6*(11), 1–9.

Ong, D. (2017). Litigation against Multinational Oil Companies in their Home State Jurisdictions: An Alternative Legal Response to Pollution Damage in Foreign Jurisdictions? In C. Tan & J. Faundez (Eds.), *Natural Resources and Sustainable Development: International Economic Law Perspectives* (pp. 278–297). Edward Elgar.

Onolememen, M. O. (2020). *Infrastructure Development in Nigeria: A Political and Economic History*. Routledge.

Onuoha, C. F. (2007). Oil Pipeline Sabotage in Nigeria: Dimensions, Actors and Implications for National Security. *African Security Review, 17*(3), 100–115.

Onuoha, C. F. (2008). Oil Pipeline Sabotage in Nigeria: Dimensions, Actors and Implications for National Security. *African Security Review, 17*(3), 100–115.

Onuoha, C. F. (2016). *The Resurgence of Militancy in Nigeria's Oil-Rich Niger Delta and the Dangers of Militarisation*. Al Jazeera Centre for Studies.

Onuoha, F. C., Alumona, I. K., & Oshita, O. O. (2019). Introduction: Understanding the Crisis of Internal Security Management in Nigeria. In O. O. Oshita, F. C. Onuoha, & I. K. Alumona (Eds.), *Internal Security Management in Nigeria: Perspectives, Challenges, and Lessons* (pp. 1–19). Palgrave Macmillan.

Ordor, A., & Abe, O. (2021). Local Content Requirements and Social Inclusion in Global Energy Markets: Towards Business and Human Rights Content. In D. S. Olawuyi (Eds.), *Local Contents, and Sustainable Development in Global Energy Markets* (pp. 392–412). Cambridge University Press.

Orere, O. (2009). Henry Okah: The Struggle of my Life, Ijaw Monitoring Group: Niger Delta Rights Defender. https://www.ijawmonitor.org/news.php?ct=4&article=113. Accessed 4 February 2022.

Oriola, B. T. (2016). *Criminal Resistance: The Politics of Kidnapping Oil Workers*. Routledge.

Oriola, T. B. (2013). *Criminal Resistance?: The Politics of Kidnapping Oil Workers*. Ashgate Publication.

Orisadare, M. A. (2019). An Assessment of the Role of Women Group in Women Political Participation, and Economic Development in Nigeria. *Frontiers in Sociology Journal, 4*(52), 1–7.

Osawaru, J. A. (2020). *Endsars Protest Hidden Truth you Need to Know*. Independent Publication.

Oseloka, O. H. (2017). *Prime Witness: Changes and Policy Challenges in Buhari's Nigeria*. Safari Books.

Oshionebo, E. (2009). *Regulating Transnational Corporations in Domestic and International Regimes: An African Case Studies*. University of Toronto Press.

Osuntogun, A. J. (2020). Rights to Development of Indigenous Peoples of Africa: A Quest for the Adoption of Resource Control Mechanism for Effective Protection. In C. C. Ngang & S. D. Kamga (Eds.), *Insights into Policies and Practices on the Right to Develop* (pp. 133–161). Rowman and Littlefield.

Oswald, S. E. S. (2009). The Impossibility of Securitizing Gender vis-à-vis 'Engendering' Security. In H. G. Brauch, H. Krummenacher, N. C. Behera, P. Kameri-Mbote, J. Grin, O. Spring, U. Chourou, & B. Mesjasz (Eds.), *Facing Global Environmental Change: Environmental, Human, Energy, Food, Health, and Water Security Concepts* (pp. 1143–1156). Springer.

Otobo, D. (2016). *Essentials of Labour Relations in Nigeria: Public Sector Labour and Employment Relations* (Vol. 3). Malthouse Press.

Otokunefor, H. O. C. (2017). *Nigerian Petroleum Industry, Policies, and Conflicts Relations* (Vol. 2). Malthouse.

Owen, T. (2004). Challenges and Opportunities for Defining and Measuring Human Security. *Disarmament Forum Journal, 3*, 15–23.

Owolabi, T. (2016, March 29). Three Killed in Oil Pipeline Explosion in Nigeria's Delta: Environment Group. *Reuters News.* https://www.reuters.com/article/us-nigeria-oil/three-killed-in-oil-pipeline-explosion-in-nigerias-delta-environment-group-idUSKCN0WV1HR. Accessed 11 April 2018.

Oxfam Report. (2017). *Even It Up: Inequality in Nigeria: Exploring the Drivers* (pp. 4–54). Oxfam International. https://oi-files-d8-prod.s3.eu-west-2.amazonaws.com/s3fs-public/file_attachments/cr-inequality-in-nigeria-170517-en.pdf. Accessed 1 January 2019.

Oxford Poverty and Human Development Initiative. (2022). *Nigeria MPI Report, 2022.* Oxford University. https://ophi.org.uk/nigeria-mpi-2022/. Accessed 3 November 2023.

Oxford Business Group. (2010). *The Report: Nigeria 2010.* Oxford Business Group.

Oyadongha, S. (2020, October 28). NOSDRA Intervenes again in SPDC/Bayelsa Community Oil Spill Face-off. *Vanguard News Paper.* https://www.vanguardngr.com/2020/10/nosdra-intervenes-again-in-spdc-bayelsa-community-oil-spill-face-off/. Accessed 28 October 2020.

Oyadongha, S., & Idio, E. (2021). Experts Link Nembe Oil Spill to Sabotage, as Bayelsa Government Kicks. https://www.vanguardngr.com/2021/12/experts-link-nembe-oil-spill-to-sabotage-as-bayelsa-govt-kicks/. Accessed 16 April 2022.

Oyadongha, S. (2021). We are Seeking International Help to Stop Nembe Oil Spill. *Vanguard News.* https://www.vanguardngr.com/2021/11/were-seeking-international-help-to-stop-nembe-oil-spill-aiteo/. Accessed 21 November 2021.

Oyewunmi, T. (2016). Security Implications of Conflicts, Crises and Disasters in the International Energy Industry: Legal and Policy Implications. In

S. C. Breau & L. H. Samuel (Eds.), *Research Handbook on Disasters and International Law* (pp. 272–294). Elgar.

Oyewunmi, T. (2018). *Regulating Gas Supply to Power Markets: Transnational Approaches to Competitiveness and Security Supply.* Wolter Kluwer.

Pabst, A. (2019). *The Demons of Liberal Democracy.* Wiley.

Paes, W. C. (2003). Oil Production and National Security in sub-Saharan Africa. In *Oil Policy in the Gulf of Guinea.* Friedrich-Ebert-Stiftung.

Pakenham, T. (2015). *The Scramble for Africa.* Hachette.

Paki, F. A. E., & Ebienfa, K. I. (2011). Militant Oil Agitations in Nigeria's Niger Delta and the Economy. *International Journal of Humanities and Social Sciences, 1*(5), 140–144.

Paleri, P. (2008). *National Security: Imperatives and Challenges.* McGraw.

Papavinasam, S. (2013). *Corrosion Control in the Oil and Gas Industry.* Elsevier.

Parkhurst, J. (2017). *The Politics of Evidence: From Evidence-Based Policy to the Good Governance of Evidence.* Routledge.

Parsons, T. H. (2004). *Race, Resistance, and the Boy Scout Movement in British Colonial Africa.* Ohio University Press.

Partain, A. (2017). *Environmental Hazards from Offshore Methane Hydrates Operations: Civil Liberties and Regulations for Efficient Governance.* Kluwer.

Pasculli, L., & Ryder, N. (2019). Corruption and Globalisation: Towards an Interdisciplinary Scientific Understanding of Corruption as a Global Crime. In L. Pasculli & N. Ryder (Eds.), *Corruption in the Global Era: Causes, Sources, and Forms of Manifestations.* Routledge.

Pashaeized, H. (2010). A Glance at the Characteristics of Mixed Methods and Importance of its Applications in LIS Researches. In A. Katsirikou & C. H. Skiades (Eds.), *Qualitative and Quantitative Methods in Libraries: Theory and Applications* (pp. 6–18). World Scientific.

Patrick, A. (2012). School Dropout Pattern amongst Secondary Schools in Delta State Nigeria. *International Education Studies Journal, 5*(2), 145–150.

Patterson, R. M., & Silverman, K. L. (2014). *Qualitative Research Methods for Community Development.* Routledge.

Patton, M. Q. (2002). *Qualitative Research and Evaluation Methods.* Sage.

Pawson, R. (2006). *Evidence-Based Policy: A Realist Perspective.* Sage.

Peace, R. (2010). *1930s Britain.* Bloomsbury.

Perrons, R. K. (2014). How Innovation and R&D Happen in the Upstream Oil and Gas Industry: Insights from a Global Survey. *Journal of Petroleum Science and Engineering, 124,* 301–312.

Persaud, R. B. (2016). Human Security. In A. Collins (Ed.), *Contemporary Security Studies* (pp. 139–153). Oxford University Press.

Peters, G. B. (2013). *Strategies for Comparative Research in Political Science: Theory and Methods.* Palgrave Macmillan.

Petroleum Industry Act, (2021). PIA: Explanatory Memorandum. Available from https://eproofing.springer.com/ePb/books/pnXXkMoim97Z_a_r MD9rZeEbrTrRUQmOXjtKXvfLWedcljNJBuXmZZBNYj-SztuHljv8yt2gL-1Cc-g7hvQhrTojgqtjLQ2jAUWQdwYTjfbm05PWXyArOed10ZI9Y9nrG YFRl5Bl8liyVB1qXexaAf17alFTrZ7252zWyo2Ivrw=. [Accessed 04/05/2024].

Petters, S. W., Nwajide, C. S., & Reijers, T. J. A. (1997). The Niger Delta Basin. In R. C. Selley (Ed.), *Sedimentary Basins of the World: African Basins* (Vol. 3, pp. 151–172). Elsevier.

Pfister, T., Reichel, A., & Schweighofer, M. (2016). *Sustainability*. Routledge.

Pharris, D. M., & Pavlish, C. P. (2012). *Community Based Collaborative Active Research*. Jones, and Bartlett.

Phelippeau, J., & Mendilow, E. (2019). Introduction: Political Corruption in a World in Transition. In J. Phelippeau & E. Phelippeau (Eds.), *Political Corruption in a World in Transition* (pp. 1–17). Vernon.

Philp, M. (2015). The Definition of Political Corruption. In P. M. Heywood (Ed.), *Routledge Handbook of Political Corruption* (pp. 17–30). Routledge.

Pickering, S., McCulloch, J., & Wright-Neville, D. (2008). *Counter-Terrorism Policing: Community, Cohesion and Security*. Springer.

Ping, G. C., & Annansingh, F. (2015). *Experiences in Applying Mixed Methods Approach in Information Systems Research*. In Management Association Information Resources.

Pirates, D. C. (2013). Ecological Security: A Conceptual Framework. In R. Floyd & R. A. Matthew (Eds.), *Environmental Security: Approaches and Issues* (pp. 139–148). Routledge.

Playfoot, J., Augustus, S., & Andrews, P. (2016). *Education and Training for the Oil and Gas Industry: Localising Oil and Gas Operations* (Vol. 4). Elsevier.

Poku, N. K., & Therkelsen, J. (2016). Globalisation, Development, and Security. In A. Collins (Ed.), *Contemporary Security Studies* (pp. 262–276). Oxford University Press.

Posner, R. (2001). Security versus Civil Liberties. *The Atlantic Monthly Magazine*. https://www.theatlantic.com/magazine/archive/2001/12/security-versus-civil-liberties/302363/. Accessed 1 December 2018.

Post, J. M. (2006). The Psychological Dynamics of Terrorism. In L. Richardson (Ed.), *The Roots of Terrorism* (pp. 17–29). Routledge.

Pottier, J., Cramer, C., & Hammond, L. (2011). Navigating the Terrain of Methods and Ethics in Conflict Research. In J. Pottier, C. Cramer, & L. Hammond (Eds.), *Researching Violence in Africa: Ethical and Methodological Challenges* (pp. 1–22). Brill.

Powell, S. (2008). *Returning to Study for a Research Degree* (2nd ed.). Open University Press.

Powers, B., and Smyth, R. (2015). Pipeline Repair. In R. W. Revie (Ed.), *Oil and Gas Pipelines: Integrity and Safety Handbook*. John Wiley & Sons Inc.

Preece, J., & Chilisa, B. (2005). *Research Methods for Adult Educators in Africa*. UNESCO Institute for Education.

Prempeh, K. (2007). Africa's 'Constitutionalism Revival': False Start or New Dawn? *International Journal of Constitutional Law, 5*(3), 465–506.

Prior, L. (2003). *Introducing Qualitative Methods: Using Documents in Social Research*. Sage.

Prno, J., & Slocombe, D. S. (2012). Exploring the Origins of Social License to Operate in the Mining Sector: Perspectives from Governance and Sustainability Theories. *Journal of Resource Policy, 37*, 346–357.

Radey, M. (2010). Secondary Data Analysis Studies. In B. Thyler (Ed.), *The Handbook of Social Work Research Methods* (2nd ed., pp. 163–182). Sage.

Ramsay, A. (2021). Climate Action is Nigeria's Chance to Free Itself from the Tyranny of Oil. *Open Democracy*. https://www.opendemocracy.net/en/climate-action-is-nigerias-chance-to-free-itself-from-the-tyranny-of-oil/. Accessed 24 November 2021.

Raphael, S., & Stokes, D. (2013). Energy Security. In A. Collins (Ed.), *Contemporary Security Studies* (3rd ed., pp. 306–319). Oxford University Press.

Ratcliffe, R. (2019, December 6). 'The Place used to be Green': The Brutal Impact of Oil in the Niger Delta. *The Guardian News*. https://www.theguardian.com/global-development/2019/dec/06/this-place-used-to-be-green-the-brutal-impact-of-oil-in-the-niger-delta. Accessed 8 July 2021.

Rauchway, E. (2008). *The Great Depression and the New Deal; A Very Short Introduction*. Oxford University Press.

Ray, S. N. (2004). *Modern Comparative Politics: Approaches, Methods and Issues*. Prentice-Hall.

*Research Methods: Concepts, Methodologies, Tools, and Applications* (pp. 910–936). IGI Global.

Rich, N. (2019). *Losing Earth: The Decade we Could have Stopped Climate Change*. Pan Macmillan.

Richards, A. (2015). *Conceptualising Terrorism*. Oxford University Press.

Richardson, L. (2006). The Roots of Terrorism: An Overview. In L. Richardson (Ed.), *The Roots of Terrorism* (pp. 1–17). Routledge.

Richmond, O. P. (2014). *Peace: A Very Short Introduction*. Oxford University Press.

Rieuwerts, J. (2017). *The Elements of Environmental Pollution*. Routledge.

Rizzo, A. (2016). From Petro-urbanism to Knowledge Megaprojects in the Persian Gulf: Qatar Foundation's Education City. In A. Shaban & A. Datta (Eds.), *Mega-urbanisation in the Global South: Fast Cities and the New Urban Utopias of the Postcolonial State* (pp. 101–115). Routledge.

Robinson, H., & Rodney, H. (2006). *Infrastructure for the Built Environment: Global Procurement Strategies*. Routledge.

Rodney, W. (2012). *How Europe Underdeveloped Africa*. Pambazuka.

Roeckelein, J. E. (1998). *Dictionary of Theories, Laws, and Concepts in Psychology*. Greenwood.

Rose-Ackerman, S., & Palifka, B. J. (2016). *Corruption and Government: Causes, Consequences, and Reforms* (2nd ed.). Cambridge University Press.

Ross, J. I. (2007). *Political Terrorism: An Interdisciplinary Approach*. Peter Lang.

Ross, M. L. (2012). *The Oil Curse: How Petroleum Wealth Shape the Development of Nations*. Princeton University Press.

Ross, M. L. (2015). What Have We Learned about the Resource Curse? *Annual Review of Political Science Journal, 18*, 239–259.

Rosthal, J. E., & Drennen, T. E. (2007). *Pathways to a Hydrogen Future*. Elsevier.

Royal Dutch Shell Report. (2012). *Royal Dutch Shell PLC: Shell in Nigeria*. Royal Dutch Shell.

Royal Ministry of Finance and Statistics Norway. (2018). *The National Budget: A Summary* (pp. 2–15). Royal Ministry of Finance.

Rubin, H. J., & Rubin, I. S. (2012). *Qualitative Interviewing: The Art of Hearing Data*. Sage.

Ruffin, S. (2012). Royal Dutch Shell Environmentally Degrades Nigeria's Niger Delta Region: A Land of Blacks. *Environmental Justice, 5*(3), 140–152.

Rugg, G., & Petre, M. (2007). *A Gentle Guide to Research Methods*. Open University.

Rukeh, R. A. (2015). Oil Spill Management in Nigeria: SWOT Analysis of the Joint Investigation Visit (JIV) Process. *Journal of Environmental Protection, 6*, 259–267.

Ruskin, M. (1976). Democracy Versus the National Security State. *Law and Contemporary Problems Journal, 4*(3), 189–220.

Rutten, M., & Mwangi, M. (2014). How Natural is Natural? Seeking Conceptual Clarity over Natural Resources and Conflicts. In M. Bavinck, L. Pellegrini, & E. Mostert (Eds.), *Conflicts Over Natural Resources in the Global South* (pp. 51–69). CRC Routledge.

Sagay, I. (2008). Nigeria: Federalism, the Constitution and Resource Control. In S. S. Azaiki, D. S. P. Alamieyeseigha, & A. A. Ikein (Eds.), *Oil, Democracy and the Promise of True Federalism in Nigeria* (pp. 370–379). University Press of America.

Sageman, M. (2016). *Misunderstanding Terrorism*. University of Pennsylvania Press.

Samuelson, P. A. (1954). The Pure Theory of Public Expenditure. *Review of Economics and Statistics Journal, 36*(4), 387–389.

Sanderson, C. A. (2010). *Social Psychology*. Wiley.

Saro-Wiwa, K. (1992). *Genocide in Nigeria: The Ogoni Tragedy*. African Books.

Sarte, B. S. (2010). *Sustainable Infrastructure: The Guide to Green Engineering and Design*. Wiley.

Sasse, J., Saab, R., Spears, R., & Tausch, N. (2016). Predicting Aggressive Collective Based on the Efficacy of Peaceful and Aggressive Actions. *European Journal of Social Psychology, 46*(5), 1–45.

Sastri, V. S., Elboujdaini, M., & Ghali, E. (2007). *Corrosion Prevention and Protection*. Wiley.

Sauer, C., & Ensink, T. (2003). *Framing and Perspectivising in Discourse*. John Benjamin.

Savasan, Z. (2019). *Paris Climate Agreement: A Deal for Better Compliance? Lessons Learned from the Compliance Mechanisms of the Kyoto and Montreal Protocols*. Springer.

Sayne, A. (2013). *Special Report: What's Next for the Security in the Niger Delta?* United States Institute of Peace.

Sayne, A., & Katsouris, C. (2015). *Nigeria's Criminal Crude: International Options to Combat the Export of Stolen Oil*. Chatham House.

Schechter, M. G. (2016). *Future Multilateralism: The Political and Social Framework*. Springer.

Scheffran, J. (2007). Tools for Stakeholder Assessment and Interaction. In S. S. Kleemann & M. Welp (Eds.), *Stakeholders Dialogues in Natural Resources Management: Theory and Practice* (pp. 153–181). Springer.

Scheffran, J., & BenDor, T. K. (2018). *Agent-Based Modeling of Environmental Conflict and Cooperation*. CRC Press.

Schertzing, P. D. (2012). Homeland Security Policing Against Terrorism: Tactics and Investigations. In J. P. I. A. G. Charvat (Ed.), *Homeland Security Organisation in Defense Against Terrorism* (pp. 117–136). IOS.

Schmid, P. A. (2004). Frameworks for Conceptualising Terrorism. *Journal of Terrorism and Political Violence, 16*(2), 197–221.

Schutt, R. K., & Bachman, R. (2008). *Fundamentals of Research in Criminology and Criminal Justice*. Sage.

Schwab, K. (2021). *Stakeholder Capitalism: A Global Economy that Works for Progress, People, and Planet*. Wiley.

Schwartz, M. S. (2011). *Corporate Social Responsibility: An Ethical Approach*. Broadview Press.

Schwegler, V. (2017). The Disposable Nature: The Case of Ecocide and Corporate Accountability. *Amsterdam Law Reform Journal, 9*(3), 72–99.

Scott, J. (2012). *Sociological Theory: Comparative Debates*. Elgar.

Scott, J. F. (2014). The Nature of Social Research and Social Knowledge. In I. Marsh (Ed.), *Theory and Practice in Sociology* (pp. 3–25). Routledge.

Seale, C. (2004). *Research Society and Culture* (2nd ed.). Saga.

Segall, M. H. (2016). *Human Behaviour and Public Policy: A Political Psychology*. Pergamon Press.

Sensing, T. (2011). *Qualitative Research: A Multi-Methods Approach to Projects Doctors of Ministry Theses*. WIPF and Stock.

Sentongo, A. (2016). The Practical Use of Early Warning and Response in Preventing Mass Atrocities and Genocide: Experiences from the Great Lakes Regions. In S. P. Rosenberg, T. Galis, & A. Zucker (Eds.), *Reconstructing Atrocity Prevention* (pp. 428–450). Cambridge University Press.

Shakespeare, W. (1807). *Julius Caesar*. John Cawthorn.

Sharma, R. A., & Sharma, R. (2006). *Experimental Psychology*. Atlantic.

Shastry, V. (2023). *The Notorious ESG: Business, Climate, and the Race to Save the Planet*. Emerald.

Shaw, P. (2019). *100 Great Leading through Frustration Ideas*. Marshall Cavendish.

Shaw, W. H. (2016). *Business Ethics: A Textbook with Cases* (9th ed.). Cengage.

Shaw, W. H., & Barry, V. (2015). *Moral Issues in Business* (13th ed.). Cengage.

Shaxson, N. (2008). *The Poisoned Wells: The Dirty Politics of African Oil*. Palgrave Macmillan.

Shearer, G., & Tusiani, M. D. (2007). *LNG: A Nontechnical Guide*. PennWell.

Sheehan, M. (2005). *International Security: An Analytical Survey*. Lynne Rienner.

Shelgba, L. K. (2011). *From My Heart to the Black Race: Myths, Realities, and complexes*. Strategic Book.

Shepard, B. (2015). *Oil in Uganda: International Lessons for Success*. Royal Institute for International Affairs.

Shepherd, L. J. (2013). Introduction: Critical Approaches to Security in Contemporary Global Politics. In L. J. Shepherd (Ed.), *Critical Approach to Security: An Introduction to Theories and Methods* (pp. 1–9). Routledge.

Shikyil, S. (2016). Legislative-Executive Relations in Presidential Democracies: Case of Nigeria. In C. M. Fombad (Ed.), *Separation of Powers in African Constitutionalism* (pp. 135–158). Oxford University Press.

Shimko, K. L. (2015). *International Relations: Perspectives, Controversies, and Readings*. Centage Learning.

Shoemaker, P. J., & Vos, T. P. (2009). *Gatekeeping Theory*. Routledge.

Shoewu, O., Akinyemi, L. A., Ayanlowo, K. A., Olatinwo, S. O., & Makanjuola, N. T. (2013). Mechatronics System: Spying and Reporting Vandalism. *Journal of Science and Engineering, 1*(2), 134–142.

Sieber, J. E. (2012). Ethical Dilemma in Social Research. In J. E. Sieber (Ed.), *The Ethics of Social Research: Surveys and Experiments* (pp. 2–28). Springer Science.

Simon, J. L. (2017). *The Art of Empirical Investigation*. Routledge.

Sinden, A. (2009). An Emerging Human Rights to Security from Climate Change: The Case Against Gas Flaring in Nigeria. In W. C. G. Burns & H. M. Osofsky (Eds.), *Adjudicating Climate Change: State, National, and International Approaches* (pp. 173–192). Cambridge University Press.

Singh, K. (2011). Corporate Accountability: Is Self-Regulation the Answer? In S. McBride & G. Teeple (Eds.), *Relations of Global Power: Neoliberal Order and Disorder* (pp. 60–72). University of Toronto Press.

Skoczylis, J. J. (2015). *The Local Prevention of Terrorism: Strategy and Practice in the Fight Against Terrorism*. Palgrave Macmillan.

Skoczylis, J., & Andrews, S. (2021). The Spectacle of Ghost Security: Security Politics and British Civil Society. In: E. T. Njoku and S. N. Romaniuk (eds.), *Counter-Terrorism and Civil Society: Post 9/11 Progress and Challenges*, Manchester, Manchester University Press, pp. 109–126.

Sloan, S., & Bunker, R. J. (2012). *Red Teams and Counterterrorism Training*. University of Oklahoma Press.

Smith, D. A. (2022). *The 6 Principles to Help Engineers Create Resilient Infrastructure*. Institute of Civil Engineers. https://www.ice.org.uk/news-insight/news-and-blogs/ice-blogs/the-civil-engineer-blog/principles-to-help-engineers-create-resilient-infrastructure. Accessed 29 October 2023.

Smith, B. (2013). *Understanding Third World Politics: Theories of Political Change and Development* (4th ed.). Palgrave Macmillan.

Smith, S. (2005). The Contested Concept of Security. In K. Booth (Ed.), *Critical Security Studies and World Politics* (pp. 31–36). Lynne Rienner.

Soysa, D. I. (2002). Paradise is a Bazaar? Greed, Creed, and Governance in Civil Wars, 1989–1999. *Journal of Peace Research, 39*(4), 395–415.

Speight, J. G. (2014). *Handbook of Offshore Oil and Gas Operations*. Elsevier.

Spellman, F. R. (2016). *Energy Infrastructure Protection and Homeland Security*. Bernan Press.

Spermann, A. (2015). How to Fight Long-Term Unemployment: Lessons from Germany. *IZA Journal of Labour Policy, 4*(1), 4–15.

Spring, O. (2009). The Impossibility of Securitising Gender vis-à-vis 'Engendering' Security. In H. G. Brauch, H. Krummenacher, U. O. Spring, J. Grin, C. Mesjasz, B. Chourou, N. C. Behera, & P. K. Mbote (Eds.), *Facing Global Environmental Change: Environmental, Human, Energy, Food, Health, and Water Security Concepts* (pp. 1142–1151). Springer.

Springael, J., Sorensen, K., Reniers, G., & Talarico, L. (2016). Pipeline Security. In S. Hakim, G. Albert, & Y. Shiftan (Eds.), *Securing Transportation Systems* (pp. 281–312). Wiley.

Stahike, S. (2018, July). Expanding on Notion of Ethical Risks to Qualitative Researchers. *International Journal of Qualitative Methods*. https://doi.org/10.1177/1609406918787309

Stahn, C. (2019). *A Critical Introduction to International Law*. Cambridge University Press.

Starman, A. B. (2013). The Case Study as a Type of Qualitative Research. *Journal of Contemporary Educational Studies, 1,* 28–43.

Stephens, D. R., & Leis, B. N. (2000). Development of an Alternative Criterion for Residual Strength of Corrosion Defects in Moderate to High-Toughness Pipe. Proceedings of the 3rd International Pipeline Conference. *Journal of American Society of Mechanical Engineers, 2,* 781–792.

Steven, R. (2008). *Sigmund Freud: Examining the Essence of his Contribution*. Palgrave Macmillan.

Steyn, P. (2014). Struggles Against Multinational Oil Companies and the Federal Government in the Nigerian Niger Delta since the 1990s. In M. Armiero & L. Sedrez (Eds.), *A History of Environmentalism: Local Struggles, Global Histories* (pp. 57–82). Bloomsbury.

Stone, J. (2007). *Aggression and World Order: A Critique of United Nations Theories of Aggression*. The Law Book Exchange.

Suberu, R. T. (2019). Constitutional Infidelity and Federalism in Nigeria. In C. M. Fombad & N. Steytler (Eds.), *Decentralisation and Constitutionalism in Africa* (pp. 101–132). Oxford Press.

Sullivant, J. (2007). *Strategies for Protecting National Critical Infrastructure Assets: A Focus on Problem-Solving*. Wiley.

Sun, Y., Zhou, K., Yi, L., & Su, X. (2023). *Environmental and Resource Protection Law*. Palgrave Macmillan.

Sunday, O., & Chukwuma, O. A. (2013). Oil Pipeline Vandalism and Nigerian National Security. *Global Journal of Human Social Science, 13*(5), 67–74.

Talus, K. (2011). *Vertical Natural Gas Transportation Capacity, Upstream Commodity Contracts, and EU Competition Law*. Kluwer.

Tame, S. C. (2018). Pre-Design Site Investigation for an Oil and Gas Facility in the Marginal Lands of the Nigerian Niger Delta Sub-region. In J. Wasowski, D. Giordan, & P. Lillino (Eds.), *Engineering Geology and Geological Engineering for Sustainable Use of the Earth's Resources* (pp. 20–40). Springer.

Tanaka, H., & Arbelaez, R. (2012). Opacity in Latin America: Argentina and Chile: A Case Study Comparison. In J. J. Choi & H. Sami (Eds.), *Transparency and Governance in a Global World, International Finance Review* (Vol. 13, pp. 337–355). Bingley.

Tarallo, M. (2019, October Issue). Is Pipeline Security Adequate? *ASIS International Security Management Magazine*.

Taureck, R. (2006). Securitization Theory and Securitization Studies. *Journal of International Relations and Development, 9,* 53–61.

Tausch, N., Becker, J., Spears, R., Christ, O., Saab, R., Singh, P., & Siddiqui, R. N. (2011). Explaining Radical group Behaviour: Developing Emotion and

Efficacy Routes to Normative and non-normative Collective Action. *Journal of Personality and Social Psychology, 101,* 129–145.

Taylor, A. (2012). *The Handbook of Family Dispute Resolution: Mediation Theory and Practice.* Wiley.

TC Energy. (2019). Life Cycle of Pipeline. https://www.tcenergy.com/about/explore-energy/understanding-how-it-works/life-cycle-of-a-pipeline/. Accessed 9 August 2020.

Temple, B., & Young, A. (2014). *Approaches to Social Research: The Case of Deaf Studies.* Oxford University Press.

Tesch, R. (2013). *Qualitative Research: Analysis Types and Software.* Routledge.

The Guardian Editor. (2023, August 28). Nigeria Still Losing 400,000 Barrels of Crude Oil Daily, Says Ribadu. *The Guardian News.* https://guardian.ng/news/nigeria-still-losing-400000-barrels-of-crude-oil-daily-says-ribadu/. Accessed 6 September 2023.

The National Conference. (2014). *CONFAB Report.* https://constitution.law nigeria.com/2018/03/26/2014-constitutional-conference-confab-report/. Accessed 19 September 2021.

The Oil and Gas Year. (2010). *The Who is Who of the Global Energy Industry: Turkey 2010.* Wildcat.

Theobald, R. (1990). *Corruption, Development and Underdevelopment.* Palgrave Macmillan.

Theodoropoulos, T. E. (2011). *Oil-Gas Exploration and Drilling.* Book Baby.

Thomas, D. (1995). Niger Delta Oil Production, Reserves, Field Sizes Assessed. *Oil and Gas Journal, 93*(46), 80–91.

Thompson, S. K. (2012). *Sampling.* Wiley.

Thomson, A. (2021, June 30). Revealed: Exxon Mobil's Lobbying War on Climate Change Legislation. *Channel 4 News.* https://www.channel4.com/news/revealed-exxonmobils-lobbying-war-on-climate-change-legislation. Accessed 8 July 2021.

Thoreau, H. D. (2016). *Civil Disobedience.* Xist Publishing.

Thorne, S. (2000). Data Analysis in Qualitative Research. *Evidenced-Based Nursing Journal, 3*(3), 68–70.

Thurston, A. (2019). *Boko Haram: The History of an African Jihadist Movement.* Princeton.

Tilly, C. (2003). *Politics of Collective Violence.* Cambridge University Press.

Timashev, S., & Bushinskaya, A. (2016a). *Diagnostic and Reliability of Pipeline Systems.* Springer International Publishing.

Timashev, S., & Bushinskaya, A. (2016b). Methods of Assessing Integrity of Pipeline Systems with Different Types of Defects. In S. Timashev & A. Bushinskaya (Eds.), *Diagnostics and Reliability of Pipeline Systems* (Vol. 30, pp. 9–43). Springer.

Tinker, P. B. H., & Corley, R. H. V. (2016). *The Oil Palm* (5th ed.). Wiley Blackwell.

Tiratsoo, J. N. H. (1999). *Pipeline Pigging Technology: Cleaning, Inspection, Fitness-for-Purpose* (2nd ed.). Gulf Professional.

Toakodi, A., & Assi, E. (2016). Corruption in the Civil Service: A Study of Payroll Fraud in Selected Ministries, Departments and Agencies (MDAS) in Bayelsa State Nigeria. *Research on Humanities and Social Sciences Journal, 6*(3), 53–69.

Tomlinson, K. (2018). Oil and Gas Companies and the Management of Social and Environmental Impacts and Issues. In T. Addison & A. Roe (Eds.), *Extractive Industries: The Management of Resources as a Driver of Sustainable Development* (pp. 422–441). Oxford University Press.

Tonunarigha, Y. D., & Oghenekohwo, J. E. (2019). Empowerment Programmes of Faith-Based Organisations (FBOs) and Socio-economic Well-being of Members in Yenagoa Community Bayelsa State, Nigeria. *International Journal of Education and Literacy Studies, 7*(4), 192–198.

Tordo, S., Tracy, B. S., & Arfaa, N. (2011). *National Oil Companies and Value Creation* (No. 218). World Bank.

Townsend, M., & Lawson, A. (2023). 'Huge Turnouts' Reported at UK Cost of Living Protests. *The Guardian News.* https://www.theguardian.com/business/2022/oct/01/huge-turnouts-reported-at-uk-cost-of-living-protests#:~:text=Thousands%20have%20gathered%20in%20dozens,seen%20in%20Britain%20for%20years. 3 November 2023.

Transparency International. (2017). Corruption Perception Index: What is Happening in Regions of the World. https://www.transparency.org/en/cpi/2017. Accessed 19 April 2022.

Transparency International. (2019). Military Involvement in Oil Theft in the Niger Delta. https://ti-defence.org/publications/military-involvement-in-oil-theft-in-the-niger-delta/. Accessed 25 November 2020.

Transparency International. (2020). Corruption Perception Index 2020. https://www.transparency.org/en/cpi/2021. Accessed 24 November 2020.

Transparency International. (2021). Corruption Perception Index 2021: Sub-Saharan Africa: How does your Country Measure Up?. https://images.transparencycdn.org/images/CPI2021_Report_EN-web.pdf. Accessed 19 April 2022.

Tudorica, D. (2018). A Comparative Analysis of Various Methods of Gas, Crude Oil, and Oil Derivatives Transportation. In *Information Management Resources Association, Intelligent Transportation and Planning: Breakthroughs in research and Practice* (pp. 563–575). IGI.

Tukur, M. M. (2016). *British Colonialisation of Northern Nigeria 1897–1914: A Reinterpretation of Colonial Sources.* Amalion.

Tysiachniouk, M. S. (2020). Disentangling Benefit-Sharing Complexities of Oil Extraction on the North Slope of Alaska. *Sustainability Journal, 12*(13), 1–31.

Ubong, U. I., Chibuogwu, E., Aroh, K. N., Umo-Otong, J. C., Harry, I. M., & Gobo, A. E. (2010). Oil Spill Incidents and Pipeline Vandalisation in Nigeria: Impact on Public Health and Negation to Attainment of Millennium Development Goals: The Ishiagu Example. *Disaster Prevention, and Management International Journal, 19*(1), 70–87.

Udeze, B. (2009). *Why Africa? A Continent in a Dilemma of Unanswered Questions*. Author Solution.

Udofia, O. O., & Joel, O. F. (2012). *Pipeline Vandalism in Nigeria: Recommended Best Practice of Checking the Menace* (pp. 1–8). Society of Petroleum Engineers. https://onepetro.org/SPENAIC/proceedings-abstract/12NAICE/All-12NAICE/SPE-162980-MS/159279. Accessed 2 August 2018.

Udoh, E. W. (2015). Insecurity in Nigeria: Political, Religious and Cultural Implications. *Journal of Philosophy Culture and Religion, 5*, 1–7.

Ughamadu, N. (2017). *Nigeria Defers 700,000bpd of Crude Oil Due to Pipeline Vandalism*. Nigeria National Petroleum Corporation.

Ugo, P. (2017). Oil Capitalism, Precarity, and Youths Resistance to Slow Violence in Nigeria's Oil Delta. In P. Ugo & L. M. Yevugah (Eds.), *African Youths Cultures in a Globalised World: Challenges, Agency and Resistance* (pp. 96–110). Routledge.

Ugochukwu, F. (2016). No, this is Not Redemption: The Biafra War Legacy in Chris Abani's Graceland. In T. Falola & O. Ezekwem (Eds.), *Writing the Nigerian Biafra War* (pp. 362–379). James Currey.

Ugochukwu, O. (2008). The Conceptual Framework and Strategy for Niger Delta Development: A Niger Delta Development Commission Perspective. In A. A. Ikein, D. S. P. Alamiesegha, & S. Azaika (Eds.), *Oil Democracy and the Promise of True Federalism in Nigeria* (pp. 95–101). University Press of America.

Ujomu. (2008). The Bounds of Security Theorising: Envisioning Discursive Inputs for the Rectification of a Post-colonial Situation. In D. Adelugba & P. O. Ujomo (Eds.), *Rethinking Security in Nigeria: Conceptual Issues in the Quest for Social Order and National Integration* (pp. 8–45). Council for the Development of Social Science Research in Africa.

Ukeje, C. (2011). Changing the Paradigm of Pacification: Oil and Militarization in Nigeria's Delta Region. In C. Obi & S. A. Rustad (Eds.), *Oil and Insurgency in the Niger Delta: Managing the Complex Politics of Petrol-Violence*. Zed Books.

Ukiwo, U. (2011). The Nigerian State, Oil, and the Niger Delta Crisis. In C. Obi & S. A. Rustad (Eds.), *Oil and Insecurity in the Niger Delta* (pp. 2–15). Zed Books.

Ukiwo, U. (2016). Timing and Sequencing in Peacebuilding: The Case of Nigeria's Niger Delta Amnesty Programme. In A. Langer & G. K. Brown (Eds.), *Building Sustainable Peace: Timing and Sequencing of Post-Conflict Reconstruction and Peacebuilding* (pp. 262–283). Oxford University Press.

Ukiwo, U. (2020). Nigeria's Oil Governance Regime: Challenges and Policies. In A. Langer, U. Ukiwo, & P. Mbabazi (Eds.), *Oil Wealth and Development in Uganda and Beyond: Prospects, Opportunities and Challenges* (pp. 309–331). Leuven University Press.

Ukpong, I. G. (2012). *Nature Under Siege: Portrait of Environmental Crisis in the Niger Delta*. Author House.

Ullman, R. (2014). Refining Security. In C. W. Hughes & L. Y. Meng (Eds.), *Security Study: A Reader* (pp. 11–17). Routledge.

Umar, A. T., & Othman, M. S. H. (2017). Causes and Consequences of Crude oil Pipeline Vandalism in the Niger Delta of Nigeria: A Confirmatory Factor Analysis Approach. *Cogent Economics and Finance Journal, 5*(1), 1–15.

Umukoro, B. (2009). Gas Flaring, Environmental Corporate Responsibility and the Right to a Healthy Environment: Case of the Niger Delta. In F. Emiri & G. Deinduomo (Eds.), *Law and Petroleum Industry in Nigeria: Current Challenges* (pp. 36–49). Malthouse.

United Nations Convention for the Suppression of the Financing of Terrorism. (1999). Special Treaty Event, 2009. https://www.unodc.org/documents/treaties/Special/1999%20International%20Convention%20for%20the%20Suppression%20of%20the%20Financing%20of%20Terrorism.pdf. Accessed 18 May 2020.

United Nations Department of Economics and Social Affairs. (2016). *Sustainable Development: Make SDGs a Reality*. https://sdgs.un.org/. Accessed 31 October 2023.

United Nations Development Programme. (1994). *Human Development Report 1994: New Dimensions of Human Security*. Oxford University Press.

United Nations Development Programme. (2017). *Human Development Report 2016: Human Development for Everyone*. United Nations.

United Nations Disaster Risk Reduction. (2022). *Principles for Resilient Infrastructure*. UNDRR. https://www.undrr.org/publication/principles-resilient-infrastructure. Accessed 29 October 2023.

United Nations Environment Programme Report. (2012). Environmental Assessment of Ogoniland: Assessment of Vegetation, Aquatic and Public Health Issues. http://hdl.handle.net/20.500.11822/25286. Accessed 9 May 2018.

United Nations Framework Convention on Climate Change. (2010). Report of the Conference of the Parties on its Sixteenth Session, held in Cancun from 29 November to 10 December 2010. https://unfccc.int/sites/default/files/resource/docs/2010/cop16/eng/07a01.pdf. Accessed 16 February 2022.

United Nations Office of Coordination of Humanitarian Affairs. (2009). *Human Security in Theory and Practice*. United Nations. https://www.unocha.org/sites/dms/HSU/Publications%20and%20Products/Human%20Security%20Tools/Human%20Security%20in%20Theory%20and%20Practice%20English.pdf. Accessed 24 January 2022.

United Nations Office on Drugs and Crime. (2018). Manual on Corruption Surveys: Methodological Guidelines on the Measurement of Bribery and Other Forms of Corruption Through Sample Survey. United Nations Office on Drugs and Crime. https://www.unodc.org/documents/data-and-analysis/Crime-statistics/CorruptionManual_2018_web.pdf. Accessed 16 October 2021.

United Nations Office on Drugs and Crime. (2019). *Corruption in Nigeria: Pattern and Trends: Second Survey on Corruption as Experienced by the Population*. https://www.unodc.org/documents/data-and-analysis/statistics/corruption/nigeria/Corruption_in_Nigeria_2019_standard_res_11MB.pdf. Accessed 16 October 2021.

United Nations Sustainable Development Goals. (2016). The Sustainable Development Agenda. https://www.un.org/sustainabledevelopment/development-agenda-retired/#:~:text=%E2%97%8F,future%20for%20people%20and%20planet. Accessed 31 October 2023.

United States Agency for International Development. (2012). Conflict Assessment Framework. https://pdf.usaid.gov/pdf_docs/pnady739.pdf. Accessed 1 October 2020.

United States Department of States. (2005). *Office of the Coordinator for Counterterrorism: Country Report on Terrorism 2004*. Government press.

University of Lincoln. (2018). Research Ethics Policy. https://secretariat.sites.lincoln.ac.uk/wp-content/uploads/sites/30/2013/08/Research-Ethics-Policy-Version-2.0-25.05.18.pdf. Accessed 19 January 2019.

Unrau, Y. A., Grinnell, J. R., & Richard, M. (2008). *Social Work Research and Evaluation: Foundations of Evidence-Based Practice* (8th ed.). Oxford University Press.

Ushie, V. (2013). Nigeria's Amnesty Programme as a Peacebuilding Infrastructure: A Silver Bullet? *Journal of Peacebuilding and Development, 8*(1), 30–45.

Usman, A. K. (2017). *Nigerian Oil and Gas Industry Laws, Policies, and Institutions* (pp. 52–54). Malthouse.

Utebor, S. (2021). Shell, Bayelsa Communities at Loggerheads Over Oil Spillages. *The Nations*. https://thenationonlineng.net/. Accessed 2 November 2021.

Uzoigwe, G. N. (1985). European Partition and Conquest of Africa: An Overview. In A. A. Boaden (Ed.), *General History of Africa: Africa under Colonial Domination 1880–1935* (pp. 19–44). University of California.

Valance, G. D., & Best, R. (2013). *Building a Value: Pre-Design Issues*. CRC.

Van Maanen, J., & Knolb, D. (1985). The Professional Apprentice: Observations on Fieldwork Role into Organisational Settings. *Research in Sociology of Organisations Journal, 4*, 1–3.

Vanguard News. (2021, February 21). State of the Nation: Nigeria No Longer Working-Obadiah, Utomi, Henshaw, Ademolekun, Others. *Vanguard News*. https://www.vanguardngr.com/2021/02/state-of-the-nation-nigeria-no-longer-working-obadiah-utomi-henshaw-adamolekun-others/. Accessed 14 February 2022.

Veolia Resourcing the World. (2016). New Challenges of the Oil and Gas Industry. https://www.veolia.com/middleeast/our-services/our-vision/new-challenges-oil-gas-industry#:~:text=With%20rising%20global%20demand%2C%20highly,and%20improve%20its%20environmental%20footprint. Accessed 27 October 2023.

Vetter, S., Endrass, J., Schweizer, I., Teng, H. M., Rossler, W., & Gallo, W. T. (2006). The Effects of Economic Deprivation on Psychological Well-being Amongst the Working Population of Switzerland. *BMC Public Health, 6*(223), 1–10.

Visser, W. (2017). *The Quest for Sustainable Business: An Epic Journey in Search of Corporate Responsibility*. Routledge.

Vorob'ev, N. N. (2012). *Foundations of Game Theory: Noncooperative Games*. Springer Basel.

Vuori, J. A., & Stritzel, H. (2016). Security. In F. Berenskoetter (Ed.), *Concepts in World Politics* (pp. 41–56). Sage.

Waever, O. (1998). Security, Insecurity and Asecurity in the West-European Non-War Community. In E. Adler & M. Barnett (Eds.), *Security Communities* (pp. 70–118). Cambridge University Press.

Waever, O. (2004). Peace and Security: Two Concepts and their Relationship. In S. Guzzini & D. Jung (Eds.), *Contemporary Security Analysis and Copenhagen Peace Research* (pp. 52–65). Routledge.

Waever, O., Buzan, B., & Jaap, D. W. (1998). *Security: A New Framework for Analysis*. Lynne Rienner.

Wakili, I., Muhammad, H., & Abbah, T. (2013). *Nigeria Lost US$ 1Billion to Pipeline Shot down in Seven Days*. Forum for African Investigative Journalism.

Walker, I., & Mendolia, S. (2015). Youth Unemployment and Personality Traits. *IZA Journal of Labour Economics, 4*(19).

Walters, G. D. (2012). Criminal Predatory Behaviour in the Federal Bureau of Prisons. In M. Delisi & P. J. Conis (Eds.), *Violent Offenders: Theory, Research, Policy, and Practice* (pp. 369–382). Jones and Bartlett.

Waltz, K. (2000). *Theory of International Politics*. McGrew Hill.

Wang, F., & Deng, Y. (2005). *China Rising: Power and Motivation in Chinese Foreign Policy*. Rowman, and Littlefield.

Wangu, J. K. (2018). *The Niger Delta Paradox: Impoverished in the Midst of Abundance*. Safari Books.

Warren, D., Biringer, B., & Vugrin, E. D. (2016). *Critical Infrastructure System Security and Resilience*. CRC.

Waschke, M. (2017). *Personal Cybersecurity: How to Avoid and Recover from Cybercrime*. Apress.

Wassenaar, D., & Singh, S. (2016). Contextualising the Role of the Gatekeeper in Social Science Research. *South African Journal of Bioethics and Law, 9*(1), 42–47.

Wasserman, J., & Jeffrey, C. (2007). *Accessing Distrustful Populations: Lesson from Ethnographic Research with Street Homeless*. Paper Presented at the Annual Meeting of the American Sociological Association, New York, TBA.

Watson, D. (1992). Correcting for Acquiescent Response Bias in the Absence of a Balance: An Application to Class Consciousness. *Journal of Sociological Methods and Research, 21*(1), 52–88.

Watts, M. (2007). Petro-Insurgency or Criminal Syndicate? Conflict and Violence in the Niger Delta. *Review of African Political Economy*, (114), 637–660.

Watts, M., & Zalik, A. (2020). Consistently Unreliable: Oil Spill Data and Transparency Discourse. *Elsevier PubMed Central Journal of Biomedical and Life Sciences, 7*(3), 790–795.

Webb, M. J. (2016). *Separatists Violence in South Asia: A Comparative Study*. Routledge.

Webel, C. P., & Barash, D. P. (2014). *Peace and Conflicts Studies* (3rd ed.). Sage.

Weinberg, L. (2009). *Global Terrorism*. Rosen Publishing.

Wells, J. (2019). Just 15% of the Oil and Gas Workforce is Female-these Women Want to Change that. *CNBC News*. https://www.cnbc.com/2019/01/04/15percent-of-oil-and-gas-workers-are-female-these-women-want-to-change-that.html. Accessed 14 November 2023.

Welp, M., & Kleemann, S. S. (2007). Integrative Theory of Reflexive Dialogue. In S. S. Kleemann & M. Welp (Eds.), *Stakeholder Dialogues in Natural Resources Management* (pp. 43–73). Springer.

Welzer, H. (2015). *Climate Wars: What People Will be Killed for in the 21st Century*. Polity Press.

Wendt, A. (1999). *Social Theory of International Relations*. Cambridge University Press.

Wengraf, T. (2001). *Qualitative Research Interviewing*. Sage.

Westermeier, C., & Goede, M. D. (2022). Infrastructural Geopolitics. *International Studies Quarterly, 66*(3).

Wetzel, J. R. M. (2016). *Human Rights in Transnational Business: Translating Human Rights Obligations into Compliance Procedures*. Springer.

Wheeldon, J., & Ahlberg, M. K. (2012). *Visualising Social Science Research: Maps, Methods, and Meaning*. Sage.

White, J. W., & Sechrist, S. M. (2010). The Form and Function of Female Aggression. In K. Osterman (Ed.), *Direct and Indirect Aggression* (pp. 85–102). Peter Lang.

Whitley, R. (2011). Qualitative Research Method in Mental Health. In G. Thornicroft, G. Szmukler, K. T. Mueser, & R. E. Drake (Eds.), *Oxford Textbook on Community Mental Health* (pp. 305–310). Oxford University Press.

Wight, J. B., & Morton, J. S. (2007). *Teaching the Ethical Foundation of Economics*. Council of Economic Education.

Wiles, R., Crow, C., Heath, S., & Charles, V. (2006). *Anonymity and Confidentiality*. ESRC National Centre for Research Methods. https://eprints.ncrm.ac.uk/id/eprint/423/1/0206_anonymity%20and%20confidentiality.pdf. Accessed 17 January 2019.

Wiles, R. (2012). *What are Qualitative Research Ethics?* Bloomsbury Academic.

William, T., & Russell, T. (2000). Linkages between Traditional Security and Human Security. In T. William, R. Thakur, & H. In-Tack (Eds.), *Asia's Emerging Regional Order*. United Nations University Press.

William, T., Dunlap, E., Johnson, B. D., & Hamid, A. (1992). Personal Safety in Dangerous Places. *Journal of Contemporary Ethnography, 21*(3), 343–374.

Williams, M. B., & Fenske, B. A. (2004). *Demonstrating Benefits of Wellhead Protections Programs*. AWWA Research Foundation Publication.

Willig, C. (2013). *Introducing Qualitative Research in Psychology* (3rd ed.). Open University Press.

Willink Commission Report. (1958). *Nigeria: Report of the Commission Appointed to Inquire into the Fears of Minorities and the Means of Allaying them*. Her Majesty's Stationary Office.

Wilson, E. A. (2017). *People Power Movements and International Human Rights: Creating a Legal Framework*. ICNC.

Wodak, R., & Meyer, M. (2004). *Methods of Critical Discourse Analysis* (Wodak and Meyer Eds.). Sage.

Wolfers, A. (1952). National Security, as an Ambiguous Symbol. *Political Science Quarterly, 67*, 483.

Wolvers, A., Tappe, O., Salverda, T., & Schwarz, T. (2015). *Concepts of the Global South-Voices from Around the World*. University of Cologne.

Wood, M. J., & Brink, P. J. (2001). *Basic Steps in Planning Nursing Research: From Question to Proposal* (5th ed.). Jones, and Bartlett.

Woodside, A. G. (2010). *Case Study Research: Theory, Methods and Practice*. Emerald Group.

World Bank Report. (1995). *Nigeria-Defining an Environmental Development Strategy for the Niger Delta* (Vol. 2). World Bank.

World Bank. (1997). *The 1997 World Bank Conference on Development Economics* (Boris Pleskovic and Joseph E. Stiglitz Eds.). World Bank.

Wormer, K. V. (2017). *Human Behaviour and the Social Environment Micro Level: Individual and Families*. Oxford University Press.

Wright, B. (2003). Race, Politics and Pollution: Environmental Justice in the Mississippi River Chemical Corridor. In J. Agyeman, R. D. Bullard, & B. Evans (Eds.), *Just Sustainabilities: Development in an Unequal World* (pp. 125–145). MIT Press.

Wutchte, T. (2012). *To Protect Critical Energy Infrastructure: Gaining Critical Insights and Discussing the Role, Strategic Objectives and Practical Measures Initiated by the Organisation for Security and Co-Operation in Europe via Their Action against Terrorism Programme*. OSCE.

Xiaofeng, Y., & Jia, L. (2016). Human Security: China's Conceptual Approaches and Policy Making Patterns. In W. T. Tow, D. Walton, & R. Kersten (Eds.), *New Approaches to Human Security in the Asia-Pacific: China, Japan, and Australia* (pp. 5–22). Routledge.

Yin, R. K. (2012). *Application of Case Study Research* (3rd ed.). Sage.

Zalik, A. (2011). Labelling Oil, Contesting Governance: The GMoU and Profiteering in the Niger Delta. In C. Obi & S. A. Rustad (Eds.), *Oil and Insurgency in the Niger Delta: Managing the Complex Politics of Petro Violence* (pp. 200–252). Zed Books.

Zecheru, G., Dumitrescu, A., & Dinita, A. (2018). Characterisation of Volumetric Surface Defects. In E. N. Barkanow, A. Dumitrescu, & I. A. Parinov (Eds.), *Non-destructive Testing and Repair of Pipelines* (pp. 117–136). Springer.

Zhao, Z. (2011). Non-Traditional Security and the New Concept of Security of China. In H. G. Brauch, J. Birkmann, U. O. Spring, J. Grin, C. Mesjasz, B. Chourou, P. Dunay, & P. K. Mbote (Eds.), *Coping with Global Environmental Change, Disasters and Security: Threats, Challenges, Vulnerabilities and Risks*. Springer.

# Index